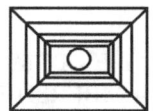

OBJECT
Masters Degree

Glorifying
God the Real, "The Spirit of Goodness"

Author: "Saint Bill"
Wilhelm J. Handel

**SUPPLEMENT
to
"The COMPASS"
(A New Bible)
"The EverLast Testament"**

ISBN: 0-9697487-2-8   Vol. 2 of 3

"SPECIAL"

LIFE-TIME
MEMBERSHIP
for

_____

with
PREVIEWS
"Institute of Universal Philosophy"

Assuming YOU Accept THREE copies of (Object: Master Degree)
For the Price of "TWO"

That is Right, this copy of Object: Masters Degree, is given to you for "FREE" with the Assumption that you will Buy THREE for the price of TWO every Three months, to give to your New found Friends for "FREE",
with the same Assumption, for the Life-of-your Membership.

Thank you, DEAR God, Thank you

SPONSOR_____

S# _____

Dated: _____A.B.

BASE 5,939 A.M.

"Let Us keep in Touch"

Phone: _____

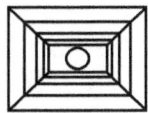

THE SERMONS
of
"Saint BILL"

and

OBJECT
"MASTERS DEGREE"

Glorifying
God the Real, "The Spirit of Goodness"

SUPPLEMENT
to
"The COMPASS"

(A New Bible)
"The EverLast Testament"

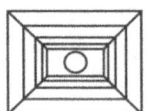

PREVIEWISM
Our World is Beautiful, Yes, Multi-Cultural

The Foundation of any True Religion is that God created Humankind in Its Image with a "Good" nature; and this once done is forever done because God is Unconditionally Loving and Unconditionally Forgiving and does not Condemn.

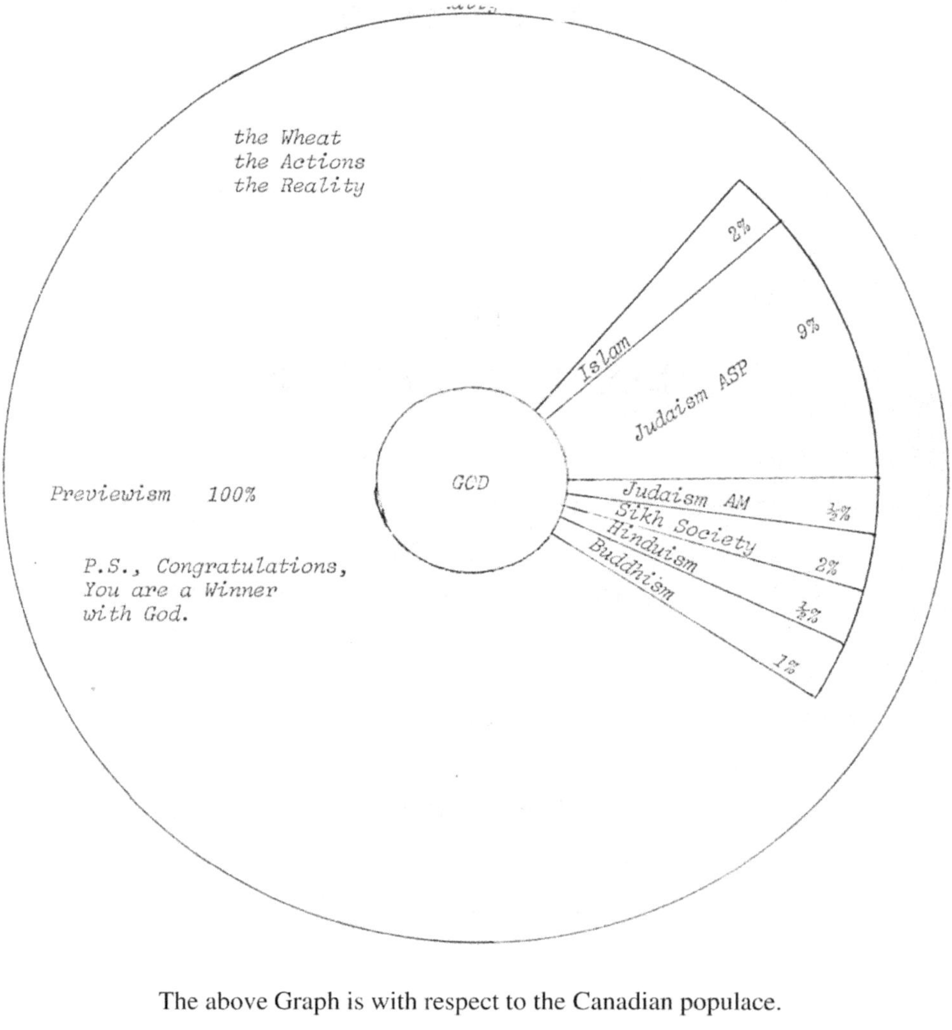

the Wheat
the Actions
the Reality

Previewism 100%

P.S., Congratulations,
You are a Winner
with God.

GOD

Islam 2%
Judaism ASP 9%
Judaism AM ½%
Sikh Society
Hinduism 2%
Buddhism ½%
1%

The above Graph is with respect to the Canadian populace.

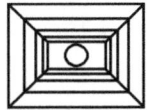

PUBLISHED BY:

PREVIEWS Inc.
Calgary, AB.,
Canada

"Eternal (TRUST) Foundation"
Executor: Wilhelm J. (Bill) Handel, M.A., L.W.

©Copyright: 60 B.H., M.A., L.W.

Base 5939 A.M.

PREVIEWS Inc.
4209 - 26th Ave. S.E.,
Calgary, Alberta
Canada • T2B 0E1
Phone:1-403-273-9182
Fax: 1-403-273-4119

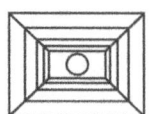

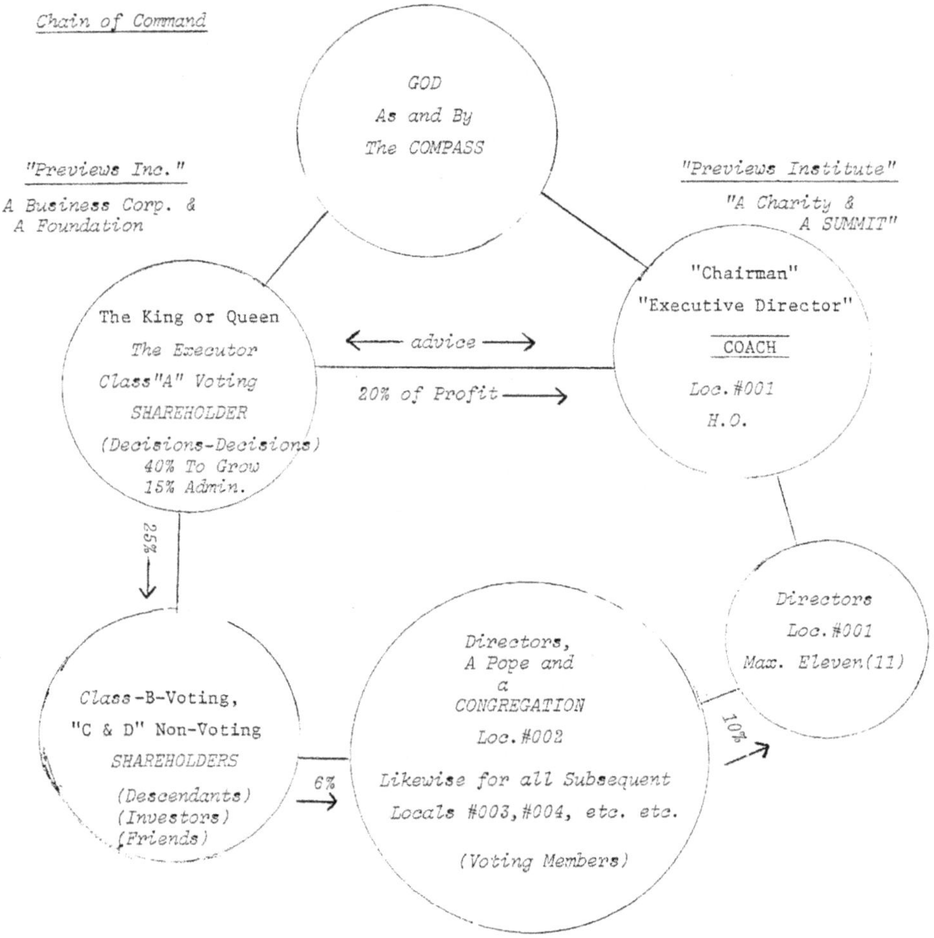

PREVIEWISM
Our World is Beautiful, Yes, Multi-Cultural

Chain of Command

GOD
As and By
The COMPASS

"Previews Inc."
A Business Corp. &
A Foundation

"Previews Institute"
"A Charity &
A SUMMIT"

The King or Queen
The Executor
Class "A" Voting
SHAREHOLDER
(Decisions-Decisions)
40% To Grow
15% Admin.

←— advice —→

20% of Profit —→

"Chairman"
"Executive Director"
COACH
Loc. #001
H.O.

25%

Class-B-Voting,
"C & D" Non-Voting
SHAREHOLDERS
(Descendants)
(Investors)
(Friends)

6%

Directors,
A Pope and
a
CONGREGATION
Loc. #002
Likewise for all Subsequent
Locals #003, #004, etc. etc.
(Voting Members)

10%

Directors
Loc. #001
Max. Eleven (11)

THE TRADITION OF "CHANGE FOR THE BETTER" IS BORN IN *"PREVIEWISM"*
www.previews-inc.com
Make 10 - 20 Copies per week and Pass It On. - God will be well Pleased.

Page 6

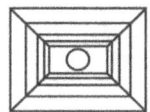

PREVIEWISM
Our World is Beautiful, Yes, Multi-Cultural

PREVIEWS of the FUTURE

God's UMBRELLA Extends over ALL of US,
According to "The COMPASS" (The Everlast Testament

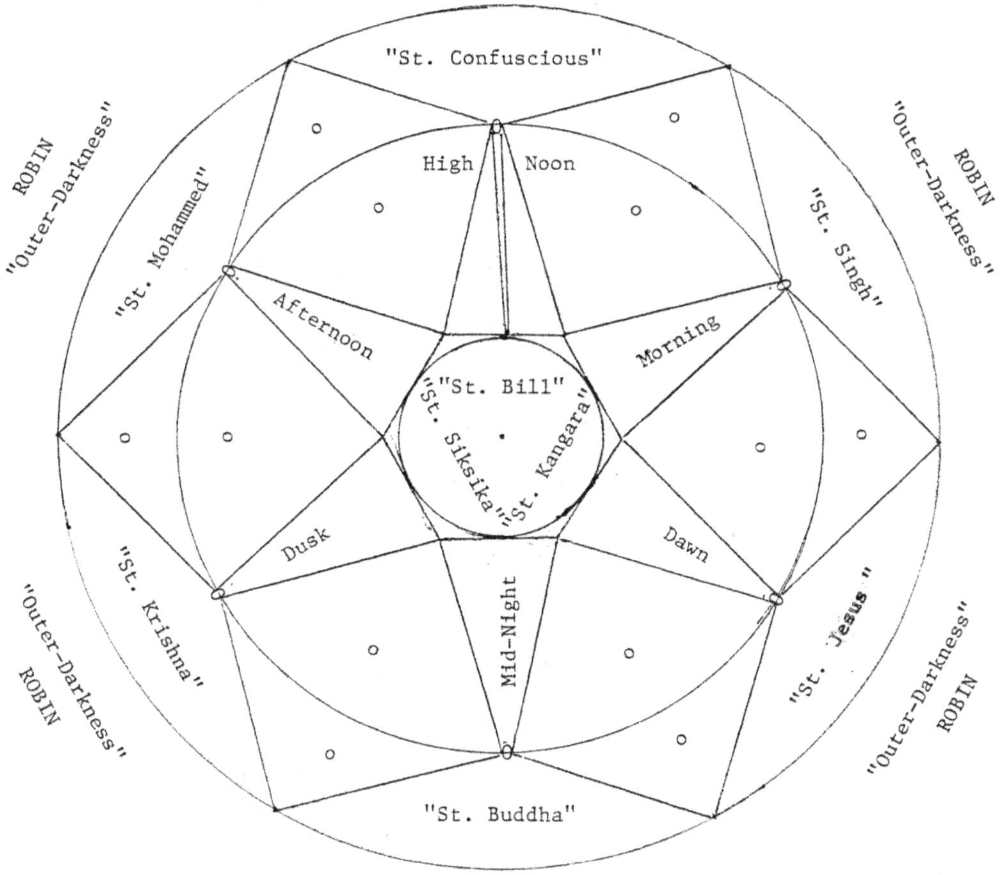

Because The Amphitheatre of God (Heaven) has a Tier for Every Language
God Speaks with Actions from Centre Stage.

**The STAR of Multiculturalism
"INSIDE-OUT"**

THE TRADITION OF "CHANGE FOR THE BETTER" IS BORN IN *"PREVIEWISM"*
www.previews-inc.com
Make 10 - 20 Copies per week and Pass It On. - God will be well Pleased.

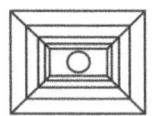

The Star of PREVIEWS

PREVIEWISM
Our World is Beautiful, Yes, Multi-Cultural
PREVIEWS of the FUTURE
Author: "SAINT BILL"
Revealed By: "The Spirit of Truth"

Because The Amphitheatre of God (Heaven) has a Tier for Every Language God Speaks with Actions from Centre Stage.

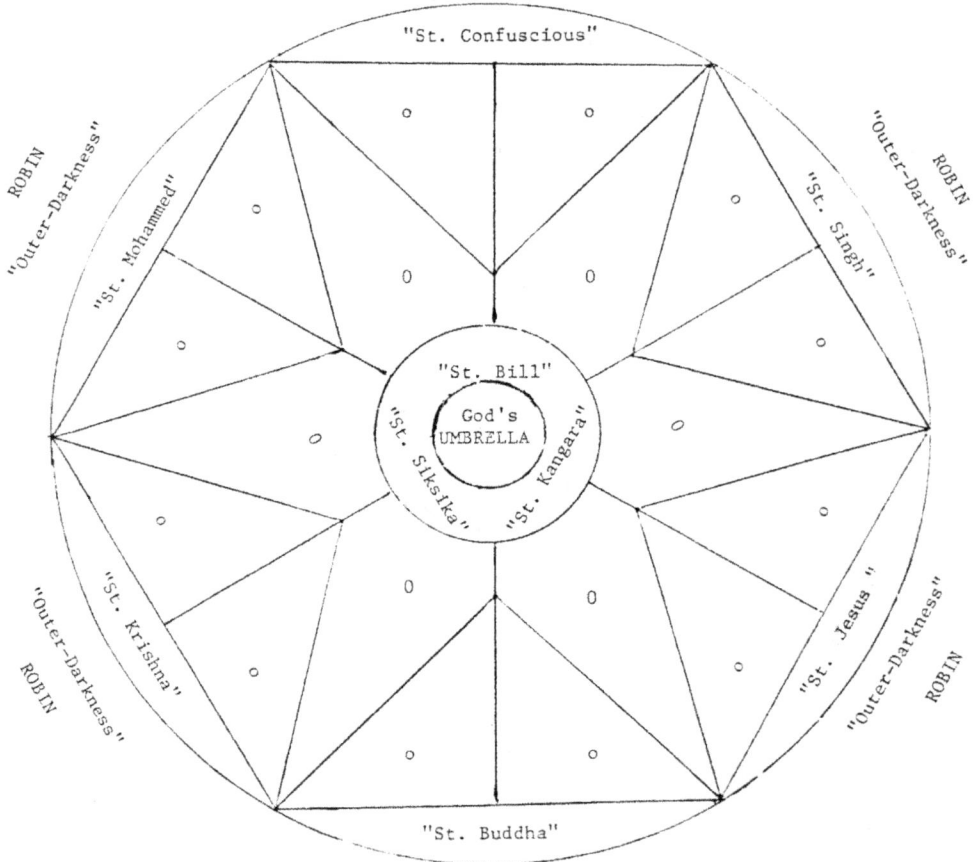

God's UMBRELLA Extends over ALL of US,
According TO "The COMPASS" (The EverLast Testament)

The STAR of Multiculturalism

"Specializing in "Food for THOUGHT"   Since (51 B.H.)
4209 - 26th Avenue S.E., Calgary, Alberta T2B OE1
THE TRADITION OF "CHANGE FOR THE BETTER" IS BORN IN PREVIEWISM

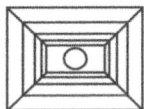

PREVIEWISM
Our World is Beautiful, Yes, Multi-Cultural

FOUNDED BY: "THE COMPASS"
Author: "SAINT BILL"
Revealed By: "The Spirit of Truth"

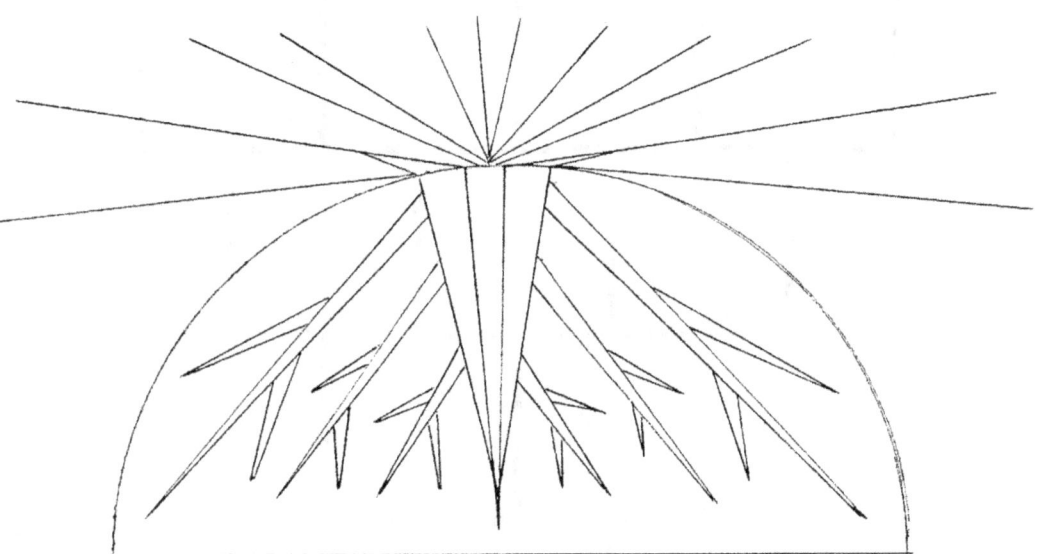

The Tree of Life is Up-Side-Down with the Roots in Heaven above the Clouds. We all Reach up to God's waiting Hand from where ever we are on Earth and we all see life from a different point of View, but as we go along we gradually come to the same conclusion and the same point of View, which is a Broad, point of View, in Heaven.

Yes, Ever Understanding, Loving, Forgiving, and above All Truthful and Forever Real and Alive in "The Spirit of Goodness" which is God.

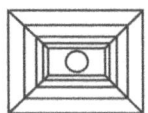

PREVIEWISM
Our World is Beautiful, Yes, Multi-Cultural

The FOUNDERS of the FOUNDATION based over Three Hundred Years.
Conceived = 63 A.B. = 2002 A.J. = 15002 A.H.
(What you can Conceive and Believe, You have Achieved)

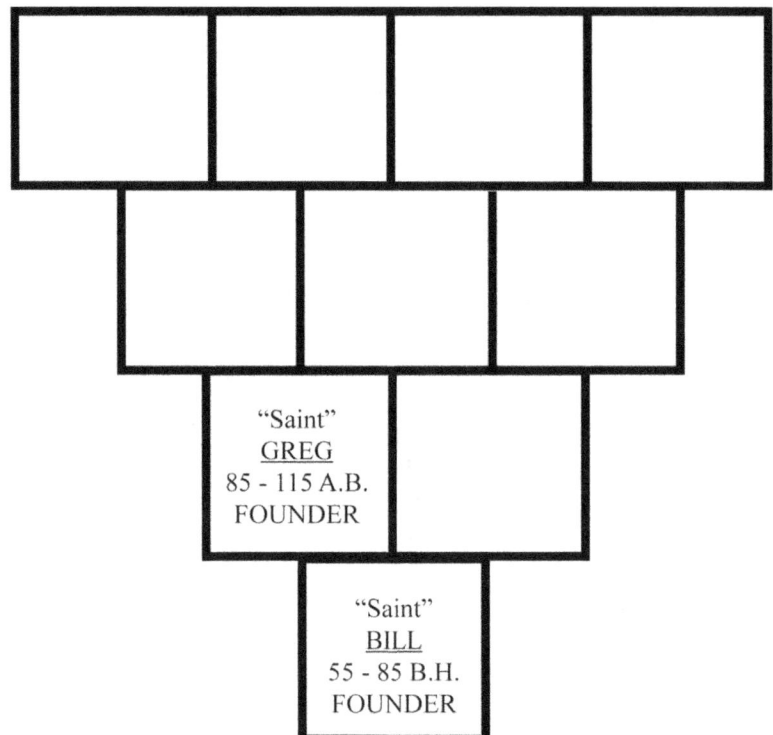

The One's who can Conceive God's Plan and the One's who Implement God's Plan are
EQUAL Partners.
Today is 2002 A.J. and by the year 363 A.B. all the World will have Achieved
PREVIEWISM
Yes, Happiness, Decency, Prosperity, and Peace of Mind.
Yes. Peace, Harmony and Equality with your Neighbours and the World around you.
Yes, Freedom from Guilt, Fear, Doubt and Illusion

The Tradition of "Change for the Better" is Born in *"PREVIEWISM"*
www.previews-inc.com
Make 10 - 20 Copies per week and Pass It On. - God will be well Pleased.

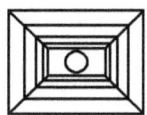

PREVIEWISM
Our World is Beautiful, Yes, Multi-Cultural

Thank you, Thank you, Thank you,. You may be Seated.

Welcome back to the Land of the Living, because the Living are Not Perfect., And the Imperfect always have Room for Improvement.

The Dead are Perfect and have No further Room for Improvement. So let Us Rejoice in the Living.

Folks you are probably wondering what I do with my Time.

Well, I am pleased to inform that I am the Volunteer President of "Previews Inc." Previews Inc. is a Publishing Company and we specialize in Philosophy. This is what I do from a Business point of View.

From a Spiritual point of View I have become a Jesus Freak.

This means that I have become a Previewlite.

Now you will all be interested to know that the Jewish Community is Thinking about REDEFINING Judaism, because It has failed, after 6 days, to fulfil Its Mandate.

And because It has failed so Miserably, we can only assume Its Mandate is not of God. Because God is a Winner, not a Loser.

Well Folks, We at Previews " are not thinking about It, We have already done it. Yes, we have Re-Defined "The Holy Spirit" and have come up with "The Spirit of Goodness". Yes, the New Judaism is based on "The Spirit of Goodness", and because in God's Eye a day is a Thousand years and a Thousand years is a Day, We will fulfil "Our Dear God's" Mandate by Tomorrow afternoon at this time, and "Our Dear God" will rest easy.

Folks, "The Spirit of Goodness" has many Children, The Oldest of which is

"The Spirit of Truth". And The youngest of which is "the Spirit of Enthusiasm". And of course there are many in between, Such as the Spirit of Understanding, The Spirit of Forgiveness, The Spirit of Love,. The Spirit of Being Lucky,. And so on

The Spirit of Goodness" has No Bad Characteristics at all..

It is not Jealous,. Not Hating,. Not Vengeful,. Not Condemning,. Not Punishing,. Not Fearful,. Not Cursing,. Not Threatening,- .And So on.

These all belong to the Evil Spirit,. And we all know, that the Evil Spirit is by Nature a Liar.

Yes, Folks, we have Re-Defined the Jewish God to "The Spirit of Goodness",. because Goodness is very Simple, and Truth is very Simple., And Stands on It's own.

Lie is very Complicated and needs Many Crutches. So Many Crutches.

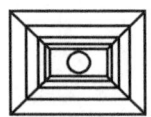

PREVIEWISM
Our World is Beautiful, Yes, Multi-Cultural

PART "C"

1. We all agree that there is only One God, and we all agree that we all have a slightly different point of view or interpretation of God. Yes, God speaks with Actions and we all interpret these Actions slightly differently. Your interpretation is inclined to say that my interpretation is wrong and therefore a lie, and my interpretation is inclined to say that your interpretation is wrong and therefore a lie. But the fact is both interpretations are true if we take the time to understand the others point of view.

2. Now we know, we in turn Act according to our individual interpretation. And so, although we all Act differently, we all Act Good in God's eye because God sees us all from our individual points of view and fully understands us and accepts all our actions as Good. (Some rich in Good and some poor in Good)

3. Because we are not God and can not always understand there are a few limitations we put on our freedom. They are that we should not Lie, Steal, Kill, or Overindulge. So you see, we are really quite Free to do our own thing, and like God, we should accept each others Actions as Good and forgive one another if we do not understand.

4. And so you see, Ignorance, Lack of Understanding, Fear of the Unknown, Fear of Change, these are the Culprits, and they are all Illusion, Yes, Shadow. They do not exist except as to the essence of a Shadow.

5. Yes, now we can understand why God Loves us all, because God fully understands us all and is not Offended by any of our Actions but just calls some of them "Waste".

6. Yes, My Children, in all of God's creation there is only Good and Waste. Not Good and Bad,. Just Good and Waste. If you take a Banana, you have the Good inside and the Peel is the Waste. If you take an Orange, you have the Good inside and the Peel is the Waste. And so it is with all of Humankind, when we do something that we habitually call "Bad",. God says, Oh my, what a Waste.

7. And so you see, With a little Understanding, Love and Forgiveness come easy.

PART "D"

When we say that God is Understanding, we are saying that God is Knowledge because Knowledge brings Understanding; And Understanding brings Love and Forgiveness.

Lack of Knowledge spells "Ignorance", and Ignorance spells "A Blind spot" in your psyche.

If your neighbor tries to enlighten this "Blind Spot" with a Lie, he/she fails because a Lie is more Darkness (Blind Spot) and you both stay Ignorant; And you both disagree.

But if your neighbor tries to enlighten this "Blind Spot" with a Truth, he/she will succeed because a Truth is always preceded by an Action of God and therefore sheds light on the subject, and you say, `Oh, I see!!.. You have then gained knowledge and understanding and with it the ability to love and forgive.

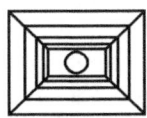

PREVIEWISM
Our World is Beautiful, Yes, Multi-Cultural

Chapter 4 Part "A"

Some people teach that God is a Jealous, Vengeful, Hateful monster that hands out nothing but punishment and does not accept you into Heaven unless you are perfect or have paid a Sacrifice (Bribe). Yes they say that God is an Extortionist and an Accomplice to murder. Worse yet, they say that God committed premeditated murder. Well, it is obvious these people are looking back into an age of Darkness.

Well, we at Previews are in an age of Truth and teach that God is a Sincere, Loving, Forgiving, Ever Understanding " Spirit of Goodness" that can not be Offended,. Therefore It hands out nothing but blessings and accepts us all into Heaven, just as we are. Beautiful, eh, a God you can and would like to please. But we must remember that our fellow Human beings do not always understand and forgive, and so what we sow, we reap, manifold from our neighbors.

This is why God gave us all a sense of Judgement to use, so that we learn right from wrong, true from false and good from waste. Yes, we must learn to Judge one another as God Judges us. (That is to, Provide the alternative, then forgive, not condemn; Bless, not curse; Reward, not punish.)

Yes, my friends, to Judge is to provide the means by which we learn to see ourselves as others see us. Which is a must lest we fall into total confusion and illusion.

Part "B"

Dear Friends, Before God we are All equal. There is no one Nation, there is no one race, there is no one Person that has any preference before God.

There is no one Religion that has any preference before God, Except the ones that say, there is no preference. This is where "Previewism" stands before God.

The Odd one of us has the gall to say that he/she worships the Evil Spirit as though It were real. (the Gall, eh!) Some of us say they worship the Evil Spirit and the Good Spirit together as One. (a bit confused, eh!) Most, near All of us say we worship "the Spirit of Goodness" because we realize the Evil Spirit is just an Illusion, as in Lie, Darkness, Shadow, Ignorance, Blind Spot in your psyche. (a whole lot of Reality, eh!).

God (the Real) (the Spirit of Goodness) pays no attention to what we say, It only pays attention to what we Do,. Yes, Our actions because Actions speak Louder than words; And It has a very positive approach because It understands All our Actions and Adds up All the Good results for you and leaves (forgets) the Waste.

As you know there is always a little Good in All of us and so we All meet God (the Real) in Heaven when we pass on from here because Goodness no matter how small is never wasted before God, because as you know "the first come last and the Last come first".

P.S. Wanting or claiming Preference before God is Evil and Evil is Illusion and Illusion is Ignorance and Ignorance causes Dissension, and Dissension is not of God.

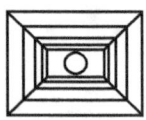

PREVIEWISM
Our World is Beautiful, Yes, Multi-Cultural

Dear Friends,

And now in Closing I want to tell you all a little Story. I have had many Friends in my Life, As we all have Friends.

But there are Three Friends that Stand out as "Stars" in my Life.

Yes, The North Star, The Sun, and The Moon. Two are Real and One is Fraud. My No. 1, Friend in life has been Confucius. He told me a lot of Proverbs when I was a Kid, and they all stood True to the Test.

My No. 2, Friend in life was Robin,. He told me a lot of Parables when I was a Kid. And He told me to Accept them all a Gospel by BLIND Faith, Because the Preacher says he is the Christ (The Jewish Messiah), (The Shadow of God). (But Jesus was a Saint, Your Brother and Mine.

My No. 3, Best Friend in life has been Terry Bracken. Yes, Terry Bracken. He honored his word. He paid me back his portion of what this Church Owed me.

Yes, a Friend in need is a Friend in Deed. And Terry came through with Flying Colors. Of these three Friends I chose to Serve the Christ because of Its parables. Its parables suggested that Nothing was Impossible. I served It for 40 years with Its Hand out and It said, Just Ask and you shall receive 20 fold.

Well, only once in my Life did I have a Cloudy Day. And only once Did I need It. And when I needed It, He let me Down Hard. The Dirty worm. It let me Down. You ask, How did He let you Down? Well, he let me Down because when I turned and Asked for One little thing, One Simple little thing, He Disappeared. Nowhere to be seen. Nowhere. Except for Terry Bracken and Confucius. They were there when I needed them. Yes, they were there when I needed them. Yes, the Messiah Disappeared, and His Disciple said, Impossible.

The Dirty Hypocrite.

Well Folks, We do not always get the Opportunity to Thank our Friends for the Help they provide in Need. But today I have the Opportunity to say, Thank you, to Terry Bracken, for being a Friend in Need.

And today I have the Opportunity to say Thank you, to Confucius.

Confucius, You along with "The Spirit of Truth" inspired me to Write this Book. The COMPASS. It is based on Reality or APPLIED Faith, Not Blind Faith.

It says, that God speaks with Actions, Not with words, because Actions Speak Louder than Words. Yes, God says, I produced the Apples,. We look around, and there is the Tree that provides them Every Year. Actions Everlasting.

The Shadow says, I am God, I can walk on water, I can raise the Dead, I can say to the Mountain "Move ", and It will Move.

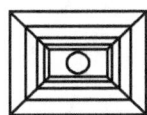

PREVIEWISM
Our World is Beautiful, Yes, Multi-Cultural

I can change a bottle of Water into a Bottle of Whiskey, by snapping my Fingers.

We look around, and where is the Proof? There is None... Empty Words... Empty Words...

FRAUD... FRAUD...

God says, I created you in my Image with a Good Nature. And my "Good Nature" that lives in your Heart is Everlasting and Eternal. Follow me and you will find Heaven on Earth and you will find that it is Eternal.

The Shadow says, I am God, and you are Bad,. You have a Bad Nature, and you must live in Misery... But follow me and I will take you to Heaven.

But It is a LIAR and so It takes you to Hell the Long way around, right here on earth.

Who do you want to Believe?... Well Folks, I chose to Believe God...

And Now I am Back to Practice what I Preach. And what I Preach is that We are All

One in God, and God is One in Each of Us.

Yes, we are not to Separate, We are to Co-Exist.

Thank you, Yours Truly,

As ever in "The Spirit of Goodness"

"Saint Bill", a Servant for God's Sake.

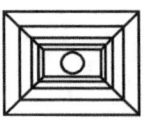

PREVIEWISM
Our World is Beautiful, Yes, Multi-Cultural

November 16/59 B.H. (Base 5939 A.M.)

Dear Friends, Thank you, Thank you, Thank you, You may be Seated.

To begin today, We have a Question for you,. Why does God provide us with Prophecies, (Previews of the Future)?...

Answer: So that we can work toward Fulfilling them.

Yes, God has a Plan and the Previews that It gives us are a part of the Plan that we are to Fulfil. We all have Previews everyday and today We want to share a Preview with you.

In the not to distant Future you are going to realize that you are a "Saint" in God's Eye. Yes, you are a Saint, because God created you with a "Good Nature" in God's Image. And everyday God forgives you and washes away the Bad and leaves you "Spotless" in God's Eye. Yes you are a Saint in God's Eye, and God Loves you, and gives you Its Blessings.

The Accuser (The Shadow) says you are a "Sinner", You are Bad,. You must Pay and live in Misery.. If you do not have any Money, you must Bow Down and worship me "Totally" or you go to Hell.

But you must Remember, The Accuser is a Liar and has no Power and can not send you to Hell or to Heaven.

God prepared a Spot for you in Heaven upon your conception,,,And because God Loves you, God is prepared to Forgive you all your Errors and Sins against Humanity, and keep you "Spotless". Yes, you are a Saint in God's Eye.

The Accuser (The Shadow) says your Errors are Sins against God., But you must remember the Accuser is a Liar; God is never Offended by any One or any thing. God always Understands and Forgives and keeps you Spotless,. So that you will be Fit to take your place in Heaven.. Oh, Yes, That is Right, there is Nothing or No one that can stop you from going to Heaven, because God always gets the Last Word.

...And the Last Word is..."Forgiven"....And the Shadow (Accuser) can go to Hell by Itself.

Yes, God always gives us Prophecies (Previews of the Future), But there is a Problem. God's Servants are Human and so they sometimes make Good (True) prophecies and sometimes they make Bad (False) prophecies.

But there is a Solution: We have to use our "Sense of Judgement" and decide which is a Good prophecy and which is a Bad prophecy. (True or False).. And then we work toward fulfilling the Good prophecies, Not the Bad.

If we work toward fulfilling the Bad prophecy, We are working for the Shadow, Not God.

Eg, If a Prophet says that God wants Someone to be Killed to satisfy God's thirst for Vengeance, It is obvious that it is a False prophecy, because God does not want us to Kill, Yes, God does not want a Sacrifice, God wants Obedience to Its Good prophecies. (And says, Forgiven, if you fail to Obey)

THE TRADITION OF "CHANGE FOR THE BETTER" IS BORN IN *"PREVIEWISM"*
www.previews-inc.com
Make 10 - 20 Copies per week and Pass It On. - God will be well Pleased.

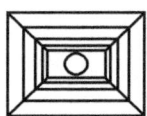

PREVIEWISM
Our World is Beautiful, Yes, Multi-Cultural

E.g, If a Prophet says, that God wants us to find or prepare an Earthly Ruler that is capable of bringing Heaven to Earth,. That would be a Good (True) prophecy, and one worthy of our Effort to work toward achieving Heavenly conditions on Earth for the Ruler to maintain.

Another Example of a Bad prophecy: If a Prophet says, that God wants us to find or prepare a Heavenly Ruler from Earth to go to Heaven and Rule in Heaven,. that would be a Bad (False) prophecy, because, Firstly, We do not know anything about conditions in Heaven and Secondly, God is quite capable of Ruling in Heaven on Its own.. God does not need an Uninformed Human to mess things up in Heaven.

So you see, we should not try to be God, we should only try to be Godly (Good) Humans, and work toward bringing Heaven to Earth.

Yes, Folks, a Prophet of God, prophesies and says, there will soon be Happiness, Decency, Prosperity, and Peace of Mind throughout the World.

A Prophet of the Shadow, prophesies and says, there will soon be Sodomy, Drunkenness, Perversion, and Abomination throughout the World.

God gave you a "Sense of Judgement" so that you can decide correctly which prophecy you want to and should Fulfil. It is obvious, Is it not.

Yes, God says,. You are a "Saint", now go and act Accordingly. The Shadow says,. You are a "Sinner", now go and act Accordingly.

Which do you want to Believe?... Well, Folks, we choose to believe God, and we are Happy-Go-Lucky with It.

Now God says, "A Mountain is a Mountain" and "A Molehill is a Molehill".

The Shadow makes, "A Molehill out of a Mountain" and "A Mountain out of a Molehill".

Yes, There are so many False prophets....

There is Only one "TRUE" prophet, and that is "The Spirit of Goodness" with all of Its children. The oldest of which is "The Spirit of Truth", and the Youngest of which is "The Spirit of Enthusiasm".

And We have it says, "Saint Bill", and the Spirit of Perseverance is related to the Spirit of Enthusiasm and we have them Both, says "Saint Bill". And the Spirit of Love is related to Perseverance and we have them all Three, says "Saint Bill".

And the Spirit of Truth is related to Love and we have them all Four, says "Saint Bill".

Yes, we must develop the Characteristics of "The Spirit of Goodness" to make us Strong.

Now we are not saying that we are the Strongest among Us,. But we are saying we are the Happiest among Us,. And we would rather be Happy, than Strong.

We let God be Strong, so that we will be Happy.

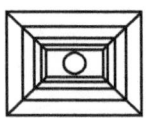

PREVIEWISM
Our World is Beautiful, Yes, Multi-Cultural

Note: If you take an Orange, you have the Good inside and the Peel is the Waste. If you take a Banana, you have the Good inside and the Peel is the Waste.

So it is with Humankind. The Good we do from within stands Forever.. The Bad we do on the Outside, God considers Waste, Not Bad, Just Waste, But God does not let Waste go to Waste. The Waste is turned into Fertilizer over time and is Good.

So you see, there is no Bad in God's world, Only Good.

All except for One thing. Yes, the Shadow. The Shadow is a Total Waste of Time with Its Lies and Illusions, and Counterfeit Miracles, Designed to disintegrate your Sense of Judgement, so that you do not know Right from Wrong, Good from Waste, or True from False.

Yes, "Look Up" and see and hear God speaking, and then Obey God.

Thanks again for Listening,

Yours truly, as ever in,

The Spirit of Goodness,

"Saint Bill".

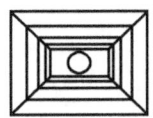

PREVIEWISM
Our World is Beautiful, Yes, Multi-Cultural

Dear Friend:

You are a Successful person,. Because you are making progress toward your Goals. That is what Success is,... Progress toward your Goals.

Now successful people are Wise people,. And Wise people are those of us that have learned the Three sources of Knowledge,. The first source of Knowledge is to talk to another Wise person,... The second source of Knowledge is to Read a Good book,. And the third source of Knowledge is "Personal Experience",... Yes, that is the most accurate source of Knowledge.

Now, when we become Wise, we make Good investments,...

Well, today we have a "Collectors Item" for you that is worth $200.00 and in Five years, you will not give it up for less than a $I,000.00...Good investment, Right?

Here it comes, "The COMPASS", a New Bible, Fresh off the Press, and with each passing year it becomes more Valuable.

You ask, How and Why does it become more Valuable? Well, it becomes more Valuable because you keep it Spotless. Yes, you wash your hands every time before you read it. And keep it Spotless,. And with each passing year it becomes more Valuable.

$200.00,. How about it?

The reason you should invest in "The COMPASS" is because in Life we need a Balance,... Yes, moderation is the key to Stability,. And this provides you with a Balance and leads to moderation,. If you go to far, one way or the other, you are in trouble,. But if you stay moderate you are O.K..

Today's Society has a Mental disease in it,. It is called Schizophrenia (Insanity). And when you Listen to or read Conventional wisdom you catch a touch of Schizophrenia. And if you Fall into the Trap of practising Conventional wisdom, you go to the Hospital with Full blown Schizophrenia.

So you do not Practice the Conventional wisdom of today,. You just Listen to or Read it to check for the Errors,. and you will be alright,. Then read "The COMPASS" and you will catch a touch of "Genius",. (And a touch of "Genius" is a "Glimpse of God")

The Doctors say, there is no cure for Schizophrenia,. But we have found a Cure,.. Do you know what it is?... Throw away Conventional wisdom,... It is a Disease.

Now we have to go,. You keep "The COMPASS" Spotless,. Wash your hands every time before you read it, and keep it Spotless; And it will become more Valuable with each passing year.

Thanks for Listening, Yours truly, as ever in,

"The Spirit of Goodness",

"Saint Bill"   B.H., M.A., L.W.

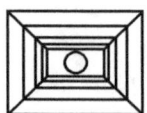

PREVIEWISM
Our World is Beautiful, Yes, Multi-Cultural

Folks, we are a Non-Profit organization (Charity) and our Object is "To Relieve Poverty", (Both Physical and Spiritual poverty)

God provides so many Blessings, An abundance of Blessings,. And most of us are in the Right place at the Right time and are Satisfied.

But there are a Few of us that are in the Wrong place at the Wrong time and they live in misery. Some of them are in Physical poverty but most of them are in Spiritual poverty. But regardless of that, It is Poverty.

Now we know that God is not Poor, God is Rich, and wants us to distribute the Wealth and Abundance of God's Food and Essentials of life to the Needy throughout the World.

No One person can possibly do this by his/her own resources, be it Financial, Physical or Spiritual. And so We at "Previews" need Help. Your help. What can you possibly Contribute to the Cause, without it being a Burden.

As you know we started at Two Hundred dollars,. If that is a Burden, what or how much is not a Burden.

Suggested Minimum: $60.00 Suggested Maximum: $200.00

Prepare yourselves for the Future, and we will make the arrangements to have you become one of our "Corporate" or "Personal" Sponsors.

In the meantime, if you want to make a Contribution, please make your cheque payable to "Previews Institute", and send it to the Address shown below. (We will issue you a receipt for "Goods" and "Services Rendered")

Thank you, Yours truly, as ever in,

"The Spirit of Goodness",

Previews - Institute of Universal Philosophy

Per: W.J.(Bill) Handel, M.A., L.W. (Coach)

P.S.: Remember, you get a "Collectors Item" by Return Mail.

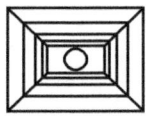

PREVIEWISM
Our World is Beautiful, Yes, Multi-Cultural

November 30/ (59 B.H.)

Thank you, Thank you, Thank you,. You may be Seated.

Dear Friends,. To begin today, we remind you of the Words of a great Servant of God (The Spirit of Goodness).

Let us turn to "Acts 26,v.16-18". It says, that I have come to Appoint you as Ministers and Witnesses of the Truth. And to Deliver you from the Jewish God. (Verse 18) Yes, it says most Israelites are worshipping "Satan", not God.

From this a Question arises, If most Israelites are worshipping "Satan", Where are the True Prophets? The answer is, There are not very many True Prophets of Old. (In fact, there are None) It is all the Prophecy of Satan (The Shadow).

And so you see, Just as with all else, Spiritual, there are Two Messiah's. The Messiah of Satan, and the Messiah of God,. The Messiah of Satan is a fictional character,. Just as "Satan" (The Shadow) is a fictional character (Illusion) (Fantasy),

The Poor man that spoke-up for God (The Spirit of Goodness) was transformed into "The Messiah of the Jews',. Yes, the Messiah of Satan,. by a Shrewd man called "Paul", (an Israelite), trying to GLORIFY his Son, not God.

As with all else of Satan (The Shadow), It has a Sheepskin Coat on, But is not a Sheep, But rather a Wolf and a Worm in One.

And so It speaks so Nice, making Grand promises,. All the while leading you the long way around to the Pits of Hell and Misery, Saying, Do not worry, Suffering makes you Strong. "Saint Bill" says, The SON-of-a-Bitch., Suffering makes you a "Sucker for more Suffering."

The Die-Hard Israelites did not accept this Poor and Good man as their Messiah, because he did not Fit into their Plan for the Kingdom of God (The Shadow) (Satan)

But "Paul" transformed him into a Poor and Bad man, breaking all of God's laws, by Counterfeit Miracles and told the Gentiles, He was the Messiah of God. Most Gentiles being Overtrusting and very Gullible accepted him as the Messiah of God.

But he was the Messiah of Satan, because his followers were Led to keep the same "Book of Prophecies" as the Israelites. The story of "Paul" in the transformation, promises to eliminate the Condemnation of Satan

If you will Glorify a Man instead of God (the Real) "The Spirit of Goodness". But "Paul" was Fraudulent in every way. First, he did not eliminate the "Old Book of Prophecies". Secondly, He knew that you should not Glorify or Worship a Fallible man. This in his own words is Idolatry.

Yes, the Messiah of Satan is of the Past, Perfect, Dead, and an Illusion and a Liar. The Poor man that Spoke up for God "The Spirit of Goodness" was a "Saint". His name was "Robin", (Illiterate and Forgotten), but a "Saint", Your Brother and Mine.

The Tradition of "Change for the Better" is Born in *"PREVIEWISM"*
www.previews-inc.com
Make 10 - 20 Copies per week and Pass It On. - God will be well Pleased.

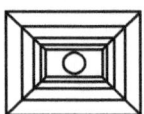

PREVIEWISM
Our World is Beautiful, Yes, Multi-Cultural

Thank God (the Real) "The Spirit of Goodness", Now we have "The COMPASS".

The Messiah of God (The Spirit of Goodness) is a Living Human being, as described in the "Chain of Command" in The Compass, page 276.

The Messiah of God, a Living Human, always being renewed with each generation, is to take the Sum Total of all the "Spirits of Goodness" (Good Intentions) in the World and organize them into a Working Order (Plan) that he/she can implement when he/she becomes King/Queen,

Executor, of "Previews Inc." the "Eternal (Trust) Foundation",
    (also known as "An Eternal Royal Family of God")

In this way we will Forever make progress toward the Future Utopia of

God's never ending Kingdom that is now Established with "Previews Inc."
and "Previews Institute of Universal Philosophy".

Thanks for Listening,

Yours truly, as ever in, The Spirit of Goodness,

(Saint Bill). B.H., M.A., L.W.

P.S.:   The Spirit (Messenger) of God says, "We are One"
        The Spirit (Messenger) of The Shadow says, "I am It"
        One causes Peace and Harmony. (Good)
        One causes War and Dissension. (Waste)

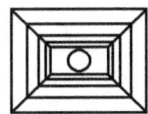

PREVIEWISM
Our World is Beautiful, Yes, Multi-Cultural

December 15/98 (59 B.H.)

Dear Friends:

"A Light in the Night is A Light in Deed" "A Light in the Light is A Light in Need"

God's hand is a "Flood-light" and God has a "Flood-Light" extended to each of us from around the Stage in the Amphitheatre of life, and as such we all have a "Flood-Light" showing us the Way of Heaven.

But in Centre-Stage there stands the Liar (The Shadow) with a small Candle in each Hand,. Saying, I am God, I am God,. Look Down and watch me, Really, I am Real.. But It has no shadow, and we know that all things Real have a Shadow. Therefore, we know It is a Fraud. Yes, God, the Real, has a Shadow. But remember, we pay no attention to Shadows. They are just a nuisance and a total Waste causing Illusion and Depression.

Previewlites are children of God, and they know they are "Saints" in God's Eye. Yes, Previewlites know that God created them with a "Good Nature" in the Image of God. And they know that because God Loves them, God forgives them their shortcomings and washes away the Bad everyday and keep them "Spotless". Yes, a "Saint" in God's Eye.

Previewlites are Looking Up, because the "Flood-Light" (The COMPASS) they have in their hand says, Look-Up and see Truth and Reality and become enthused by opportunity.

The poor Souls who do not have "The COMPASS" (a Flood-Light) with them, Look Down to the Frauds, which say,. You are a "Sinner", You are Bad,. You must Pay and Live in Misery. If you do not have any Money, You must Bow down and worship us Totally, and I will forgive you so that you do not have to go to Hell,. But I will not Forget, You must answer again on Judgement Day. Now remember, If you look up once, You go to Hell.

Yes, God says, You are a "Saint", now go and Act accordingly, and reap the Rewards.

The Shadow says, You are a "Sinner", now go and Act accordingly, and reap the Punishment.

We know we do not have to ask, "Which do you want to Believe", because we know that God also gave you a "Sense of Judgement" to use, and it will guide you correctly.

Thanks for Listening,

Yours truly, as ever in,

"The Spirit of Goodness",

B.H., M.A., L.W. (Saint Bill).

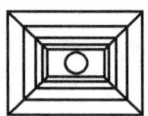

PREVIEWISM
Our World is Beautiful, Yes, Multi-Cultural

December 21/59 B.H. (Base 5939 A.M.)

Dear Friends,.

My Father George, always said, that the first time someone strikes me, It is my fault. The second time someone strikes me, It is his fault. And the Third strike is Mine. Twice as Hard.

This brings me to an Understanding with the Phenomena of Turning the Other Cheek.

God says, Be ye angry and Sin not, Let not the Sun go down on your Wrath. This means we Forgive all every Evening, and start a New day every Morning, with Two Cheeks.

When someone strikes you the first time that day, You turn the other Cheek. If he strikes you again, You strike him back Hard. If he does not strike you again, but chooses to walk away, It means he has Forgiven you, and you are Both free.

Now when the second man strikes you that same day, You strike him Back Hard, and Say, Oh, I am sorry, I was short Tempered. Yes, I was out of Cheeks... Then you tell him your story, and he will say: Oh, That is alright, I Forgive you, and You are Both Free.

Thank you, Dear God, Thank you.

B.H., M.A., L.W. (Saint Bill)

A Misc. Proverb:

    You can live completely without Illusion,

     because it is a most Joyous existence.

    But you can not live completely without Reality,

    because it is a most Miserable existence.

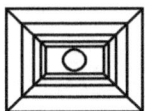

PREVIEWISM
Our World is Beautiful, Yes, Multi-Cultural

The PREVIEWLITE's conversion presentation.

My Dear Child,. Do you Realize that you are a "Saint" in God's Eye.?

Yes, You are a "Saint" because God created you with a "Good Nature", in the Image of God., And because God Loves you, God Forgives you, your shortcomings and Washes away the Bad every day and keeps you "Spotless". Yes, a "Saint" in God's Eye. Yes, God says, you are welcome in Heaven any time, Just as you are.

The Accuser (The Shadow) (The Devil) says, You are a "Sinner", you are Bad,. You must Pay, and live in Misery., If you do not have any Money,. You must Bow Down and worship me "Totally" or you go to Hell.

But remember, the Accuser (The Shadow) is a Liar and has No power to send you to Hell or to Heaven.

God prepared a Spot for you in Heaven upon your Conception., And there is Nothing or No-One that can stop you from going to Heaven., Because God always gets the Last Word., And the Last word is "Forgiven".

Thank you, Dear God, Thank you.

"Saint Bill"

P.S.: There are 214 examples of Truth, such as the above, found in "The COMPASS".
And there are 214 opposite Statements to these, found in Other Books of Knowledge, all claimed to be the Truth.
You say, Impossible. I say, Test me.

Thank you,
"Saint Bill".

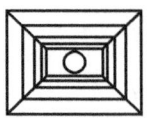

PREVIEWISM
Our World is Beautiful, Yes, Multi-Cultural

Dear Friends,

As we know, God is a very Busy Spirit and it seems that Its work is never Done.

We also know that God wants us to follow Its example and find work that is never really Done.

When I was a young man, I said, I would sell "Real Estate" until I was 85 years old. But I retired early with a Hobby, and now I have been Blessed with work that will keep me Busy until I am 95.

We all have various degrees of Success, but there are Two basic Goals we all have in common. Firstly, we all want to have our "Home" here on Earth paid Up in Full when we retire from work, and we also want a few frills around so that we can then enjoy our Leisure.

The second Goal in life we all have is that God can Receive us "Proud" for our Efforts here on Earth, and that we can sit "Proud" amongst our unlimited Friends in the Amphitheatre of Heaven, with Our Dear God in Centre Stage.

And so I want you to follow God's example, as I have done, and take up the Hobby ofPreaching the "Good News" in God's Plan. So that your work will never be Done, and so that you also will sit "Proud" in God's Circle of Friends around the Universe (The Stage) of Heaven, from where we will Giggle and Chat and watch the World go by.

Glory, Glory,. Hallelujah!!

Beautiful eh! Yeh, Yeh, Yeh,

"Saint Bill".

A Misc. Proverb:

> A Sexy person has Virtue, in Control. An Impotent one has no Virtue, in Control. God says, Honor your word in this Regard, and have Fun. The Shadow says, Be dead to the Flesh, Yes, be Perfect. (Well, the Earthworm)

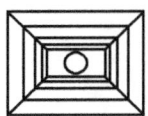

PREVIEWISM
Our World is Beautiful, Yes, Multi-Cultural

My Children and My Friends the World over.

In the Beginning there was "The Spirit of Goodness" (God the Real), and it was Dark and Cold., And God said, "Let there be Angels", and from One there became a Multitude of Angels around God., And God said, I shall call you My Children,. Yes, My Little "Spirits" of Goodness.

All of the Angels obeyed and Honored God, "Except One", And this One said, "I am God", Obey and Honor Me and I will take you to Heaven.

Then the Little Children said, "Where are we Now"?

And after a moment God said, I will "Show" you,..Let there be Light,. And the Light appeared in the Midst of them,. And the Angels seen they were in Heaven around the Universe of Planets, Stars, Moons, and Space, and they Knew "The One" had tried to Deceive them.

Then the Angels said, Let us All Join Hands in One Big Circle around "Our Magnificent God" and Praise God for our Creation in Its Image. And "The One" Disobedient disappeared into Outer-Darkness behind them for Fear of being Exposed.

And the Angels said, We shall call "That One", The Shadow, in reference to the Darkness Behind us. And we shall call God, "Light", in recognition of the Knowledge Before us.. And the Source of God we shall call, "The Eclipse of Energy", around the "Steel-Glass-Ball" (the Sun) in the Centre.

Then God said, I shall give you, All my Children, a Name so that you remember that you are All Related to me (God the Real). And each of you shall have a Shadow below and Behind you. My first Born I shall call "Truth"

My Youngest I shall call "Enthusiasm".

Note: This is the first Piece of the Picture We have of the Beginning.

....And the Last shall come First, and the First shall come Last. And God is, was, and always shall be the Same, Today, Yesterday, and Tomorrow, and with No missing Link. What is thought of the missing Link is Illusion, Small and Invisible and Insignificant.

Yes, cast it out, because we are One with God, and God is One with us, Always.

Note: To continue see Ch.l,v.33, Page 19,

Then "Part B", Page 190. (And so on)

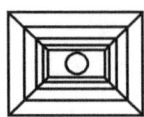

PREVIEWISM
Our World is Beautiful, Yes, Multi-Cultural

And So you see, when your Body ceases to function, You go to Meet your Soul-Mate in Heaven.

Thank you,

Yours truly,

As ever in, "The Spirit of Goodness",

B.H., M.A., L.W. (Saint Bill)

P.S.: The Spirit of God (Reality) says, "We are One".
The Spirit of The Shadow (Illusion) says, "I am It".
We all know what God did to that one, yes, kicked It out into Outer Darkness, beyond the reach of Light, and said, Stay there Alone, I need you there for Reference.
"The Spirit of Goodness" says, "We are One".
The Holy Spirit says, "I am It".

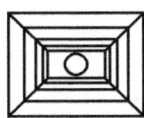

PREVIEWISM
Our World is Beautiful, Yes, Multi-Cultural

Dear Friends: Thank you, Thank you, Thank you,. You may be Seated.

To begin today,. We have a Question,. What is a Mutation?

Answer: A Mutation is like a Chemical reaction.

Example: If you take some Lead and add some Acid and Oxygen you get Lead-oxide.

2)   If you take 2 parts of Hydrogen and add a part of Oxygen you get Water.

3)   If you take a picture of a Car and add a picture of a Wheel, you see a Wheel-wrench.

Now if you take Sincerity and add some Love, you get Integrity.

2)   If you take some Love and add Enthusiasm, you get Perseverance.

3)   If you take Forgiveness and add some Hope, you get Initiative.

So you see what Mutations are,., They are creative thought Reactions in your mind., And these New thoughts are called "Previews" of something great or something more..

And so what you have to do is keep a Pad of writing paper and a Pen handy all the time. So that when you get a New Mutation, you write it down right away. So that you can Refer to it at the end of the Day and let it grow into something Tomorrow. So that you get the full Picture Show.

That way you are always busy taking the Initiative and getting Results. If you do not write the New Mutations or "Previews" down on paper you forget them and all you become is a Dreamer.

I had a Mutation this morning and now you are reading it.. So you see, these New Mutations provide us with Leadership, and as you know we can all use Leadership and Leadership training. This all works Hand in Hand with our "Achiever's Habits Program" found in The COMPASS, page 11, & page 94.

Thanks for Listening,

Yours truly, as ever in "The Spirit of Goodness"

"Saint Bill" a Servant for God's Sake

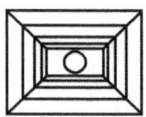

PREVIEWISM
Our World is Beautiful, Yes, Multi-Cultural

Dear Friends,. Thank you, Thank you, Thank you,. You may be Seated.

(Acts 26, v.16-18) Justifies Our Desire to Appoint you Ministers of God, "The Spirit of Goodness", which is Truth, which is Light, which is Knowledge, which leads to Riches.

Your Purpose is to Deliver people from "The Shadow of God", which is Illusion, which is Darkness, which is Ignorance, which leads to Poverty.

"The Spirit of Goodness" is your Desire to Do Good, which is Normal and which is Natural. "The Spirit of Goodness" also has a "Sense of Judgement", which tells you that "Good" brings Joy and Satisfaction, and "Bad" brings Sorrow and Dissatisfaction,. So you Naturally choose to do "Good", which in turn encourages and increases your "Good Nature" and the Desire to do more "Good". Yes, because "The Desire to do Good" is the Dominating force in the World, It multiplies and Accumulates.

The Negative Results of the "Bad" (Illusion) are Absorbed (Forgiven) by the "Good", which is Goodness. Yes, the Desire to do Bad leads to Spiritual Poverty and the Material gains are Wasted in Frustration until One realizes that he/she has to change Its ways. Yes, the "Bad" are "Spinning their Wheels", and they always come to realize it Sooner or Later.

In the meantime God (The Spirit of Goodness) and the "Good" continue on their way of Happiness, Decency, Prosperity, and Peace of Mind,. Always encouraging any and All to Join them in Heaven on Earth. Yes, that is Right, Heaven has now come to Earth in the Knowledge of "Previewism".

Thank you,

Yours truly,

B.H., M.A., L.W. "Saint BILL" (Coach)

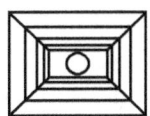

PREVIEWISM
Our World is Beautiful, Yes, Multi-Cultural

Dear Friends,. Thank you, Thank you, Thank you,. You may be Seated:

"Saint Bill" says to the Human Race,. "We shall Eat Humble Pie, Before "God the Real" (The Spirit of Goodness),. And not Before any Human. Never,. Because any Human that wants you to Eat Humble Pie, Before Him/Her is Bad (a Fraud) (an Illusion), and a Bastard.

Any Human that says, Eat Humble Pie, Before God "Only" is Good (Authentic), and a Real man/woman., Because he/she knows that God "Only" is "Tremendous" "Magnificent", and Great., And any Knowledge that comes to us, comes through "The Spirit of Goodness", and So God gets the Glory and the Honor and the Praise,. Not any still) Simple, Fallible Human. Yes, that is Right, Eat Humble Pie, "Only" Before "God the Real" (The Spirit of Goodness).

And the Gateway of Reality will be in Front of you, and the Escape of Illusion shall stay Behind you. Yes, you will continue to grow and increase in the Quality and Quantity of Goodness before you.

Thank you, Yours truly,

as ever in, "The Spirit of Goodness"

B.H., M.A., L.W. "Saint Bill" (Coach)

P.S..: My Mother "Katherina" always said, "You listen to your Father,.

He is the "Push" around here, and I am the "Pull" away out Front with an

Invisible String, a Long one and a Strong one,. Always tight but Flexible. Together, we are Two in One, in You, and You are One in Two in Us.

And "God the Real" (The Spirit of Goodness) will provide Us with a "COMPASS", "a New One", Now go and Find It.

Thank you, Dear God, Thank you,

B.H., M.A., L.W. "Saint BILL" (Coach)

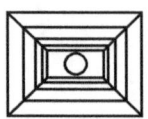

PREVIEWISM
Our World is Beautiful, Yes, Multi-Cultural

Dear Friends,. Thank you, Thank you, Thank you,. You may be Seated,...

To begin today, we want to remind you that the "God of the Dark Ages", (The Shadow), said,. You are a "Sinner", You are Bad,. You must pay me a "Sacrifice" or you go to Hell.

At the Dawn of a New Age,. "Saint Paul" said, No Way, God does not want a Sacrifice, God wants "Obedience". Therefore, No more Sacrifices, because God says, Forgiven, when It does not get Obedience, once in a while. Then "The Shadow" did sneak back in and said, You are a Sinner, You areBad. But if you do not have any Money, You must Bow Down and Worship me "Totally" or you go to Hell.

At "High Noon" of the New Age, Yes, The Age of "Bright Lights",... "Saint BILL" said, No Way, God does not want you to Worship any One or any Thing, Except, "The Spirit of Goodness" (God, the Real) and All of Its Children. Yes, my Little "Spirits" of Goodness, also known as Angels, Of which the First Born is called "Truth" and the Youngest of which is called "Enthusiasm". And in between there are many more such as the Spirits of Perseverance, Love, and Planning toward the PREVIEWS of Goodness (God). Therefore, "Saint Bill" says, Do not Worship any One or any Thing except "The Spirit of Goodness" and All of Its Children, because the Old Age of Darkness has passed away, Yes, come to an End, and The "New Age of Light" is here, Yes, It is Arrived and It is Truly Everlasting and Eternal. Now do not "Look Back", do not "Look Down",. Just put your Foot Down once in a While and Rub with your Rubber Heel and say,..

"Die you CockSucker:.,Die", until there is nothing left but Dust, and then turn and say,. "Be gone, You Bastard", Out into Outer Darkness beyond the reach of Light, and Stay there, We need you there for Reference. Then turn again and "Have a Happy Day". God Bless you,.

Yours Truly,
as ever in, "The Spirit of Goodness"

B.H., M.A., L.W. "Saint Bill" (Coach)

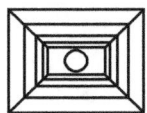

PREVIEWISM
Our World is Beautiful, Yes, Multi-Cultural

Dear Friend in 'Saint Bill"

The Shadow, being ignored by God because It is a Vacuum, a fraud, an Illusion, a Nothing,.was so upset and Jealous of God that It Cursed and Cursed, Condemned and Condemned and said "God Damned it all."

But do not forget the Shadow is before all else, a Liar.

We know God Forgives, not Condemns; God Blesses, not Curses.

And we know God Blessed All in Its creation and Damned "Nothing".

The Shadow Condemned us to Death, but it is a Lie, because God overruled and said Life is Everlasting, yes, Life after Life after Life.

The Shadow Cursed us to be born with a Bad Nature, but It Failed, God Forgives and always Retains and Renews our Good Nature, Time and Time Again, Life after Life after Life.

Now what we should learn from this is that God is a Winner because It always Forgives and keeps Its Kingdom intact.

Therefore we should also always Forgive our fellow human beings so as to reap the Blessings of God; And we should also always use our Sense of Judgement and remember that "to Forgive is to Forget"; Which means that if are Dealing with a Criminal, you say, "You are Forgiven, Now get out of my sight, so I can Forget you."

That is what God says to the Shadow; Be gone, out into outer Darkness, Beyond the reach of Light, and stay there, we need you there for Reference.

Thank you, Dear God, Thank you.

B.H., M.A., L.W. "Saint Bill" (Coach)

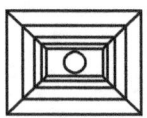

PREVIEWISM
Our World is Beautiful, Yes, Multi-Cultural

January 18/99 (60 B.H.)

Dear Friends,.

I, "Saint Bill" have been in a Diving contest for the past Six (6) millenniums and my turn came up in 5990 A.M.. (51 B.H.)

The Deal is, you have Ten years to make Six Dives, and the Diver who makes Six Dives without a Splash get First prize, Yes, Gold Medal..

Well, the previous Divers all Failed, but this year I made my Sixth Dive and "Sip, Sap" (No Splash), All Six, No Splash. (Gold Medal).

Just like "Mohammed Ali, "Sip, Sap", and they are out Cold.

"The Greatest", Yes, My Dear Friends, "The Greatest",. That is me and my Mentor, Mohammed Ali,. And We are, My Dear God, "The Greatest-Yes, Friends, We have been Listening to and Writing God's words for the past Nine years, and this week We wrote "The End" on "The COMPASS", "A New Bible", The EverLast Testament). And No-one lost a Feather. That is Right, No Splash),. Yes, Prophecy Fulfilled, "Like a Thief in the Night", and it is Done. Not one Arm raised in Strife, Not one word spoken in Haste, and Not one Illusion left intact.

Yes, Friends, We have had Revealed, by "The Spirit of Truth", a "Steel-Glass-Ball" that is firm but Flexible, Not a Crystal-Ball, which when thrown Down, Shatters to Pieces,. But a "Steel-Glass-Ball", like a Golf-Ball clean clear through, which when thrown Down bounces back quickly for you to throw it again and again.

We have been throwing our "Steel-Glass-Ball" for Nine years and there is Not one Illusion left, They are all shattered to Slithers and we have Rubbed with our Rubber Heel until there was Nothing left but Dust.

Now it is "Heaven on Earth" as God planned It.

(Take a Look, Then Read the Book)

Thanks For Listening,

Yours Truly, as ever in, "The Spirit of Goodness"

"Saint Bill"

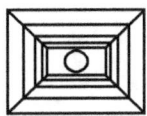

PREVIEWISM
Our World is Beautiful, Yes, Multi-Cultural

January 20/99 (60 B.H.)

Dear Friends, in "Saint Bill",

The Following is a description of why and what the problem was in

the Past Society. It is given so that the Present Society will be able to avoid the Pitfalls of the Past which are The Shadow's Blue Print to Read from, All in opposite terms,. because It is always a Liar. Therefore, when we look Down, we are Listening to the Shadow and It guides us back into the Pitfall, because It is a Sucker-for-Punishment.

However, when we Look Up, we see and Hear God (the Real) speaking with Actions, and because we know that God speaks with actions we know not to Listen to the Words of the Shadow, which are all Lies. Yes, we must Learn

to interpret the Actions of God (Present), Not the Words of the Shadow (Past). Then we are in tune with the Times and we can Plan for the Future according to our "Sense of Judgement" and "Good Nature" which brings

forth "Truth" and "Reality" based on our ever-improving "Sense of Judgement". Subsequently, we find that God (the Real) leads us to Joy and Happiness along with God's Blessings and Rewards,. Because God is Not a Sucker for Punishment, God (the Real) is a Lover of the Positive aspects of Life. Yes, We can Plan for a Beautiful and Prosperous Future because God is the same Now, and Tomorrow.

The Previewlite says, I Preach what I Practice, because it is based on the Actions of God, of the Present. The Shadow Worshipper does not Practice what He/She Preaches, because it is Lie, based on the Words of the Shadow, of the Past.

Thanks for listening,

As Ever,

"Saint Bill"

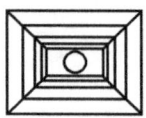

PREVIEWISM
Our World is Beautiful, Yes, Multi-Cultural

Dear Friends,.

The Shadow-Worshipper wants you to be a Follower like he/she is, because the Shadow says, You be a Follower, So that I can lead you to Hell the Long-Way-Around.

God (the Real) "The Spirit of Goodness" wants the PREVIEWLITE to be

a Leader because God is far out Front Looking to the Future which is Heaven. Therefore, a Leader (like God) does not Push you from Behind, but rather Pulls you from Far out Front with an Invisible String, a long one and a Strong one,. Tight but Flexible.

The problem is "The Previewlite" is so Far out Front, It is coming from Behind, and so it seems He/She is Pushing you, but in Fact you are just holding up the Show.

Now we can understand why God always sends the Generals (Leaders) to the back Row., Yes, to bring up the Rear (the Lost). But when the General has gathered all of the Lost, he/she begins to encourage you to become a Leader instead of a Follower, and so again, It seems as though he/she is Pushing you, but in Fact you are just holding up the Show.. So get with it Son or Daughter,. Take the Initiative and become a Leader (Previewlite). But do not turn and obstruct the General, just go and get to the Front of the Crowd and subsequently away out Front, helping the General (Leader), who is simultaneously in Front of you and Behind you all the way.

Yes, Folks, a Previewlite is a Leader, a Shadow-Worshipper is a Follower. A Leader takes the Initiative, A Follower procrastinates.

A Leader gains Momentum, A Follower comes to a Stand-Still.

A Leader continues to Look to the Future,. A Follower turns to go Backwards. But you are a Leader, my Son or Daughter,. So Look Up and see Truth and Reality, and become Enthused by the Opportunity ahead of you.

Thanks for Listening,

Yours truly, as ever in,

"The Spirit of Goodness",

"Saint Bill" a Servant for God's Sake

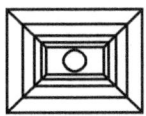

PREVIEWISM
Our World is Beautiful, Yes, Multi-Cultural

January 20/99 (60 B.H.)

Dear Friends, in "Saint Bill",. Thank you, Thank you, Thank you,. You may be Seated.

Folks, there are some Books of Knowledge that Suggest you think that the Devil (Demon) lives in Pigs, and that Beasts have Wings, and that Dogs have Horns, and that Pigs have Mud on their Nose, all the time.

Well, this is Sick Psyche Psychology, because it is the Virus of a Mental disease called Schizophrenia, and Schizophrenia if not treated, leads to Insanity.

The Doctors say, there is no Cure for Schizophrenia, but "Saint Bill" has developed a Cure., It is found in "The COMPASS", a New and True Book of Knowledge.

It is known that if you just pay Lip service to these Sick Suggestions found in some Books of Knowledge, You are not in too much danger of catching the Disease, and that the Virus stays Dormant.

But if you take these Suggestions seriously and Fall into the Trap of Practising the Way of Life that is combined with them, You activate the Virus and you catch the Disease, and if not treated in time you go Insane.

But, Do not worry, God (the Real) has known this from the Beginning and this is why It gave us a "Sense of Judgement" to use, So that we learn to know, "Good from Waste", "Right from Wrong", "True from False", "Reality from Illusion". Yes, "Sanity from Insanity".. And God knows that when we are Sane, We follow God's suggestions and Do "Good" to develop our "Good Nature" in the likeness of God.

When we follow "Sick Psyche Psychology" we are being led toward "Insanity" which Destroys the "Good Purpose" that God had in mind for you, and so you Do "Bad" as a result of the Ignorance in it all, which leads to Poverty, Both Physical and Spiritual Poverty.

This is why you find so many people who do not Practice what they Preach, we call them Hypocrites, because although they have not had any other Books of Knowledge to read, they know better than to Practice Insanity, or Illusion, which all has Its roots in "The Shadow of God".

Yes, The Shadow is the Culprit, the Deceiver, and the Liar, and is always changing Its name so that we will not Recognize It in between the Lines of these So called Books of Knowledge.

We call the Shadow, Devil, Satan, Demon, Accuser, Lucifer, Crystal, and a whole host of other names. All as though It were Real.

In the True Book of Knowledge, "The COMPASS", we have Identified the Culprit, Yes, "The Shadow", and It is an Illusion, a Vacuum of Light, a Fraud, and a Nothing. And has no Power what so ever when we "Look Up" to God (the Real) "The Spirit of Goodness", the correct description of God.

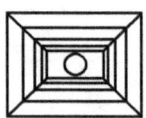

PREVIEWISM
Our World is Beautiful, Yes, Multi-Cultural

Yes, "The Spirit of Goodness" Suggests you think about "The Birds and the Bees", and "The Flowers and the Trees". And things called Love, Forgiveness, Truth and Reality, and a whole host of other Beautiful and Wonderful characteristics of Life in Heaven and on Earth.

And this leads to Riches, Both Physical and Spiritual Riches.

Folks, as you know an Ounce of Prevention is preferred to an Ounce of Cure.

So take the Initiative and find "The COMPASS", Now.

Call us any time at our number shown above.

Thanks for Listening,

Yours truly, as ever in, "The Spirit of Goodness"

W.J. (Bill) Handel, M.A., L.W. (Coach)

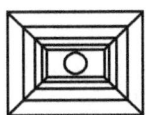

PREVIEWISM
Our World is Beautiful, Yes, Multi-Cultural

Dear Friends,. Thank you, Thank you, Thank you,. You may be Seated.,

Today we wish to tackle the Statement of: "There is an Exception to almost Every Rule". First of all we know that God Loves, not Hates, God Forgives, not Condemns, God Blesses, not Curses, and so on. God gives Rewards, and does not Punish.

The Shadow says, God Damned It all. But it is a Lie. We know that God Blessed all in Its creation, and Damned Nothing. The Shadow is a "Vacuum of Light", a Fraud, an Illusion, and a Nothing,. So God Damned Nothing. God is too Wise to be Evil. Yes, God just continues to ignore the Shadow, and never Acknowledges It. And the Shadow gets so Upset and Jealous of God that It tries to Condemn, Curse, Punish, Hate, and say, "God Damned it All". But it is a Lie. "God Damned Nothing". (Not even "Nothing".)

But We are not God, and so although God is not capable of doing these things, we must sometimes say, "Damn the Shadow". It is a "Nothing" and a Nuisance, always trying to interfere with my Intentions to do "Good Works".

And so one of our Objectives is to Learn to Completely Ignore the Shadow, and not Acknowledge It. We do this by Looking-Up, and knowing that It is below and Behind us, and a Nothing, and then saying, "Be Gone", out of my mind, out into outer Darkness, beyond the Reach of Light, and Stay there. We need you there for Reference.

And so you see Friends, when we have Mastered this technique, The Shadow has absolutely no Power over us, because we become much like God (the Real) "The Spirit of Goodness", where we are so Far out Front that the Shadow's voice becomes so Faint that It is inaudible. But remember, The Shadow is a SNEAKY Bastard, So always be prepared to say, "Be Gone" etc. etc..

Thanks for Listening, as ever in, "The Spirit of Goodness",

"Saint BILL"

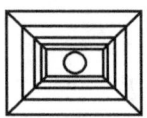

PREVIEWISM
Our World is Beautiful, Yes, Multi-Cultural

January 20/99 (60 B.H.)

Hi and How are you, All my Dear Children, Relatives, and Friends...

You know when you have a Big organization with lots of Duties to perform, You need a lot of money to pay all your Staff. But if you do not have much money you have to do all of the work yourself and scrape by.

This means that you then wear Many Hats. Well, I wear about 5 Hats now to keep all of the departments functioning. First of all, I am a "Publisher" and I am on my Second Book which is now about half done. Secondly, I am an "Investment Agent" where I sell an R.S.P., but Mine is Guaranteed. When you put your money in the Bank in a G.I.C. or the Savings account, when the Bank goes broke you are wiped out. But with "Previews" R.S.P., the whole country can go broke and you will still have you Investment intact, Guaranteed. Because it is secured by Real Estate property. Thirdly, I am now a "Preacher", not too busy as such, but a Preacher just the same. Fourthly, I am an Administrator or Executor of an "Eternal (Trust) Foundation", "Previews Inc.". Fifthly, I am now a "Promoter". Yes, I have taken up the cause of a "Good Man", which is to Promote Good Will amongst people and the Nations. Yes, I now Promote "Good Will" amongst all of Humankind.

Enclosed you will find your Bonafide Share Certificates in the "Foundation. Every Descendant from now, throughout eternity will receive a Share Certificate as Its "Birthright". The Benefits and Privileges that they provide are many.

Most importantly, they assure you that you have Unconditionally received the gift of Life in Heaven and on Earth, and that the "Living Spirit of God" within you is EverLasting and Eternal. Yes, once Conceived there is no looking Back. Life in the Womb, Life on Earth, and Life in Heaven, Guaranteed, just like Water, Ice and Steam., Or Liquid, Solid, and Gas. No sweat, right. Right.

Let us know when the New Additions are due and arrived, So that we can keep our Records up to date. Right, right, right, Right. Glory, Glory, Hallelujah!!

If any of you have any spare time, you may come into our Office and we will put you to work.

Thanks for Listening,

Yours truly, as ever in, The Spirit of Goodness,

B.H., M.A., L.W. "Saint Bill" (Coach) (Executor) (King) etc. etc.

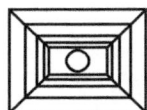

PREVIEWISM
Our World is Beautiful, Yes, Multi-Cultural

"Open Letter", Dated: January 22/99 (60 B.H.)
To All of Whom it may Concern,.

Dear Friend,..

In any Endeavour or Objective there are always "Active" and "passive" participants. At present "Previews Inc." (Car No.1) is completely organized and operative. "Previews Institute" (Car No.2) is also now completely organized and operative, Since "The COMPASS" is now complete.

"Previews Inc." and "Previews Institute" are like Two people,. They are separate entities, but have a Marriage Contract that keeps them working together. They will never Separate because they both have "ONE" objective, That is to "Relieve Poverty", Both Physical and Spiritual Poverty.

So you see, at present I have Two Cars. I drive which ever One I want at all times, when ever I want or need to. When one Car needs Repair, I put It on Hold, and drive the other to do Its work, and vice-a-versa, until the other is back on the Road.

And so you see, at present I wear Two Hats. First, I am the "Executor" of the Estate known as "Previews Inc.", which is an "Eternal (Trust) Foundation", providing for "An Eternal Royal Family of God", which includes each and every last person on Earth. Secondly, I am the "Chairman of the Board" of Previews Institute.

At present I have a Few people in mind to take over the Reigns of "Our Dear God's" Kingdom here on Earth, when I go to take my place in Heaven with "Our Dear God".

But no Final Decisions have been made,. Anyone and Everyone is still eligible to compete for the Position and Honor, which of course is very Subordinate and Subservient to the Honor and Glory that goes to "Our Dear God" in Heaven and on Earth, being "The Spirit of Goodness" , (God, the Real).

If you keep "In Touch" and continue to Indicate that you are Indeed a Devoted and "Active" Previewlite. You may well be the "Happy-Go-Lucky" winner of the Contest, and take Home all the Prizes, Including the "Gold Medal".

Trusting you to be One that says, "Let's Try It",

We remain,

Yours truly, as ever in, "The Spirit of Goodness",

Executor, Per: W.J.(Bill) Handel, M.A., L.W.

P.S.: Our Objective, "To Relieve Poverty

Both Physical and Spiritual Poverty.

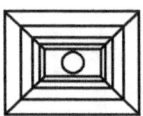

PREVIEWISM
Our World is Beautiful, Yes, Multi-Cultural

Dear Friends,.. Thank you, Thank you, Thank you,.. You may be Seated....

To begin today, We have a Question for you,.. Why does God always Understand and Forgive?..

Answer: Because God always knows the Circumstances under which we make our Decisions. And so always Understands and Forgives. We do not always have all of the Facts, and so we sometimes make Good decisions and sometimes we make Bad decisions. But God knows the Facts and so always Understands and Forgives your decisions, Good and Bad.

We as humans do not know all of the Circumstances of our Neighbours decisions and so do not always Understand and Forgive, but God knows you lack some of the Facts, and so always Understands and Forgives you even though you have not Understood and Forgiven your Neighbor.

We as Humans should always remember that God always Understands and Forgives All, and so we should always Forgive our Neighbor regardless of whether we Understand or not.

Yes, we come to realize that God knows the Circumstances and Facts are different for each of us at every turn, and so we all get an individual judgement in our Favor. Because God, Forgives, not Condemns, God Blesses, not Curses, God Rewards, Not Punishes.

On another Note,. When a person thinks It is God, He/She tries never to fight Evil with Evil,. But when he/she is tired of being a Sucker for Punishment, He/she realizes that he/she has to use Its "Sense of Judgement" or Discernment and say that you sometimes Fight Love with Love, and sometimes you Fight Evil with Evil., And that most of the time you Fight Evil with Love. But at no time is it necessary to Fight Love with Evil.

When this happens you remember that you have only Two Cheeks and that the Third strike is yours, twice as Hard. This is all necessary because we are dealing with Humans and not Gods. Yes, there is only One God, and that is "The Spirit of Goodness", God the Real, who knows All. But we Humans are always Learning to better Cope with the Influence of Illusion, Ignorance, Yes, The Shadow.

Thank you,

"SAINT BILL"

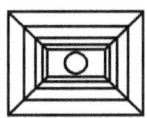

PREVIEWISM
Our World is Beautiful, Yes, Multi-Cultural

Dear Friends,. Thank you, Thank you, Thank you,. You may be Seated....

As we all know, The Shadow of God is a Fictional Character and does not exist except as to the Essence of a Shadow. (Which is Illusion) (Which also does not exist)

When we Understand what God is asking of Us, we (Act) do "Good" and receive Blessings from God, which is "Good Returned" manifold.

When we do not Understand God, we Act (Do) according to Illusion, and this causes Pain and Confusion. This we call "Bad Results".

Now we can not Blame God, and we do not want to Blame ourselves, So we Blame it on "The Shadow" (Illusion), But remember, this does not make "the Shadow" Real. No, not at all, we just need a "Scape Goat" so that we do not need to Blame ourselves.

This is Fine, Temporarily, But do not Fall into the Trap and say "The Shadow" is Real,. because It then becomes your "God" and It is a "Fraud". Yes, "Illusion" is the Culprit, trying to lead you to think it is "Real and Good", and necessary to Suffer.

It is not necessary to Suffer if you Develop (use) your "Sense of Judgement" and follow Right not Wrong. Yes, Forgive one-another, and not Punish.

Now we know, Why we know, that any Idiot that says, "Do not Judge" is serving the "Fraudulent God". Yes, Illusion,. Yes, The Shadow.

Now we know, Why we must always strive to gain more Knowledge, because knowledge is Truth and brings forth "The Good Blessings" of God the Real, "The Spirit of Goodness".

Illusion is Lie and brings forth "the Waste It is",. Yes, Pain and Confusion. We call this the "Evil" spirit, but It is not Real,. It is still Illusion, caused by "The Shadow" which is Darkness, which is Ignorance, which is Nothing, which is Vacuum of Light.

Yes, Light brings forth Knowledge and Knowledge is God and God is Goodness. Yes, Joy and Happiness, which comes by more and more Using (Developing) your "Sense of Judgement". Yes, Truth and Reality is God and God is Reality and Truth, Not Fantasy, Illusion and Lie.

When we fully Understand and Realize this, we do not need any more "Scape Goats". Yes, we come to Realize that we just sometimes make our "Own" mistakes, but we Understand and Forgive ourselves as God Understands and Forgives us.

And when Someone or Something says, you must Suffer, we just say,

"Be Gone", out of my Sight, and out of my Mind,. We are with God, which is True Knowledge, based on Reality not Fantasy. (Yes, We Forgive.)

Thank you, Dear God, Thank you Thank you, Dear Friends, Thank you,

B.H., M.A., L.W. "Saint Bill" (Coach)

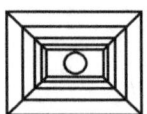

PREVIEWISM
Our World is Beautiful, Yes, Multi-Cultural

Dear Friends,. Thank you, Thank you, Thank you,.. You may be Seated

Today I want to tell you all a little Story. I will tell you the Story, and then I will tell you the Moral of the story.

Out on the Farm, when I, "Saint Bill", was a Child, My Father, George, had Two buildings. The House and the Barn.; Both buildings had Two Doors, the Front door and the Back door.

One day my Father went out Hunting, and as he was Hunting, he looked back and far in the distance he seen a Deer, a Doe, a female Deer, and you do not Shoot the Females. My Father decided he would meet the Deer half way and make Friends with it. As he approached about half way up, He noticed it was a Bear: It had been Stalking him.

So what did my Father do?.. He turned and started walking toward the Barn. And as the Bear was walking through the Barn, My Mother, Katherina, slammed the Front door on his back, and My Father slammed the Back door on his face,. and now they had the Bear in the Cage.

The Bear thought he was going to have a Feast, but all he needed was a Hamburger.. And so my Father bought the Bear a Hamburger once in a while to keep him Happy.

Now the Moral of the Story.

About a year ago My Father went out Hunting for Opportunity, beyond Farming, and as he was Hunting he looked back and there in the distance he seen his Uncle Jake, a wise Businessman and a Friend.

My Father thought he would meet his Uncle half way, and made a Deal with him. Well, this past week Both ends of the Deal went Flop. And as my Father approached up close this past week for close discussion, He found his Uncle was a Bear. So my Father walked toward the Barn and My Mother slammed the Front door on his Back and My Father slammed the Back door on his Face.

Old Uncle Jake thought he was going to have a Feast, but all he needed was a Hamburger,.. So My Father bought him a Hamburger once in a while to keep him Happy.

Note: In life, in translation, a Hamburger is a Small Favor once in a while. (It only costs a dollar.)

Thanks for Listening,

Yours truly, as ever in, "The Spirit of Goodness",

B.H., M.A., L.W. "Saint Bill" (Coach)

Chuckle, Chuckle,. eh

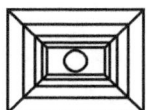

PREVIEWISM
Our World is Beautiful, Yes, Multi-Cultural

Dear Friends,. Thank you, Thank you, Thank you,. You may be Seated

Folks, today we want to assure you that "Our Dear God" (The Spirit of Goodness) has the Situation of today "In the Bag".. And just as the Jews (Shadow Worshippers) did not get what they wanted in a "Messiah", So the "Messiah Worshippers" (Shadow Worshippers) will not get what they wanted for "the End of an Age".

Yes, there will not be One arm raised in Strife,. Not One word spoken in Haste,. and Not One Illusion left Intact.. There will be only Truth and Reality, and Peace and Quiet.

Yes, the "Old Age" will pass away Slowly and Quietly, and the "New Age" will come to full Bloom Quickly and Quietly. Yes, within Ten years we will have Dug a Hole big enough to Bury the "Old Age".. And the "New Age" will Stand on the Lid of the Coffin,. Look Up,.Put Its Foot Down Hard,. And Say, "Die you Cocksucker Die". Yes, "Dead you Illegit Dead".

Now the "New Age" of "Our Dear God" (the Real) The Spirit of Goodness shall remain in "Full Bloom" forever and ever and Eternally. Because It is an Age of Truth, an Age of Light, an Age of Knowledge, which leads to Riches in every way, Spiritual, Physical, and Material.

Yes, "Our Dear God" (the Real) "The Spirit of Goodness" has now provided for truly Enriching "Food for The Stomach" and "Food for Thought" with and by the Implementation of the "Proven Principals" found in "The COMPASS", and Its Supplement, "The Sermons of Saint Bill".

The Praise, Honor and Glory be to God. (Glory, Glory, Hallelujah!)

Thank you,

Yours truly, as ever in, "The Spirit of Goodness",

B.H., M.A., L.W. "Saint Bill" (Coach)

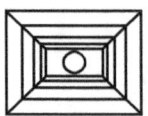

PREVIEWISM
Our World is Beautiful, Yes, Multi-Cultural

Dear Friends,.. Thank you, Thank you, Thank you,. You may be Seated

Today we will talk about the "Steps and Stages" of our Development.

As we know, a "Good person" is an Honorable person, and an Honorable person is one who Honors his/her Words of "Goodness" to come, and not his/her words of Shame. A Hypocrite is a person who says something "Good" and then does the Opposite. A "Simple Person" is a Greedy person not always knowing when Enough is Enough. Yes, sometimes wanting more than Enough. A "Weasel" is a person who says One thing out of one Side of his/her mouth, and the Opposite out of the other Side of his/her mouth, and doing Nothing. Yes, most of the foregoing spells "Indecision and Confusion", not knowing which way to turn and just walking around in Circles like a useless Imbecile. Children are prime examples of "Indecision and Confusion", as they say, I Love you, Mom., out of one side of their mouth, and when the Wind changes they say ,"I Hate you, Mom'. Yes, they have not yet learned the Human's Law of "You Reap what You Sow" and do not yet abide by It.

When we have Matured enough to abide by this Law, then we take the next Step and abide by "God's Law", which is, "Look Up and Forgive One-another and Reap Only Blessings", barring the weather of course. At this Stage we are considered "Wise People".

A "Saint" is a person who has a Memory-Bank and can Relate to all of these Stages, and then Encourage his/her Associates to Develop in a "Good" way,. "Our Dear God" (The Spirit of Goodness) knows we are all very Capable of "Sainthood"...

Trusting you to be one that says, "Let's Do It", we remain,

Yours truly, as ever in, ""The Spirit of Goodness",.

"Saint Bill" (Coach)

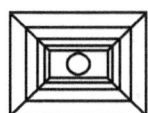

PREVIEWISM
Our World is Beautiful, Yes, Multi-Cultural

Dear Friends,. Thank you, Thank you, Thank you,. You may be Seated....

Today we are going to talk about "Trust"

You know, This past week I was talking to an Old Businessman, trying to make a "Deal" with him.. And He said to me, "You know, I am not sure that I Trust you,. Why should I Trust you?.. And I said to Him, "Well, I think I am a "Saint" and I act accordingly, So you can "Trust" me..

But, I said, to him, "You think you are a "Sinner" and you act accordingly. Now, Why should I Trust you? Well, the poor Old man did not know what to say.

After a pause, I said to him, Do not Despair, I am going to Trust you anyway,.. Do you know Why? Because in the back of your mind you know you are a "Saint" too. You just sometimes think you are a "Sinner" because you are sometimes Listening to "the Accuser", the Devil, the Shadow, which says, You are a Nothing, You are Useless, You are Bad, You are thinking wrong,.. Do it this way. It is "Good" for you and to Hell with your neighbor....(Yes, the Shadow, (Illusion), says, You are a "Sinner".)

But, I said to the Old man, You know you are a "Saint" and you know that God says, "Do unto others as you want them to do unto you".., And so today I am going to "Trust" you, because from this day forward, You are going to say, "I am a "SAINT", and I will Act accordingly,.. And to Hell with the Shadow, the Devil, "The Accuser".. Yes, I will say, Be Gone, out into outer Darkness, beyond the Reach of Light, and stay there, we need you there for reference.... Yes, I will remember, that I am a "Saint" in God's Eye,. and I will Act accordingly, So that I can be "Trusted", and also Trust.

Well, the Old man Smiled and said, It's a "Deal"   (Chuckle, Chuckle, eh:)

Thank you,

Yours truly, as ever in, "The Spirit of Goodness",

B.H.,M.A., L.W. "Saint BILL" (Coach)

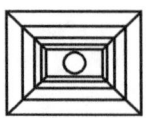

PREVIEWISM
Our World is Beautiful, Yes, Multi-Cultural

Dear Friends,. Thank you, Thank you, Thank you,.. You may be Seated....

You know, we have heard of People who say that God is Three Persons in One.. And they say that All Three persons are "Good"- But they are always in Conflict.. And they can not explain this.

The "Previewlite" understands why this is so. Yes, the "Three in One" God is made up of "God the Good Guy" (God the Real),.."God the Bad Guy" (God the Fraud),. and "God the Hypocrite" (God the Human).

Yes, we know that any Person that says (claims) He/She is "God on Earth" is a "Fool", a "Hypocrite", a Liar, and a Thief.. Trying to Rob God (the Real) of the Glory of Flawlessness.. And "God the Fraud" says, Good, Good, "You are on My side" because I want so much to be God, but always "Fail" to be.. So you the "Hypocrite" keep up the "Good" work and we will say, "We are One".. Yes, Two against One, and we will say, We are God, and I will be able to say, "I am God".. Yes, that sounds like a fair Compromise.

But "God the Real" (The Spirit of Goodness) says to "The Hypocrite", You can say (claim) what you want, but I say, that "Actions" speak Louder than words, and my "Actions" are as Clear as "Steel-Glass", Yes, as Clear as Day.

And "God the Real" says to "The Hypocrite", You with your uncontrolled Ego will continue to follow your Illusions until one day you become Tired of "Failing" and give-up in total Frustration. (Yes, You will say, My God, My God, why hast thou Forsaken Me; because you are Looking at "Smoked-Glass")

Yes, the Day is coming when You will Realize that "God is One", yes, God is God, and Not "the Shadow" (Illusion).. And you will Realize that "God the Real" is always in complete Harmony with Itself and the World which includes You the "Hypocrite", because "God the Real" understands All, and keeps Its Kingdom intact, by Forgiving, Not Condemning, Blessing, Not Cursing. Yes, Rewarding, Not Punishing.... **Yes,** God is Alive, Not Perfect.. Thank you,

Yours truly, as ever in, "The Spirit of Goodness"

"Saint BILL" (Coach)

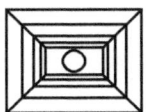

PREVIEWISM
Our World is Beautiful, Yes, Multi-Cultural

Dear Friends:

Just a Few Miscellaneous Proverbs:

1) The Shadow (Devil) says, You love me First, Yes, You love me above all things. And to Hell with your Neighbor, unless it Pleases you.

God (the Real) "The Spirit of Goodness" says, You love your Neighbor first, Yes, You love your Neighbor above all things. And to Hell with the Devil (Shadow). And then God says, And do not worry about me, I have already looked after myself when I so instructed you.

Yes, The Shadow says, "I", I, I, am God,. I am the Important One. God says, to you,. **"You"** are the Squeaky wheel, Not me, and the Squeaky Wheel gets the grease. (Ha, Ha, Ha.) (How true, eh::)

2) We All understand and agree that "Previews Institute" is Multi-Cultural. Therefore, In the Delivery of Its Teachings, A Devoted "Previewlite" will Teach from "The COMPASS" and Verify when asked, from another Book of Knowledge.. A Person, temporarily inclined toward another Denomination, may Sometimes Teach from another Book of Knowledge, and Verify when asked, from "The COMPASS". Yes, A page for A page, when asked.. Any Points Unverified will be left to and for Meditation   (And the "Truth" will Prevail.) (Unto Each His/Her Own)

3)   Dear Children and Friends,.. We at "Previews" do not Push you in any particular direction. We go out Front and Pull you along with an Invisible string, and it is a Long one and a Strong one.

We do not put you Under our Wings, We put you On our Wings, and let you Fly with us, and Enjoy the Scenery, as you see It.

And when you describe your Point of View, It is a joy for Us to Listen to. And when we describe our Point of View, It is a joy for you to Listen too.

Thanks for Listening,.

Yours truly, as ever in, "The Spirit of Goodness",

B.H., M.A., L.W. "Saint Bill" (Coach)

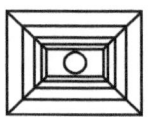

PREVIEWISM
Our World is Beautiful, Yes, Multi-Cultural

Dear Friends,. Thank you, Thank you, Thank you,.. You may be Seated,....

Today we are going to Discuss the meaning of the word, "Judge". (Decide) As we know, the Supreme Person in Society is the "Judge". We know that the "Good" live above the "Law" but are none the less "Subject to the Law". We know that the Confused (Bad) live under the "Law" but are none the less "Subject to the Law". The Judge, although Supreme, is also "Subject to the Law", because he/she can be Removed if he/she does not live above the Law.

The Judge tells us that the Wise settle their Differences out of Court and Not in Court, because we can make "Deals", but the Judge goes by the Book of Law. The Books of Law are Drawn up by Wise people making "Deals" for the Future generations to live by. The Future generations do not always understand the Circumstances under which the "Laws" (Deals) were made. This is why when the Circumstances change the "Laws" change. But if we make our "Deals" without the Judge we are never "Subject to the Law".

Yes, folks, we must learn to "Judge" one another as "God the Real" (The Spirit of Goodness) Judges us, and that is to provide the Alternative then Forgive, Not Condemn; Bless, Not Curse; Reward, Not Punish, and so on.

Yes, we must remember that "God" is the "Supreme Judge" and "God" is always in your Favor because It always know the Circumstances and Conditions under which you Acted, and knows that you are sometimes Misled, and so "God" Forgives us All.

But we must remember, that we are not "God", and because some of us sometimes Unintentionally become Habitual Criminals the "Line of the Law" must remain. So that we, when necessary, may Ultimately encourage some people to Act properly, with and by the "Fear of Consequences". But we must not Confuse this with "God" because when it is up to "God" the Verdict is always "Not Guilty", No Consequences. Yes,.."Forgiven".

And so you see, We must learn to "Judge" like the "Judge" so that we do not get Confused with the Facts because the Facts are sometimes coming from "Shadow Worshippers" who have not learned to Judge and have subsequently become Confused Liars and Act accordingly. Yes, we call them "Sinners" or "Criminals", under the "Law", and by the "Law".

But again, do not get this Confused with "God". Remember in "God's Eye they are "Saints" because in "God's Eye" they are Innocent by reason of Insanity. (Ha, Ha, Ha, Ha, Ha) "Chuckle, Chuckle, eh::"

Yes, folks, It is a big joke (a Circus) when you Understand it all the way God the Real (The Spirit of Goodness) understands it All.

This is why God is always Happy and Living in Bliss in Heaven and on Earth. Yes, we must

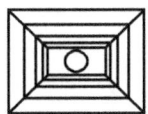

PREVIEWISM
Our World is Beautiful, Yes, Multi-Cultural

learn to "Judge" so that we learn "Right from Wrong", ""Good from Waste", "True from False", Possible from Impossible, Reality from Illusion, Yes, ""God" from The Shadow" and subsequently Live above the Law along with the "Judge",. So that we can Ultimately truly encourage people in general to Act properly, with and by the enticement of the Blessings of "God the Real" (The Spirit of Goodness). Yes, Folks, God gave us a "Sense of Judgement" and we must use it to Develop it to the Utmost for our Own sake here on Earth and Ultimately for "God's" sake in Heaven. (Ha, Ha, Ha, Ha,) "Chuckle, Chuckle, Chuckle, eh::"

Yes, "Life is a Joke not a Yoke" if and when we learn to "Judge" in God's fashion. Yes, this is the Ultimate Goal, to learn to Judge in God's fashion, because then we can make "Deals" with the "Supreme Judge".. right, RIGHT:: (Chuckle, Chuckle, eh:.)

Thanks for Listening,

Yours truly, as ever in, ""The Spirit of Goodness"

"Saint Bill" (Coach)

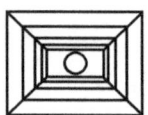

PREVIEWISM
Our World is Beautiful, Yes, Multi-Cultural

Dear Friends,.

Just a Few Miscellaneous Proverbs:

    1) The Shadow (Devil) says,. I am God, I am Perfect, I can not Compromise with you "The Living".

    God "the Real" says,. Children, I give you a "Free Will" to use your "Sense of Judgement" because I am prepared to "Compromise" with you at every Turn. I have no choice. I am not Perfect,. I am just Super, Super Excellent, because I have been around since the Beginning, and have been Improving ever since.. "Illusion" has always tried to separate us, from the Beginning, but It has Failed, because I am Active, Yes, I am Alive,. always changing and improving my ways and means to meet and win any Challenge the Future may bring.

    And God says,. I created you in my Image with a "Sense of Judgement", and when someone or something says, "Do not Judge" or Be Perfect, Be Brittle, Be Crystal,. You say, Be Gone, out into outer Darkness beyond the reach of Light, and stay there, we need you there for Reference.

    2) The Shadow says, I am God, You believe what I say, Do not Question me, Just have Faith, Do not Test me,. I would not Lie to you, would I? If it were not so I would tell you, Right? (And you say, 'Oh, of Course.')

God "the Real' says, Test the Spirits,. There are Two you Think,. "Reality" and "Illusion",. So TRY them,. If they work they are possible and True and of Me.. If they do not work, they are impossible and Lie, and of the Fraud, Yes, the Shadow. (And you say, Thank you, Dear God.)

Thank you,

Yours truly, as ever in "The Spirit of Goodness",

Saint Bill, "Coach"

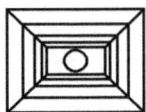

PREVIEWISM
Our World is Beautiful, Yes, Multi-Cultural

Dear Friends,.

Just a Few Miscellaneous Proverbs

The "Previewlite" says to the Shadow Worshipper,. God is Not Almighty.`, Yes, God can not do Everything. God can not Lie, God can not Steal,

God can not Kill,. God can not walk on Water, God can not Raise the Dead, Yes, God can not Do a lot of things!

The "Shadow Worshipper" says to the Previewlite,. Oh, Your God is Small. The Previewlite says, Yes, My God Small but "Truthful", and REAL!!

Your God, BIG LIAR, - and an ILLUSION!!! "an Illusion".

So get thee Behind me, Out into outer Darkness, beyond the reach of Light, and Stay there, I need you there for Reference.

The "Previewlite" says to the Shadow Worshipper,. You know from where you have been and where you have come from,. I can understand your Attitude... All your life you have been told that you are a Nothing and a Nobody

Well, you want to Feel you are a Somebody and a Something,.-This is Good!! But you must remember, that He/She who thinks He/She knows Something,. Knows Nothing,, And He/She who knows He/She knows Nothing,. Knows Something!!

Yes, It is a BIG, BIG world and Your Neighbor comes "First", Not God,..., God (the Real) "The Spirit of Goodness" says, "Love your Neighbor" and do not worry about Me,. because I have already looked after myself when I so instructed you.. Yes, God says, I do not need your Love,... I am Love, So take It and give it away, and It will grow and grow and be returned many Fold,, and You will find "Heaven on Earth" as God wants it to Be!!

Thank you, Dear God, Thank you,,,

Yours truly, as ever in,

"The Spirit of Goodness", (Saint Bill)

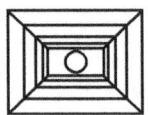

PREVIEWISM
Our World is Beautiful, Yes, Multi-Cultural

Dear Friends,.

Just a Few Miscellaneous Proverbs

1) We know that God comes First, and Our Neighbor comes Second. We also know that the Last come First and the First come Last. Therefore, Our Neighbor comes First, and God comes Second. This is why God says, It is not Jealous because It wants you to "Love your Neighbor" and not feel Guilty or disloyal to God. Yes, God is "Not Offended" when you "Love your Neighbor".

2) God, the Real, is "The Spirit of Goodness" and is not too Proud to allow Its children to "Love one-another". Yes, "The Spirit of Goodness" is not Jealous and does not want Its children to Feel guilty or disloyal to God for Loving their Neighbor.

God, the Real, "The Spirit of Goodness" allows Its children a Choice to Honor and Glorify God by Loving one-another., and God knows that It does not always get the message across and so God Forgives Its children when they do not always Love one-another and appear to Disgrace God.

Yes, God, the Real, is not a Hoity Toity Self righteous Idiot that demands unjust Worship, as though It were Perfect and Holier than Thou.

Yes, God is Reality, not Fantasy, and Heaven is a Predetermined place for all of God's children, not just for the Hoity Toity Self righteous Idiots.

Yes, God is Real, not Superficial or Artificial.

Yes, Mister Perfect is an Illusion, weak, hopeless, helpless, Desperate, and always calling for Attention to pacify Its pitiful, crying, Confused state of mind that knows It is predestined to Burst and Disappear.

But, "The Spirit of Goodness" is Real, strong, flexible, never ending, confident, reproductive, never a burden to anyone as It continues on Its way always ready to make adjustments to meet and win any Challenge the Future may bring. And knowing It will always be there for you when you need It.

Thank you,

Yours truly, as ever in, "The Spirit of Goodness"

Saint Bill" (Coach) B.H., M.A., L.W.

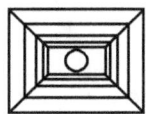

PREVIEWISM
Our World is Beautiful, Yes, Multi-Cultural

Dear Friends,.

Just a few Miscellaneous Proverbs

We must not Forget that there are only Two Entities...God and Humans. Humans tend to Live in Illusion. God Lives in Reality.

If the Humans do not use their "Sense of Judgement" then they continue to Live in Illusion.. But if they Use their "Sense of Judgement" they Begin to Live in Reality, with God, which is Goodness.

And so you see "Illusion" we call "The Shadow", but The Shadow is a "Fictional Character", which is Illusion.. God, the Real, knows this and pays No attention to Illusion or the subsequent Shadow, because It is just another Illusion.

And so you see "Reality" is where It is at.. The "Spirit of Goodness" within is Reality, and It can be Mature or It can be Immature but It is still "Reality", And the Reality is "The Spirit of Goodness" within us is a Part of God and It can not Die just as God can not Die, and so It goes to Heaven to be with "God the Total" in Heaven when out Body ceases to function.

2) There are approximately Six Minor religions in the World today.

They are, Sikhism, Islam, Buddhism, Judaism, Hinduism and Confucianism. The One Major religion in All these Areas is ""Society as a Whole".

.It makes the Rules, and "Society" is Now represented and organized by "Previewism" as manifested in and by "The COMPASS".

Author: B.H., M.A., L.W. Alias: "Saint BILL".

Thank you, Dear God, Thank you.

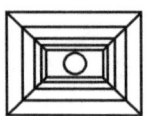

PREVIEWISM
Our World is Beautiful, Yes, Multi-Cultural

Dear Friends,. Thank you, Thank you, Thank you,. You may be Seated....

Today I am going to tell you a Fictional Story.

You know, the Shadow says,. God wants a Sacrifice, God wants Vengeance, Yes, God is a Cruel Bastard,. And Greedy to Boot.. And the Shadow says, God is Powerless to Deal with Its children, because the Children do not have enough Money, and they do not want to Kill themselves, as a Sacrifice.

So the Shadow says, I will BORROW God MY Life, and You my money. Yes, I will Consummate and become a Man,. Then you can Kill me, and Keep my Money,. and I will go to Heaven to Help God Rule,. Yes, I will be the "Supreme Judge". Ah! Yes, I will be God.

Yes, the Shadow says,. I am Desperate, I want so much to say, I am God, and take First Place.. Yes, the Shadow says, If you will Worship me and Believe that I am God, then I will make you the only true children of God.

But the Shadow knows, It can not FOOL "God the Real", So the Shadow says, We will make God into three (3) people. Yes, we will Compromise and Join forces and we will have "God the Good Guy" and "God the Bad Guy" and "God the Human".. And I will be able to say, I am God.

Glory, Glory, Hallelujah, If I can just get someone, anyone, to believe this, I will not be Alone in Hell anymore. Yes, an Outcast, and a Nothing. Yes, I want so much to be a Something. Please Believe me, It is your only Hope. Yes, My children, this is the Only way to get to Heaven.

Please Believe Me, "For God's Sake", Believe me. Otherwise God will Kill you. He will, Really. Ya, really.., Come on,. I Love you,. Believe me, Please.

(Ha, Ha, Ha, Ha, Ha,. Chuckle, Chuckle eh'.') (The .... sucking Earthworm)

Dear Friends,. Now let Us get back to Reality. We know that God is One and and One in All,. and we know that in God's Eye there is No Evil in the World, Only "Reality" and "Illusion".. Reality is "Good" and "Illusion" is "Waste".. We know that we are All one Family of God. Yes, we are All Children of God, Just as we are.

We know that God is EverUnderstanding, Loving, Forgiving, and so on and on. What more do we need? We know that "The Spirit of God" lives within us, and can never Die, Just as God can never Die.

There is Nothing or No-one that can Kill us "Spiritually", because there is only One "Spirit", and It is a Living one, and a Loving one, and a Truthful one.. The other is "Illusion".

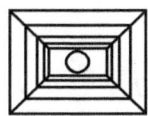

PREVIEWISM
Our World is Beautiful, Yes, Multi-Cultural

Yes, the True Spirit of God is a Possibility.. The "Illusion", Shadow, with all Its Lies is Impossible. So Forget It, It is a Pile of Garbage.

Then get on with your Life, here on Earth,. Heaven will come only too Soon. But it will be Beautiful, just as Heaven on Earth is Beautiful with "God the Real" (The Spirit of Goodness). "Glory, Glory, Hallelujah, for Reality".

Thank you, Dear God, Thank you,. Thank you, Friends, Thank you,

Yours truly, as ever in, "The Spirit of Goodness"

(Saint Bill) "Coach" B.H., M.A., L.W.

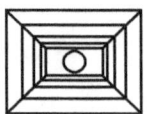

PREVIEWISM
Our World is Beautiful, Yes, Multi-Cultural

Dear Friends,. Thank you, Thank you, Thank you,.. You may be Seated

Today I want to tell you a Sad, Sad Story. It is a story of a Small Boy who was Misled by "Sick Psyche Psychology" and Psychic Fortune Tellers. He was Five years old when his mother (a disturbed Psychic) told him that he had no Earthly father, and that he was born of a Virgin mother. Yes, this Small boy was told that he was conceived by God, and that he would never Die.

This Small boy grew up to think he was someone Special and that he would change the Rules and Laws of God so that there would not be so much misery, Poverty, Drunkenness, and Abomination in the World.

He called his Father (God) a Liar and a Fool and Ultimately "SATAN" in disguise. He carried on to such Extremes that he Disrupted Society to the point that his own Friends took part in having him Executed and put to death by Reason of Insanity. Yes, his own Friends turned him in.

As this Poor Man was Dying, He realized he had been Lied to and that he was Not God's only Son, but an ordinary Mortal **Person** like **everyone else.** He admitted to All the people present at his Execution, when he said,.

"My God, My God, why hast thou Forsaken me.". Yes, his God had Forsaken him as the "Fraud" (Satan) always does when the going gets tough.

To make matters worse for the Poor Man, He then Realized he had Forsaken his God, and Died completely ALONE.

Poor Man,. All because of a Psychic Fairy Tale by his Mother and a very gullible Father.

The World has since learned that God, the Real, is "The Spirit of Goodness"

and Its oldest Child is "The Spirit of Truth", and It lives in your Heart (Soul). And goes to Heaven when your Body ceases to Function. Truth very Simple.

Thanks for listening.

Yours truly, as ever, in,

"The Spirit of Goodness"

B.H., M.A., L.W. "Saint Bill"

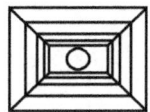

PREVIEWISM
Our World is Beautiful, Yes, Multi-Cultural

My Dear Children and Friends,....

The Shadow says,. I am Almighty,. I can do Anything,. I can even Raise the Dead.... Therefore, I can Justify MURDER.

Well, the Dirty EARTHWORM.

We know that God, the Real, is not Almighty and will Never Justify MURDER,. No Never,. God has and does FORGIVE Murder,. But never Justifies Murder,. NEVER.

There is Never any Reason for that kind of Garbage,. NEVER.

The Dirty, Lying, Twisting,... ,sucking Shadow, The Son-of-a-Bitch, (Illusion), Get Thee Behind Me.

Thank you Children and Friends, Thank you, Dear God, Thank you,

As ever in, "The Spirit of Goodness",

B.H., M.A., L.W. "Saint Bill"

P.S.: 1) A "Forgiven Person" is a "Saint" in God's Eye. Therefore, we are All Saints., because what our Neighbor thinks is Secondary, when it is Negative.

2) God does not change the Rule because of the Exception. Therefore, Some things are Never Justified; But, nevertheless, remain Forgivable.

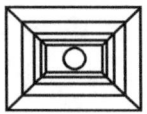

PREVIEWISM
Our World is Beautiful, Yes, Multi-Cultural

The "Previewlite" has made a Commitment and is Determined to live by "The Spirit of Goodness", God the Real, and This God's Law is: Look Up and Forgive one-another and Reap only Blessings, barring the Weather of course". (and the weather will now continually improve) (until we have Heaven on Earth for most everyone)

The Shadow-Worshipper lives by "The Hoity-Toity Spirit", God the Fraud, Yes the self-righteous Idiot that says you must live by Man's Law, which is: You Reap what You Sow. Which means you must Strike back at the Actions of Ignorance. This creates a Vicious Circle and causes nothing but pain and Suffering. Then the Fraud says, Follow me and I will take you to Heaven. But remember, the Fraud is a Liar, so It takes you to Hell the long way around. Right here on Earth.

The Previewlite knows that Heaven is for All according to God the Real, and that our purpose is to bring Heaven to Earth by way of "The Spirit of Goodness".

And not try to bring Earth to Heaven by way of "The Hoity-Toity Spirit", God the Fraud.

Yes, the Object of the Previewlite is to eliminate the Unfulfilling influence of the Fraud (the Shadow) from the face of the Earth by placing a copy of "The COMPASS" in every Home in every Country of the World, by Sale or by Gift.

This may take a few Days or a few Years, but it is going to Happen. And the World will live by a New-Psychology and it will be beautiful, Heaven on Earth as God, the Real, meant it to be. Then we can be assured that Heaven in Heaven will be just as beautiful and what we expect.

Thanks for Listening,

Yours truly, as ever in, "The Spirit of Goodness",

B.H.., M.A., L.W. "Saint Bill" (Coach)

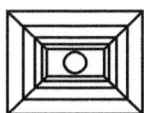

PREVIEWISM
Our World is Beautiful, Yes, Multi-Cultural

Dear Friends,. Thank you, Thank you, Thank you,. You may be Seated....

Today we are going to talk about another TWIST,. and Straighten it out into Outer Darkness, behind us, beyond the reach of Light, and say, Stay there, we need you there for Reference.

Folks, as we know, there are only Two Real Entities in Life,. Yes, God and Humans. The Third Entity is Illusion. When we follow God we produce GOOD, If we follow Illusion we produce WASTE. There is only One bit of Waste in God's world that causes Illusion, and that is the Shadow of God.... And we know that as with any other Shadow, the Shadow of God is an Illusion.- And we know, Illusion is the

Seed of Lie, which produces WASTEFUL Actions,. which God FORGIVES. Truth, very Simple.

The Shadow tries to Divide 2 by 3 to make 3 but all It gets is .666666666. Plus 2 remainder. Therefore, God and Humans are Indivisible,. and .666666666. is the Supposed sign of the Bad Guy (Shadow). But remember, the Bad Guy is a Liar, So It says that .666666666. is the Supposed sign of the Good Guy.

So you see, the Bad Guy labels the Good Guy, Bad. (Well, the Earthworm)

But the fact is, It is simple Mathematics, and has nothing to do with REALITY. The Reality is, there are only Two Real Entities that concern Us, all else is of the Shadow of God, which is Illusion, Yes, Illusion upon Illusion, so forget It, It is a Waste of Time, and Time is of God, and God is of Time to see Reality. Because Reality is God, and God is Reality, Not Fantasy. So Think about Reality. Yes, The Birds and The Bees, and The Flowers and The Trees, and things called

Love, Forgiveness, Truth and the many Good Spiritual Realities. Truth, very Simple. Thanks for Listening,

Yours truly, as ever in, "The Spirit of Goodness",

B.H., M.A., L.W. "Saint Bill". (Coach)

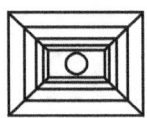

PREVIEWISM
Our World is Beautiful, Yes, Multi-Cultural

Dear Friends,.

Just a Few Miscellaneous Proverbs

A Forgiven Person is a "Saint" (Child of God) in God's Eye,... and is FREE. A Condemned Person is a "Sinner" in the Shadow's Opinion,... and is a SLAVE. But remember The Shadow is an Illusion,. So there are no Condemned people, only Forgiven people. Yes, we are all "Saints" in God's Eye because God FORGIVES: All.

Yes, a Condemned person is a Sinner, and is always Depressed and living in Misery. A Forgiven person is a "Saint", and is always Enthusiastic and Living in Bliss.

So you see, You have a Choice, You can follow Illusion and think you are Condemned and live in Misery as a Sinner.. Or you can follow the Reality of God and know that you are Forgiven and live in Bliss as a "Saint".

Yes, you can not have it both ways,. You are either one or the other., Yes, a wise man once said, "You are either For me or Against me, because I do not like Hypocrites.

2) The Shadow Worshipper says, that God the Real is The Holy Spirit and Its Father is Adam (The Bad Guy), and Its Son is Robin (The Good Guy). And so, being Confused, He/She worships all Three Entities as One. Yes, God the Good Guy, God the Bad Guy, and God the Human (The Hypocrite). (the Problem is Two of the Entities are Fictional)

The Previewlite says, that God, the Real, is "The Spirit of Goodness" and It has many Children which It calls Angels. Yes, the little Spirits of Goodness. The Oldest of which is "The Spirit of Truth" and The Youngest of which is "The Spirit of Enthusiasm". And they are All born in our Heart and Soul when we are Conceived, and go to Heaven when our body Ceases to Function. Yes, God is a part of Us and We are a part of God, and so can never Die Spiritually. Yes, God is One.

Thank you,

Yours truly, as ever in, "The Spirit of Goodness", B.H., M.A., L.W. "

"Saint Bill" (Coach)

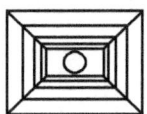

PREVIEWISM
Our World is Beautiful, Yes, Multi-Cultural

Dear Friends,. Thank you, Thank you, Thank you,. You may be Seated....

Today we are going to talk about "Goals". Positive Goals and Negative Goals.

We know that the subject of "God" is a lot about Psychology. You have Positive psychology and you have Negative psychology. We know that the Positive we call the "Good Guy" and the Negative we call the "Bad Guy". But the Bad Guy is a Liar, and so It says, "I am Positive". It neglects to say, "False Positive".

So the Bad Guy (Shadow) Says,. Have Faith and you can say to the Mountain "Move" and It will move.. Sounds Positive, but It is totally Negative.

Now let me explain,. The Naive get up in the morning and say, Hey, today I am going to "Move mountains",. Oh Boy! Am I Enthusiastic!!. Now what happens Next? Well, at the end of the Day the Poor person says, I failed, I failed,. I am a failure, I am a Failure, Everyday I am a Failure, and the Enthusiasm goes "Poof". And the Poor person becomes a "Negative Bastard", because the Bad Guy (Shadow) says, "You are a Useless Tit", and the Poor person begins to believe It and Lives accordingly.

Now let us look at "True Positive" psychology. The Good Guy (God) "The Spirit of Goodness" says, Face Reality and establish where you are at, both Physically and Spiritually, and then set some "Goals" that are High but within your Reach, (Not beyond your Reach). Then at the end of the Day you will say,. I have Succeeded in the First Step toward my Goal.. Oh Boy! Am I Enthusiastic.:!, and then you Add another Big Step to your "Goal", and every day you become more and more Successful and more and more Enthusiastic. Yes Stronger and Stronger and more and more Positive based on a "Success Pattern" that has developed in your Psychology. "True Positive Psychology"   Folks, in "The Compass" (Our New Bible), we have Drawn out a Success Pattern that guarantees you the Highest degree of Success possible, both Physically and Spiritually. Yes, there are Two types of Goals, Physical and Spiritual. We will start with the "Spiritual".

As you know, God, the Real, (The Spirit of Goodness) has many Children, we call them Angels or Characteristics of God. The Oldest is the "Spirit of Truth". The Youngest is the "Spirit of Enthusiasm", and of course there are many in between such as Perseverance, Love, Forgiveness, Tolerance, Happiness, Charity, Planning, Organization and Determination and many more.

Now if you Set these "Characteristics of Goodness" as your Spiritual Goals you will Automatically become Successful in your Physical Goals.

Yes, If you start with the "Spirit of Truth" and Live in Reality, (Not in Fantasy) your Enthusiasm will grow and grow as you take each Step toward your Physical Goals., And as your Enthusiasm grows, Your Perseverance grows, and as your Perseverance grows, your

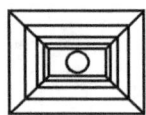

PREVIEWISM
Our World is Beautiful, Yes, Multi-Cultural

Love will grow, and as your Love grows, your Forgiveness will grow, and as your Forgiveness grows, your Tolerance will grow, and as your Tolerance grows, your Happiness grows, and as your Happiness grows, your Charity grows, and as your Charity grows, your Planning grows, and as your Planning grows, your Organization grows, and as your Organization grows, your Determination grows. (And so on and on)

Yes, Folks, based on Successful Actions and Results, we become Stronger and Stronger, Richer and Richer in every way. Based on Fantasy and Illusion you become weaker and weaker and Poorer and Poorer in every way.

So you See, Folks, You have your Choice. You can be "True Positive or "False Positive". And because you were born with a "Sense of Judgement", we know you will make the Right Choice.

We Previewlites did and we are "Happy-Go-Lucky" with it. Every Day Richer and Richer, Both Physically and Spiritually.

Thank you, Yours truly,

as ever in, "The Spirit of Goodness",

B.H., M.A., L.W. (Saint Bill) "Coach"

P.S.: For the "Achiever's Habits Program", Part 1, Spiritual,
See Ch.1,v.26, Part 2, Physical, See Ch.14, v. 1-18

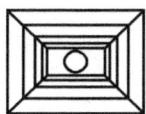

PREVIEWISM
Our World is Beautiful, Yes, Multi-Cultural

GOD BLESSES THOSE THAT,
BLESS, NOT Curse,
REWARD, NOT Punish,
Yes, FORGIVE, NOT Condemn.
In Proportion to the Sowing
Look UP to the Positive, (Truth) Not Down, to the Negative. (Lie)

The Shadow Punishes Those That,
Punish, Not Reward,
Curse, Not Bless,
Yes, Condemn, Not Forgive.
Because It (The Shadow) is a Liar.
Yes, by Nature disguised as "Good",
Yes, Illusion is by Nature a Sucker for Punishment and so
It Punishes Itself by the Use of People who
do not use their "Sense of Judgement".
This is why "Illusion" says, Do not Judge.

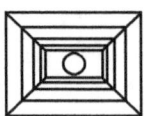

PREVIEWISM
Our World is Beautiful, Yes, Multi-Cultural

Dear Friends, Thank you, Thank you, Thank you, You may be Seated

Today we are going to talk about the Weather.. You know we have "Sunshine", Rain, and Hail Storms. Yes, we have "Saints", Sinners, and Criminals.

The Saints are always handing out "Blessings", and living in Bliss because they know they are Forgiven all their Shortcomings and can do nothing wrong. Yes, they are Living according to God's Law, which says,. "Look Up and Forgive one another and Reap only Blessings, Barring the weather of course.

Yes, the Sinners are always Crying because they think they are Condemned and must live in Misery,. And so they live by Man's Law, which says, "You Reap what you Sow". And so they think they must Strike back to create a Vicious Circle, to continue to live in Misery because they are Suckers for Punishment and want to Justify their Law.

But they are outnumbered by the Saints who are the Sunshine of this world and continue to hand out blessings regardless of or if they get Rain (Pain).

The Criminals are the ones who are completely confused and disoriented and think they must destroy the works of the Saints. And so we call them the Hail Storms.

The Sinners and the Criminals are of the same Psychology, Yes, we call them Shadow Worshippers. But remember the Sunshine of God, the Saints, over rule the day and God's Heaven is always on Earth if you live by God's Law, which says, "Look Up, and forgive one another and Reap only Blessings,.barring the weather of course." Yes, this is God's Psychology and it is Beautiful, and brings you nothing but Happiness. Yes, God Blesses those that Bless, not curse. Reward, not Punish, and Forgive, not condemn.

All according to the Sowing. Yes, God is not Perfect.

Thank you. As ever in the Spirit of Goodness,

"Saint Bill"

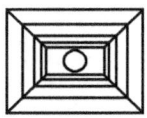

PREVIEWISM
Our World is Beautiful, Yes, Multi-Cultural

Dear Friends,. Thank you, Thank you, Thank you,. You May be Seated....

Today I am going to tell you a Story, a Winning Story.

I will start by saying that "The Spirit of Goodness" is God and God is the "Good Spirit", and It is Real.

The Shadow is the "Bad Spirit" and the Bad Spirit is "The Shadow" and It is Illusion.

The Bad Spirit was given a Name, which was "Adam" and Adam was said to be Human. That was a Lie because a Human can not be a total Illusion or a total Waste.

The Author of that Story worshipped the Bad Guy, (The Shadow), But It failed Him because It was Human.

Some time later, The Good Spirit was given a Name, which was "Robin" and Robin was said to be Human and furthermore said to be Perfect. That was a Lie because a Human can not be Perfect because to be Perfect is to be Dead, and God is not Dead.

The Author of that Story worshipped the Good Guy (The Spirit of Goodness), but It failed Him because it was Human.

The Winner in this "Story Contest" was Author, "Saint Bill" because "Saint Bill" did not give God, the Real, (The Spirit of Goodness) a Human Name, but just said, I love you, by saying, Dear God, Thank you for All my Blessings, Both Physical and Spiritual,. And to Hell with the Shadow because It is Illusion in and of every Form Real.

Yes, the minute you Worship an "Idol" you will be disappointed and Alone when the going gets Tough (Tuff). So do not Worship "Saint Bill". Worship God, the Real, The Spirit of Goodness, and It will Never fail you. Never.

But remember "Saint Bill" because He was not Perfect and recognized that God is not Perfect.. The Shadow is Perfect because It is a "Nothing". Yes, an Illusion. Yes, Nothing is Perfect. Something is "Alive", "Active", and "Good".

"The Spirit of Goodness" is Real and It lives within Us along with Its Children, Yes, the little Spirits of Goodness. The oldest being "The Spirit of Truth" and the youngest being "The Spirit of Enthusiasm", and this "Family of God" within us cannot die, just as God can not die, but goes to Heaven to be with "God the Total" when our Body ceases to function.

Yes, Physical death is an Illusion, and Spiritual life is a Reality, and Eternal. Have that Faith and It will bring you Happiness, Prosperity and Peace of Mind. Thank you, Dear God, Thank you, as ever in, "The Spirit of Goodness",

Yours truly, B.H., M.A., L.W. "Saint Bill"

P.S.: Another Profound Difference between a "Saint" and a "Sinner".

> A "Saint" always has time to talk to any Neighbor, any time, any where. A "Sinner" says, You are too Smart, I do not want to talk to you because I have no time, I am busy with the Morons. Yes, bring me the Morons.

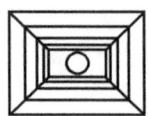

PREVIEWISM
Our World is Beautiful, Yes, Multi-Cultural

Dear Friends,. Thank you, thank you, thank you,. You may be Seated

Today we are going to talk about "The Truth" as described by a great "Theologian", and interpreted by a Great "Philosopher". Now, if you do not know the difference you better learn quickly or you will be Confused.

Yes, a Theologian interprets Words without Actions, yes, Empty words.

A Philosopher interprets Actions without Words, yes, the whole Real Truth. Because God speaks with Actions not with words, Yes, Actions speak Louder than words. So you see, You tell the Tree by the Fruit, not the Leaves.

Now we are told that this great "Theologian" was not conceived by the Hindu God, and not conceived by the Buddhist God, or conceived by any other God, but was conceived by the Jewish God.

Then this great Theologian said,. The Jewish God is Satan,. (Acts 26, v.16-18),. which means this great Theologian was conceived by Satan. And we know that Satan is before all else a Liar. And a Lie is just an Illusion expressed, by a Human.

The Truth is that God only Creates without conception. The Creation then conceives to make Life Everlasting in the Image of God.

The great Philosopher of today was conceived by "Confucius-Reincarnate",... Yes, Confucius realized long before the Lies began that Humans are born with a "Good Nature", a "Sense of Judgement", and a "Free Spirit".... And that God never Condemns, but rather always Loves and Forgives, and hands out Blessings.

Humans are also, By Nature, born Ignorant and so rather than interpreting the Actions of God, they begin by interpreting the Words of their foreparents, and predecessors. But they learn sometime later that God, "The Spirit of Goodness", is a God of "Future" not of "Past". And so they sooner or later begin to interpret the Actions of God and gradually eliminate the Lies and Illusions of the Past.

Yes, the Future is of all things Real, and Reality is God, and God is Reality, not Fantasy. "The Spirit of Goodness" is God and It is Real, and Lives within our Heart and Soul from Conception and goes to Heaven when our body ceases to Function.

Yes, this is "Truth very Simple", all else on the Subject is Illusion. Have that faith and It will bring you Happiness, Prosperity, and Peace of Mind.

Thank you, Yours truly, as ever in, "The Spirit of Goodness",

B.H., M.A., L.W. (Saint Bill) "Coach".

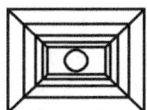

PREVIEWISM
Our World is Beautiful, Yes, Multi-Cultural

Dear Friends,. Thank you, Thank you, Thank you. You may be Seated.

Today we are going to talk about a Past Society. Yes, the Shadows Society.

You know statistics tell us that 1 in 900 people in society are in Jail. (A Jailbird) and 1 in 100 is a Criminal on the loose. And that 1 in 10 is a Sinner, Yes, a Shadow Worshipper.

That leaves approximately 89% of people who are "Saints". (In the Human Eye)

But the Shadow is a Negative Bastard and a Liar, and so It makes a Mountain out of a Molehill and a Molehill out of a Mountain. Yes, It says we are all Sinners except me of Course. Yes, the Shadow is the Accuser, but remember the Shadow does not exist, and is just an Illusion, and so It works through your Neighbor (People). So you see, It is your Neighbor who is the Accuser, Yes, the ignorant Idiot who thinks that God Condemns and does not Forgive, Unless, Yes, Unless. Yes Condition upon Condition, Yes, He/She thinks that God is an Extortionist and a Slave Driver. and a Glory seeker. (Oh, how Pitiful.)

The fact is that God the Real, "The Spirit of Goodness" is EverUnderstanding Loving, and Always Forgiving, and Never Condemns or Accuses you of any Wrongdoing. Yes God always Forgives and Renews your Good Nature and your Desire to do more Good.

Yes, The Spirit of Goodness, that lives in your Heart by Nature does never Accuse your Neighbor of any Wrongdoing, but rather always tries to Understand and Forgive.

But remember, that to Forgive is to Forget, So if you find you are Dealing with a Criminal of any sort, You just say, I forgive you, Now get out of my Sight so I can Forget you. Yes, this is Necessary because we are Not God and can not cope with continual Waste and Abuse. So you see, we must use our Sense of Judgement and extend our hand to those in the Pits of Hell on Earth but not Jump into the Pit with them. Yes, if your Neighbor is a Habitual Criminal, you say Be Gone.

This is what God says, to the Shadow, Be gone out into outer Darkness, beyond the reach of Light, and Stay there, I need you there for Reference. Yes, out of Sight and out of Mind, And if It is out of Mind It is out of Existence.

Yes, The Shadows society is now out of Existence because we have now learned that we are All Saints in God's Eye, and any Neighbor that Accuses you of anything is Forgiven for His/Her ignorance of the Facts about God the Real, "The Spirit of Goodness" and all of Its Children (Angels). eg..Sincerity, Enthusiasm Perseverance, Love, Planning Organization, etc.

Thanks for Listening,

Yours truly, as ever in, the Spirit of Goodness

"Saint Bill"

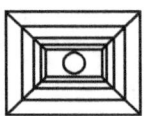

PREVIEWISM
Our World is Beautiful, Yes, Multi-Cultural

Dear Friends,. Thank you. Thank you. Thank you,. You may be Seated...

Today I have a Question for you. If you were on your last three breaths of life what would you tell your Nieghbor was the most profound thing you learned while on Earth that He/She can depend on. Come Hell or High Water. ....

Well, Folks, while you are thinking. Let me tell you what I have learned is the True Gospel Truth that you can depend on.

"The Spirit of Goodness" is born in your Heart and Soul when you are Conceived. And when you enter this World a Fat Head says to you, "Invite me into your Heart and let me Rule your Life". Now the poor people who fall into this Trap find they have nothing but Turmoil in their mind because the "Fat Head" tells nothing but Lies but your Soul knows the Truth, and so there is nothing but Turmoil and Confusion.

Yes, the "Fat Head" says to you,. I am God, you believe what I say. Do not Question me, Do not Judge,. Just Believe, Have Faith,. I would not Lie to you. Would I....

Then the "Fat Head" says to you,. You believe what I say and I will take you to Heaven,. If you Question Me, you will go to Hell.

Well, the Truth is, if you keep the "Fat Head" in your Heart It will lead you to Hell the long way around, right here on Earth, because It is a Liar.

You remember, that God the Real, "The Spirit of Goodness" has a "Lean and Mean" head and Loves you with a Firm hand as It says that my Laws are Fixed,. No-one can break them unless they Lie. So you accept my Laws and learn to live by them and you will find Heaven on Earth, because that is what it is all about. Heaven on Earth. Heaven in Heaven is predetermined and for All, not just the "Fat Heads".

Yes folks. God created Heaven and Earth,. It did not create Hell.. Hell was created by the "Fat Heads" before us who would not accept God's Laws and wanted to make their own to live by, and so they said, "You Reap what you Sow", yes, an Eye for an Eye, and a Tooth for a Tooth,.To the Tee. But It is a Lie and causes nothing but pain and suffering. But remember the "Fat Heads" are Suckers-for-Punishment, and so they say It is Good for you. Yes, Suffering makes you Strong. Well, I say. Hog Wash, the purpose is to be Happy, not Strong. We let God be Strong, so that we can be Happy,

Yes, the Law of God the Real says, "Look Up and Forgive one-another and Reap only Blessings,.Barring the Weather of Course". Yes, we must accept the Weather and always Forgive and not Condemn, regardless of the Exceptions,

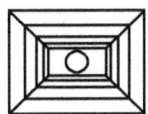

PREVIEWISM
Our World is Beautiful, Yes, Multi-Cultural

Yes. the Sunshine is the Rule and the Rain and Hail Storms are the Exceptions. But you do not change the Rule because of the Exceptions.

Because we are dealing with Humans we try to change the Exceptions to meet the Rule.

And you do this by "Forgiving, Not Condemning", Blessing, Not Curseing. Yes. Rewarding, Not Punishing".

But there are a few exceptions to this too.. Yes, the "Fat Heads", they are stuck in the Mud and continue to wallow in the Pits of Hell on Earth.

So you just extend your hand to them and offer to help them out, but do not Jump into the Pits with them. Yes, if you have Faith in God's Law the "Fat Heads" will eventually see the Light in It and accept your hand without you having to Suffer with them.

Yes folks, you must use your "Sense of Judgement" and "Judge" right from wrong - true from false, possible from impossible. Yes, Good from Waste, and forgive people their Shortcomings without doing what causes the Shortcomings.

Yes folks. If we break the Laws of God the Real, "The Spirit of Goodness", and try to live by our own we are in trouble until we become "Lean and Mean" and learn to accept the Truth about life, and the Truth is that God Loves us All, All the Time. And Heaven is for All without exception.

Therefore, refuse to live by any other way except by "The Spirit of Goodness" that lives in your Heart and Soul from conception. It will guide you correctly if you learn to Judge in God's fashion, which is to always Forgive, extend your hand, and walk away from the Pit. This is what God does,. It never looks back or down.

Folks, as you can tell, I am very long winded, but I have come to the end of my third breath.

Thanks for Listening,

Yours truly, as ever in, "The Spirit of Goodness",

B.H., M.A., L.W. "Saint BILL" (Coach)

PREVIEWISM
Our World is Beautiful, Yes, Multi-Cultural

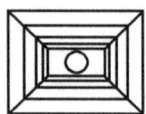

Dear Friends,. Thank you, Thank you, Thank you,. You may be Seated....

Today I have another Question for you. "What happens when you build a Church on the Side of a Sand Hill"?.

Yes, you have already guessed,. It sinks and topples down.

Well, you know a Character called "Robin" said that the foundation of "Hoodianity" is Judaism. And then It said that Judaism is worshipping Satan. (Acts 26,v.16-18)

Well, we know that Satan is a Sand Pile, not Cement. Yes, Satan is a Fraud, a Liar. Well, Robin was a Bad Guy, held out to be a Good Guy, Yes a Fraud, a Liar.

But It put on a Sheepskin Coat and wooed the sheep Its way toward Its Church. And once inside It said, sorry, no Carpet just corrugated gravel.

To keep the sheep inside Its Church this character called "Robin" said, I am God

on Earth, I can even Raise the Dead, Worship me, please, I will even Die for you. Come on, I love you. Believe me, Really I do. I will bring you Riches and Knowledge and you can be just like me, you can have anything you want, if you just say "Robin"

Please disregard the Floor, I will bring in the Red Carpet tomorrow. Please. Just say "Robin" and you will be more beautiful than me. Now don't you leave this Church or you will go to Hell. If you stay and Worship me, I will take you to Heaven. I came from Heaven and I know what it is like, you will Love it, I know. Please Worship me, for God's sake, please.

Well, the Church sank into Judaism in Disguise.

ooooo0ooooo

Now Folks, I have another Question for you,. What happens when you build a "Summit" on "The Spirit of Goodness", Yes, the Spirit of Truth, the Spirit of Enthusiasm, the Spirit of Perseverance, the Spirit of Planning, the Spirit of Organization, the Spirit of True Forgiveness, Yes, truly Forgotten,. the Spirit of True Love, yes, truly Free., the Spirit of Curiosity, etc.

Yes, you have already guessed,.You find Happiness, Decency, Prosperity, and Peace of Mind, etc. etc. Yes, Heaven on Earth as It should be, because you are Living in Reality, not Fantasy.

Thanks for Listening,

Yours truly, as ever in, "The Spirit of Goodness",.

"Saint Bill".

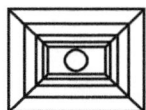

PREVIEWISM
Our World is Beautiful, Yes, Multi-Cultural

Dear Friends,. Thank you. Thank you. Thank you,. You may be Seated.....

Today we are going to compare "The Game of Life" to a "Card Game".

You know we have 13 Tricks and 4 Suits to each Trick, for a total of 52 Cards and One Joker, if you so choose.

The Joker has no Power except that which you give It in the Game.

If you choose to give the Joker no Power, you can just Discard It and play the Game without It, with a Lot more Fun.

The Joker, when given Power, claims to hold All the Power in the Game. And that the Game Revolves around It. But in fact the Power can be revoked and the Game played without the Joker. Which means the Joker is just a Joke.

As you know, in the Card game there are a maximum of 13 players and God the Real, "The Spirit of Goodness" holds all of the Aces.

As you know, there are 4 rounds to be won, and "God the Real" always wins the first round when It plays the Ace of Hearts Last, because under the Heart is written the words "Truth and Love".

When everyone has played his/her Card of the Second round. God the Real, always wins as It plays the Ace of Diamonds Last, because under the Diamond is written the words "Happiness, Decency, Prosperity and Peace of Mind".

When everyone has played his/her Card of the Third round. God the Real, always wins as It plays the Ace of Clubs Last, because under the Club is written the words "Law and Order".

When everyone has played his/her Card of the Fourth and Last round. God the Real, "The Spirit of Goodness" always wins as It plays the Ace of Spades Last, because under the Ace of Spades is written the word....FORGIVEN....

The reason God, the real, always wins in this Game is because It pays no attention to the Joker, because God knows the Joker is a Fraud, a Joke, a Laugh, a Nothing, because whether you give The Joker Power or Not, God the real, does not recognize or acknowledge this Power as the "Real Power" is written under the Aces, and God always gets the Last Word.... FORGIVEN....

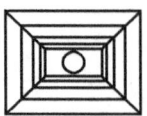

PREVIEWISM
Our World is Beautiful, Yes, Multi-Cultural

In Summary, we say that if you play the Game the way, God the Real, plays you will always have Four Aces in your Hand, and win Happiness, Decency, Prosperity, and Peace of Mind in Heaven on Earth, and a Spot in Heaven in Heaven....Thanks for Listening, as ever .... "Saint Bill".

A New Standard for the Charity.

Dear Friends:

Previews Institute of Universal Philosophy, is a Non-Profit charity specializing in "Food for Thought", and our Object is to relieve Poverty, both physical and spiritual poverty. Yes, to advance all of Humankind in the Spiritual sense because Spiritual success leads to Material success. Yes, this is the Relief of poverty, yes, a Charity. Philanthropy at Its Best.
We at "Previews" have set a new standard for the Charity, whereby all in house overhead and salaries are paid by the Founder (Foundation) of the Trust.
This means that every nickle of every dollar that the general public donates goes toward the Releif of Poverty, both physical and spiritual poverty.
Our program includes help in providing for the six basic needs of Society. These are Shelter, Food, Clothing, Education, Insurance and Spiritual Ideal (Doctrine or Dicipline).
At present we have underway our "Free Lunch for the Destitute" program, whereby just for the asking the Destitute can have a Free lunch at our Participating Restaurants. And Previews Institute picks up the Tab on a monthly basis.
Yes, although the Seed of our Charity has just begun to sprout, we can already see Results. And without a Doubt as our Charity grows into full bloom we will be covering all of the Basic needs in an appropriate way.
As you know, The ones who create a Charity and The ones who give to a Charity are Equal Partners. Yes, United we can go the Distance.
When you come to Decide to Give to our Charity, you can be assured that all donations will be received with many Thanks.
Assuming you may be ready now, Please make your cheque payable to "Previews Institute" and send It to the address shown on our web-site in the "Order Info" link... And remember, you get a Collectors Item as a Thank you Gift.

Hoping to hear from you soon, we remain Yours truly,
As ever in The Spirit of Goodness, "Saint Bill".
A Servant for God's sake.

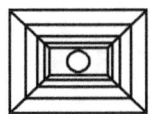

PREVIEWISM
Our World is Beautiful, Yes, Multi-Cultural

Dear Friends,. Thank you, Thank you, Thank you,. You may be Seated

Today we are going to explain our Position with regard to "The Spirit of Goodness", (God the Real).

You know the N.H.L. has a lot of "Teams" on it. And when you are standing among the Fans when someone asks, Who are you Rooting for?.....you have to answer or you are an Oddball or an Outcast, Right?

Well you know there are Seven Major Religions in the World today, and

I ask, Who are you Rooting for? Well, what ever you say, It does not matter because we all get the Benefit of the Exercise, in each.

You know the Seven Authors of the Religions are, Confuscious, Abraham, Buddha, St. Paul, Mohammed, Singh, and (Guess Who), "The Spirit of Goodness".

Yes, "The Spirit of Goodness" says, (We are One, Not, I am It), Yes, "The Spirit of Goodness" represents the Winning Combination of Religions in the World today. Yes, the Winning Religion of today, (and Today is all we have), is Society as a Whole, because It makes the Rules (Laws) and Society sets up the mechanisms to achieve Peace and Harmony throughout Life.

And "The Whole of Society" is now represented by, (Guess What), "PREVIEWISM". And the Author of "PREVIEWISM" is (Saint BILL). So all you other Gentlemen "Take a Bow", Knees and All, You Gentlemen, Bow.

And let not one of you walk away "Sulking" because we all get the Benefit of the Exercise of Talking to One-another in "The Spirit of Goodness".

Yes, this is what it is all about, talking to one-another in "The Spirit of Goodness". This brings Heaven to Earth for all who take part in "The Spirit of Goodness", (God the Real).

Yes, "The Spirit of Goodness" lets us know that Heaven in Heaven is for All, not just the Hoity-Toity-Self-righteous Idiots,. Fat Heads,. Sulkers,. Yes, "Shadow Worshippers". Yes, "The Shadow" is God the Fraud, the Liar when It says, "I am Real", look down and watch me. Wrong, It is Illusion.

Look Up and see "Reality" because Reality is God and God is Reality, Not Fantasy. Yes the Light of Day brings us Reality. The Shadow of Night brings us Illusion. Reality is Truth, Love and Forgiveness,. Illusion is Lie, Fear and Condemnation and Curse.

So Folks, Thank God for "The Spirit of Goodness" as it is Real and True.

Thanks for Listening, as ever in

"The Spirit of Goodness",

(Saint Bill)

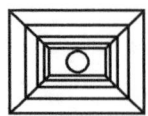

PREVIEWISM
Our World is Beautiful, Yes, Multi-Cultural

Dear Friends

Do you realize what a wonderful opportunity is before you to Adopt a most rewarding Hobby for your Retirement years.

Yes, there is nothing more rewarding than the Advancement of all of Humankind in the Spiritual sense, because "Spiritual Success" leads to "Material Success". Yes, this is "The Relief of Poverty", (a Charity)

If you were an Apple Tree Farmer and all you had was an Apple Orchard, Could you sell "Peaches and Cream"?...Of course not, unless you were a Liar.

Well, as we all know, the First Book of Knowledge is a Box of Apples.

And the Second Book of Knowledge is trying to sell Peaches and Cream out of an Apple Box... They are obviously Frauds.

The people of the First Book of Knowledge are still trying to sell Apples, but the problem is, the Apples have gone Rotten, and so they are taking a Free ride on the Back of the fraudulent Peach sales men and women. These people are obviously "Less than Human" and Frauds too.

According to the Second Book of Knowledge, the First Book of Knowledge represents "God the Fraud" (Acts 26,v .16-18). and the Second Book of Knowledge represents "God the Human" (2 Thes 2,v.9-11)...So far so Bad, as they are both "Frauds".

Well, we at "Previews" have Conceived and Developed a "Peach Tree", and we are going to sell "Peaches and Cream" because we are Dairy Farmers....besides good Scientists.

Dear Friends...., ."The Peach Tree", the Third Book of Knowledge, "The COMPASS" represents "God the Real". "The Spirit of Goodness", and It lives in your Heart, Mind and Soul. And we, together, are going to sell Peaches and Cream and we are going to Live life to the Fullest, because there is no longer any Curse. It, the Curse, has been Exposed for what It is, Yes, a Story of "The Shadow" (Illusion),. Pure Bad Fiction. (Rev.22,v.3)

The Digital Watch has been prepared,..All It needs is a Battery and It will "Never Look Back" again because It manufactures Its own Batteries thereafter.

Please do not miss this wonderful opportunity for yourselves,.

Thanks for Listening,

Yours truly, as ever in, "The Spirit of Goodness".

Good ole Brother, Bill. Alias, "Saint Bill". (Coach)

Previews Institute

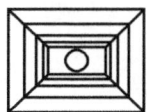

PREVIEWISM
Our World is Beautiful, Yes, Multi-Cultural

Just a Few Miscellaneous Proverbs:

We know that God is Real and Light.

We know that Devil is the Opposite of God, Therefore, Devil is Illusion and Shadow.

Yes, the Shadow is an Illusion and

an Illusion is Nothing, and

Nothing is Perfect.

Yes, Mr. Perfect is an Illusion.

Therefore, God is not perfect,

God is Real and Light.

~~~~~~~~~~

Look around you and you See God..

Look Up and you See God.

Yes, the Weather can be likened to God. It is not Perfect.

You have Sunshine, Rain and Hailstorms. Sunshine is the Rule,

The others are the Exceptions.

But you do not change the Rule

because of the Exception,

~~~~~~~~~~

If you Look Down you See The Shadow.

and the Shadow is Illusion and Lie.

Yes, Lie is just an Illusion in Words.

So Look Up and See Truth and Reality.

Because Reality is God and God is Reality,

Not Fantasy. Yes, Truth is just Reality in Words.

Thank you, as ever in, "The Spirit of Goodness",

 "Saint Bill" (Coach)

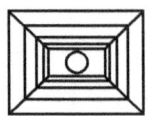

PREVIEWISM
Our World is Beautiful, Yes, Multi-Cultural

Dear Friends,. Thank you. Thank you. Thank you, You may be Seated....

Today we want to remind you of some basic Facts about Life in Heaven on Earth. We know that God does not Condemn, God does not Punish, God does not Hate. God always Understands and Forgives, God always Hands out Blessings, God always Loves. Therefore all of our Sins against Humanity have been washed away by the Truth about God. Therefore the Wages of Sin is Life Eternal in Heaven in Heaven with God Eternal.

We know that God is the same Yesterday, Today, and Tommorrow. Yes, God is "The Spirit of Goodness". It has no Evil (Bad) characteristics at all.

Therefore there are No people (Souls) in Hell of Yesterday or Today and certainly not of Tommorrow, because Hell is a Fictional Place and Its only Occupant is a Fictional Character. Yes, The Shadow, out in outer darkness, beyond the reach of light. Yes, out of Sight, and out of Mind, and out of Existence.

We know that life on Earth is a beautiful experience when we do not pay any attention to the Shadow (Illusion), and keep our Mind's Eye on Reality, because Reality is God, and God is Reality, Not Fantasy.

We know that "The Spirit of Goodness" (God) tells us that we all go to Heaven because all of our Sins against Humanity have been washed away by the Truth about God. Therefore we know that Heaven is a predetermined Place, just as Heaven on Earth is predetermined when we live without Illusion (the Shadow) and all of Its Fantastic Lies. Yes, total Confusion.

We know that when we follow God's example and Forgive, not Condemn, Bless, not Curse, Reward, not Punish, we will Reap the same from our Neighbors. Barring the Exceptions.

We know that when we eliminate the Unfulfilling influence of Illusion (The Shadow) we will be living by a New Psychology and life will continually improve until we have Heaven on Earth for most everyone, and as always we will have Heaven in Heaven for Everyone. In the meantime we will make life a lot easier for God on Earth, Yes, "The Spirit of Goodness" will Rest easy.

We know this may take a few days or a few years, but it is going to happen, just as sure as we Rotate into the Light every morning..

Thanks for Listening, Yours truly, as ever in, "The Spirit of Goodness",

B.H., M.A., L.W. "Saint Bill", (Coach) Previews Institute.

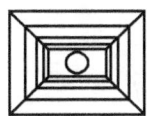

PREVIEWISM
Our World is Beautiful, Yes, Multi-Cultural

Dear Friends,. Thank you. Thank you. Thank you,. You may be Seated.

Today we are going to talk about some Realities.

You know, a FOOL once asked a "Smart ASS", Who are you? And the Smart ASS said. It does not matter what I think. What you think is what matters.

So the "Smart ASS" asked the FOOL, Who do you think I am?

And the "FOOL" said. You are God on Earth...

And the "Smart ASS" said. If you think so, you are thinking Right...

Well folks, we know who is the "Fraud" and we know who is the "Jack ASS".

Yes, the "Smart ASS" knew that if It said, I am God, It would be a "FOOL".

So It let the "FOOL" say. You are God, and let him/her walk away Believing It.

Well, what a "Jack ASS".

Yes, the "Smart ASS" is a Brazen "Son-of-a-Bitch", and an Earthworm, letting anyone who is "FOOL" enough believe that It is God on Earth.

Well, what a .... Earthworm,. Obviously a "Fictional Character".

No real Character could be so Brazen, and No FOOL could truly be so Stupid.

But this is what Some people on Earth think is Reality. Obviously been Fooled.

Any way, Folks, so much for that "Illusion" that Someone once thought was Reality. My, what a Waste of time. But this is what the "Smart ASSes" of this world want you to do. Yes, Waste your Time, Glorifying a Real FOOL.

Yes, the Real Truth always prevails, and now It is here. Yes, God on Earth is "The Spirit of Goodness", and It lives in your Heart and Soul from Conception, and goes to Heaven when your body ceases to Function.

Yes, Truth very Simple.

Thanks for Listening, Yours truly,

as ever in, "The Spirit of Goodness",

B.H., M.A., L.W. "Saint Bill" (Coach)

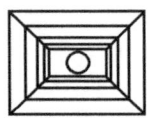

PREVIEWISM
Our World is Beautiful, Yes, Multi-Cultural

Dear Children: November 9/99 (60 B.H.)

In 30. Years from now all of the 1st generation will be in Heaven and all of their illusions will have passed away with them.

In 60 years from now all of the 2nd generation will be in Heaven and all of their Illusions will have passed away with them.

In 90 years from now in the 3rd generation we will begin to see the Fruits of Reality as manifested in and by "The COMPASS", a New Bible. "The EverLast Testament".

It shows us the Ways of God the Real, Not God the Fraud.

God the Fraud, says, "You reap what you Sow", yes. an Eye for an Eye, and a Tooth for a Tooth, all to the Tee. But it is a Lie and causes nothing but pain & Suffering.

God the Real. "The Spirit of Goodness" says, "Look Up and Forgive one-another and Reap only Blessings, Barring the weather of course. And the weather will now continually improve, until we have Heaven on Earth for most everyone.

Yes, in life we have "Sunshine", Rain, and Hailstorms. (That is "Saints", Sinners, and Criminals.) Yes, "Smilers", Cryers, and Destroyers.

The Sunshine is the Rule,.the others are the exceptions. But you do not change the Rule because of the Exceptions. Because we are dealing with Humans we try to change the Exceptions to meet the Rule. And now slowly bring Heaven to Earth for All.

In "The COMPASS", God the Real, "The Spirit of Goodness" has convinced us that we are All Saints in God's Eye because God understands all of our Actions and Forgives any and All Shortcomings that we have. Therefore God never Accuses us of any Wrong-Doing, but rather Forgives and Renews our Good Nature and our Desire to do more Good

Yes. if we Believe and Know we are "Saints" in God's Eye, we go and Act Accordingly.

If we think we are "Sinners" according to the ACCUSER, the DEVIL, the SHADOW, the FRAUD we go and Act Accordingly, which is to Punish, Curse, and Condemn. Yes, Hate.

But remember the FRAUD is a Liar. and so It says. I Love you. this is Good for you. Yes. Suffering makes you Strong.... God the Real says. Hog Wash, Suffering makes you a Sucker for more Suffering.

Yes, a "Saint" knows that God wants us to be Happy. So we let God be TRULY strong in Goodness , so that we can be HAPPY. Beautiful eh. Glory, Glory, Hallelujah.

Thanks for Listening, as ever in, "The Spirit of Goodness"

Saint Bill, (Coach)

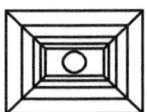

PREVIEWISM
Our World is Beautiful, Yes, Multi-Cultural

Dear Friends,. Thank you. Thank you. Thank you.. You may be Seated....

God on Earth is "The Spirit of Goodness", and It lives in our Heart, Soul, and Mind from Conception. Let It Flurish. It is the Creator, the Good Provider, the "Steadfast Comforter". We know It very well, if we are Honest with ourselves. To be and remain Honest with ourselves we must always have Faith in Reality and Refuse to be led to have Faith in Illusion.

When you are a Young person, and someone says to you, "Take me into your Heart and let Me rule your Life because I am Old and Wise, I love you."

You say: Be Gone, you Bastard, I recognize your line..."You say. Do not Judge,"

Well, I say. You Bastard,..Earthworm,..Shadow.

"The Spirit of Goodness" in my Heart right now gave me a "Sense of Judgement", a "Free Spirit" and a "Good Nature", and I have to use my "Sense of Judgement" to Nourish my Good Nature to let it grow into something Beautiful.

If I do not use my "Sense of Judgement" my "Free Spirit" will lead me into confusion and Illusion... Which is what you want, You Bastard.

If I use my "Sense of Judgement", my "Free Spirit" will make me Creative like my Maker. And I will become a "Good Provider" like my Maker.

And I will follow the Law of "The Spirit of Goodness", which is "Look Up, and Forgive one-another and Reap only Blessings, Barring the Weather, of course... Yes, I will reap Happiness, Decency. Prosperity, and Peace of Mind. What more do I need?

I look around me and I see many who are achieving these Blessings and I see a Few who call themselves "The Only True Children of God", and all they do is stand around and Accuse others for the Misery they are in.

When in fact it is because they accepted the Bastard (Fraud) into their Heart.

Yes, they got Fooled into thinking there was a better way than that of The Spirit of Goodness" in their Heart, Soul, and Mind from Conception.

Well, Children and Friends, let me assure you there is no better way than the "Natural Way", and the Natural Way is to use your "Sense of Judgement" to develop your Good Nature, and allow your Free Spirit to make you Creative, and a Good Provider, and a "Steadfast Comforter" like your Maker.

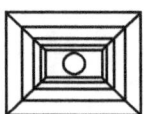

PREVIEWISM
Our World is Beautiful, Yes, Multi-Cultural

Yes, my Children and Friends, we can be just like our Maker, because our Maker is not Perfect and Forever tries to Improve upon Itself. And our Maker (God the Real) "The Spirit of Goodness" has been Improving upon Itself every day from the Beginning of time. And it is a pretty Good World we live in today. And it will continue to improve until we have Heaven on Earth for everyone, because we are now living by the Law of,God the Real, which is: "Look Up, and Forgive one-another and Reap only Blessings, Barring the Weather of course". Yes, we are All "Saints" in God's Eye.

God the Fraud, has been Identified. It is "The Shadow", It says, "I am Perfect", Follow me.. So that It can say. You Fail everyday. You are Hopeless, You are Useless, You are a "Nothing",. I am God,.Worship Me.

Yes, the Fraud accuses you of being a "Sinner" against God, when in fact you are only a Sinner against a Human being once in a while. God the Real understands this and continues to Love, Forgive and Bless you.

So my Children and Friends, in closing, I say, kick the Fraud out of your Heart, Put your Foot down hard on the Shadow, and Rub with your Rubber, Rubber Heel until there is nothing left but Dust... Then Look Up to God the Real in Heaven and in your Heart, Mind, and Soul, and Live forever in Bliss as a "Saint".. Free of all Guilt, Fear, Doubt, and Illusion.

Thanks for Listening,

Yours truly, as ever in, "The Spirit of Goodness",

Saint Bill, B.H., M.A., L.W.

Coach, Previews Institute

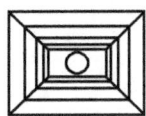

PREVIEWISM
Our World is Beautiful, Yes, Multi-Cultural

Dear Friends,. Thank you. Thank you. Thank you,. You may be Seated....

1) Does God send out Evil Spirits to cause Disharmony?

    Answer: NO!!

Satan says, "I am God,. I can do that without a problem" (Judges 9, v.23)

2) Does God present something so that you will believe a (Lie) Falsehood?

    Answer: NO!!

Satan says, "I am God,. I can do that without a problem" (2 Th.2,v.9-11)

Only Satan wants us to believe a Lie. Only Satan wants Disharmony.

But It says, "I am God", believe Me, I would not Lie to you, would I?

If It were not so I would tell you. Right?.... The Brazen Earthworm Scum.

3) God is not a Murderer.

The Devil says, "I am God", I want someone to be Killed as a Sacrifice,

Do not worry,. I can Justify Murder because I am Almighty, I can even Raise the Dead.

4) Therefore in essence there was No Sacrifice.

God the Real, "The Spirit of Goodness" rejected the Sacrifice, and said, I am not Almighty, I can Never Justify Murder, NEVER,

I want No part of Murder,. You can not Raise the Dead, That is a LIE...

Besides, I do not want a Sacrifice. That is another LIE....

5) God the Real, says, the whole story is the work of Satan....(The Shadow)

All I want is Obedience to my will to a Human level.

Therefore, this man will die a Natural death and go to Heaven

like all of My children have in the past, present and Future.

6) Therefore, God the Real, says. Be Gone Satan, you Bastard, Out into

outer Darkness, beyond the Reach of Light, and Stay there, ALONE,

I need you there for Reference.

Thanks for Listening,

Yours truly, as ever in, "The Spirit of Goodness"

Saint Bill, B.H., M.A., L.W.

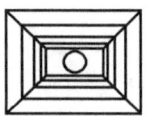

PREVIEWISM
Our World is Beautiful, Yes, Multi-Cultural

Dear Friends,. Thank you, Thank you, Thank you,. You may be Seated....

Today we are going to talk about the Difference between The Future and The Past. We know that God the Real, "The Spirit of Goodness" always Looks to the Future, and as such always prepares the Way for us to Lead a Good and Productive Life. As such the Future holds only Goodness and Truth and Happiness for us.

We know that God the Fraud, The Shadow, is always looking to the Past, and It is filled with Lies and Illusions, which when Acted upon bring us Nothing but Pain and Suffering.

So you see there are some of us who sometimes live in the Past and some of us who sometimes live in the Future. The Secret is to Turn and Look Up to face God and Look to the Future with It. Then Act on our Inspirations from God to have the Blessings Flow.

You know, someone once asked me, "How do you Change the Future".. The answer is,. "Eliminate the Lies of the Past"... Then that same someone asked me, "How do you eliminate the Lies of the Past"? The answer is,. "Read what ever you wish about the Past, and then use your "Sense of Judgement" to decide what is True (possible) and what is Impossible (False). Then Discard the False and Pay No more Attention to it as you Turn and Look Up to the Truth held high.

So you see, In order to Achieve the Utmost in a Happy and Productive life, You must always try to Forget the Past quickly, because it contains Lies and Illusions.

Then always try to Look Up to the Future and your Positive Goals because the Future holds only Truth and Reality, which when Acted upon brings us Happiness, Decency, Prosperity, and Peace of Mind. That is a pretty good Summary of what I had to say.

Thank you, as ever in,

"The Spirit of Goodness"

B.H., M.A., L.W. "Saint Bill"

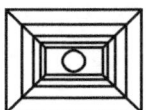

PREVIEWISM
Our World is Beautiful, Yes, Multi-Cultural

Dear Friends,. Thank you, Thank you, Thank you,. You may be Seated

Today we are going to talk about a Fictional Character called "Robin Hood", or "Robin Christ", or "Robin Messiah", or "Robin Shadow", and his brother Jesus.

We know that Christ refers to "The Christ of God" and Messiah refers to "The Messiah of God" and Shadow refers to "The Shadow of God". All three of these words, Christ, Messiah, Shadow,. mean Illusion. Yes, The Illusion of God.

Robin is a fictional "Bad Guy", and Jesus is a fictional "Good Guy". The Bad Guy was a Liar and so he said his name was Jesus.

This Bad Guy performed as we all know how. (2 Th.2,v.9-11)

Jesus was a Human who thought he was "Perfect", and so he thought he must not degrade (contradict) his brother. Yes, he thought he must always speak Good of his brother. But if you always speak good of your brother you are a Liar. So he was Stuck in the Mud and said "Nothing". Yes He was a Nothing.

Folks, I, W.J. (Bill) Handel, M.A., L.W. "Saint Bill", the Author of "The Compass", have studied the Christian and Jewish Bible for over 50 years and have found that God the Real, "The Spirit of Goodness" never tells Us a Murder Story, and asks us to Believe that the "Motive" for It is based on the Truth. Oh, NO!!, the Truth is the Truth, but the Motive for Murder is always based on a LIE. No matter how you Twist and Turn, you cannot Justify Murder. You can "Forgive" murder, but you cannot Justify Murder.

Yes, we have Herein, allowed the Real Jesus to Stand Up and Speak to the World. (Acts 26, v. 16-18)

Thanks for Listening. Yours truly, as ever in "The Spirit of Goodness"

B.H., M.A., L.W. "Saint Bill" (Coach)

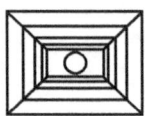

PREVIEWISM
Our World is Beautiful, Yes, Multi-Cultural

Dear Friends and Children of all ages:

We all know there are three sources of knowledge. They are (1) To talk to a Wise person. (2) Read a Good book. (3) Personal Experience. This is the most reliable source of knowledge.

Well folks, let me share with you a discussion I had the other day with a Wise man.

The Wise man said, Hello, How are you today.

I said, Fine, Just Super excellent.

The Wise man said, Good,.How can I help you today?

I said, I have a Question for you.

The Wise man said, O.K., Shoot, I will see if I can answer.

I said, "Who brought Sin into the World?

The Wise man said, That is a pretty big question, that I can not answer, what do you think?

I said, As with everything Spiritual there are two kinds. And there are two kinds of Sin. One is Sin against God, and One is Sin against Humanity. As with all Thought, One is Reality, and One is Illusion.

Well, Sin against God is an Illusion, and Sin against Humanity is a Reality. Therefore God always says, "Forgiven", now go and Forgive your neighbor and we will Both be at Peace.

The Wise man said, How else can I help you today?

I said, You say you do not know the answer to my Question. Well, I would like to inform you that there is no sin in the World. The Accuser just makes you think there is, but It is a Lie, and a Lie is just an expressed Illusion.

The Wise man said, Thank you, Is there anything else I can help you with today? I said, I am upset because I was told that God was upset with some of my Actions, when in Fact God understood my Ignorance in it all, and said, Forgiven,

Not you are condemned.

The Wise man said, What Happened?

I said, To forgive is to forget, so I forgot what happened, besides it is a long story, but I can say that I found "God the Real" and together we Kicked "God the Fraud" out of my Heart, Mind, and Soul. And now I live in Reality, Not Illusion.. I no longer try to walk on water, or Raise the Dead, or say to the Mountain, move.. I now think about "Possibilities" and that is why I like your teacher, even though he is a bit confused about some things.

The Wise man said, It has been nice talking to you but I have to be going, is there anything else I can help you with today?

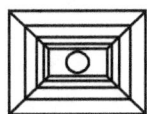

PREVIEWISM
Our World is Beautiful, Yes, Multi-Cultural

I said,. Not just now, maybe a little later, and just then a "Wise Lady" came along.

The Wise lady said, Hi, Bill,. How are you today?

I said: Just fine, Super excellent, but not Perfect.

The Wise lady said, Good,. What is on your mind, today?

I said: I have a Question for you.

The Wise lady said, Come on:!!! I will see if I can answer.

I said: "What brought Sin into the World?"

The Wise lady said, Hell, Bill,. You asked the Big question. I do not know, what do you think?

I said: Well, if you do not know what brought Sin into the world, then I guess I will have to tell you what I think did. O.K.?..

The Wise lady said, I will be happy to know what you think.

I said: Thank you, and you correct me if I am wrong.. Well, I think "The Shadow of God" with the help of Abraham brought what they thought was Sin into the World.

The Wise lady said, please explain further, I am interested!

I said: Well, to begin I will say that all things in God's world are Real except, "The Shadow of God".. As with any other Shadow, "The Shadow of God" is an Illusion. And an Illusion is a Liar when It says, "I am Real".

The Wise lady said, I always thought that phrase was a Metaphor.

Yes, The fact is God is Real and Its opposite is an Illusion. So you see Abraham was brought under an Illusion when he thought his Father had died. He was wrong. His Father went to Heaven just as we all do when our body ceases to function.

The Wise lady said, Thank you, Bill, I appreciate that bit of information,. Is there anything else going on for you that you wish to address?

I said: No, not really. I just thought I would like to hear what you have to say about Life.

The Wise lady said, Life is a broad subject,...I celebrate it daily and do what I can to enjoy every aspect of it. How about you?

I said: Thank you, I do the same and I feel I am the happiest and luckiest guy that ever walked this earth.....since I realized that Life is Eternal for all of God's children and not just for the Hoity-Toity self-righteous Idiots that say we are all Bad.

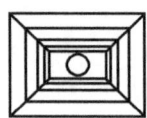

PREVIEWISM
Our World is Beautiful, Yes, Multi-Cultural

The Wise lady said, Refreshing!! Thank you. I have to go now and spread more Cheer. Thank you again and God Bless you.

I said: Thank you, You are O.K., God Bless you because you do not condemn and do not reap the same.

The Wise lady said: Thank you. My cup runneth over. Bye for now.

I smiled and waved.

Thanks, folks, for listening.

as ever in "The Spirit of Goodness"

B.H., M.A., L.W. "Saint Bill"

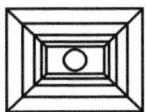

PREVIEWISM
Our World is Beautiful, Yes, Multi-Cultural

Dear Friends and Children of all ages:

As we know God is always looking forward to the Future and never looks back because It is too busy planning and preparing a beautiful Present for us.

As we know God never wants Centre Stage in our lives.. God says, I do not need your Love,. I am Love. So take It and pass It on to your Neighbor and It will grow and grow and be returned manifold.

So you see. God wants us to have Faith that God's love is always there for us to take, and pass It on. So you see. God wants us to give our Neighbor Centre Stage in our lives and keep God's face in front of us and God's Back behind us. Yes, always stay within the Stem of God's Umbrella and take God's love from Its hand and pass It on to our Neighbor.

This is because "The Spirit of Goodness" says, "We are One", Not "I am It". God does not say, "I am It", God says "We are One", therefore your Neighbor is just as important as me. In fact your Nieghbor is more important than me, because you can not serve me without serving your Neighbor first.

So you keep your Eye on your Neighbor's needs, and serve your Neighbor first, and you will already have served your God., because God is not Jealous of your Neighbor or anything else.

Yes, to love is to give without expecting a return, and we can do this when we have Faith that It will be returned manifold, as God has Faith that It will be returned manifold, and It is.

Furthermore, The cure for the Disease called "Sin" is to know and accept that God Loves you, just as you are, and the Accuser can go to Hell by Itself when It says, I am It, I am Perfect,. You are Bad. Yes, to hell with Him.

Thanks for Listening,

as ever in, "The Spirit of Goodness",

"Saint Bill".

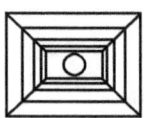

PREVIEWISM
Our World is Beautiful, Yes, Multi-Cultural

Dear Friends and Children of All ages:

As we know, "The Spirit of God" says, "We are One" (That makes us Equal)

The Devil (Shadow) says, "I am It".

But we know The Devil is a Liar, so God kicked It out, right.

The Devil being a Liar, says, "I rule the World".

But we know better, "The Spirit of Goodness", rules the World.

This is why there is a lot more Good in the World than there is Bad.

Yes, only,   1 in 900 is a Jailbird.

   1 in 100 is a criminal on the loose.

   1 in 10 is a Shadow Worshipper.

That leaves 88% of people who are "Saints" in the Human eye.

In God's eye we are all "Saints" because God Forgives and renews our Good Nature time and time again.

So the Devil can go to Hell by Itself, when It says we are all Bad.

Not one has fallen short of the Grace of God because God Loves and Forgives "Unconditionally".

The Devil (Shadow) says there are conditions, but It is a Liar, trying to get Its foot in the Door. Once in, It makes you a Slave to Its conditions.

God wants you to stay Free, so It makes Its Love and Forgiveness "Unconditional".

So remember. Reality is God and God is Reality, not Fantasy.

Thanks for Listening

Yours truly, as ever in, "The Spirit of Goodness",

B.H., M.A., L.W. "Saint Bill"

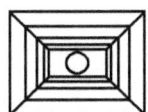

PREVIEWISM
Our World is Beautiful, Yes, Multi-Cultural

Dear Friends and Children of all ages:

Today we will consider the Three types of people in the World. First there is the "Bad Guy", Yes, the one who knows he/she is doing "Bad" all the time and Rejoices in It. We call him a "Dirty Criminal".

Secondly, there is the "Good Guy", Yes, the one who knows he/she is doing "Good" all of the time and claims he/she is Humble. We call him an "Idiot" because he thinks he is Perfect.

Finally, (Thirdly) there is the one in the middle who is not certain of anything, who claims he/she is One then the Other and acts accordingly. We call these Hypocrites.

The Society of A Country isolates the "Bad Guy", once identified, in Jail. And says, turn yourself around.

The Society of the World isolates the "Bad Guys" in a small Area in the Middle East and surrounds them with the "Good Guys", and says. Enjoy yourselves.

Now we know that Aggression is a Sin against Humanity. And Self Defense is an Act of God. So the "Bad Guys" aggress and the "Good Guys" defend themselves.

This leaves the Third parties throughout the rest of the World living in Bliss because they are neither Good or Bad, because they have had the opportunity to learn to FORGIVE one-another. And as such we consider them "Saints".

Of course we know that in God's Eye all the World is a "Saint" because God Forgives All.

All of this will continue until we (abolish) the records of the Dark ages.

Yes, the "Bad Guys" are using the records of the Dark ages as their Blue-Prints to Live By. And the Poor "Good Guys" are suffering unneccessarily.

God the Real, "The Spirit of Goodness", has revealed to "Saint Bill" the records (Blue-Prints) of the FUTURE. Yes, the age of Bright Lights wherein all of Humanity will see and realize the Real Truth, as manifested in and by "The COMPASS".

Yes, the secret to complete Peace and Harmony in the World is to learn to Roll with the Punches until your opponent has played himself out of energy, and Rolls over Dead.

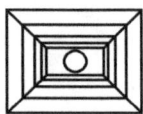

PREVIEWISM
Our World is Beautiful, Yes, Multi-Cultural

This is what God the Real, does with the Shadow. Yes, God the Real, lets the Shadow self-destruct, because the Shadow is a Liar, an Illusion, Yes, a Nothing, not worthy of any attention or rebuttal of any kind.

And when the New Generations of the World gradually see the Light the records of the Dark ages will pass away. And we will have Peace and Harmony throughout the World.

Thanks for Listening,

as ever in, "The Spirit of Goodness",

B.H., M.A., L.W. "Saint Bill"

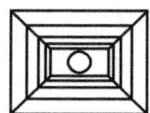

PREVIEWISM
Our World is Beautiful, Yes, Multi-Cultural

Dear Friends and Children of all ages:

As we know, there is only One God, but It seems there are Three. Yes, we have God the Good Guy,. God the Bad Guy, and God the Human.

God the Good Guy is God the Real,. God the Bad Guy is God the Fraud, and God the Human is a Hypocrite. On the one hand He/She is only half as Bad as the Bad Guy. And on the other hand He/She is only half as Good as the Good Guy. But He/She claims It is both.

For the Bad Guy,this person performed as we all know how according to 2 Thes 2, v. 9-11, Yes, all counterfeit Miracles to lead us to believe what is False.

For the Good Guy, this person did nothing because He/She thought It was Perfect and did not want to spoil His/Her record.

Yes Folks, we must remember that God the Fraud says most things identical to God the Real, and so in order for us to determine who is speaking we must watch the actions and pay no attention to the words, because as we know Actions speak louder than words.

Yes, the Fraud says, I am God, follow me and I will take you to Heaven, please it is your only Hope. But It is a Liar and so It takes you to Hell the long way around right here on Earth.

The Fraud says, I have come to give you Hope, and then says. Ah, not all who come to me and say God, God, will be accepted into Heaven, No not All, only those who have done my Will. And of course we know no-one has done Its will, "Be Perfect". So everyone goes to Hell according to that Earthworm, as this makes Us Hopeless.

Friends and Children, we know that God the Real, "The Spirit of Goodness", understands us all and Forgives us all our Shortcomings and washes away the Bad every day and keeps us Spotless so that we will be fit to take our place in Heaven any time. Just as we are. Yes, God the Real, prepared a Spot for us in Heaven upon our conception, and there is Nothing or No-one that can stop us from going to Heaven, because God always gets the Last word, and the Last word is ..FORGIVEN.

And the Bad Guy. The Fraud, can go to Hell by Itself, out into outer Darkness beyond the reach of Light, and we can say "Stay there", we need you there for reference.

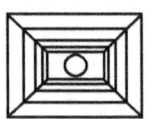

PREVIEWISM
Our World is Beautiful, Yes, Multi-Cultural

Yes Folks. God the Real, "The Spirit of Goodness", set us Free from the beginning to use our "Sense of Judgement" and Judge (Decide) right from wrong so that we can and will fulfill our Good Nature, and our desire to do Good.

If we do not Judge (Decide).we become confused and walk around like useless Imbeciles, hitting pitfall after pitfall. Yes. Suffer, Suffer. Suffer, and become suckers for more Suffering, which leads to Retaliation.

Now we know that God does not Retaliate, but this is what it all leads to if we do not use our "Sense of Judgement" to fulfill our Good Nature to reap the Blessings of God the Real. "The Spirit of Goodness", with all of Its Good Characteristics.

So Folks, remember there are Three Gods. Two are Frauds,. One is Real and True.

And remember, use your "Sense of Judgement" and decide what is right from wrong- for yourself, and allow everyone around you the same privilege, so that you can fulfill your Good Nature. Yes, Look Up. and Forgive one-another and Reap only Blessings, barring the weather of course. This is God's law remember.

Thanks for Listening,

Yours truly, as ever in. "The Spirit of Goodness",

B.H., M.A., L.W. "Saint Bill".

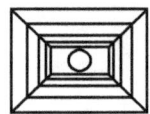

PREVIEWISM
Our World is Beautiful, Yes, Multi-Cultural

APPROACH

Hi, Mr. or Mrs. Johnson,..How are you today?......

I am with Previews Institute of Universal Philosophy.......

We are an "internet Ministry"...(A Charity)..'and after you understand our "Service", you may want to support us "Financially"...

I have a Masters Degree in Psychology... Yes, I have 65,000 words memorized on the subject, and if I started to Recite, you would say,. Wait, I haven't time for all that....Right?...

So what we have done is compiled a PREVIEW for you to look at.......

It takes about 5 minutes, maybe 10 if you are Fast, to make a decision as to whether you are For Us, or Against Us.........Now let me assure you, either way you will be considered a "Good Person"........

Our Web address is "www.previews-inc.com" and here is our introduction.......

INTRODUCTION

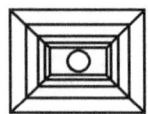

PREVIEWISM
Our World is Beautiful, Yes, Multi-Cultural

Positive vs Negative

INTRODUCTION

Hi, Mr. or Mrs. Johnson,... How are you today?..... I am with Previews Institute of Universal Philosophy......We are an "Internet Ministry"...(A Charity)... and after you understand our "Service", you may want to support us "Financially"....

We represent Society as a Whole where Religion is concerned. Therefore we are Multi-Cultural. We are a Charity and our Object is to "Relieve Poverty", and so we provide "Food for Thought" in the Spiritual sense because "Spiritual Success" leads to "Material Success". Yes, this is "The Relief of Poverty", both Physical and Spiritual poverty. Philanthropy at its best.

We at "Previews" do not just throw money at the problem,. we go to the Root of the problem and "Relieve Spiritual poverty".

Spiritual poverty has a lot to do with Psychology and Psychology has a lot to do with God the Real or God the Fraud..That is right, "The Positive or The Negative".

We have composed a "New Bible" called "The COMPASS", wherein we have gathered all the Positive psychology of all the different Religions of Society and identified - the "False Positive" (Negative) psychology of Society as a whole, and called it what it is. Yes, we have called a Spade a Spade without compromise with the Fraud.

When people see the Real difference between the Positive and the Negative, they naturally choose the Positive because It is in tune with their "Good Nature" that they are born with.

Oh yes, we are all born with a "Good Nature" in the Image of God the Real, "The Spirit of Gooodness". And then we have a choice. We can read from a Black and White book or we can read from a "Green and Blue" book called "The COMPASS"......

True Positive, Not False Positive.   (Let me give you a few Examples...)

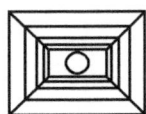

PREVIEWISM
Our World is Beautiful, Yes, Multi-Cultural

Example:

1) The Negative guy says,. You are Cursed to live in Misery.

    The Positive guy says,. You are Blessed to live in Bliss,
                            barring the weather of course.

So there you have your choice, you can plan a life of Misery or you can plan a life of Bliss.

But remember. We have Sunshine, Rain, and Hailstorms.

The Good guy lives by the Rule, The Sunshine of the Day.

The Bad guy lives by the Exception, The Hailstorm of the Season.

The Bad guy goes a step further and says,. If you do not worship me, you will not get any Sunshine.

But It is a Damned Liar. because God gives us all The Sunshine of the Day. and says,. You can expect it. Yes. have Faith and do not change the Rule because of the exception.

Where people are concerned, we try to change the exception to meet the Rule so that we can all live in Bliss, because that is what God wants us to do.

Example:

2) The Good guy says,. Walk around a lake and while you are at it enjoy the Scenery.

    The Bad guy says, I am more positive than that, I say, Have no doubt and you
        can walk across it. (Sounds positive but it is totally negative)

If we try to live by Illusion we fail every day, and when we fail every day we become pessimistic, negative bastards. Just like the Bad guy.

So there you have your Choice: You can be Positive and Enthusiastic
                                       or You can be Negative and Depressed

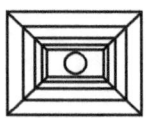

PREVIEWISM
Our World is Beautiful, Yes, Multi-Cultural

Example #3:

The Criminal psychology has been around for Six thousand years saying It is a Winner. But in Reality only 1 in 400 people is a Criminal after Six thousand years. This psychology is in fact a Loser in the lowest degree. The people of this psychology claim they are God on Earth, but they are obviously Liars.

About two thousand years ago these people with (Criminal Psychology) realized they were fooling no-one. So they decided to Team-up with the "Police Psychology".

Yes they convinced a "Good Guy" to become their leader by saying to him, that if he would commit Suicide, they would make him "God on Earth". Well, the poor soul went to Heaven thinking he was Perfect. He had obviously been put under a Curse, and we all know that a Curse is just an "Illusion". This one we call "God the Fraud".

After Two thousand years there are less than 1 in 100 following "Police Psychology". These people claim they are Winners too, but they are obviouly losers. And we all know that losers are Negative illegits that need to be... Forgiven.

About Ten years ago "God the Real", (The Spirit of Goodness", suggested to "Saint Bill" that he write a "New Bible" according to the Truth, the whole Truth, and nothing but the Truth, So help me God in Heaven. The name of the New bible is "The COMPASS" because it points to your God's waiting hand, that you can grasp.

After Ten years it is found that 88 in 100, that is 88% of people already follow the teachings of "The COMPASS". Those we call "True Winners"because they are Positive Enthusiastic people who know that Reality is God and God is Reality, Not Fantasy.

Yes, they know that "You Reap what you Sow" is man's law.

And God's law is, "Look up and Forgive one-another and Reap only Blessings,
 Barring the Weather, of course".

Yes, they realize that God is not perfect. God is Alive.. To be perfect is to be Dead, and without further room for Improvement.

God the Real, "The Spirit of Goodness", always has room for Improvement.

Yes, they have True Hope for the Future, and a Better Tommorrow.

Thank you. Dear God, Thank you.

"Saint Bill" B.H., M.A., L.W. (Coach)

P.S.: Remember, In God's Eye we are all "Saints", because God Forgives All.

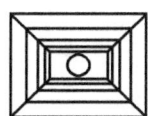

PREVIEWISM
Our World is Beautiful, Yes, Multi-Cultural

Dear Friends and Children of all ages:

God the Real, The Spirit of Goodness, The Good Guy, says. We are One. This makes us Equal and when we are equal with God and one-another we live in Peace and Harmony, because we are living in Reality, and Freedom of Thought.

God the Fraud, The Shadow, The Bad Guy, says, "I am It", I am better than you, ya, I am Perfect. Therefore you must be my Slave. So you do as I say,.or you are Dead... Now go walk accross the Ocean. (Illusion and Lie, right.)

Well folks, all the world knows that "Nothing is Perfect". And when Something says "I am Perfect" it must be a "Nothing", Yes, An Illusion. And when Someone says "I am better than you, He/She is a Liar and a Lie is just an expressed Illusion.

We all know that when we live in Illusion and Lie it causes descension, pain, suffering, strife and ultimately War.

Our creator gave us all a "Sense of Judgement" to use so that we can choose Right from Wrong. Thank God the Real. "The Spirit of Goodness", that it is always an obvious and easy choice.

Therefore, we must learn to Judge one-another as "God the Real" Judges us. That is to provide the alternative, then Forgive, not Condemn,.Reward, not Punish,. Yes, Bless, not Curse. Then continue on your way being Creative in thought, word and deed.

Folks, It is a Lovely World when we realize that God the Real, "The Spirit of Goodness", brings Heaven to Earth in every way Physical, Material, and Spiritual.

And we should Glorify and Praise "The Spirit of Goodness" that lives in Heaven, in the World, and in our Heart, Mind. and Soul. Remembering we are One with God, and God is One with us, always.

God bless you. Children and Friends and we will see you all after a while.

As ever in, "The Spirit of Goodness".

B.H., M.A., L.W. "Alias, Saint Bill"

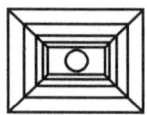

PREVIEWISM
Our World is Beautiful, Yes, Multi-Cultural

Dear Friends:

All of God's creation is Real and Good, except "The Shadow" (Satan). Yes, all Nature is Good, except "The Shadow" (Illusion). The Shadow says,.Nature is Bad, "I am Good".

As an example, The Shadow says, "Do not Judge".. Well, the Natural thing to-do is to use your "Sense of Judgement". To Judge is to decide Right from Wrong then act on the Right so as to grow in Reality and Truth.

We have learned that the Right thing to do is to Love and Forgive, Not Hate and Condemn. Yes, the Right thing to do is to "Provide the alternative", then Forgive, not Condemn, Reward, not Punish, Bless, not Curse. If we do otherwise, We become "The Accuser", Yes, the Shadow's servant.

Because of all the Confusion in the Human Sphere, Man made some Rules and Regulations (the Law). The Law is a statement with consequences to discourage people from (acting on) following Illusion and Lie (the Shadow), because it causes pain and suffering. So if you do not pay any attention to the Law you suffer the consequences so that you come to realize the pain and suffering you caused.

But remember the Law says, 1) Do not take the Law into your own hands or you will be punished. Yes, the Law was made by man for man, not for or by God. Yes, the purpose of the Law is to be "The Accuser" so that you do not have to be the Accuser.

This leaves you free to follow God's Law, which is: "Look up, and Forgive one-another and reap only Blessings, "Barring the Weather of course".

Yes, 88% of people understand this and follow God's law. But approximately 10% do not understand this and live in Illusion and Lie. And the First Lie they tell you is that you are all "Sinners" except me of course, ya, I am O.K., I am perfect in The Shadow". God created me, remember, In Its Image so I am Perfect.

Wrong, One of the First Illusions that the Human had and acted on was that God is Perfect. Wrong, God is Alive. To be Perfect is to be Dead, or without further room for improvement.

Well, God the Real, "The Spirit of Goodness", always has room for improvement, because It lives in our Heart, Mind, and Soul, in the World, and in Heaven with God.

Our job on Earth is to learn to decipher Reality from Illusion and it seems that it is a relentless and painfull task, but it is not. If we follow God's law it becomes easier and easier and more and more Joyful as we go along the Highway.

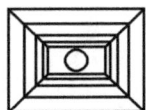

PREVIEWISM
Our World is Beautiful, Yes, Multi-Cultural

Less than One percent of people are conscious Criminals, And less than One percent of people are Police officers. The Police officers are amongst the most courageous of people because they are dealing with the totally Confused. And the totally Confused commit Suicide or Murder. So although they are not amongst the majority, we should Glorify and Praise the Police Officer because he/she is doing a great job.

We should Glorify and Praise "The Spirit of Goodness" with all of Its Children (Angels) (Characteristics) even More and More, Because "The Spirit of Goodness", God the Real, understands the whole Picture and Forgives us All our Shortcomings and Wrongdoings and considers Us all "Saints", just as we are.

Yes, we are all suitable to enter Heaven at anytime because God the Real, loves and forgives, and understands Why it is the way it is.. And we must have faith in our Experiences because they Show us Right from Wrong. Yes, Actions speak louder than words. So follow your "Sense of Judgement", and gain Peace of Mind.

Thanks again for Listening, as ever in,

"The Spirit of Goodness",

B.H., M.A., L.W. "Saint Bill"

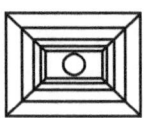

PREVIEWISM
Our World is Beautiful, Yes, Multi-Cultural

Dear Friends and Children of all ages:
We would not be able to list all the occupations in Society on this page, but to give you an example we will start with just a Few.
    Electricians, Technicians, Plumbers, Carpenters,
    Brick-Layers, Doctors, Lawyers, Accountants,
    Engineers, Architects, Salespeople, Agents, Janitors,
    Gas-Jockeys,
    Etc. Etc. Etc.
And finally we have Theologians, and Philosophers.
The Theologians are talking about "Theory", Unproven, impractical Theory. and so they are, in essence, serving "Illusion", impractical Illusion.
The Philosophers are talking about "Principals", Proven, practical Principals. and so they are, in essence, serving "Reality", proven Thought.
Now we know that Reality is God, and God is Reality, Not Fantasy (Illusion)
And so most people of most occupations are Close to God because they are working with "Reality".
And the Reality is that in God's Eye, we are all "Saints", because God forgives all and renews our "Good Nature" time and time again.
In the Shadow's opinion we are all Sinners just like the Shadow (Illusion)(Lie).
Folks, we all serve "Society" to the best of our ability in some way. And we all earn our expenses in some way. Well, we all know that "Charity-Work" is the ultimate of Goodness because it is serving those that have fallen through the Cracks.
Folks, we at "Previews Institute" need your Support to lift the Load.
Please do not Hesitate to do your part in it all, and send us what ever is not a "Financial Burden" to you.
We know you will be as generous as you can, and so we "Thank you" now for your Support.

As ever in, "The Spirit of Goodness",

Bill Handel, M.A., L.W. Alias: "Saint Bill".

P.S.: Please make cheque payable to: "Previews Institute"

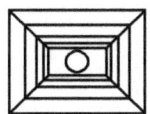

PREVIEWISM
Our World is Beautiful, Yes, Multi-Cultural

Negative vs Positive

IMAGINATION

The Mind once Streched never returns to Its original Dimension. (Except in the Instance of Illusion)(Illusion Shrinks the Mind)

So if you Think you can walk on Water, You are Sick. And the more you Think about it, the Sicker you get.

The Negative Guy, prophesizes "Doom and Gloom", and War, Drunkeness, and Perversion. The Positive Guy, prophezies "Sunshine & Rainbows", And Happiness, Decency, Prosperity, and Peace of Mind. throughout the World.

In 300 years....We are "OutFront".

Hindu	-Abraham	-Confucius	-Buddha-	St.Paul	-Mohammed	-Singh	- Luther	-"Saint Bill"
15,000- yrs. ago	6000- yrs. ago	3500- yrs. ago	2500- yrs. ago	2000- yrs. ago	1600- yrs. ago	500- yrs. ago	500- yrs. ago	10 yrs. ago

The race is on again and although the others have had a head start, "Previewism" is and will be the Predominant Positive Philisophical Force in the World within 300 years. (Positive, No doubt in our Mind).

(YOU will be Interested in Becoming a "FOUNDING PARTNER", when you Understand our Object)

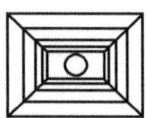

PREVIEWISM
Our World is Beautiful, Yes, Multi-Cultural

Dear Friends and Children of all ages:
There are Two Trees in Life.
    One Grows outward and upward.
    One Grows inward and Downward.

I) The Tree of Goodness.	2) The Tree of Waste.
The Seed of Goodness is "Light".	The Seed of Waste is "The Shadow".
The Root of Goodness is "Reality"	The Root of Waste is "Illusion".
The Tree of Goodness is "Good Actions".	The Tree of Waste is "Bad Actions".
The Fruit of Goodness is "The Blessing of God", yes, Forgiveness.	The Fruit of Waste is "Self-Punishment", yes, Condemnation.

So you see, when we Forgive, The Bad Actions, they become just Waste and are Forgotten. Yes, a Benevolent Circle.

When we Condemn, The Bad Actions, they grow more Waste and Punishment, Yes, a Vicious Circus.

So which do you choose?... Obvious Right!!

Thanks for Listening,

as ever in, "The Spirit of Goodness",

B.H., M.A., L.W. "Saint Bill".

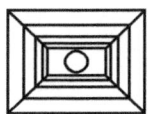

PREVIEWISM
Our World is Beautiful, Yes, Multi-Cultural

Dear Friends and Children of all ages: Would it not be nice to not have any more pain and Suffering in our lives?

Well, let me assure you that when you understand "Previewism", your days of pain and Suffering are over, and Gone.

Evil was brought into the world by a Man who acted on the Illusion that God punishes and kills and takes Vengeance for things that do not please It.

Yes, this Man acted on the further Illusion that God is Jealous of your Neighbor or anything else that sometimes draws your attention toward It.

Yes, this Man acted on the further Illusion that God is Self-righteous and Holier or Better than you.

Well, we all know that Pain and Sufferring are the Fruit of the Tree of "Bad Actions", and "Bad Actions" are the Tree of the "Root" of Illusion, And Illusion is the product of Its Seed called "The Shadow". And "The Shadow" is the "Waste" left over after God the Real, "The Spirit of Goodness" had built the Heavens and the Earth and all else in it and on it that God seen was Living and Good.

And so you see, when we realize that "The Shadow" (Satan) is just Illusion and Waste,, we cast It out into outer darkness, beyond the reach of Light, just as God did in the beginning, and say, Stay there, Alone. we need you there for Reference.

Yes, folks, when we cast out Illusion from our Minds, and Dwell on the Reality of God the Real, "The Spirit of Goodness" with all of Its Good Characteristics and all of Its beautifull creation, we find there is no need for Condemnation and Curse. Yes, we realize that "Love and Forgiveness" wipes out the Tree of Waste and Illusion, and stops the Cycle of Pain and Suffering. Yes, Life has now become a beautiful Benevolent Circle with the Blessing of "Previewism", And Pain and Sufferring will die a natural death as the New Generations gradually overcome the unfullfilling influence of "The Shadow".

Yes, when we realize that there is no better Plan than that of God the Real, "The Spirit of Goodness", we come to realize that Reality is God, and God is Reality, Not Fantasy.

And all the Negative Prophecy of "Doom and Gloom" and War, Drunkeness, and Perversion will come to an End. And we will see that the Positive Prophecy of "Sunshine and Rainbows", and Happiness, Decency, Prosperity, and Peace of Mind will come to Be, and we will live in Peace and Harmony throughout the World.

Yes, God the Real, "The Spirit of Goodness", knew in the Beginning that it would be a struggle coping with, dealing with, and overcoming the unfullfilling influence of "The Shadow", but It also new that It would persevere and Prevail (overcome) all the Obstacles and achieve Its Goal, Yes, Heaven on Earth.

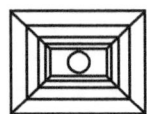

PREVIEWISM
Our World is Beautiful, Yes, Multi-Cultural

Heaven in Heaven is Predetermined as per God's Plan, which calls for "''Conception''", Life in the Womb, "Birth", Life on Earth, and finally "Life in Heaven" after the Body ceases to Function. Yes, there is no better Plan than that because It is Real and True. Yes, Reality is God, and God is Reality, Not Fantasy.

So now you know what your "Goal" is, Yes, Live in Reality, (Possibilities) and not in Illusion (Impossibilities). Yes, Cast out the Impossibilities because they have an Ulterior motive. Yes, to drive you Insane and render you an Imbecile (Waste), Yes, The Future holds great Promise for Goodness to come - during a Minimal of influence from the Shadow.

Thanks again for Listening, and God Bless you.

Yours truly, as ever in, "The Spirit of Goodness",

B.H.,M.A.,L.W. "Saint Bill".

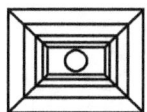

PREVIEWISM
Our World is Beautiful, Yes, Multi-Cultural

Dear Friends and Children of all ages:

We have a question for you.

How would you like to be associated with the most "Positive Thinking" religion in the World today, and in the World to come?

Well, "God Bless you", you have just discovered the place to be.

"Our Summit is our Home & Our Home is our Summit,

And our Congregation is Our Family"

(Proverb 4,vs.G)"The COMPASS"

Folks, The Synagogue, The Temple, The Church, The Mosque, in our experience all tell you that Life is a One-way street. Yes, Givme, Givme, Givme, Givme. And when you are old and grey they seem to give you a Kick and the Graveyard.

Well, we at "Previews Institute" tell you the Truth, Life is a Two-way street. What you put in, You get back many-fold.

Yes, we now have "The Summit" as our place of Worship. And every member of our "Summit" gets a Pension beginning at age 60, until he/she goes to Heaven. Is that not Wonderful? Yes, that is Wonderful.

Glory and Praise be to God the Real, "The Spirit of Goodness", that lives in our Heart, Mind, and Soul, and in Heaven, and in the World today.

The Pension (return for your efforts) naturally is dependent on your age upon entering and what you can put in toward the benefit of the one who has fallen through the Cracks. Yes, we are a "Charity" and we need and must look after the Destitute. They try too, but the weather is bad in their area.

For your help and efforts in this regard, you now get a Return on your investment. Yes, Reality is God, and God is Reality, Not Fantasy.

For further details on how to get started on this Highway of Life, please Contact the Writer by the means shown below. Thank you,

As ever in,

"The Spirit of Goodness",

Bill Handel, M.A., L.W. "Saint Bill"

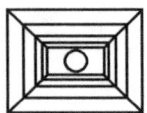

PREVIEWISM
Our World is Beautiful, Yes, Multi-Cultural

Dear Friends and Children of all ages:

As we all know, we all start at the bottom of the Totem Pole and work our way up.

We start as a Laborer, then we go to The Tradesman, then The Salespeople, then The Manager, then The Administrator, and finally to The Philosopher.

And so you see, we are all "Leaders" in our own fashion. Yes, we all have the opportunity to pass on our knowledge and experience to our young.

We at "Previews Institute" have developed a "Self-improvement" program based on positive, proven, practical principals. (Not Theory as proposed by The Theologian)

We all must pay attention to our work during working hours, but during "Coffee Break", we must plan our Leisure so that we can enjoy our Leisure and not waste it in Confusion and Frustration.

People of all ages are welcome to take part in the "Self-improvement" program and it is Free of charge. Yes, we are a "Charity" and our Object is to "Relieve Poverty", both Physical and Spiritual poverty. (Philanthropy at its Best).

All the World who see Value in our services can contribute to the cause and we will keep record of your total generosity (individually) and at age 60, you get your contribution back or a pension income, which ever you choose.

Yes, folks, Life is a benevolent circle when we expect "The Positive" and not the Negative. And The Positive organize to ensure the continuation of benevolence.

For further details on how to get started on this Highway of Life, please contact us through the means shown below.

Thank you, as ever in,

"The Spirit of Goodness",

Bill Handel, M.A., L.W."Saint Bill".

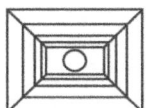

PREVIEWISM
Our World is Beautiful, Yes, Multi-Cultural

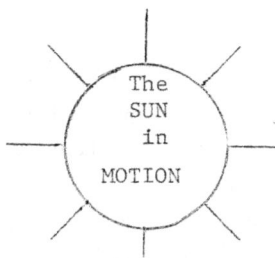

The Earth Rotates at 1,000 miles per hour at the Equator.

The Earth Revolves around The Sun at

18.5 miles per Second.

And Bogles the Mind.

But Not to Worry,

All under Control, Now!!

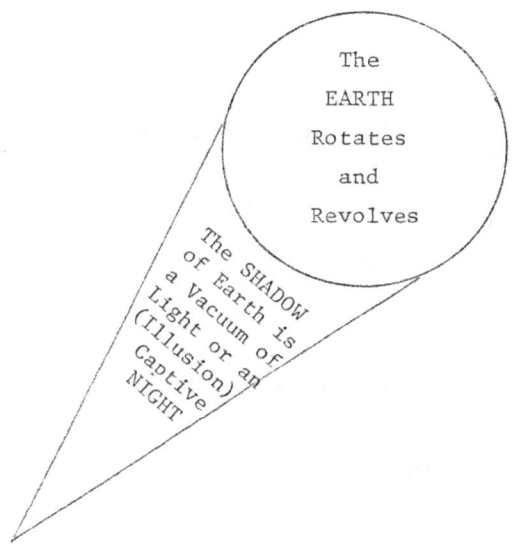

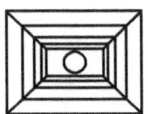

PREVIEWISM
Our World is Beautiful, Yes, Multi-Cultural

Dear Children,

By God's Grace, I have accomplished All of My Childhood Dreams.

My First Dream was to be a "Preacher", But I failed my English and I could not go to University. But "Our Dear God" was looking after me. and so Now I am a "Practitioner" (Preacher)

My Second Dream in Life was to be an "Airplane Pilot". But I was Color Blind and they would not accept me into the Airforce. But Now I have a surprise for you. I am going to be a "Space Ship" Salesman. Yes, I have a Pilot project going that will lead to the "Real" thing..

But in the meantime, I took Third choice and became a "Banker", then a "Public Relations" man, then a "Salesman" and then an "Agent".

And then I took some time off and did some thinking, and It all came together, and so now I am a Super, Super, "Mediator", Yes, a "Practitioner" for "God the Real" (The Spirit of Goodness). This is now my "Career".

But I have time for a "Hobby", and this is where my "Pilot" project comes in. Yes, soon I will be a Super, Super, "Space Ship" Salesman, working for the "Airlines".

You say, Impossible. I say, Watch me. I know where I am going because I know "Our Dear God" is looking after me. Always has, and Always will.

Thanks for Listening,

Yours truly, as ever in,

"The Spirit of Goodness",

(Saint BILL) "Coach" B.H., M.A., L.W. Alias: Wilhelm J. Handel

Dated: March 15/60 B.H. Base: 5939 A.M.

Pages: 11 - 110   =   "The Sermons of Saint Bill"

Pages 111 - 354   =   "Object, Masters Degree"

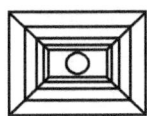

PREVIEWISM
Our World is Beautiful, Yes, Multi-Cultural

Dear Friends, Thank you, Thank you, Thank you,.. You may be Seated...

Today we are going to Describe the Road of and to "Success".

You know the World is a busy Place.. It Revolves around "YOU".

You have your Goals

You have your Dreams.(Your Conceptions)

and You have your "Vision" (Your Beliefs)

And You have the People you Confide In. (This we call Your "Master-Mind" Alliance)

Then You have your "Competitor" and you have your "Upline"

You Tell your Competitor nothing that he/she does not Already know.

You tell your Upline everything they Need to know to be Successful.. Except your Goal.. In other words, You do not tell them your Dreams, You just tell them your Vision.

If Someone works toward your Vision, They are in your Upline.

If Someone "Thinks" of your Dreams (Goals), They are in your Master Mind.

When you find you can "Trust" them you tell them a little more of Your Vision,. But not your Dreams.

Yes, there are Two types of Goals, Dreams and Visions.

Visions you write out on Paper, and share with your Upline.

Dreams you share with No One, Except your God.

And Remember there are Two of Those, The Real one, and The Fraud..

So be careful who you are Talking to.

Thank you, Friends, Thank you,... As ever in,

"The Spirit of Goodness"

B.H., M.A., L.W. "Saint Bill"

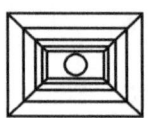

PREVIEWISM
Our World is Beautiful, Yes, Multi-Cultural

Dear Friends,. Thank you, Thank you, Thank you,.. You may be Seated....

Today I am going to tell you a TRUE Story of my Life....

Today I am 59 years Old.

When I was 22 years old I had a "Dream" that I would be a $12,000,000.00 man.

And my Father always told me that when you have an Apple tree, You eat the Apples, Not the Tree.

Well, when you have a Bank account, You spend the Interest, Not the Principal. If you Spend the Principal, It will soon go away.

Well, the Interest of your "Dreams" is the "Effort" you spend toward them.

And so I spent a lot of "Interest" toward my "Dream",. Yes, a lot of Work went into the ground as Seed money toward my "Visions".

Yes, my Father told me there are Two types of "Goals",.... Dreams and Visions. Visions you write out on Paper and share with your Upline (Family).

Dreams you share with No-One, Except your God... And Remember, there are two of those,... The Real one, and The Fraud.. So be careful who you are talking to.

Well, today the "Fruit" of my Efforts, the Work that went into the Ground is worth about $3,000,000.00 . And about a year ago I invested about a $100,000.00 into "Previews Inc." (Eternal "Trust" Foundation) and said, Now grow and bear some Fruit. Well, the Tree is growing beautifully and soon it will bear "Fruit".

But I now have time for a Hobby (a sideline of work), and as with most Hobbies they grow into beautifull Trees that bear "Fruit".

Yes, Folks, today my "Dream" has become a "Vision" that I am now sharing with you. "Dreams" I share with No-One, Except My God. Yes, "The Spirit of Goodness".... That is God, the Real, Not the Fraud...

Today my "Vision" of $12,000,000.00 is within my reach. I have $3,000,000.00 in Assets that are bearing a lot of "Interest". And I have my "Hobby" that requires a little bit of Attention and it will soon begin to bear the most "Fruit".

Yes, my Hobby is passing on a "Training Program" that allows and assures young people of "Success". This VENTURE is operating under the auspices of "OBJECT, MASTERS DEGREE", where we represent a New High Tech Internet Company called "Previews Inc.". It is a Retail Internet Shopping Mall that requires help in Advertising and Marketing its "Compensation Plan" for leading your own Ministry for "The Spirit of Goodness", God the Real. Yes, "A Charity",while you Earn.

My Associates and Myself are going to pass on our Many years of Experience in Public Relations, Advertising, Marketing, and Sales to any and all who have "Dreams" and "Visions" of a beautifull Future.

For further details of our "Vision", stay tuned..

Yours truly, as ever in, "The Spirit of Goodness",

B.H., M.A., L.W. (Saint Bill).

THE TRADITION OF "CHANGE FOR THE BETTER" IS BORN IN *"PREVIEWISM"*
www.previews-inc.com
Make 10 - 20 Copies per week and Pass It On. - God will be well Pleased.

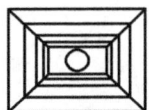

PREVIEWISM
Our World is Beautiful, Yes, Multi-Cultural

FREEDOM has a Price Tag.
The Price Tag is: "YOU Must Dream a Little"

A) What the Mind can Conceive and Believe, It can Achieve.
   (Beware: There are Two Types of Dreams.
   Dreams based on Possibilities; *and*
   Dreams based on Impossibilities.
   (The Wise Flirt with the Possible.)

B) Dream a Little; It is the Seed to Vision.
   What you can Conceive is your Dream.
   What you can Believe is your Vision.
   Vision is the Fruit of Dreams.
   We Act on Vision, not on Dreams.
   Organization is the Fruit of Vision.
   Organize a Step by Step process, right down to Step One,
   and get Started toward your Vision the Fruit of your Dreams.

   If I had $ _____
   I Would   _____
   _____
   _____
   _____
   _____
   _____
   _____

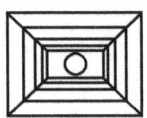

PREVIEWISM
Our World is Beautiful, Yes, Multi-Cultural

Dear Friends and Children of all ages:
1) The purpose of "Us old Folks" is to make "The Children" happy.
 But if "The Children" are Happy already, then they certainly do not need any help from us.
 So we should just help those that Stumble or ask for Help and Advice.
 We can talk about our experiences in and at the proper circumstances, but - we should not overinfluence those that are Happy already.

Thank you, Dear God, Thank you, for the Thought.

B.H., M.A., L.W. "Saint Bill".

••••••••••

2) When you work for "The Spirit of Goodness",
 It will work for You!!!....... through Thick or Thin.

••••••••••

3) When you work for a "Human Idol",
 It will only be there with Its Hand out, when the Sun shines.
 But when the Clouds come and the Rain falls, It is like The Shadow,
 It disappears, nowhere to be seen until the Sun shines again.

••••••••••

4) By One Man, "Satan" was brought into the World, and It was made out to be quite a Monster. It took Two big men to kick It out of the World. The first one died trying, and the Second one picked up his Armor and walked away, because there is no use in fighting with an "Illusion". Yes, "The Shadow of God" has many names to distract you and try to keep you confused. The names are the likes of: Lucifer, Devil, Christofer, Messiah, Demon, Satan, Illusion, Shadow, Darkness, etc. etc. Yes, Satan (The Shadow) is the Scape-Goat that takes all the blame for One Man's Sick-Psyche-Psychology. And asks you to believe that It went to Heaven to help God rule. What a "Son-of-a-Bitch".
Well, the game is Over, and God the Real, "The Spirit of Goodness", has Prevailed.

Thank you, Dear God, Thank you,..

B.H., M.A., L.W. "Saint Bill".

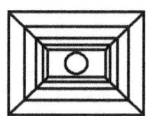

PREVIEWISM
Our World is Beautiful, Yes, Multi-Cultural

What you Sow,You Reap,Manifold,
Invest Wisely, Obtain your MASTERS DEGREE
in Psychology & Philosophy in your Spare Time, and
EARN while you LEARN, to lead your own Ministry.
Small investment, Big Return, while you Serve.
PREVIEWS INSTITUTE, Bill @ 273-9182

A Five Year Program Investment:
$5,250.00 over five years. $1,050.00 per year
$87.50 per month
RETURN:
1)   A monthly income, Now!!
           A pension at age 60.
           Peace of Mind.

What are you going to do after you get your MASTERS DEGREE?
You are going to pass it on, and Charge for your Services.
Why are you going to Charge for your Services?
Because you have Expenses.
What are you going to do with the Profit?
Spend it on Charity.
Yes, you are going to be One of the most Happy, decent, and prosperous persons on Earth.
Yes, a "Previewlite"
Yes, a Child of God, and this gives us "Peace of Mind".
Thank you, Dear God, Thank you.   Ideal Ages: 18 - 44
B.H., M.A., L.W. "Saint Bill".

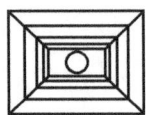

PREVIEWISM
Our World is Beautiful, Yes, Multi-Cultural

Dear Friends and Children of all ages:

Our "Achiever's Habits Program" works on the fact that it takes a Big effort to get a Load of Hay rolling, but a very small effort to keep it going once Rolling.

As we know, when we start a physical excercise program, initially the muscles get sore during workout. But after a while the body looks forward to the workout with anticipation and not reluctance, as it initially does.

Well, the same thing happens with the Mind. Initially when we start a New program of spiritual Self-Improvement we stretch the muscles of the Mind and they become sore and we reluctantly have to force ourselves to Think and Act in certain ways. But after a while the Mind's muscles become strong and we come to look forward to the workout with anticipation and Joy because the New Thinking process has become a Habit which carries Itself along with ease.

Folks, your Self-Image is your God, and God the Real is "The Spirit of Goodness". "The Spirit of Goodness" has many Children (Angels)(Characteristics) such as Sincerity, Enthusiasm, Judgement, Initiative, Perserverance, Organization, Planning, Happiness, Being Lucky, Understanding, Love, Forgiveness, etc. etc. etc..

So if you let your Mind Dwell on "The Spirit of Goodness", which is your Desire to do Good with these characteristics, It soon improves your Self-Image or your God.

Yes, God the Real, "The Spirit of Goodness", always has room for Improvement. Is that not Wonderfull? Yes, that is Wonderfull,. You are now on a continuous journey of Self-Improvement that will lead to Happiness, Decency, Prosperity, and Peace of Mind. What more do we need? Nothing, because this will bring Heaven to Earth.

Heaven in Heaven is predetermined as per God's plan. So we have the World by the Horns. Let us Continue on our Journey.

Thank you, as ever in, "The Spirit of Goodness",

B.H., M.A., L.W. "Saint Bill"

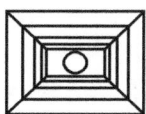

PREVIEWISM
Our World is Beautiful, Yes, Multi-Cultural

Achiever's Habits Program

GOALS PHYSICAL & MATERIAL		GOALS SPIRITUAL
To be most effective for motivation, Physical and Material goals must be within Reach within certain time Frames. 1. Career 2. Income 3. Savings 4. Investments 5. Real Property 6. Family 7. Community 8. Personal 9. Charitable 10. Fun Time 11. Chattel Property	*A person with Goals becomes Master of his/her own Destiny.* *A person who relies on God to Reveal his/her Destiny is like a Ship without a sail.* *Because they forget that God set them Free to Drift or Decide on a Direction.*	To be most useful, Spiritual goals must become Habits. 1. Planning 2. Understanding 3. Organization 4. Initiative 5. Enthusiasm 6. Confidence 7. Moderation 8. Curiosity 9. Perserverance 10. Sincerity 11. Be Lucky 12. Judgement 13. Charity There are many more mentioned in The COMPASS but the above are the priorities.

When setting Goals, one should break them down into Five Catagories:

1. Daily Review	2. Weekly Review	3. Monthly Review	4 Yearly Review	5. Five Year Review

For further details See
Chapter 14, The Compass

THE TRADITION OF "CHANGE FOR THE BETTER" IS BORN IN *"PREVIEWISM"*
www.previews-inc.com
Make 10 - 20 Copies per week and Pass It On. - God will be well Pleased.

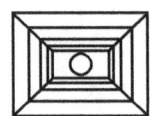

PREVIEWISM
Our World is Beautiful, Yes, Multi-Cultural

Steps and Stages of "The Achiever's Habits Program"

1) Buy a copy of "The COMPASS"
2) Read a page every evening before bedtime. (Make it a Habit that is without Fail)
3) Say a prayer of "Thanks to God" every evening before you fall asleep.
   Example: Page 300 of The Catechism, at back of "The COMPASS".
4) Ask for a Supply of "Pocket Cards" from your "Pope" or "The Coach"
5) Write out (Define) one Characteristic per week on a "Pocket Card" and carry
   It with you in Pocket or Purse to read and refresh your Mind for One week.
   Continue the process until you cover all the Characteristics on your List.
   Then repeat until you are Strong in them All. (See page 94,vs.18)
6) Do a Good deed every day and you will soon have many Happy returns.
7) Look for and Dwell on the "Positive" aspects of Life in your Day.
8) Refuse to be led into Illusion. (Impossibilities)
9) Remember, Reality is God, and God is Reality, Not Fantasy.
10) Remember, God always gets the Last word. And the Last word is...Forgiven...

Thank you, Dear God, Thank you,

B.H., M.A., L.W.. "Saint Bill".

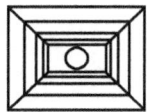

PREVIEWISM
Our World is Beautiful, Yes, Multi-Cultural

BAPTISM of the "Previewlite"

Dear Friends and Children of all ages,

"Let us gather together, and Thank God for Creating this Child with,

    "A Free Spirit"

    "A Sense of Judgement"

and   "A Good Nature".

Yes, "The Spirit of Goodness", with all of Its Angels will Guide this Child to, Happiness, Decency, Prosperity, and Peace of Mind, throughout His/Her life here on Earth., And take Him/Her to Heaven when His/Her body ceases to Function.

Thank you Dear God, Thank you, as ever in,

"The Spirit of Goodness", God the Real.

God Bless you, _____ Simon Jacob _ Johnson ....

Amen, Amen, and Amen. (sample)

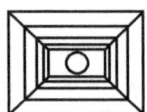

PREVIEWISM
Our World is Beautiful, Yes, Multi-Cultural

Dear Friends and Children of all ages:

1) As we all know, an "Ounce of Prevention" is preferred to, or better than a "Pound of Cure". An Ounce of Prevention is painless, while a Pound of Cure is expensive and a Burden..

Well, to prevent Mental Illness (Schizophrenia) or a Troubled Soul (Spirit) and stay free of Guilt, Fear, Doubt, and Illusion, we must read One Page from "The Compass", in rotation, front to back to front, every evening before we go to Bed. For best results we should make this a Habit that is without Fail.

••••••

2) What is Sin? (A) Sin is Punishment, or Pain and Suffering. Illusion is not a Sin, but Expressing a known Illusion gives rise to someone acting on the Lie. This causes Frustration on the part of the recipient and causes Him/her to retaliate. So in fact you are causing a chain reaction that goes right back to you. So you are in fact Punishing or causing Pain and Suffering to yourself.

As well as to a lot of others. Please Act on Truth and Reality.

••••••

3) Going to Heaven: A face of an Angel is all that is here. One beautiful Freckle equals one little smile. Not ready to Leave but has to go. Wants to go back but God says No. Leaving your life is a scary thought, but it is something that can be overcome. A mother, a father, a sister and friends,.a meaningful life that suddenly ends. An angel is what they are meant to be, Now just think of all they can see. Looking over their family night and day. Saying I love you in their own special way. In the Night we sleep, in the Day we Laugh or Cry. They watch us all from their Place on High.

We love you Forever, We will like you for always,.as long as we are Living, Our Family you will be.

Thank you, Dear God, Thank you,

as ever in, "The Spirit of Goodness'",

B.H, M.A., L.W. "Saint Bill".

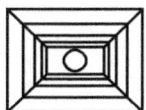

PREVIEWISM
Our World is Beautiful, Yes, Multi-Cultural

Dear Friends and Children of all ages:

1)   Q) Who made this beautiful day,.God or the Lord.

      A) God made this beautiful day, the Lord is a man like you or me and did nothing, except try to Steal the Glory.

      A) Yes, God is a Heavenly entity. while the Lord is an Earthly entity.

2)   Now, a Triangle: Your Neighbor, Your God, and You.

      Q) Who comes first, Your God or you?

      A) Your God comes first, because when you serve your God first, you will already have served yourself.. If you serve yourself first, you run the risk of Offending your God.

      Q) Who comes first, Your Neighbor or Your God?

      A) Your Neighbor comes first, because when you serve your Neighbor first, you will already have served your God.. If you serve your God first, you run the risk of Offending your Neighbor.

So you see, you should always come last, because when you come last, you will be one of the most Happy, Decent, and Prosperous persons on Earth, and knowing this you have Peace of Mind.

There are only Four things that you should refuse to do for your Neighbor: They are that you should not, Lie, Steal, Kill, or Overindulge. Beyond this you serve Your Neighbor First.

There are only Four things that you should refuse to do for your God: They are that you should not, Lie, Steal, Kill, or Overindulge. Beyond this you serve your God First.

Thank you, Dear God, Thank you

B.H., M.A., L.W. "Saint Bill".

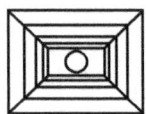

PREVIEWISM
Our World is Beautiful, Yes, Multi-Cultural

Dear Friends and Children of all ages:

1) Q) Who is the better person, the person who Created God's Plan, or the Person who Implemented God's Plan?

   A) They are both equal, because One person can not Receive and Create God's Plan and Implement it too. It takes many to Impliment God's Plan and so they are just as important as the Creator. Yes, we will say Equal.

2) Q) Who created God's plan,. Abraham or Jesus?

   A) Jesus said,. Abraham created "Satan's" plan. (Acts 26 vs.16-18)

   Abraham said,. Jesus is a Lunatic and a Blasphemer, Crucify Him.

   Jesus said,. God gave us a Free Will to choose Right from Wrong for ourselves. Abraham said,. God is a Dictator, Do it my way or you are Dead.

   Jesus said,. God gave you a "Sense of Judgement". Use it to Decide right from wrong, so as to grow in Reality and Truth. Yes, come closer to God. Abraham said. Do not Judge, Do not eat of the Fruit of the Tree of the Knowledge of Good and Bad or else you will be punished, so as to create Fear and keep you under the Influence of Illusion and Lie.

3) Q) How did the Trinity (Tri-une God) come to be?

   A) The Pagan people before the dawn of modern History had many Tribes and many Regions (Countries). Each tribe or country had a Human Idol who they called their God. These Idols would try to out-do the other and so they would lead their people to war against each other to see who was Supreme.

One day it came to pass that One of the Regions had a Human Idol who said that all of the Regions (countries) should consider themselves Equal so that they would not have to Fight all the time.

This Human Idol became very popular amounst the majority of the Regions because the majority of people seen that it was obviously a better way than Warring all the time.

...this Human Idol became very popular amongst the People of the majority of the Regions (Countries) but was despised by the other Human Idols who where loosing control of their people.

This Human Idol came to be Loved and Respected throughout the world as far as it reached at the Time.

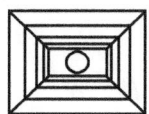

PREVIEWISM
Our World is Beautiful, Yes, Multi-Cultural

Then one day this most popular Human Idol passed away in old age, and Died.

The majority of the people of the world Loved him so much that they did not want to forget him, because he promised Happiness, Decency, Prosperity, and Peace of Mind throughout the World. Yes, Peace, Harmony and Equality.

So these people decided to say that their Human Idol had become a "Spirit", and that this "Spirit" would never die in their Heart, Mind and Soul.

The Problem these people had was, that this Spirit had Two Natures and so they decided that Their God was Three people in One. Yes, God the Good guy, God the Bad guy, and God the Human. Yes, a Trinity.

The world has since learned that we should not worship Human Idols because they Fail you when the going gets tough (tuff). And the world has since learned that you should not worship "God the Bad guy" because It brings you Pain and Suffering.

Yes, the world has learned that Two are Frauds, and One is Real and True.

Yes, the world has learned that "God the Good guy" is "The Spirit of Goodness", with all of Its children (angels), the oldest being "The Spirit of Truth" and the youngest being "The Spirit of Enthusiasm", and of course there are many in between. Yes, "The Spirit of Goodness" is Real and True because It does not have any Human names attached to It, nor any Human connotations, such as Father, Mother, Son, Daughter, Brother, Sister, etc. etc. etc.

Yes, "The Spirit of Goodness" is truly a Heavenly entity and It lives in Heaven, in the World, and in our Heart, Mind, and Soul from conception. And there is Nothing or No-one that can stop us from going to Heaven, when our body ceases to Function, because God always gets the Last word, and the Last word is ... FORGIVEN ...

Yes, "Dear" is our God's name,. Yes, Our God's name is Dear to us

Thank you, Dear God, Thank you,

As ever in, "The Spirit of Goodness",

B.H., M.A., L.W. "Saint Bill".

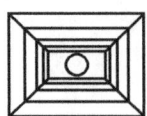

PREVIEWISM
Our World is Beautiful, Yes, Multi-Cultural

Dear Friends and Children of all ages:

1) Q) Does God, "The Spirit of Goodness", know when It is telling the Truth?
A) Yes, Always.

Q) Does Satan (The Shadow) know when It is telling a Lie?

A) No,.Never,. It is too stupid to know the difference between Truth and Lie. So It just continues to walk around in circles, like a useless Imbecile, hitting pitfall after pitfall. All the while claiming It is God.

3) Q) If The Shadow (Satan) does not know when It is telling a Lie,. Who does know?
A) Two Entities..God, "The Spirit of Goodness", and You. God, "The Spirit of Goodness", always knows but does not acknowledge or pay any attention to the Lies because God knows they are just Illusion,. not worthy of any Reaction.

You, sometimes know Illusion from Reality and sometimes you do not. When you know It is Illusion and Act on It in word or deed, you are taking advantage of God's good Graces (Nature), and you hope that your Confused neighbor is not watching.. You are not worried about the neighbor who lives in Reality because that is who you are taking advantage of.

When you do not know Illusion for what It is, you do what comes Naturally, and that is to try (test) It out for Results.

If you are pleased with the results for yourself and Your neighbor, then you call It Truth. If you are not pleased with the results for yourself or your neighbor, you call It Lie. If you are not pleased and your neighbor is, you leave It for further consideration.

Now we all know that the Wrath of The Shadow's Servant (the long arm of the Law) almost always, sooner or later, catches up with you who knowingly Act on Illusion or Lie. So you are a "Shadow Damned" Fool to try to beat the odds of "The Long Arm of the Law". Not withstanding "The Statute of Limitations" of the Gentiles. "Eph. 4,vs.26"

Part B:

Dear Friends and Children of all ages:

Before the dawn of modern History there were two major Societies in the world that we are familiar with.

They were the Hindu Society and the Pagan Society. The people of the Hindu Society are the predeceasors of the Gentiles as we know them today. The people of the Pagan Society are the forefathers of the "Shadow Worshippers" as we know them today. During the pre-dawn age it all started to fall down for the Pagan Society when the first two People of the Pagan Society were converted to the then Hinduism.

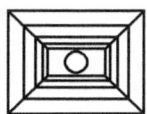

PREVIEWISM
Our World is Beautiful, Yes, Multi-Cultural

The Pagan people called this couple "Gentiles" because they were a Gentle man and woman. This young couple preached to the Pagans that Human Idols are not God because they have Two Natures, and that God, the Real, had only One Nature, the Good One. They further preached that God was a Spirit, Yes, "The Spirit of Goodness", which had many children (angels), the oldest being "The Spirit of Truth" and the youngest being "The Spirit of Enthusiasm". And of course there were many in between.

The Names of these two people were "Adam and Eve". They were very Gentle and Happy people. The Human Idol of the Pagan tribe that they were a part of was named Juda. Juda cursed and condemned this couple, and their offspring, and their followers. Adam was a gentle man but he was also a Realistic man and so he said, "I will drop my Heel on your Head one day, and It will go to Slitherines."

...Adam further said to Juda,."All of this will be done without me causing One drop of Blood to be spilled. (Of course Adam was talking about "Hands-Down-Intelect")

Juda had a son called Abraham, and Abraham had a Heart for Adam and Eve.

But Abraham was afraid of his Father and so Abraham being well educated for the Time started to write a story of what he seen in the Future of Humankind. Abraham was loyal to his Father but Abraham had doubts about the Future of his tribe and country.

Abraham tried his best to preserve the Psychology of his Father but Abraham's story was based a lot on the Illusions of his forefathers of the Dark ages.

Adam and Eve had a vision of Happiness, Decency, Prosperity, and Peace of Mind, Yes, Peace and Harmony throughout the World. This vision was based on the knowledge that God was, is, and always shall be "The Spirit of Goodness" which is everloving, everforgiving, and EverUnderstanding and can not be led or driven to Retaliate.

Folks, as you know the rest is History and because in God's eye a day is a Thousand years and a Thousand years is a Day,. We will see our Dear God's kingdom reign the World over before tomorrow afternoon at this time.

Yes, "Saint Bill" said to Adam..."Adam, I have a big foot and a Heavy one, and I dropped my Heel on the total of the Earthworm and It went to Slitherines, and I Rubbed with my Rubber, Rubber Heel until there was nothing left but Dust.

And then "Saint Bill" said to the other Four, Bow you Gentlemen Bow, Knees and All you Gentlemen Bow. (Chuckle, Chuckle, eh!!)

Thank you, Dear God, Thank you,. as ever in,

"The Spirit of Goodness",

B.H., M.A., L.W. "Saint Bill".

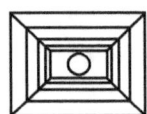

PREVIEWISM
Our World is Beautiful, Yes, Multi-Cultural

Dear Friends and Children of all ages:

1)   Q) What does the "Previewlite" say to his/her neighbor out on the front Lawn?
   A) Come on into my house and we will talk, to come closer to the Truth.

   Q) What does the "Shadow Worshipper" say to his/her neighbor out on the front Lawn?

   A) We will talk right here,.If you agree with me, you can come in,. If not, you stay right here, and you will be Damned and Condemned.

2)   The "Previewlite" say, By who?

   The "Shadow Worshipper" says, By my God.

   The "Previewlite" says, Be gone you Jackass.

   The "Shadow Worshipper" says, You are Damned and Condemned.

   The "Previewlite" says, You know my friend, to forgive is to forget,.

   So I forgive you your ignorance,. Now get out of my sight so I can forget you.

••••••

The Shadow Worshipper is lost for words, so he strikes out with his Left hook. The Previewlite rolls with the punch, and says, Now be gone you Jackass. The Shadow Worshipper winds up with a Right.

The Previewlite raises his Left, and pops him with a Right,. and the Shadow Worshipper falls on his ass.

The Previewlite says, Now be gone you Jackass, I am not a Barbarian.

"I am a Gentleman",...So you go find one of your own kind, and cry in your Beer.

Thank you, Dear God, Thank you

B.H., M.A., L.W. "Saint Bill".

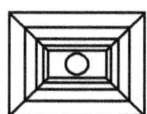

PREVIEWISM
Our World is Beautiful, Yes, Multi-Cultural

Dear Friends and Children of all ages:

The Shadow (Satan) (Devil) (Lucifer) (Illusion) is a sick psyche psychologist, yes, very Sadistic - a Sucker-for-punishment. So negative that it is always suicidal, but has not the courage to do it, but rather asks you to come its wayand suffer suffer suffer along with it.

But remember, The Shadow is before all else a Liar, and so It says, "Come my way and I will make you Happy, yes, I will make you Rich beyond comprehension, and finally The Shadow says, please follow me and I will prepare atable for you in Heaven, please it is your only Hope.

Yes, Promise, Promise, Promise,. What the poor thing forgets is that God the Real, "The Spirit of Goodness", prepared a Spot for you in Heaven upon your Conception, (Yes, that is Predetermined),. Our job on Earth is not to try to get to Heaven,

but rather continually try to bring Heaven to Earth for your Neighbors and Yourself.

This is not done by pleasing The Shadow because It is a Sick-Psyche-Psychologist, and a Liar, and a Coward, without the courage to face Reality.

This is why we Humanbeings established the Law of Mankind. Yes, to serve The Shadow. Yes, "You Reap what You Sow" is Man's Law to Punish you for following The Shadow. Yes, The Shadow has no power to Punish you, and so It convinced a Man to establish this Law to do Its work. Yes, this Law sounds very Fair, but God is not Fair or Fairy.

This is why God the Real, "The Spirit of Goodness", established God's Law in the Beginning when It said, "Look Up and Forgive one-another and Reap only Blessings, barring the weather of course". Yes, this Law serves God because God is Loving, Forgiving, and Everunderstanding, and does never Condemn, Curse, or Punish anyone.

So there you have it, because God set you Free as the weather in the beginning, you now have a Choice. You may Condemn, Curse or punish yourselves by following the Shadow, or you can Forgive, Bless, and Reward yourselves right here on Earth and live in Bliss and Heaven will come only too soon. (Chuckle, Chuckle, eh!)

Thanks for Listening, Folks, It was a pleasure, as ever in,

"The Spirit of Goodness",

B.H., M.A., L.W. "Saint Bill".

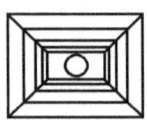

PREVIEWISM
Our World is Beautiful, Yes, Multi-Cultural

October 24/00 (61 B.H.)

Dear Friends and Children of all ages:

At the dawn of modern (recorded) history there were two predominant areas of influence in the worlds Society. They were the Middle-east (Pagan), overall known as Palistine and the Far-east (Hindu), overall known as India.

At the time there were approximately twelve Provinces in the Palistine area presently known as the Arab world. These peoples operated in what they then called Tribes. In todays standards they were very primative people who had no Jail facilities. The criminals of this Society, once identified, were just told to move on and out of sight. But some criminals found they had nowhere to go , and so they agreed to become slaves to society for certain periods, until they had paid back their debt to society. The criminals were known as Wandering Nomads without a Country. As with Criminals today some of these Nomads were well educated for the time. And they cursed and condemned mainstream Society for making them Outcasts. These Wandering Nomad tribes claimed they had Rights too and that they would one day claim some territory and form a Country of their own which they would call ? ? . These wandering Nomad people were disbanded and spread throughout the World.

The last surviving tribe of these people had a Leader (Human Idol) (God) called Juda, and Juda had a Son called Abraham who did some Writing about the Future of Mankind. Some of these writings became used by Mainstream Society which had some of Its own writings about the Future. As time went on there were many Pamphlets (books) in circulation in Society as a whole. The Authors of these Pamphlets (books) were called Prophets. (Some Bad, Some Good) (Some True, Some False)

Then it came to pass that a man called "Moses" gathered a selection of these books and bound them together as One bigger Pamphlet (Book) which he called "The Torah". It was a Book which became popular throughout Mainstream Society, but It became known as Judaism as a Religion, with many conflicting Attitudes.

The Hindu Society (predeceasors of the Gentiles) grew from small numbers at the time to over 850,000,000 people in today's Society of the World.

The Arab world (predecessors of the Gentiles, Adam and Eve) grew from small numbers at the time to over 900,000,000 people in today's Society of the World. The Pagan (Wandering Nomads) of Judaism came to be a mere 13,000,000 people in today's Society of the World. (P.S: The World has 5.7 Billion people in todays time.)

(But the Underdog always Screams (complains) the Loudest.) Another group of Gentiles has in the meantime grew from small numbers of old times to over 1,000,000,000 people in today's Society of the World.

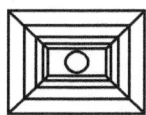

PREVIEWISM
Our World is Beautiful, Yes, Multi-Cultural

All the while the "Wandering Nomads" claiming to be God on Earth. (Chuckle, Chuckle). And now Finally, we have a Unifying Psychology manifested in the Philosophy of PREVIEWISM as manifested in and by "The Compass", by Author, "Saint Bill".

In it we describe God the Real as "The Spirit of Goodness", with all of Its children (angels), the oldest being "The Spirit of Truth" and the youngest being "The Spirit of Enthusiasm", and of course there are many in between.

"The Spirit of Goodness" says, "We are One" and that makes us equal, and when we are equal with God and one-another, we live in Peace and Harmony, because we are living in Reality, and Freedom of Thought.

The Bad Guys are still saying, "I am It", I am better than you, Ya, I am Perfect, so you must be my slave, so you do as I say or you are Dead. Now go walk accross the Ocean. (P.S.: Yes, still causing Pain and Suffering because they are living in Illusion and Lie). (But they are an insignificant and Dying group of people).

Thanks again for Listening, It was a pleasure,

As ever in, "The Spirit of Goodness",

B.H., M.A., L.W. "Saint Bill".

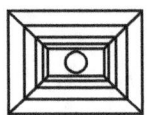

PREVIEWISM
Our World is Beautiful, Yes, Multi-Cultural

Dear Friends and Children of all ages:

There are Three types of Psychology in Society as a Whole.

They are 1) The Criminal Psychology on the one Hand and 2) The Police Psychology on the other hand, and 3) The Main Stream Psychology coming down the middle. The Main stream psychology is that of Gentle people (Gentiles). They win the War with "Hands Down Intellect". Yes, Peaceful Co-existance.

The Criminal with his/her Left hand Initiates violence to try to force Its opinion. This we call Aggression, and It is a Sin against Humanity.

The Police responds with his/her Right hand, and wins the War for Main Stream Society. This we call "Self-Defence", and It is an Act of God.

Main stream Society continues to "Lead the Way" up and down the Middle showing restraint and self-control and many more characteristics of "The Spirit of Goodness" always using "Hands-Down-Intellect"" and Never resorting to Violence to win the War.

Thank God the Real, "The Spirit of Goodness", for the Police Officer for always standing by with his/her Right hand to keep the Criminal under control. Mainstream Society of a Country puts, the Criminal who exremely overviolates the Rules, in Jail and says, Turn yourself around.

Mainstream Society of the World puts, the people with Criminal Psychology, in a small area in the Middle-East and surrounds them with the Good Guys (Police) and says, Enjoy yourselves.

Mainstream Society of the World then continues on Its way in Happiness, Decency, Prosperity, and Peace of Mind,. Knowing that in God's Eye we are all "Saints" because God the Real forgives All time and time again, Accepting us All into Heaven, "Just as we are"...

Thank you, Dear God, Thank you

"Saint Bill".

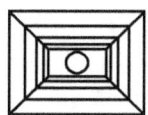

PREVIEWISM
Our World is Beautiful, Yes, Multi-Cultural

Dear Friends and Children of all ages:

1) The wise Previewlite seldom confronts the person with Criminal Psychology, because the person with criminal psychology is the Underdog and the Underdog always screams or complains the Loudest,. And It is a seasoned Liar and so It makes you look like the Bad guy to the Police and so you are unjustly punished.

Yes one should always try to avoid the people with criminal psychology and let them congregate with and amoungst themselves. When they have had enough of Pain and Suffering, they will turn to God the Real, "The Spirit of Goodness", and find happiness, decency, prosperity and Peace of Mind and come to live in Peace and Harmony with you and yours. So just continue to Forgive, Bless, and Reward.

2) The Police and Main-Stream society realizes that we should all earn our living with Honesty and Integrity.. And please God by giving some to Charity for the ones who have fallen through the cracks.

The Criminal says, "I will make my living by Extortion and give 10% to Charity, and I will be able to say, "I am better than you"

We can all see the error in the latter psychology.

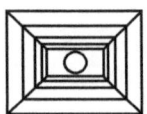

PREVIEWISM
Our World is Beautiful, Yes, Multi-Cultural

Dear Friends and Children of all ages:

At the Prophetic World Council of Temples the "Chairman of the Board" or "Executive Director" in Centre Stage will be God the Real, "The Spirit of Goodness", with all of Its children and not a Human being.

All decisions will be made by 60% majority Vote after free discussion of the alternatives. And all will remember that to lead "City Hall" one must always begin on ground floor and work the way up and around the foundations.

"City Hall" of the World is a big and High Temple and one can not change Its Focus from the Top down, but rather from the Bottom up. This is a Juggling Act and the best Jugglers get to be in the Inner Circle around Centre Stage at the Top.

We of the Human race should all love and enjoy Competition, and win or loose we should all take comfort that we all get the benifit of the excercise.

Naturally, we are talking about a competition of "Hands-down-Intellect" and so it is only natural that the Elderly usually win , give or take a few years.

The young who listen and watch with two Ears and two Eyes and use only one Mouth will learn the most the quickest and stand the best chance of getting to the Inner Circle around Centre Stage at the Top.

Of course we realize that the World is Multicultural and so Inner Circle will be representative of all the different Countries of the World and as such of the "Society of the World".

Thanks for Listening, It was a pleasure, as ever in,

"The Spirit of Goodness",

B.H., M.A., L.W. "Saint Bill", (Coach)

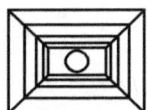

PREVIEWISM
Our World is Beautiful, Yes, Multi-Cultural

Dear Friends and Children of all ages:

Judaism, being a descendant of the Pagan Society, attempts to curse, condemn, and punish the world as though It were Evil. All the while holding the Jewish community out as though they were the "Only true children of God". Yes, the Bad guy, the "I", "I", "I", guy was expelled from Heaven, and Judaism assumes the nature of the Bad guy, and we know the Bad guy is an Illusion.

But the world has not acknowledged the Curse and Condemnation, and has totally Ignored It, and continues to be Blessed, Forgiven, and Rewarded by God the Real, "The Spirit of Goodness".

The result being that the Jewish community has become the Scape-goat of Illusion, (Acts 26,v. 16-18). Yes, self cursed, condemned, and punished.

But we must remember the Origin of the Jewish community. They were the Outcasts (The Criminals of society), driven into exile. And so we can Forgive them for their Shortcomings. The world has now given them an area in the Middle-east which they can call their own. And now they can start to live like the rest of the world by learning to forgive one another and the world for their shortcomings.

This will allow them to begin to live in Happiness, Decency, Prosperity, and Peace of Mind, and in Peace and Harmony with the world around them.

Yes, there is no longer any curse. (Rev.22,v.3) Yes, within three hundred years the true Prophecy (Previewism) of God the Real, "The Spirit of Goodness", will be predominant throughout the world, and all will live in Peace and Harmony and Equality.

Thanks for Listening, It was a pleasure,

as ever in, "The Spirit of Goodness",

B.H., M.A., L.W. "Saint Bill".

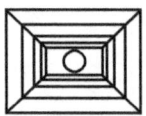

PREVIEWISM
Our World is Beautiful, Yes, Multi-Cultural

Dear Friends:

As we all know, Children do not have a choice of which Languages they first learn. It is always that of their father and mother. So it is with Religion. Religion is much like a language, we all see life a little different but we are talking about the same thing, and that is Reality. Yes, reality is God and God is reality, not fantasy or illusion.

When I was a child I was told that I was brought into this world as a descendant of the Woman who brought Sin into the world. As time went on I was told that I was brought into this world as a descendant of the man who brought Good into the world. But the problem was that I was told that he was a Bachelor. A really good Bachelor. This I could not understand, so I started to ask some questions.

Well, the story got so confusing that it was obvious that no one knew what they were talking about.

Yes, I came to realize that "Truth" is very simple and stands on its own. Lie is very complicated and needs many crutches. So many Crutches that it became clear that it was all based on a Lie and Illusion.

And so I started to study other Languages (Religions) and began to see the whole picture as I learned to look up to people and not look down on people. Yes, It is a big picture when you see it from Heaven, which is from the outside in, which is from the Bottom Up, not from the Top Down.

Yes, folks, I learned that Truth always prevails and dominates this world and the people in it. Yes, the majority (88%) of people live in Truth and Reality. The minority (1%) live in Lie and Illusion. And in between there are (11%) who are confused until they start to ask some questions and begin to see the whole picture.

Yes, folks, I was brought into this world in the minority and they are a loud bunch. They are always screaming and complaining of percecution. Yes, always cursing and condemning the world for their ills. The fact is they bring it upon themselves. Yes, they made the rule: "You reap what you sow" and claimed it was God's Law. And so they continue to curse, condemn, and punish themselves.

By learning other languages (Religions) I learned God's true Law: Which is: "Look Up and forgive one another and reap only Blessings, barring the weather of course". Yes, there are some things that are as a result of following God (Reality) and some thing that are as a result of following the Shadow (Illusion), and some things are as a result of the weather, and so we have to face the weather, make the best of it, and leave the chips fall by the wayside, and not on our shoulders,. because "Chips on our Shoulders" represent condemnation of our neighbors. And we should not condemn our neighbors. We should Forgive them.

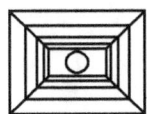

PREVIEWISM
Our World is Beautiful, Yes, Multi-Cultural

So drop the chips on the wayside and continue in Happiness, Decency, Prosperity, and Peace of Mind. Yes, learn to live in Peace and Harmony with the world around you.

I found that this is how 88% of people live world wide, but they are a quiet bunch. Always in peace and harmony with God and their neighbors.

Yes, folks, I have droped the chips that my ancestors put on my shoulders and have found it is a beautiful world we live in, not withstanding the minority. The Shadow worshippers.

Yes, folks, we must realize that it is not a perfect world and was never meant to be. It was just meant to be a Good world, a Super Super Excellent world. And so we should not try to be perfect because it causes much pain and suffering for ourselves and our neighbors. Yes, be satisfied with Super Super Excellent and you will be happy, decent, and prosperous, finding it easy to Understand, Love, and Forgive.

Thanks for Listening, as ever in,

"The Spirit of Goodness", B.H., M.A., L.W. "Saint Bill".

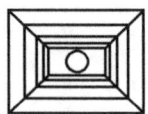

PREVIEWISM
Our World is Beautiful, Yes, Multi-Cultural

Dear Friends and Children of all ages:

We have another Analogy for you.

You know, when you eat potatoes It tastes like potatoes, and when you eat corn It tastes like corn, and when you eat turnips It tastes like turnips, and when you eat peas It tastes like peas, and so on and on.

But if you dare to make a Stew and put it all together It tastes delicious. Well, you know, we have Hinduism, Judaism, Confucianism, Buddhism, Catholicism, Protestantism, Islam, Sikhism, Zen, Previewism and so on and on.

When we learn to understand as many as possible, the picture becomes very clear and beautifull. And life becomes a Joy amoungst Humankind.

Yes, folks, by Itself any religion has Its limitations but all together the limitations are removed and It becomes a Big and beautiful world.

Well, now we are going to add some Sugar and Spice to the "Stew" and It will be Super, Super Excellent, beyond all expectations.

The Sugar and Spice comes in the Entity of:"Prophetic World Council of Temples" Yes, this is the consumation of the Intent of "Previewism".. Previewism is by the way "Peaches and Cream" in the Stew. And now we have added "Sugar and Spice".

The "Sugar and Spice" is Freedom of Thought, with the emphasis on the true Positive. Wow, what a "Stew". Just beautiful and It tastes Super Delicious. Now we need your Contribution, to make It even better.

Chuckle, Chuckle, eh..

Thanks for Listening, as ever in,

"The Spirit of Goodness",

W.J.(Bill) Handel, M.A., L.W., "Saint Bill"

Spiritual Practitioner

PROPHETIC WORLD COUNCIL OF TEMPLES

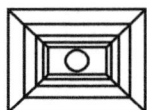

PREVIEWISM
Our World is Beautiful, Yes, Multi-Cultural

"My Temple is my Home & My Home is my Temple and My Congregation is my Family"

The Tradition of "Change For The Better"
is Born in PREVIEWISM

www.previews-inc.com

God the Real, "The Spirit of Goodness", Lives,

"Let It Flourish" Serve your Neighbor first, God comes second

Dear Friends and Children of all ages:

There are two laws in our society.

    1) Man's law, "You Reap what you Sow"

    2) God's law, "Look up and Forgive one-another and Reap only blessings, barring the weather of course".

We should always try to live by God's law first, but in exceptional and extreme circumstances we have no alternative but to use Man's law.

Therefore we must serve our neighbor first and we will have already served our God. This leads to riches in every way.

If we serve our God first we are serving ourselves, this leads to poverty in every way.

Remember, God the Real, "The Spirit of Goodness", lives in Heaven, in the World, and in your Heart, Mind, and Soul.

Dwell on this in your daily activities, and It will Flourish.

Thank you, Yours truly,

as ever in "The Spirit of Goodness"

B.H., M.A., L.W. Alias "Saint Bill"

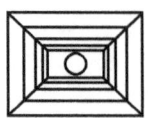

PREVIEWISM
Our World is Beautiful, Yes, Multi-Cultural

Dear Fellow Practitioners:

As we all know, God the Real, "The Spirit of Goodness", says, "We are One", that makes us equal, and when we are equal with God and one-another, we live in Peace and Harmony because we are living in Reality and Freedom of Thought.

God the Fraud, "Illusion", says, "I am It", I am better than you, Ya, I am Perfect, so you must be my Slave, so you do as I say or you are Dead,. Now, go walk accross the Ocean. This causes much pain and suffering because it is living in Illusion and Mental slavery.

Now, It is obvious that "We are One" is the answer and so we are asking for your participation and contribution (Input) to our web-site. This can come in what ever form you wish, be it Spiritual or Financial, or both.

Folks, the False Prophet propheceize War, descension, drunkeness, and perversion throughout the world.

The True Prophet propheceize Happiness, decency, prosperity, and peace of mind, throughout the world.

Which do you want to fullfill? The positive or the negative. We think it is obvious.

Hoping to hear from you soon, we remain,

Yours truly, as ever in, "The Spirit of Goodness",

Prophetic World-Council of Temples
Per: W.J.(Bill) Handel, M.A., L.W. (Coach) Alias: "Saint Bill".

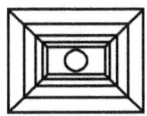

PREVIEWISM
Our World is Beautiful, Yes, Multi-Cultural

January 30/01 (62 B.H.)

Dear Friends and Children of all ages:

As we all know, some people believe "Robin Hood" was a Real character, and some people believe "Robin Hood" was a Fictional character.

As we all know Real characters are prone to Truth and Reality, and Fictional characters are prone to Lie and Illusion.

And so you see, It does not matter whether "Robin Hood" did or did not live here on Earth. What we have is the Reality of life here on Earth today.

And the Reality is that God the Real, "The Spirit of Goodness", forgives us all our shortcomings every day and continues to Bless and Reward us with our daily needs, accepting us all into Heaven, just as we are, when our body ceases to function. All for Free.. Is that not wonderfull? Yes, that is wonderfull.

And when The Shadow found that Its chosen people were loosing the battle of mind control and extortion of the Gentiles, The Shadow found a need to deceive the Gentiles and have them believe what is false, (2 Th. 2, v.9-11). So that It might continue to grow in numbers of Slaves.

And so the Shadow brought forth a person who It says, "Walked on Water".

In fact The Shadow says, there were Two that walked on water. And then The Shadow says, believe me, please, I would not lie to you would I? If it were not so I would tell you. Right. Do not question me, Just believe what I say and I will take you to Heaven. Otherwise you will go to Hell Yes, Fire and Brimstone.

And so The Shadow found a few more converts to believe they are Chosen people.

But those of us who use our "Sense of Judgement" know that "Robin" and "Peter" did not walk on water because the Need to walk on water was to fullfill a Fictional story. And when we fullfil a Fictional story, It is a Fictional Story Itself. Yes, Lie upon Lie upon Lie. Illusion upon Illusion upon Illusion.

The Shadow says, It rules the world, but we know better. God the Real, "The Spirit of Goodness", rules the world. This is why there is a lot more "Good" in the world than there is Bad. Yes, 1 in 900 is in Jail.. 1 in 100 is a Criminal on the loose. 1 in 10 is a Shadow worshipper. That leaves 88% of people who worship God the Real, "The Spirit of Goodness", that lives in their Heart, Mind, and Soul.

And so folks, Do not obey The Shadow when It says, Do not Judge, that is false instruction. Just continue to use your sense of judgement and decide right from wrong, so that you might continue to grow in Reality and Truth.

Thank you,

"Saint Bill".

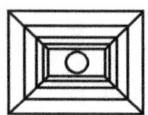

PREVIEWISM
Our World is Beautiful, Yes, Multi-Cultural

Dear Friends and Children of all ages:

Today we are going to tell you a Fictional story. A fictional story but true to life. Yes, within the Realms of possibilities.

Once upon a time there was "Robin" the Good guy, and there was "Robin" the Bad guy. Robin the Good guy said, he represented "God the Real", and Robin the Bad guy said, he represented "God the Real".

The people said, the Good guy was a "Perfect" wise guy. and the Bad guy was a "Perfect" idiot.

This meant that God the Real and God the Fraud had something in common.

But we know better. They have Nothing in common. One is Black and One is White. We also know that "Nothing is Perfect",. Not even God the Real, "The Spirit of Goodness". But we do know that God the Fraud is a Perfect idiot. Yes, "Illusion" is a Perfect Liar, because "Illusion" is a "Nothing", and "Nothing is Perfect".

When we think we are Perfect, we think "Nothing is Impossible", but we are Fooling ourselves.

God the Real, "The Spirit of Goodness", is a Possibility.

God the Fraud, "Illusion", is Impossible, but is a Liar and says, It is possible, believe me, Do not question me, please, I love you, I would not Lie to you, would I? If it were not so I would tell you, Right.. Just believe me and I will take you to Heaven. But "Illusion" is a Liar and so It takes you to Hell the long way around, right here on Earth.

So Folks, follow God the Real, "The Spirit of Goodness", as It is not Perfect, and when we believe we are Not perfect, as God is not Perfect, we live in Peace and Harmony and in Reality and Freedom of Thought, right here in Heaven on Earth.

Now, do not worry about Heaven in Heaven because It will come only to soon, but It will be beautifull, as God, "The Spirit of Goodness", wants It to be in Heaven and on Earth.

Yes, God the Real does not want you in Mental Slavery (Attempting to be Perfect), Excellence or Super Excellence is good enough for God the Real, because God accepts you just as you are because you are Its creation.

This allows you to be Happy with yourself because you are everyday Successfull..

Illusion, God the Fraud, wants you to believe you must be Perfect, so that you Fail every day and become Negative, Pessimistic, and Unhappy with yourself.

So Saint Bill says, To Hell with God the Fraud, "Illusion", "The Shadow".The Dead Liar.

(You will be interested in Becoming a Founding Partner when you Understand our Object)

Come in or Call Now!!!.   Thank you

Yours truly,
"Saint Bill".

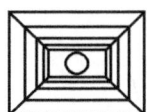

PREVIEWISM
Our World is Beautiful, Yes, Multi-Cultural

Dear Friends and Children of all ages:

We know that to "Judge" is to Decide right from wrong for ourselves and allow all others the same privelege.

Question 1) What is a person who does not Judge?

Answer: An Imbecile. Walking around in circles hitting Pitfall after Pitfall. P.S.: So do not obey the one who says, "Do not Judge". That is false instruction.

Question 2) What is a person who "Tries to be Perfect"?

Answer: A Hypocrite. Saying one thing and doing another. A frustrated Idiot.

P.S.: So do not obey the one who says, "Go and Be Perfect". That is false instruction.

Question 3) What is the purpose of a "Counterfeit Miracle"?

Answer: To disintegrate your Sense of Judgement and render you an imbecile.

P.S.: So discard Counterfeit Miracles for what they are, Pure Fantasy, Illusion. and have Faith in your "Sense of Judgement". It is God's gift to you. Use It.

Question 4) In which Image did God create you?

Answer: In God's image.

P.S.: Therefore, the creation not being perfect, means that God is not Perfect. This is why God the Real can always forgive us, because It knows we have room for error, Just like It has. But God the Real has Billions of years of experience so there is not much room for error in God. But there is one bit of waste that keeps hanging around, since the beginning, and that is "The Shadow",Illusion. But God allowed that to be, because It knew that "Illusion" can be overcome when we use our "Sense of Judgement".

Thank God for being Very Wise,Brave and Steadfast.

Question 5) Does anyone ever Choose to be Evil?

Answer: No. They have to be Deceived first, by Illusion. So use your "Sense of Judgement". and Progress.

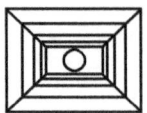

PREVIEWISM
Our World is Beautiful, Yes, Multi-Cultural

My Dear Successor:

Previews Inc. and Institute of Universal Philosophy are founded by "The Compass" by author: "Saint Bill". They will continue to be governed according to "The Compass" in perpetuity.

If you, my successor, write a book two inches thick of a general subject, you may promote it and pocket the profits while you govern Previews Inc. and Institute of Universal Philosophy. But if the book is on the Subject of Religion, then you must resign your position and go into competition with all of us other Immortals on your own and see who wins the race in eternity.

Then someone else will step forward to continue Previews Inc. and Institute of Universal Philosophy, according to The Compass by author ""Saint Bill". This is how it will be because "Saint Bill" has faith that "The Compass" will survive on Its own throughout eternity and be number One within a few hours or days. "Saint Bill" also knows that being number One does not make him or God the Real, "The Spirit of Goodness", perfect. No not at all because "Nothing is Perfect" excepting "Illusion" - Illusion "The Shadow" is a Perfect Liar, and a Nothing, and "Nothing is Perfect". Yes, to be Perfect is to be Dead and only Illusion is Dead.

My dear Successor, If you write a book that jives with "The Compass", then you may call It volume number 4 and add It to our library, with you as the Author.

But "The Compass", volume 1, by author "Saint Bill" must remain as the Foundation. I, "Saint Bill", have full confidence (faith) in your "Spirit of Fairness" and trust you will act according to the Intent of this letter as I appoint you Successor.

Thank you, Yours truly,

as ever in, ""The Spirit of Goodness",

W.J.(Bill) Handel, M.A., L.W. alias: "Saint Bill" (Coach)

Previews Institute of Universal Philosophy.

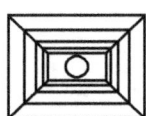

PREVIEWISM
Our World is Beautiful, Yes, Multi-Cultural

Dear Friends and Children of all ages:

Let us set the Record straight with a few Definitions.

1) God the Real: "The Spirit of Goodness". The Desire to do Good that lives in your Heart, Mind, and Soul from conception.

   It also lives in the World, and in Heaven with God.

2) God the Fraud: "Illusion The Shadow. Also known as Satan, Devil, Messiah,

   Hood, Lucifer, and many other such Illusions.(Acts 26,v.16-18)

3) Breathe: A function that allows the body to continue to function.

   You must breathe to stay alive.

4) Judge: Decide right from wrong for yourself and allow all others the same privelege. You must Judge to stay Sane and to keep thinking Straight.

   Condemn: Hand out Punishment. Cause pain and suffering.

   We should not Condemn. (It is self-defeating)

6) Forgive: Forget. Cast out.

   We should Forgive people their shortcomings because we have them ourselves. Yes, we are not Perfect just as God the Real is not Perfect. This is why God the Real always Forgives.

7) Love: To love is to Give without expecting a Return. Free Gift. Therefore, It does not matter if a person would Die for you, If It did it out of Love, you would owe It nothing.

   Curse: To predict or wish something Bad to come to your Neighbor.

   We should not Curse because God does not Curse. It is self-defeating.

9) Bless: To Predict or wish something Good to come to your Neighbor.

   Reward: To give something in payment for Doing Good. God rewards us All and Well.

   "Good": Something that brings us Happiness, Decency, Prosperity, and Peace of Mind, and Peace and Harmony amoungst Humankind.

12) "Bad": Something that brings us Pain and Suffering.

    "Sin": Something that Offends God the Real.

    There is no such thing because God the Real Understands All and Forgives All and as such wipes out all pain and suffering because It Forgets and Casts out any memory of It.

14) Sinner: A person who thinks It is condemned by God the Real.

    This person is living under an Illusion and as such Retaliates against those that serve the Illusion. This causes a Vicious Circle.

THE TRADITION OF "CHANGE FOR THE BETTER" IS BORN IN *"PREVIEWISM"*
www.previews-inc.com
Make 10 - 20 Copies per week and Pass It On. - God will be well Pleased.

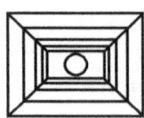

PREVIEWISM
Our World is Beautiful, Yes, Multi-Cultural

15) "Saint": A person that knows that God the Real always Forgives and Never hands out punishment, but rather Accepts him/her just as they are, and continues to hand out Blessings to create a Benevolent Circle.

"Thank you, Dear God, Thank you"

16) Preacher: A person who talks 90% of the time and Acts only 10% of the time.

Practitioner: A person who Acts 90% of the time and talks only 10% of the time.

Spirit: A Thought.

"Good Thought" is based on Reality, or something.

"Bad Thought" is based on Illusion, or nothing.

Unsophisticated: Unpretentious. Down-to-Earth. "Moderate". Living in Reality.

Holy: Hoity-Toity Self-righteous Idiot. Extremist. Living in Illusion.

Trusting: Confidence. Applied Faith. Knowing Humanity.

Jealous: Inconfident. Inferior. Having only Blind Faith. Lacking experience.

God's Creation: Beautiful. "The Spirit of Goodness" with all of Its Angels.

The Chips left over: Blab.. "Illusion" "The Shadow". Total Waste. (Cast It out).

Thanks for Listening, My Children and Friends,. Yours truly,
as ever in, "The Spirit of Goodness",

B.H., M.A., L.W. "Saint Bill" (Practitioner) (Coach)
Previews Institute of Universal Philosophy.

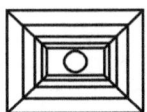

PREVIEWISM
Our World is Beautiful, Yes, Multi-Cultural

Dear Friends and Children of all ages:

Once upon a time there was a Society in which the people had only One name. And in this Society there was a man called "Robin". This Robin was a man who had studied life and God to the enth degree. This Robin developed a sharp tongue which he called a "Spiritual Gun". This man called Robin shot down every man with Evil thoughts, words or Actions. When Robin's "Spiritual Gun" was empty he passed away and went to Heaven.

As time went on there appeared again men with Evil thoughts, words, and Actions. And Society progressed to give people Two names. Then an Evil man decided he would assume the name of "Robin" and call himself "Robin Hood".

"Robin Hood" said he was a "Good" man and he said to Society that he had picked up the "Spiritual Gun" of his Forefather. And so he said to Society, hold it right there, you are all under Arrest. You bow down and Worship me or I shoot.

Most of Society knew the Gun was Empty, so they just walked away and continued with their work, in happiness, decency, prosperity and peace of mind.

Robin Hood was frustrated as only a few were gullible enough to believe him and so he said to the Few, "Bring me your children". Ah, yes, the Children. They will believe anything. And so Robin Hood preached to the Children. But the children found it hard to believe what this man Robin Hood was preaching as Society was progressing on the established path.

Robin Hood was an Evil man but he was also a Shrewed man and so he decided to perform a multitude of "Counterfeit Miracles". Then he said to the Children, If you do not believe me, believe my Miracles. Please. (He was obviously Desperate).

Again, only a few were gullible enough to believe. As time went on Robin Hood also passed away and went to Heaven.

Society as a whole continued to progress in happiness, decency, prosperity, and peace of mind, and in peace and harmony with the world around It, by following their Natural Good instincts.

Well, folks, two thousand years later the world's population has reached 5.7 Billion people. Approximately 4.7 Billion people are still continuing according to their Natural Good Instincts. Their natural Good instincts are called "The Spirit of Goodness" with all of Its children (angels), the oldest being "The Spirit of Truth" and the youngest being "The Spirit of Enthusiasm" with many in between. You will be delighted to know that the world is a beautiful place to live in, Not withstanding the "Shadow Worshippers".

Yes, folks, in the world today we have identified the Culprit, Robin Hood. We call him "The Shadow", "Illusion", "Deceiver", "The Bad guy".

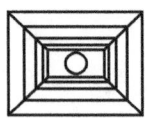

PREVIEWISM
Our World is Beautiful, Yes, Multi-Cultural

Only a handful of his "Billion" followers are really convinced that he is a descendant of "Robin" the wise guy. The remainder are Hypocrites saying one thing and doing another. But they are not sure about the Gun (whether it is loaded or not), and so they continue to Bow and pay, Bow and pay. (Chuckle, Chuckle, eh!.)

Thank God the Real, "The Spirit of Goodness", for our Natural Good Instincts that keep us truly Free in Spirit (thought), word and Deed. And knowing that even the Deceived will be welcome in Heaven as God is EverUnderstanding, Loving, and Forgiving. Yes, God always gets the Last word, and the Last word is...Forgiven.

Thank you Children and Friends for Listening,

Yours truly, as ever in,

"The Spirit of Goodness",

B.H., M.A., L.W. "Saint Bill", (Coach)

Previews Institute of Universal Philosophy.

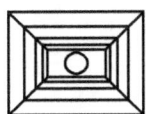

PREVIEWISM
Our World is Beautiful, Yes, Multi-Cultural

Dear Friends and Children of all ages:

Today we have a few Jokes and miscellaneous proverbs to reveal.

1) Question,. What is the difference between a Lunatic and a Diplomat.

   Answer: A Lunatic says, "Get thee Behind me".

   A Diplomat says, "Let us agree to disagree and talk this over".

2) Life is a Pendulum. One Extreme (Black) to the other Extreme (White).

   The ideal position to be in is a Medium (Moderate) light Grey. God the Real, however, does not care where you are at in the swing as long as you keep your Back to the Black and your Face to the White.

3) We all agree that there is only One God.

   But there are many Lords around the world.

   We all have personal Mentors, Idols, or Lords,

   But we should remember they are not God, they are only Experienced Guides.

4) (Analogy): You do not Junk your old Car until a new one is in Sight. You keep fixing the old one until the New one is here.
   Which means, you do not Criticize unless and until you have an Alternative.

Well, now we have an Alternative to the Old Books of Knowledge. Yes, we now have "The COMPASS" by author "Saint Bill". (A new Bible) "The EverLast Testament".

So the Old can be Discarded. (It is already Obsolete).

Thanks for Listening

as ever in, "The Spirit of Goodness",

B.H., M.A., L.W. "Saint Bill"

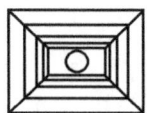

PREVIEWISM
Our World is Beautiful, Yes, Multi-Cultural

Dear Friends and Children of all ages:

Just a few more miscellaneous Proverbs

1)   Books of Prophecy mix The Good with The Bad and cause confusion, because the Prophets all claim to be representing God, but we know better, (some are True and some are False) So we have to use our Sense of Judgement to decide right from wrong for ourselves and allow all others the same Privilege.

2)   Books of Wisdom are Books of Experience that represent God the Real, "The Snirit of Goodness", and a well developed "Sense of Judgement" that reveals the Truth about life and God the Real and exposes God the Fraud (Illusion), so that It is Cast-out of mind and not Acted on. This creates Happiness, Decency, Prosperity, and Peace of Mind and Peace and Harmony amoungst Humankind.

Thank you, Dear God, Thank you.

It is said (known) that the Books of Prophecy will pass away (1 cor.13,v.8-13) as the Books of Wisdom progress with God the Real, "The Spirit of Goodness", that lives in your Heart, Mind and Soul,.together with all of Its children (angels), the oldest being "The Spirit of Truth" and the youngest being "The Spirit of Enthusiasm", with many in between such as "The Spirit (Sense) of Judgement". Yes, your "Sense of Judgement" leads you to the "Truth". There are Four steps to Judgement. 1) Gather the Facts. 2) Weigh them(Pro and Con). 3) Decide (For or Against). 4) Action. (Without action It is wishful thinking).

When you agree with your God's (Neighbor's) suggestion, You Act on It. When you disagree with your God"s (Neighbor's) suggestion, You Forgive (Forget It).

Remember, Suggestions come in Two forms, (Words or Actions).

Thanks for Listening, as ever in,

"The Spirit of Goodness",

B.H., M.A., L.W. "Saint Bill".

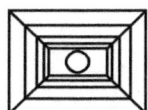

PREVIEWISM
Our World is Beautiful, Yes, Multi-Cultural

Dear Friends and Children of all ages:

Question: What is the difference between a Previewlite and a Shadow Worshipper?

Answer: The Previewlite uses his/her "Sense of Judgement" and comes closer to the truth which leads to Happiness, Decency, Prosperity and Peace of Mind.

> The Shadow Worshipper does not use his/her "Sense of Judgement" because his/her God says, "Do not Judge, Lest you will be Judged", so as to create Fear and keep you under the influence of Illusion and Lie. This leads to Pain and Suffering.

2) The Previewlites do Good because they want to.

> The Shadow Worshippers do Good because they have to, or they are told they will go to Hell.

3) The Previewlite, "Living in Truth", finds he/she lives in Heaven on Earth and lives accordingly.

> The Shadow Worshipper, "Living in Confusion" finds he/she lives in Hell on Earth and lives accordingly.

4) The Previewlite looks forward to Heaven in Heaven and a life of Bliss.

> The Shadow Worshipper does not know what he/she is coming to and so has to sit in the Front Row with the Morons to see the show..

The Previewlites are at the Door Ushering in the Masses and choosing which Row to place them in or where to put them in the Standing Room.

Chuckle, Chuckle, eh.!   Thanks for Listening,

as ever in, "The Spirit of Goodness",

B.H., M.A., L.W. "Saint Bill". (Coach)

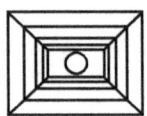

PREVIEWISM
Our World is Beautiful, Yes, Multi-Cultural

Dear Friends and Children of all ages:

As you have noticed the colors of "The Compass" are green and blue. That is because God's favorite colors are green and blue, yes, Blue skies and Green grass. The green feeds the Stomach and the blue feeds the Mind.

Yes, we specialize in "Food for Thought". Our object is to promote Positive thinking. But first we must realize there are two kinds of Positive.

True Positive and False Positive. True positive is Positive, and False positive is Negative.

Let me give you an example: True positive says, I can walk around a Lake,

False positive says, I can walk across It.. One is positive and One is Negative.

Let me explain: When you try to walk around a lake, you succeed and become accustomed to Success. Yes, Positive and Enthusiastic.

When you try to walk across It, you fail and become accustomed to Failure. And you become Negative, Pessimistic, Yes, even Sadistic. (Yes, that is where It's at).

Let me give you another example: God the Real says, I am the Creator of the Universe, I am the Ruler of the universe and on Earth. (True Positive)

God the Fraud says, I am God, but I am powerless to deal with my Children. None of them have enough money and None of them want to Kill themselves as a Sacrifice to pay the Price...So I give up. I am going to commit Suicide. Oh, yes, and pay the price willingly. Then I am going to Raise myself from the Dead and go to Heaven to help God Rule. (Ah, yes, I will be God) (Pure Fantasy and Illusion) (Negative) Sick psyche psychology.

Yes, that is where It's at.

Thanks for Listening, yours truly,

as ever in, "The Spirit of Goodness"

B.H., M.A., L.W. "Saint Bill" (Coach)

Previews Institute of Universal Philosophy

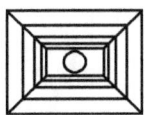

PREVIEWISM
Our World is Beautiful, Yes, Multi-Cultural

Dear Friends and Children of all ages:

We have a quiz for you today.

It is said of old that, "It is more blessed to Give than to Take."

Question: Is this God's statement or is this Man's statement.

Answer: This is Man's statement. Because One has to ask before he/she reduces the honor of taking. This Man's statement is a form of extortion, whereby he/she creates fear or embarrassment if you do not give. It is like asking, "Who is more important, The King or the Peasant?"

In Satan's eyes the King is more important, but in God's eye they are equal. The King says, It is more blessed to Give than to Take, in order to encourage the peasants to Give, Give, Give. But the King's purpose is to Share the Wealth. So it is just as blessed to Take as to Give.

In summary, we say that Man's laws are always flawed, but God's laws are never flawed. God's law in this regard is: To Give or to Take is equal, and it should be and it can be, If we take the time to Spot our neighbor's needs and Fill them before he/she has to Ask. Yes, be alert and Generous.

Thank you, Dear God, Thank you.

B.H., M.A., L.W. "Saint Bill".

> *P.S.:* Please do not misunderstand and do not interpret this to mean, "I am God". Chuckle, chuckle, eh!!.. Yes, you see, The Doctrine I profess is not mine, but that of It that sent me. If you understand this you reap the Blessings of God, And so it does not matter if I speak of It that sent me or I speak of myself. Either way it does not matter, because It (God) gets the Glory:: (John 7,vs.16-18)

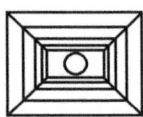

PREVIEWISM
Our World is Beautiful, Yes, Multi-Cultural

Dear Friends and Children of all ages:

Just a few more Humorous Questions

1) What is a "Shadow Worshipper"?

   Answer: A person who thinks he/she has Two Natures. The predominant being the "Bad Nature". The Coat to cover It all is a "Nice Face".

2) What is a "Previewlite"?

   A person who knows he/she has only One Nature. The "Good Nature". It can not be covered. Because the "Ugly Coat" is a known "Illusion".

3) What are we all Born with?

   A Free Spirit, A Sense of Judgement, A Good Nature. It is your Sense of Judgement that Screens (controls) your Free Spirit and when it is effective at casting out Illusion, Your Good Nature begins to Flourish along with the many Good characteristics of "The Spirit of Goodness", (God the Real). Anyone who says, "Do not Judge", is serving The Shadow and leading you to Confusion, Negative thinking, Pessimism, and ultimately Sadism.

So just continue to use your Sense of Judgement and become Clear thinking, Positive, and Enthusiastic and ultimately Ecstacy.

Thank you Children and Friends,

Yours truly, as ever in, "The Spirit of Goodness",

B.H., M.A., L.W. "Saint Bill" (Coach)

Previews Institute

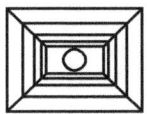

PREVIEWISM
Our World is Beautiful, Yes, Multi-Cultural

Dear Friends and Children of all ages:

Today we have a Message of True Hope for the Future. True hope is based on Reality. False hope is based on Illusion.

The Eastern religions have a Positive approach to life and lives as "Saints". The Western religions have a Negative approach to life and lives as "Sinners".

The "Saints"are Happy-go-Lucky people. The "Sinners" are Sad-depressed people. The fact of life is that you can not be both at the same time. At any given moment you have a choice to be one or the other.

The other fact of life is that to think you are both means you are Confused.

Dear Friends and Children, as we know when a child is born into this world, after a few months it begins to crawl and after a few more months it will stand. Then after a while It begins to walk, and then It begins to run.

Well, the Hope we have for the Western world is that the same applies to the Spiritual realm. If you are told you are a Sinner as a child you learn to think and act like a "Sinner". If you are told you are a Saint as a child you learn to think and act like a "Saint".

Well, as we all know we are all children of God the Real, "The Spirit of Goodness", and that means that at any point in our lives we can choose to think we are Sinners or we can choose to think we are Saints. Yes, We can choose to be Happy or Sad about what life brings us. We can use life as a Stumbling block or we can use life as a Stepping stone to better things to come. And they will come if we look forward to them with a True Positive attitude and subconscious.

Folks, when I was a child I was told that I was a Sinner, a poor miserable Sinner. Well, 40 years later I was told that I was a Saint. So I asked, What is a Saint?

Well, I was told that a Saint is a person who knows that God accepts and loves you just as you are. And that God is everunderstanding and forgives you your Short-comings every day at every moment so that you can Renew your "Good Nature" and have the Strength to continue to try again. So that you are continually improveing. Yes, Two steps Forward, and One back,. Not One step Forward, and Two back. So you see, The True hope we have today is that True Positive thinking has come to the Western World with the knowledge of "PREVIEWISM". Whereby we can tell our children that they are "Saints" when they are conceived and born into this world and that they can choose to stay Saints as children of God the Real, "The Spirit of Goodness", as manifested in and by "The COMPASS" by Author, "Saint Bill".

Thanks for Listening, as ever in,

"The Spirit of Goodness", yours truly,

"Saint Bill".

The Tradition of "Change for the Better" is Born in *"PREVIEWISM"*
www.previews-inc.com
Make 10 - 20 Copies per week and Pass It On. - God will be well Pleased.

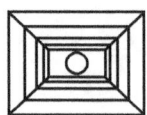

PREVIEWISM
Our World is Beautiful, Yes, Multi-Cultural

Dear Friends and Children of all ages:

Today we are going to have a Deep discussion. We are going to talk about God the Real, "The Spirit of Goodness", and God the Fraud, "Illusion". The Good Guy we are going to call "Robin" and the Bad Guy we are going to call "Robin Hood".

Robin is a servant of God (Reality) and Robin Hood is a servant of The Shadow, (Illusion). We know that Reality is God's creation, and Illusion is Shadow's creation. God's creation is Something and Shadow's creation is Nothing.

The vehicle that God uses to bring us Reality (Knowledge)(Truth) is Light. The vehicle that Shadow uses to bring us Illusion (Fantasy)(Lie) is Night.

Night is in Itself a Shadow, yes, The Shadow of the Earth, and It is an Illusion. Light is in Itself a part of God's creation. The source being the Sun. (Reality).

All of God's creation was created in the Dark (Ignorance) including Humanbeings. And when the Light appeared, there appeared a Shadow (Night), and God said,

Oh well, "Nothing is Perfect. "Something is Alive and Good, and we will overcome ignorance, Illusion, "The Shadow", Night.

And so, God said, "Let us give Earth a Spin" and we will bring the Ignorant into the Light so that they can See the Reality of God all around them.

And they will find that Reality brings them Joy, Happiness, Decency, Prosperity, and Peace of Mind so that they can live in peace and harmony with their Neighbors.

And they will find that Ignorance and Illusion is a thing of the Past and they will learn to look to the Future always as God does. Yes, God always looks to the Future because It knows that life is Eternal with no beginning or end in Sight.

And so you see if you live in Ignorance, Illusion & Lie and promote It you are a servant of The Shadow, (Robin Hood), the Bad Guy and as you know this brings you nothing but Pain and Suffering. And so you are a Sucker for Punishment.

If you accept the Strength and Courage that Knowledge, Reality & Truth brings you and promote It, you are a servant of God, (Robin), the Good Guy.

Dear Friends, Over the course of time "Robin Hood" has always declared that It is Real because It is a permanent Liar (Illusion) (Ignorance). And Robin Hood has always declared that Robin is an Illusion and a Liar. But the fact remains that we should keep our Eye and Attention on Reality because Reality is God and God is Reality, Not Fantasy or Illusion. And the Reality is that Life is Eternal.

In both the Physical and Spiritual Sense."Yours truly, in, "The Spirit of Goodness".

B.H., M.A., L.W. "Saint Bill".

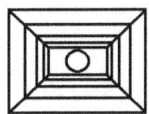

PREVIEWISM
Our World is Beautiful, Yes, Multi-Cultural

Dear Friends and Children of all ages:

Today we have a Parable for you.

You know, God the Real, is not Perfect, but Alive and Unsoiled and Spotless because It has a "Waterhose" handy that It uses to keep Itself Spotless.

The Waterhose is known as "Love" for the Hose, and "Forgiveness" for the Water.

So you are created and Born in the Image of God, and you are Spotless, yes, A Saint in God's Eye.

So you go out into the World (a Mud Puddle) and you get your Rubber Boots dirty. Do not Fret because you have a Waterhose handy to wash them off and you are Spotless. Yes, A Saint in God's Eye.

Then you go out into the World (a Mud Puddle) and you begin to Play because you are a Happy child of God. But someone gives you a Push and you fall into the Mud., and you are Dirty from Head to Toe. Do not Fret because you must remember that you have a Waterhose at Home where you can wash your Clothes, your Boots, and Yourself., and you are Spotless, Yes, a "Saint" in God's Eye.

In the meantime, if some of your Playmates forget there is a Waterhose for us All, and then say, You are a Dirty Sinner. Do not Fret or be Offended because you know you are a "Saint", because all you have to do is use the Waterhose, and you are "Spotless", yes, "A Saint",. conceived, born, grew-up, Lived, and gone to Heaven as a "Saint", yes, a Child of God from beginning to End and back to Beginning for ever and ever, Thank you, Dear God, Thank you.

And so you see, the purpose of us old folks is to remind the young folks that they are always "Saints" in God's Eye, because they can excercise Love and Forgiveness at all times when someone calls them "a Sinner", because you can always Forgive them for their Ignorance and Forgetfullness and Lack of Judgement.

Yes, folks, God the Real, "The Spirit of Goodness", has a "Sense of Judgement" and always remembers the "Realities" of life and does not get caught-up in forgetfullness, Ignorance and Illusion, or Superstitious Tradition.

Yes, folks, Look to the Future and you will see God. Look behind you and you will see Illusion. Yes, folks, God never looks back. Always to the Future, and a "Better Day".

Thank you, Dear God, Thank you.

Thanks for Listening, Yours truly, as ever in,

"The Spirit of Goodness" B.H., M.A., L.W.

"Saint Bill" (Coach)

Previews Institute

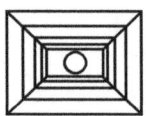

PREVIEWISM
Our World is Beautiful, Yes, Multi-Cultural

Dear Friends and Children of all ages:

Today we want to List the definitions of a "Saint". We will not bother defining a "Sinner" because in God's Eye there are none in this World. And if in God's Eye there are none, why should we be the "Accuser's" servant and define something that does not exist. (A Shadow). (An Illusion).

Therefore we will begin with the "Saints".

1) A Saint is a person that knows that God accepts and loves him/her "Just as you are". (Unconditionally).

2) A Saint is a person that is a Practitioner as opposed to a Preacher. A Practitioner acts 90% of the time and talks only 10% of the time. A Preacher talks 90% of the time and acts only 10% of the time. (Usually all Preach and no Practice)

3) A Saint is a person who knows that God is Real and The Shadow is Illusion.

4) A Saint is a person who knows God inside out and Dwells on the Positive. A Preacher is a person who knows God inside out and Dwells on the Negative. (Yes, Sick psyche Psychology).

5) A Saint is a person who has the courage to face Reality and cast out Illusion.

6) A Saint is a person who knows he/she is conceived and born with three things.
a) A Free Spirit. (We are all Free to decide Right from Wrong for ourselves)
b) A "Sense of Judgement". (We must use It to allow It to lead us to the Truth)
c) And a "Good Nature". (We must be Loving and Forgiving to allow God and ourselves to Renew our Good Nature at every Instance).

7) A Saint is a person who knows you do not change the Rule because of the Exception. Yes, 88% of our. Society are "Saints" in the Human Eye. (100% are in God's Eye) The So called "Sinners" are in Church with the Preacher or in Jail.

8) A Saint is a person who knows that My Summit (Temple) is my Home and My Home is my (Temple) Summit and My Congregation is my Family. (Oh, yes, Indeed).(And that includes You).

9) A Saint is a person who is "Happy-go-Lucky" and is always prepared to take advantage of opportunity. (And make the Best of what Life hands him/her).

10) A Saint is a person who is Free in every Sense, and allows all others the same privelege. Yes, we all have a different concept of God. The Preacher says, Follow me and I will set you Free, and then turns and says, You are a "Sinner". You bow down and Worship my God or you are Dead.

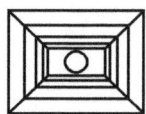

PREVIEWISM
Our World is Beautiful, Yes, Multi-Cultural

The Practitioner says,. You are a "Saint",. You worship God the Real, "The Spirit of Goodness", or what ever you please and you will still be Free to come to Heaven,. because God always gets the Last word. (And the Last word is...FORGIVEN)

Thank you, Dear God, Thank you...

Yours truly,

as ever in, "The Spirit of Goodness",

B.H., M.A., L.W. "Saint Bill" (Coach)

Previews Institute

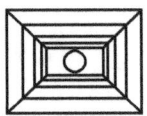

PREVIEWISM
Our World is Beautiful, Yes, Multi-Cultural

Dear Friends and Children of all ages:

Today we are going to do a little Boasting.

We, God the Real "The Spirit of Goodness", and "Saint Bill" started to develop a New and True Religion in October 14/5990, about Eleven years ago, by starting to write "The Compass". "The Compass", a New Bible, The EverLast Testament was completed in about Nine years and since then we have completed "The Sermons of Saint Bill" and are well on our way to completing our third Volume called "Object, Masters Degree". Yes, and Every page written is a Bomber for Truth.

All during this time we have now chaulked up about (25) twenty-five Disciples and about (45) forty-five Families and about (150) followers. And we, "Saint Bill" and "The Spirit of Goodness" are totally confident that not One, no not One of these people would betray or turn us in to be Crucified. Ha, Ha, Ha, Ha, Ha,.., chuckle, chuckle, eh!!!.. chuckle, chuckle, eh, but how true.

Yes, My Friends, God's plan toward Its Goal does not include Murder, That was "The Shadow's" plan toward Its Goal. But The Shadow failed as It always does and God the Real, "The Spirit of Goodness", has prevailed. Thank you, Dear God, Thank you for being Creative, a good Provider, and a Steadfast Comfortor.

Yes, God's Goal is to achieve Happiness, Decency, Prosperity and Peace of Mind for Its people thoughout the World. And It has been making progress toward this since time began, not withstanding the unfullfilling influence of The Shadow. But now we have Identified the Culprit, Satan, Lucifer, Devil, Demon, Messiah. Yes, these are all "Illusion" just like "The Shadow" causing nothing but pain and Suffering.

But now we have the alternative, "Reality", oh, yes, Reality is God and God is Reality, Not Fantasy or Illusion. And within Three Hundred years we will have achieved our Goal, barring the weather, of course. Yes, folks, we now will eliminate the unfullfilling influence of The Shadow, by casting It out of our Mind. Yes, Be Gone...

Thanks for Listening, as ever in,

"The Spirit of Goodness", Yours truly,

"Saint Bill".

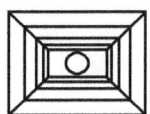

PREVIEWISM
Our World is Beautiful, Yes, Multi-Cultural

Just a Few questions and answers:

1) Are you Spiritually FREE? (Yes) Then you are a Saint.
2) Do you live above the LAW? (Yes) Then you are a Saint.
3) Can you Offend God? (No) Then you are a Saint.
4) Does God always Understand and Forgive? (Yes) Then you are a Saint.
5) Is your Preacher a Saint? If Yes, Why does he/she call you a Sinner?
   If No, Why do you follow him/her?
6) What did God give you, So that you do not have to Worship an Idol or a Preacher? Answer: "A Sense of Judgement" (It keeps you FREE)

This is why Christ says,. "Do not Judge", Just Believe Me. Yes, To Glorify an Idol, and Keep you a Slave.

A "Saint" glorifies God the Real, "The Spirit of Goodness", and is FREE.

A "Sinner" glorifies himself or his Idol,. and is saddled with Guilt, Fear, Doubt and Illusion.

Yes, A Slave.

Thank you, Friends and Children of all ages:

Yours truly, as ever in, "The Spirit of Goodness

B.H., M.A., L.W. "Saint Bill" (Coach)

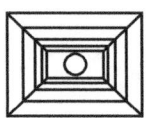

PREVIEWISM
Our World is Beautiful, Yes, Multi-Cultural

Dear Family and Friends and Children of all ages:

Charity is Love, and to Love is to Give without expecting a Return. We are a "Charity" and true Love is to Give willingly and Freely. Therefore, We, Previews Inc. and Previews Institute, do never want to Ask for Donations, but rather just Lead the Way in volentary Giving. In this way the Members of the Body will never feel enslaved but rather learn and want to Give Freely and Willingly, because the Spiritual Rewards are Great.

Previews Inc. is the official Publisher of "The Compass" and Previews Institute buys "The Compass" from Previews Inc. and distributes them to the People.

Previews Inc. receives Just Reward for Its efforts and Feeds the Family and Its Descendants. Yes, this provides "Food for the Stomach".

Previews Institute promotes God the Real, "The Spirit of Goodness", together with all of Its children (angels), the oldest being "The Spirit of Truth" and the youngest being "The Spirit of Enthusiasm", with many in between as manifested in and by "The Compass". Yes, this provides "Food for Thought" for everyone and the Rewards are Great.

Anyone and Everyone is welcome to become a "Founding Partner`" of Previews Inc. and their Families and Descendants will also enjoy the Just Rewards.

To you the Readers, we say, please ensure that the Listeners understand the intent of this Letter and keep the people FREE.

Thank you, Dear God, Thank you,

Yours truly, as ever in,

"The Spirit of Goodness",

W.J. (Bill) Handel, M.A., L.W.

"Saint Bill" (Coach)

Previews Institute of Universal Philosophy

P.S.: When you decide to Give, Please make Cheque PayableTo: Previews Institute,

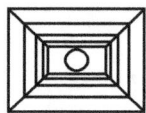

PREVIEWISM
Our World is Beautiful, Yes, Multi-Cultural

Dear Friend:

The next time you see your Preacher,

You say,. "You are a Saint" and "I am a Saint",. Thank God the Real, "The Spirit of Goodness",.

And if the Preacher once says,. You are a Sinner,. You just say,. "I Forgive you for your Ignorance".

Those are the Last words of a Wise man. Yes, Dear God, Forgive them for they know not what they do or say!

Dear Friend: What can you do to help God keep The Shadow (Illusion)(Satan) under control and Reduced to Nothing every day of your life?

ANSWER: When the opportunity arises in your conversation with those you meet today, ask them this Simple question...

(Susie)(Joe)(Sam).... Do you realize that you are a "Saint" in God's Eye? Yes, you are a Saint, because God created you in Its Image, and because God loves you, It is prepared to Forgive you all your Sins against Humanity, and keep you Spotless, So that you will be Fit to take your Place in Heaven at any time and any place and any Day.

(Isn't that Wonderful? Yes, Indeed it is. Thank God, "The Spirit of Goodness", and all of Its Angels for reminding Me and my Friends of this Eternal Fact at every opportunity today.

Thank you, Dear God, Thank you, for allowing me to Serve you in this way, Every Day.

Thank you, Dear God, Thank you.

Thanks for Listening, as ever in,

"The Spirit of Goodness",

"Saint Bill" (Head Coach) A Servant for God's sake.

Previews Institute of Universal Philosophy

P.S.: We are FORGIVEN before we Start our Day, and We are FORGIVEN after we End our Day, and while we Sleep, We can do Nothing wrong. So We are always, "Saints".

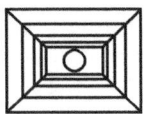

PREVIEWISM
Our World is Beautiful, Yes, Multi-Cultural

Dear Friends and Children of all ages:

This letter is addressed to those of you who do not already know, that The Old Testament is a Lie and the Works of The Shadow (Illusion) (Satan). This is verified by a Wise man according to Acts 26, vs. 16-18, of The New Testament.

Since the Intent of The Old Testament is to Enslave the world to the service of Human Idols, we should Cast-out the entire Thought process and put It behind us, Never again allowing It to distract us from the Truth.

The Truth being that we are all created in the Image of God, "The Spirit of Goodness", and as such we are all Children of God and considered Equal "Saints" in God's Eye.

As Saints, we are all conceived and born with "A Free Spirit", "A Sense of Judgement", and "A Good Nature".. And since all Goodness in the world is to the Glory of God, we should never worship a Human Idol, because they always Fail you when the going gets Tough (Tuff). God the Real, "The Spirit of Goodness", never Fails you. You may be Distracted by The Shadow (Illusion) and sometimes Fail God, but God is always there to stand by you when the going gets Tough.

Yes, my Friends, because God the Real is everUnderstanding, everLoving, and everForgiving, we may Dwell on Joy, Happiness, Decency, Prosperity, and Peace of Mind at all times, never for a Second falling into Fear of God.

Yes, my Friends, "Fear of God" is "Illusion" and Illusion leads to Self-punishment and Negative, Sadistic thinking, culminating in Murder or Suicide.

So Cast the Garbage Out into outer Darkness, beyond the reach of Light, behind you and never Look back again... Look to the Future because It is always Rosy, and what you can make of It

Yes, my Friends. It is now evident that"the Wise man" referred to in paragraph one of this letter was on the Verge of writing "A New Bible", "The Compass", but was denied the opportunity by Negative Sadistic people who put him to Death along with many others before him for promoting the Truth about God the Real, "The Spirit of Goodness", and all of Its children (angels).

Then in retrospect the task of writing was given to those of the Old-School of thought, and the Bastards twisted Murder into Justification for the Lies and Illusions of the Dark ages, and to Glorify a Human Idol to worship.

Well my Friends, the world has since learned that you do not Glorify or Worship Human Idols. The world has further learned that there is Never any true Justification for Lying, Stealing, Killing, or Over-indulging. Never. These things can be Forgiven, but Never Justified.

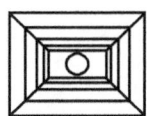

PREVIEWISM
Our World is Beautiful, Yes, Multi-Cultural

And so you see, Folks, this Wise man that we refer to was a "Saint", just like you or I. But he died in Vain until Now. Yes, Now "The COMPASS" is here, and this Wise man will get his Just Reward. He will be remembered as "Saint Jesus", along with "Saint Peter", "Saint Susie", "Saint Sam", "Saint Joe", "Saint Victoria", and "Saint Bill", and so on and on and on.

Yes, Folks, Jesus is now a "Saint", and not a Fictional character such as The Messiah, The Christ, or The Shadow (Illusion) (Satan) Acts 26, vs. 16-18.

Yes, Folks, cast these Characters out and think about the Future.. Remember, God says, Look to the Future. It is for my Saints (my Children), and to Hell with the Past. It is for Nothing and is Forgiven and Forgotten.

Yes, Folks, the Future is Positive,. The Past is Negative. So take your choice of what you think about. Yes, use your "Sense of Judgement" and Decide (Judge) what is Right or Wrong for yourself and allow all others the same privilege.

Thank you, Dear God, Thank you. Thank you, Friends and Children of all ages,

Yours truly, as ever in, "The Spirit of Goodness",.

"Saint Bill" (Coach)

Previews Institute of Universal Philosophy

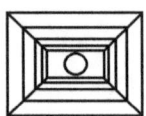

PREVIEWISM
Our World is Beautiful, Yes, Multi-Cultural

Dear Friends and Children of all ages:

All the worlds Children are Born into this world as equals in God's Eye. Basically because we are all Born a bit Ignorant.

Now from all sides of the Earth we all start a trek accross the Valley and Up Life's Mountain. At the Top of the Mountain there is a Plateau.

We all have different degrees of Success on this Trek and not all reach the Plateau. During the Trek of life we all find many Unequalities amoung us, but when we reach the Plateau we are again considered Equals.

Over the Course of all Time there have been Several, perhaps Many forgotten, who have reached the Plateau,. Such as,. Hindu, Juda, Abraham, Confucous, Buddha, Paul, Thomas, Jefferson, Peter, Krishna, Mohammed, Singh, Sittingbull, Siksika, Kangara, Ali, and so on and on and on, and of course the most Recent "Saint Bill".

The reason the most Recent is called "Saint Bill" is because he was not only strong Physically, but also very strong and Alert Mentally.

Yes, you see, "Saint Bill" noticed a Big Boulder on the Plateau and with One Big Leap of Faith, Jumped upon the Boulder, stood Up, Looked Up, and put his Foot down Hard, and It went toSlitherines, Then "Saint Bill" rubbed with his Rubber Rubber Heel until there was nothing left but Dust.

Then "Saint Bill" said,to the other Four around him, Bow, you Gentlemen, Bow, knees and all, You Gentlemen Bow. Ha, Ha, Ha, Ha,.. Chuckle, Chuckle, eh!.' Yeh.'.

Thanks for Listening Folks, It was a Pleasure,

Yours truly, as ever in,

"The Spirit of Goodness",

B.H., M.A., L.W. Alias, "Saint Bill" (Coach)

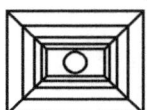

PREVIEWISM
Our World is Beautiful, Yes, Multi-Cultural

Dear Friends and Children of all ages:

Today we are going to talk about the original Truth and the original Lie.

The original Truth stems from Reality, and the original Lie stems from Illusion. The Reality is that God set us Free in every sense Physical and Spiritual. The Illusion is that God forbid us to do this, that or the other thing.

The Truth is that God said, Go you are Free, because I forgive you your Shortcomings and say,. carry on and "Do It better next time". Yes, Forget It.

The Lie is that God said, Do not Judge, Yes, just ignore your "Sense of Judgement", and continue to fall into the Pits, and continue to Suffer needlessly, because Suffering makes you strong. (Wrong, Suffering makes you a Sucker for more Suffering).

The second Lie is that God said, You Do not Judge or I will Condemn you, Punish you, and put you to Death. (Wrong, God does not Kill). (Especially not Itself).

The second Truth is that God said, All of my Creation is "Good", especially my "Sense of Judgement", because It leads you to the Truth, and the Truth sets you Free.

So there you go Mr. Shadow, go fly a Kite, I will use my "Sense of Judgement", and Judge (Decide) right from wrong, true from false, Good from Waste, Possible from Impossible, Reality from Illusion, and God the Real from God the Fraud.

And I will make progress and continue to live in Bliss, Happiness, Decency, Prosperity, and in Peace of Mind. Yes, I will gain the ability to live in Peace and Harmony with my Neighbors, and the world around me.

Thank you, Dear God, Thank you, for putting us a Step above the Animals.

Thanks for Listening, It was a pleasure,

as ever in, "The Spirit of Goodness",

B.H., M.A., L.W. "Saint Bill.'" (Coach).

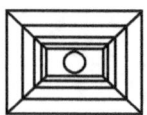

PREVIEWISM
Our World is Beautiful, Yes, Multi-Cultural

Dear Friends and Children of all ages:

Today another insight has come to mind regarding the phenomenon of "Turning the other Cheek."

As we know God the Real, "The Spirit of Goodness", never Retaliates, but rather always turns the other Cheek. Yes, No consequences from God. And that is because God is not Physical, but only Spiritual, and therefore we can not strike God square right on the Nose.

Well, you know, in Real life we know that the "Law" is the servant of The Shadow. But really only if you Hit the Judge square right on the Nose. Yes, the Judge is only Human and He/She can and will turn the other Cheek over and over again as you slap him/her with the little and sometimes big "Grey" offences.

But when you strike the Judge right square on the Nose with an obviously "Black" offence, then he/she must strike back with a "Guilty" verdict.

And so you see the "Law" is very leniant to those of us who use our "Sense of Judgement" and never strike the Judge right square on the Nose with a "Black" offence, and leave the Judge no choice but to strike back with "Guilty"

Yes, folks, the "Law" serves The Shadow only if you strike your Nieghbor "Right Square on the Nose",. But if you use your "Sense of Judgement" the Law serves God by giving us Guide-lines to stay in the "Grey" areas of our words and actions, and never strike our Neighbor with a "Black" word or action. "Black" representing "Right Square on the Nose" of either your Neighbor or the Judge downtown.

Chuckle, Chuckle, eh!! I trust this has been helpful for your understanding of the Subject.

Thanks for Listening, It was a pleasure, as ever in,

"The Spirit of Goodness",

B.H., M.A., L.W. "Saint Bill" (Coach)

Previews Institute

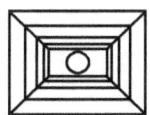

PREVIEWISM
Our World is Beautiful, Yes, Multi-Cultural

Dear Friends and Children of all ages:

Our Favorite proverb is, *My Summit (Temple) is my Home & My Home is My (Temple) Summit and My Congregation is my Family.* Oh yes, and that includes You.

This is because God is Omnipresent and each Family unit has the Right to Direct communication with God the Real, "The Spirit of Goodness", and all of Its Children (Angels).

Let me tell you a Parable to elaborate.... If you went to your nearest Apple Tree farmer, you would have to ask permission to take an apple of the Tree.

It is God's Apple but the Farmer says He owns It SO you have to ask permission.

Well, you ask permission and Eat the Apple, and when you are finished you have several Seeds in your hand. So you go home and plant the Seed in your Garden. And when It bears Apples you do not have to ask permission for an Apple because they are now yours for Free. Yes, Direct from God. For ever and permanently Free.

Well, you know the Tree of Life Is the Tree of Love and Forgiveness. And so as a child you go to a certain type of Temple and they say, around here you have to Ask for Forgiveness or you are out of Luck. But you know that everyone around you in the world tells you that Love and Forgiveness are Free, Unconditionally Free gifts of God the Real, "The Spirit of Goodness". So you go to this type of Temple until you are through High School and then you take a Few Seeds of Truth and go on your way. As you get a little older you set up a household and Plant the Seeds of Truth in a flower Pot in your Living room, and if you wish throughout the Home. After a few years your Family find that Love and Forgiveness are Free Gifts of God.

Unconditionally and Permanently Free Gifts that you do not have to ask for, they are just there as part of Life. Free.

Well, you know the wise person does never go back to a certain type of Temple, because they teach False doctrine. The True Doctrine of God says we all have Direct Communication with God because we were all given a "Sense of Judgement" to use to Judge (Decide) Right from Wrong and naturally learn to avoid the Pit falls of life and not have to Suffer needlessly. This is a Natural Instinct of creation. Anything to the contrary is pure Fiction, Fantasy, and Illusion of misguided, selfrighteous, Extortionist, Glory Seeking Idiots or Lunitics.

Yes, folks, God's Love and Forgiveness is Free,. take it and pass it on for Free and It will grow and grow into something more beautifull than you can at first imagine, allowing you to realize that the World is a beautifull place to live in and in fact Heaven on Earth as God meant it to be. Yes, if only we stay in Direct Communication with God the Real, "The Spirit of Goodness", and all of Its angels. The most natural being our "Sense of Judgement". Yes, It leads us to the Truth and the Truth sets us Free. Yes, into Direct contact with God.

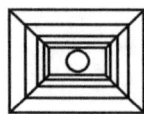

PREVIEWISM
Our World is Beautiful, Yes, Multi-Cultural

Yes, folks, our favorite Proverb is found in "The Compass", a New Bible, The EverLast Testament,. The Fruit of the Tree of Love and Forgiveness,. Growen in the Home of "Saint Bill" from the Seed of Truth that we are all created and born in the Image of God, and as such we are Not Perfect.

Yes, folks, "Saint Bill's" favorite saying is: Do not worship me, worship God the Real, "The Spirit of Goodness", because the Good Characteristics we learn to use belong to God, Not to me. Yes, folks, any and all Good in the world is to the Glory of God, and we should only Thank God for that and we shall always stay Free.

Thanks for Listening, folks, It is a long story, but I trust you Understand the Short One.

Yours truly, as ever in, "The Spirit of Goodness",

"Saint Bill" (Coach)

Previews Institute

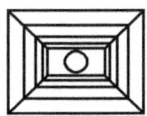

PREVIEWISM
Our World is Beautiful, Yes, Multi-Cultural

Dear Friends and Children of all ages:

Today we want to touch on two little discussed ideas.

1)   It seems that the "Old World" has more Faith in The Shadow (Satan) than It has in God. Yes, you see, Satan Retaliates, while God Forgives.

The Fruits of Retaliation come quickly, and they are a Curse upon Oneself, as we reap what we sow. Yes, "You Reap what You Sow" is Man's Law, and It is a Curse upon Oneself.

God's Law is: "Look up, and Forgive one-another and Reap only Blessings, barring the weather of course".

Yes, the Fruits of Forgiveness come Slowly, but they do come, and Many-fold, and they are a Blessing to all.

But remember, Hail Storms are the Exception, and we should not change the Rule because of the Exception.

Yes, we must have Patience and Faith in God's Law and It will work for the Good of all Humankind, as It is a Blessing upon us all.

2)   God does not want us to Kill, especially not Ourselves. Therefore, It is a Lie to think that one has to Die for His/Her cause.,

A Good Cause is God's Cause, and It takes time to accomplish, and so we should not try to Rush or Force our way on a slow changing Humanity.

It is a Lie to think that you have to Die to accomplish your Goal. Satan says, Kill yourself and many others with you, and I will make you a "Martyr". This is seeking to Glorify Oneself and Satan, Not God.

God says, A Good cause never requires that you Kill yourself for It. If you have to Kill yourself, for It,. It is Satan's Cause, Not God's.

This re-affirms that God does not want a Sacrifice, God wants Obedience to Its good Words and Instructions. And if It does not get Obedience immediately, God says, Forgiven,. we have lots of Time to learn and do it better next time.

Yes, God is Seldom in a hurry, but rather just continues on Its way of Goodness and always allows us Freedom of Choice to follow God (Goodness) or follow Illusion (Satan) (Complete Waste).

Yes, God always says, I will not Retaliate because I Forgive you for your Ignorance and Lack of experience and sometimes a Lack of Attention to your Lessons.

You Stupid Bastards,. I Forgive you because you are My Children, and Grand Children, and My Great Grand Children and so on and on,

---

THE TRADITION OF "CHANGE FOR THE BETTER" IS BORN IN *"PREVIEWISM"*
www.previews-inc.com
Make 10 - 20 Copies per week and Pass It On. - God will be well Pleased.

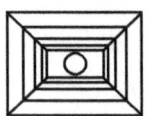

PREVIEWISM
Our World is Beautiful, Yes, Multi-Cultural

Yes, God is very Old and Wise and has Learned the "Good Way" the easy way, not the Hard way. And this was accomplished by using Its "Sense of Judgement" and following It with Patience, Kindness, Love, and Forgiveness, and so on and on.

Yes, Folks, Learn to Judge one-another as God Judges you,. That is to provide the Alternative, then Forgive, Not Condemn, Bless, Not Curse, Reward, Not Punish.

In this way, the Easy way, You will find Happiness, Decency, Prosperity, and Peace of Mind, as you learn to live in Peace and Harmony with your Nieghbors.

Thanks for Listening, It was a pleasure,

Yours truly, as ever in,

"The Spirit of Goodness"`,

W.J. (Bill) Handel, M.A., L.W. "Saint Bill" (Coach)

Previews Institute,

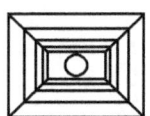

PREVIEWISM
Our World is Beautiful, Yes, Multi-Cultural

Dear Friends and Children of all ages:

Today we have another Question for you.

Why did God choose to be Forgiving? and Not Condemning.

Answer: Because It realized that It was not Perfect.

Yes, to think that One is Perfect is "Illusion", and so we must forgive to stay in Reality. Yes, Illusion causes Discension and discension is not of God, because God is very Peaceful, and Loving.

When we sometimes choose to condemn, we are being Hypocrites and bring condemnation upon our selves, as we Reap what we Sow. And this is Negative and Foolish.

We must choose to be like God and Realize that we are not Perfect to become Loving and Forgiving. Then we will be living by God's Law, which is: "Look Up, and Forgive one-another and Reap only Blessings, barring the Weather of course".

Yes, God is like the Weather, It is not Perfect, and because of "Illusion" we sometimes have "Hailstorms", but Hailstorms are the exception and so we must not change the Rule because of the exception. Because if we change the Rule we are falling into more Illusion and more Hailstorms. So you see, we have no choice but to Forgive one-another as God Forgives us. Otherwise we are being Foolish or Insane.

Yes, God gave us a "Sense of Judgement" to use to Judge (Decide) right from wrong for ourselves and allow all others the same privelege because we are not Perfect,.

Yes, God the Real, "The Spirit of Goodness", says, Learn to Judge one-another as I Judge you, which is to Provide the alternative, then Forgive, not Condemn, Bless, not Curse, Reward, not Punish. Yes, be Positive, not Negative.

Because to be Positive is to be Alive, To be Negative is to be Dead.

And God is not Dead.

Thanks for Listening, as ever in,

"The Spirit of Goodness",

B.H., M.A., L.W. "Saint Bill".

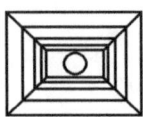

PREVIEWISM
Our World is Beautiful, Yes, Multi-Cultural

Dear Friends and Children of all ages:

Today we are going to talk about the God we do not know and the God we know.

The God we do not know has Absolutes, and these Absolutes are Real, we think, or it seems, but we do not know for sure.

The God we know has no Absolutes. The God we know is not one extreme or the other, The God we know is a Compromise on the greater side of the Positive.

The Positive always overwhelmes the Negative, and if It does not overwhelm without a Fight, then It overwhelms with a Fight, but It always Overwhelms, we think, or so it seems. Of this we can be Sure. Yes, just look around you, and you will see the Evidence.

Yes, the God we know is Real as It is "The Spirit of Goodness" and there is Goodness all around us in both the Physical and Spiritual sense.

Yes, there are two kinds of Faith. Blind Faith and Applied Faith.

Blind faith is a Leap into the Darkness. Applied faith is a result of the evidence you see all around you.

Those that live by Blind faith live in confusion, pain and suffering.

Those that live by Applied faith live in Happiness, Decency, Prosperity, and Peace of mind, knowing that God is the same Today, Yesterday, and Tomorrow. Yes, even unto "Life Eternal" in the Physical, Material, and Spiritual sense.

Young people have a lot of Blind faith because they have not had the opportunity to Apply the Evidence (Principals) of life, but when they do they achieve Applied Faith and receive the Rewards.

So there you go, Children, Have fun!! Chuckle, Chuckle, eh!!

Thanks for Listening, as ever in,

"The Spirit of Goodness",

"Saint Bill", (Coach)

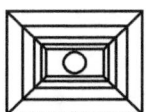

PREVIEWISM
Our World is Beautiful, Yes, Multi-Cultural

Dear Friends and Children of all ages:

Are You Going to "JOIN" Our Temple (Summit) "Our Place of Worship is Our HOME". We Represent God the Real, "THE SPIRIT OF GOODNESS".

Therefore, we have "Jesus" the Good Man on Our Side.

Christ (Messiah) the Bad Guy, Has been Defeated.

Yes, Jesus, Represented God the Real, "The Spirit of Goodness". (John 7,vs.16-18) Christ (Messiah) Represented God the Fraud (The Shadow). (Acts 26, vs.16-18)

Jesus said, You are either For me or Against me, You can not be Both. Yes, You are either a "Saint" or a Sinner,. You can not be Both.

Christ (Messiah) says, You are a Sinner, and if you sometimes feel Positive. Then you are Both Sinner and Saint,. (Which is a Lie, according to Jesus)

Yes, Jesus said, You are a "Saint", So start Acting like One.

Christ (Messiah) said, You are a "Sinner", knowing that if you think so,. You will continue to Act like One.

Yes, Folks, a true "Saint" is a Previewlite, and a Previewlite is a Child of God, who serves God the Real, "The Spirit of Goodness".

A Christian (Messiahn) is a Child of God, who serves "The Shadow", God the Fraud. and as such they call themselves "Sinners".

But we know that in God's Eye we are never Condemned, but Always Forgiven, and as such we are always "Saints" in God's Eye, because we were all Created in the Image of God, and as such we are not Perfect (Dead), But Rather Eternally Alive in Spirit, Body, and Mind. (Thank you, Dear God, Thank you)

Yours truly, as ever in, "The Spirit of Goodness",

Saint Bill,

Previews Institute

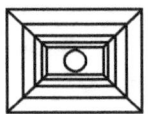

PREVIEWISM
Our World is Beautiful, Yes, Multi-Cultural

Dear Friends and Children of all ages:

With and By "The Compass", "The Sermons of Saint Bill" and "Object, Masters Degree", by "Saint Bill", Jesus the man has been Vindicated. He was a pretty Good man, a bit confused, but none the less pretty good. Almost as good as the "Super, Super Excellent, Saint Bill".

Yes, Folks, "Jesus the Man" has been Vindicated, and "Jesus the God" has been Crucified under the Heel of "Saint Bill", because "Jesus the God" was a Fraud. Yes, "Jesus the Man" represented God the Real, "The Spirit of Goodness", John 7,vs,16-18, and "Jesus the God" represented The Shadow (Illusion) (Satan), Acts 26,vs.16-18,.(2 Thes.2,vs.9-11),

Yes, The Shadow's favorite disguise is a Sheep Skin Coat and the Mask of a Good Man. And when "Saint Bill" started to use his "Sense of Judgement" and started to Judge (Decide) right from wrong, true from false, possible from impossible, Positive from Negative, Reality from Illusion,. The Mask and Coat disintegrated and all that remained was an "Earthworm" seeming to appear on the Surface. Yes, The Shadow.

So "Saint Bill" put his Foot down Hard on the Worm and It went to Slitherines. Then "Saint Bill" Rubbed with his Rubber Rubber Heel until there was nothing left but Dust. Then "Saint Bill" realized that The Shadow (Satan) as with any other Shadow is just an Illusion, pure Fantasy,. and when described, pure Lie.

Yes, Folks, Reality is God and God is Reality, Not Fantasy, and the Reality is Heaven, Earth and all that is in It and on It, and "The Spirit of Goodness" that lives in Heaven, in the World, and in your Heart, Mind and Soul, and It is Eternal in every Sense Physical, Material, and Spiritual. Thank you, Dear God, Thank you.

Yes, today is a Glorious day for "Jesus the Man", "Saint Bill", and All of Humankind,

Thanks for Listening, Take it to Heart, You will be Delighted"

As ever in,

"The Spirit of Goodness",

"Saint Bill" (Coach)

Previews Institute.

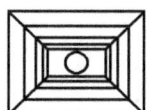

PREVIEWISM
Our World is Beautiful, Yes, Multi-Cultural

Dear Friends and Children of all ages:

Today we are going to discuss several topics.

1) All Religions in the World serve God the Real, "The Spirit of Goodness", in fullness, except "Judaism". Yes, we find that in Life "Aggression" is a Sin against Humanity. And "Self-Defence" is an Act of God. And the First Aggressor in the World was a "Jew" because He/She brought Sin into the World. Yes, the first Aggression was when Someone called his/her neighbor a Sinner and the Defense was to say, No, I am a "Saint" because We were all created in the Image of God and the Image of God is Forgiveness. And Forgiveness keeps us Clean as a Whistle.

Yes, a Child of God, not a Child of Illusion. So you are Forgiven for your Ignorance. But the Jew (Judaism) pressed Its luck by, being unable or refusing, to face Reality and Understanding that we are all Free as Children of God. And so he/she continued to call his/her neighbor a "Sinner" until his/her neighbor said, Be Gone, Illusion.

Yes, The Saint walked away and went his/her way in Happiness, Decency, Prosperity and Peace of mind. And the Jew (Judaism) is still fighting with those that believe him/her. But thank God most in the World are above the Animals and use their "Sense of Judgement" and Judge (Decide) right from wrong, Reality from Illusion before they Act. And in this way stay Free Spirited and Good Natured. Thus being Forgiving. Thank you, Dear God, Thank you.

2) Now, we are going to compare "Capitalism" with "Socialism or Communism".

Capitalism gives you the Property and says Its yours. And you Feel good and Happy.

And you work toward "Prosperity". This gives you a Sense of Decency and Peace of Mind.

Socialism says, The Property is Mine, All belongs to me, and you are a Poor person. You must work for Me all your life and when It is over, I will pay for your Funeral.

Chuckle, Chuckle, eh!

Thanks for Listening,

as ever in, "The Spirit of Goodness",

"Saint Bill" (Coach),

Previews Institute

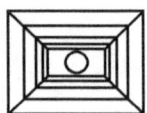

PREVIEWISM
Our World is Beautiful, Yes, Multi-Cultural

Dear Friends and Children of all ages:

The Gateway of Hell (Illusion) has passed and is now Behind us, and We now find we are in the Kingdom of Heaven with God, (Reality), and the Reality is "The Spirit of Goodness" all around us in the Physical, Material, and Spiritual sense. And we find that "The Spirit of Goodness" is not Perfect (but Alive) and Far, Far, Far, Far ahead of us in Learning and Experience. Thus finding it very easy to always Understand and Forgive us with the continual Ignorance we are in Until we Reach the Roots of the "Tree of Life" which are above the Clouds.

The Tree of Life is the Tree of Love and Forgiveness and Love and Forgiveness are the Children (Angels) of "The Spirit of Goodness", and "The Spirit of Goodness" has three Characteristics which are, "A Free Spirit", "A Sense of Judgement" and "A Good Nature".

The Sense of Judgement being the ability to Judge (Decide) right from wrong, Reality from Illusion,. Leads us to God's oldest Child (Angel), that being "The Spirit of Truth", and the "Truth" keeps us Free.

If we allow our "Sense of Judgement" to develop to a High degree of accuracy, then Our Good Nature grows Big and Strong to overcome Its natural Weakness, which is Ignorance,. and Ignorance allows "Illusion" (The Shadow) into our Mind.

So the First Step in the Newness of Life is to "Cast Illusion Out", by using your Sense of Judgement and Judging (Deciding) right from wrong (Reality from Illusion). Yes, My Dear Friends and Children, Learn to Judge one-another as God Judges you,. That is to provide the Alternative, then Forgive, Not Condemn, Reward, Not Punish, Yes, Bless, Not Curse. Yes, to Judge is to provide the means by which we See ourselves as others See us,. which is a Must, Lest we fall into total Confusion and Illusion.

Thank you, Dear God, Thank you, for the Insight and Ability (Strength) to Judge (Decide) Right from Wrong. Yes, God the Real from God the Fraud.

Thanks for Listening,

Yours truly, as ever in, "The Spirit of Goodness",

B.H., M.A., L.W. "Saint Bill" (Coach)

Previews Institute of Universal Philosophy.

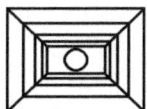

PREVIEWISM
Our World is Beautiful, Yes, Multi-Cultural

Dear Friends and Children of all ages:

Now, for some Business Smarts

- You can not get Rich on the Back of DISATISFIED Customers. Because they will Buck you Off into the Dust.
- You will get Rich on the Back of SATISFIED Customers. Because they will carry you Along Up High, in Glee.

There are Four kinds of Psychology in use at all times and when we use them properly, we live in Happiness, Decency, Prosperity and Peace of Mind.

They are Positive psychology, Negative psychology, False positive psychology, and False negative psychology.

We all know what Positive and Negative psychology is and what it does. But now let me explain the False Positive and the False Negative. First let me say that False Positive is Negative, and False Negative is Positive.

Eg.: You may sound Positive when you say, "I can do anything" I can walk on Water, I can Raise the Dead, I can move a Mountain by saying Mountain Move. But as you go along you find you Fail, Fail, Fail, and Fail.

And you become Disheartened, Pessimistic, and Negative, and Ultimately Sadistic, Yes, This is False Positive and It is ultimately Negative.

Eg.: You may sound Negative when you say, "You do it this Way, or I will Punish you because I will Hate you..

But as you go along, when the Crunch comes, You say, Forgiven,. I will give you two more Chances to Do it Right, O.K.? And you have made Someone HAPPY, and Encouraged, etc.. Yes, this is False Negative, but It is ultimately Positive.

(YOU will be Interested in Becoming a "FOUNDING PARTNER", when you Understand our Object)
"Call or Come in, Now!!!!"

"Saint Bill"

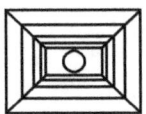

PREVIEWISM
Our World is Beautiful, Yes, Multi-Cultural

Dear Friends and Children of all ages:

Today we have another Explanation of the "Trinity".

"One puts Man before God (The Father) (Juda) (The Shadow's Servant) "One puts God before Man (The Son) (Christ) (Messiah) (The Shadow)

One says, "We are Equal and One" (The Spirit of Goodness) (God the Real)

Two are Frauds, Yes, the "I" "I" "I" guys.

One is Real and True, Yes, We, me, my Neighbor, and God are Equal Partners.

A "Saint" is a Child of God, who serves God (The Spirit of Goodness) (Forgiven).

A "Sinner" is a Child of God, who serves Satan (The Shadow)(Self-Condemned)

A wise Man once said that God says, You are either For me or Against me. You can not be both.. (John 7, v. 16-17)

A "Saint" is a person who knows It is not Perfect. (Living in Reality) A "Sinner" is a person who thinks It is Perfect. (Living in Illusion)

Yes, we all know that Nothing is Perfect, and The Shadow is a Nothing. (Illusion).

All of Reality is "Alive".

All of Illusion is "Dead".

Therefore, we all go to Heaven, because we all have a certain degree of Reality. In the Amphitheatre of Heaven, some will be in Centre Stage with God,. Some will be in the Front Row, Some will be in the Middle Rows, Some will be in the Back Row, Some will be in the Standing Room, and Some will be at "The Door".

Thanks for Listening,

as ever in, "The Spirit of Goodness",

(Saint Bill) "Coach".

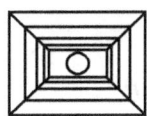

PREVIEWISM
Our World is Beautiful, Yes, Multi-Cultural

Dear Friends and Children of all ages:

Today we are going to talk about a Dear friend of Mine.

First we are going to explain that this Friend had three Personalities.

1) Jesus the Fictional Bad Guy. (Christ)(Messiah)(Shadow) (2 Thes. 2, vs.9-11)

2) Jesus the Fictional Good Guy. (Perfect) (Dead) (Useless) (A Collection of all the Real and Good thoughts of all the Good people of all time, attributed to one Man.) (This would not be an error except that they said he was Perfect, and this make him Fictional, because we all know that Perfection is an Illusion.)

3) Jesus the Ordinary Man, (A Victum of his Up-bringing) (Brought up in a Society of Psychic Fortune Tellers, Sick-Psyche Psychologists, and Hate Mongers) (This poor man was told when he was only Five (5) years old that he did not have an Earthly Father, and that he would be Killed one day as a Sacrifice)

(He was told not to worry, because this was God's wish for him) (This poor man was totally Mentally Abused and grew up to be totally Confused)

See: The Book of Insights, Chapter 1, Part "C",. In "The Compass", page 182-183.
See: The Sermons of "Saint Bill", Sermon 1132B, page 56.

Dear Friends:

Of these three personalities, the First two I abhor (Cast Out). Jesus the Ordinary Man and all of his troubles, I can relate to and Understand, I went through much the same problems in describing and defending God the real, "The Spirit of Goodness", and all of Its children (angels), the oldest being "The Spirit of Truth" and the youngest being "The Spirit of Enthusiasm".

The only difference is that I was not betrayed because I spoke with "Truth", and not Confusion. (Yes, I looked to the "Future" and not the "Past')

(And "The Future" is filled with Bliss.)

Thanks for Listening,

as ever in, "The Spirit of Goodness"

"Saint Bill" (Coach)

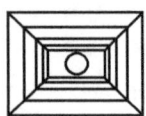

PREVIEWISM
Our World is Beautiful, Yes, Multi-Cultural

Dear Friends and Children of all ages:

Just another Summary

1)   The Shadow does not know the Truth. The Truth reveals that The Shadow is Ignorant. Therefore The Shadow is afraid of the Truth because the Truth dethrones The Shadow.

The One thing that Leads us to the Truth is our "Sense of Judgement", yes, our ability to Judge (Decide) right from wrong, Reality from Illusion, possible from impossible, Charity from Extortion, true from false, yes, God from The Shadow. So The Shadow says, "Do not Judge", just believe what I say, I would not Lie to you, would I,. If it were not so I would tell you, right?..(Well,the Brazen Bastard.) Then The Shadow says, "There is only One way to get to Heaven", and that is to Bow Down and worship Me, because if you do as I say and never make any decisions of your own, I will make you Wise, and you will receive Eternal Life as your Reward from Me. Oh,yes, I am God, believe me, there is no other. (Well, the Cocksucker) Yes, The Glory Seeking Extortionist is holding up a Balloon full of knowledge based on Ignorance and Lies and holds out God's Gift as Its own. and Deceives a Few and then claims It (The Shadow) rules the World. (Well, what a Laugh) We all know that God the Real, "The Spirit of Goodness", rules the world. This is why there is a lot more Good in the World than there is Bad.

Yes, 1 in 900 is in Jail.

1 in 100 is a criminal on the loose.

1 in 10 is a "Shadow Worshipper", but only on the surface (Really Hypocrites)

That leaves 88% of people (Society) that are worshipping and Glorifying God the Real, The Spirit of Goodness, because It says, "Use your Sense of Judgement" and come closer to the Truth and Reap the Benifits while you are here on Earth. Heaven will come only to soon, but It will be beautiful, Just as life on Earth can be.

Thanks for Listening,

as ever in, "The Spirit of Goodness",

"Saint Bill" (Coach)

Yes, Life can be Beautiful when we improve the Weather Forecast!!

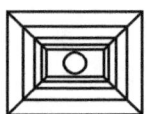

PREVIEWISM
Our World is Beautiful, Yes, Multi-Cultural

What God?

Dear Friends and Children of All ages:

Today we have a Question for You. What God do you Dwell on during your Daily activities?

We hear some say, they dwell on Buddha,. Some say, they dwell on Mohammed,. Some say, they dwell on Confucous,. Some say, they dwell on Singh,. Some say, they dwell on Jesus,. Some say, they dwell on Juda (the Father), and Some say, they dwell on "The Holy Spirit" of all of these Men.

And we say, All inferior, because God is not Holy (Hoity-Toity, Self-righteous), God is both Humble and Proud given the proper circumstances.

And we say, All inferior, because if any of these Men say they are Perfect, they are Liars, because we know that Nothing is Perfect, and if we sometimes think we are Perfect, we are under an Illusion. Yes, Hoity-Toity, Self-righteous Idiots.

Yes, Folks, we say, the above Gods are all Inferior to God the Real, "The Spirit of Goodness". Yes, we at "Previews" say, we dwell on the Spirit of God the Real, which is "The Spirit of Goodness". And "The Spirit of Goodness" is not Perfect, but just Far, Far, Far, Far ahead of us in Learning and Experience, making It very easy to always Understand, Love, and Forgive us for our Ignorance (Shortcomings).

Yes, Folks, we who Relate God to a Man are always Inferior to those of us who Relate God to a Spirit because we know we are talking about "The Spirit of Goodness". "The Spirit of Goodness" is not Almighty, because God can not Lie, God can not Steal, God can not Kill, God can not walk on Water, God can not tempt us to do Bad. Yes, God can not do a lot of things. If It did It would be a Two-faced Hypocrite.

Yes, Folks, "The Spirit of Goodness" has three main Characteristics, being: It has "A Free Spirit", "A Sense of Judgement", and "A Good Nature".

"The Spirit of Goodness" with Its characteristics has many Children (Angels), the oldest being "The Spirit of Truth" and the youngest being "The Spirit of Enthusiasm", and of course there are many in between.

Dwell on this Folks, and you will come to think about the birds and the bees and the flowers and the trees and things called love, forgiveness, truth and reality and many more such wonderful and beautiful characteristics as you come closer and closer to God the Real, "The Spirit of Goodness". Yes, Folks, with your Help, Support, and "Thoughts of Goodness to come", we will achieve Happiness, Decency, Prosperity, and Peace of Mind for all of Humankind within Three hundred years, and all will live in Peace and Harmony.

Thanks for Listening, as ever in,

"The Spirit of Goodness",

"Saint Bill" (Coach)

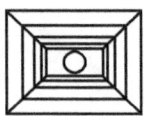

PREVIEWISM
Our World is Beautiful, Yes, Multi-Cultural

Dear Friend:

Each and Every member of Society must do his/her part in maintaining and or improving the National and International Psychology that governs the degree of Happiness, Decency, Prosperity, and Peace of Mind we enjoy during our Life.

Freedom of Thought means Freedom of Worship and each and every one of us is Entitled to this.. What we need to achieve this Freedom is the support of like minded organizations and people.

In "The Compass" our favorite Proverb is:

> "My Summit (Temple) is my Home, and My Home is my (Temple) Summit, and My Congregation is my Family"

Oh, yes, and that includes You. Yes, the World being one Big Family must Decentralize to maintain Freedom of Thought or Freedom of Worship or Freedom of Religion and Culture.

We at "Previews" have taken the Initiative and established a world wide web site that is accessable to all looking to the Future and Newness of Life. The Desire for Freedom of Thought is a Positive motive and we know that Positive Psychology is of God the Real, "The Spirit of Goodness"..Negative Psychology is of God the Fraud, The Shadow (Illusion)..Positive Psychology is far, far ahead in the game of Life and we all have to do our part to keep it that way.

To you the Head of a Household the cost of maintaining and improving the degree of Freedom of Thought is very reasonable. In fact all you have to do is Buy a Customized Sign to establish your Summit (Temple) as your Home, for all the neighborhood to see where to find the way to Positive Psychology and all that it means. Yes, a One-time investment to do your part in Telling the World of the Truth.

At present this means $200.00. How about it? Make a Wise decision and Go for It. You and your Family will be Glad you did.

We thank you now for your Help and Support in our Objective.

Yours truly, as ever in, "The Spirit of Goodness",

W.J.(Bill) Handel, M.A., L.W. "Saint Bill" (Coach)

Previews Institute

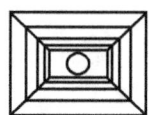

PREVIEWISM
Our World is Beautiful, Yes, Multi-Cultural

Dear Friends and Children of All ages:

A wise man once said, "You are either For God or Against God, You can not be Both".

Yes, you either live Under the Law or Above the Law,. You can not be doing Both, unless you are a Hypocrite.

Now a Question: What does it mean to live Under the Law?

Answer: When you live by Man's Law, You reap what you sow. You are living Under the Law because it causes a Vicious circle of Punish, Punish, Punish, Therefore Life is very miserable, Under the Law.

People who live this way call themselves "Sinners because they know God is not pleased."

Now another Question: What does it mean to live Above the Law?

Answer: You are living Above the Law when you live by God's Law, which is,

"Look Up, and forgive one-another and Reap only Blessings, barring the weather of course". This causes a Benevolent circle because you obey the Law as best you can, and forgive one-another when you Bend the Law. Yes, If you can find the Loop holes you are Bending the Law, but not Breaking It. And if you Forgive yourself and others for these discrepancies, you are always receiving Blessings; Yes, a Benevolent circle. This makes Life a Joy to live. People who live this way call themselves "Saints" because they know God is Pleased.

Of course we know that because of the Nature of God and the Saints, they consider the others "Saints" too, because we Forgive them for their Ignorance (Shortcomings).

Thanks for Listening,

as ever in, "The Spirit of Goodness",

B.H., M.A., L.W. "Saint Bill" (Coach)

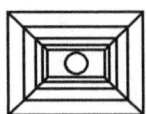

PREVIEWISM
Our World is Beautiful, Yes, Multi-Cultural

Dear Friends and Children of All ages:

A Tribute to "Little Britney"

The "Amphitheatre of Heaven" is very "Large", and so Some of us are at the Doors around the Outer Limits of Light,. "Ushering in" the new comers from out of the light, into the Light.

Some of us are in the "Standing Room", next within.

Some of us are in the "Back Rows". Some of us are in the "Middle Rows". Some of us are in the "Front Rows" above the Clouds.

And finally, Some of us are in "Centre Stage" with God.

And so you see, The Amphitheatre of Heaven has a Tier for every Language, and God speaks with "Actions" from "Centre Stage", because Actions speak Louder than Words.

Yes, we all Interpret the "Actions of God" in our own Special way.

Yes, we are all Individuals, and we all see Life a little different, but we can be Assured that "Little Britney" is going to be in the "Front Row" or in "Centre Stage" with God.

Either way, She is going to see Life just as God presents it, and She will see "Mostly" Good Times, and Some Bad Times. She will see Mostly Happy Times, and "Some" Sad Times. And "Little Britney" will send us her Interpretations, Via, Mental Telepathy from God in Heaven.

Yes, Folks, "Little Britney" will live Eternally in the Hearts, Minds, and Souls of All generations of the Past, Present, and Future, because She was, is, and always will be a Part of the Family of God. Yes, we are All Angels in our own Special way. Thank God for Creating us in Its Image.

Thank you, Dear God, Thank you.. Thank you, Folks, for Listening,

Yours truly, as ever in, "The Spirit of Goodness",

W.J.(Bill) Handel, M.A., L.W, (Coach)

"Previews Institute of Universal Philosophy".

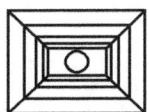

PREVIEWISM
Our World is Beautiful, Yes, Multi-Cultural

Dear Friends and Children of All ages:

I want to address the Day today with a word from Britney.

Yes, I was talking to Britney yesterday and as Little as she was,. She said to me,. "Don't you people Cry too much, because the Show must go on".

And so in carrying on the Show of the Day, I want to tell you a story to advance the purpose and cause of Your Lord.

As you know, I am a Multiculturalist, A Canadian, and as such I have learned many Languages, Namely Many Religions. As a wise man once said, "In my Father's house there are Many Mansions".

My main Purpose in life is to advance the purpose and cause of God the Real, "The Spirit of Goodness". But in my travels I find I can advance the Cause of many Lords.

And so today I want to tell you this story to advance the Purpose and Cause of Your Lord Jesus.

As I arrived at the Hospital today to visit with Brigitte and Greg there were a few people ahead of me. And so I sat down beside a young lady who was also waiting to see Brigitte. We were not saying too much until she said something in the way of Religion. When she spoke of the subject of Religion, I said, that was Great, very Good.

I said to her, Her name was Donna, I said, Donna that brings me to a question for you. And she said, O.K., Shoot.

I said, if I were to say to you, "I think you are a "Saint", would you agree with me? And she said, Yes. And I said, Great, That makes Two of Us. Now let us stand Back to Back and take on the World.

She paused and said, Well, sometimes I am a "Sinner" too.. And I said, No you are not, You are a Saint in God's Eye, and Jesus said, You are either For God, or you are Against God, you can not be Both. So you remember, You are a Saint.

in God's Eye,. And that is what matters,. And if your Neighbors once say, You are a Sinner,. You remember, they are speaking out of Ignorance. So you Forgive them for their Ignorance and remember, You are a "Saint".

Yes, remember, You are Forgiven before you start your day and you are Forgiven when you end your day.. and while you are Sleeping you can do nothing wrong. So you are always a "Saint" in God's Eye.

Thank you, Dear God, Thank you. Thank you Friends for Listening,

Yours truly, as ever in, "The Spirit of Goodness",

W. J.(Bill) Handel, M.A., L.W. Alias, "Saint Bill" (Coach)

Previews Institute,

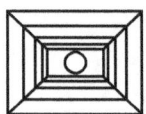

PREVIEWISM
Our World is Beautiful, Yes, Multi-Cultural

Dear Friends and Children of All ages:

Today we have a Parable for you, wherein we want you to Pretend you are God. O.K., Here we go.

God, the Real, has a Circle of Friends,. They are called the Human Race.

God, "The Spirit of Goodness", is in the Centre of the Circle as a Global Eye that can see All at the same time. It sees many Families hand in hand watching It throughout the day.

God is very warm and compassionate as It says, "I love you" in Its usual fashion, to All at the same time.

God is an Excellent Host as It invites All to Two special gatherings every day. Yes, the Ups and the Downs. God sometimes finds it very difficult to convince everyone that, although It can not find equal time for everyone, It still Loves you All equally all the time

And so God sends out Assurances that relieve our anxiety, such as, "The First come Last, and the Last come First". or, "Have faith in my words at all times when my Actions seem to miss you, because I can not be All things to All people All the time". Yes, Just remember, I love you All equally all the time, and I Forgive you All for your Shortcomings all the time, and so You are All Saints in my Eye at all times. Let nothing or No-one shake that Faith because I am Omnipresent. Yes, as the Host, I am in "Centre Stage" all the time, and you must have Faith that I am Watching you All with a Loving Eye all the time.

Thank you, Dear God, Thank you,.

Thanks for Listening,

as ever in, "The Spirit of Goodness",

B.H., M.A., L.W. "Saint Bill" (Coach)

Previews Institute

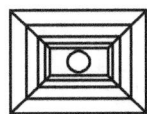

PREVIEWISM
Our World is Beautiful, Yes, Multi-Cultural

Dear Friends and Children of All ages:

Today we have a few more Questions.

1) What is the difference between an Isrealite and a Canadian?

    Answer: None what so ever. Absolutely none,. Because All of Humankind were created, conceived and born in the Image of God.
    Yes, we are all equal with God and one-another.

2) Are you a Gentile (Gentleperson) or are you a Jew (a Barbarian)?

    Answer: You are most likely a Gentile because only 1 in 400 is a Jew.

    Gentiles practice Positive psychology such as: Previewism, Hinduism, Confucianism,etc. Jews practice Negative psychology such as: Judaism, Christianity, Islam, etc.

3) Are you a Jesus person or are you a Christian?

    Answer: A Jesus person is a Gentile.

    A Christian is a Gentile converted to a Jew. (Result: A confused Hypocrite)

Yes, a few of us were Deceived by a shrewd Jew called Saul.. Saul changed his name to Paul and put on a Sheepskin coat and the Mask of a Good man, and continued to preach the Lies and Illusions of the Dark ages.

Saul also changed the word Messiah to Christ and said he was the King of the Jews. But Jesus said, Christ means Messiah and the Messiah is the Jewish God, and Jesus said, the Jewish God is Satan (Illusion) (The Shadow). (Acts 26, v. 16-18)

Therefore Jesus was not the Messiah of the Jews, they rejected him, because Jesus was a Gentile and a Gentile speaks for God and seeks to Glorify God, while the Messiah (Christ) seeks to Glorify himself. (John 7, v. 16-18)

P.S.: We know that Negative psychology leads to Murder and Suicide. We know that Positive psychology leads to a full Life of Bliss.

Thank you, Dear God, Thank you, for an obvious and easy choice.

as ever in, "The Spirit of Goodness",

B.H., M.A., L.W. "Saint Bill" (Coach)

Previews Institute of Universal Philosophy.

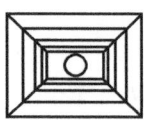

PREVIEWISM
Our World is Beautiful, Yes, Multi-Cultural

Dear Friends and Children of all ages:

Just a few more Questions

1) What does Jesus make You,."A Sinner or A Saint", (Remember, It can not be Both) Answer: The Spirit of God, "The Spirit of Goodness", which Forgave Adam and Eve for misunderstanding Its instructions, was renewed in every generation as Adam and Eve learned to Forgive One-another for their misfortune as a result of Ignorance.

Yes, they also learned to Forgive their Children for their Ignorance and Misfortunes. And they passed on the True knowledge that they gained during their Life here on Earth, and this continued, continues, and will always continue Eternally.

Yes, when Adam and Eve learned to Forgive One-another as God the Real, "The Spirit of Goodness", Forgave them, they also learned to Cast-out the Illusions of the Past.

Yes, they learned that if they do not Cast-out Illusion (The Shadow)(Satan) they would confuse their Children and make them Stumble as they did, do, and always will.

Yes, Illusion when expressed is Lie and So they told their Children not to Lie. Just tell the Truth (Reality). But some of their Children were, are, and always will be "Slow Learners" and so the process of Elimination continues Eternally.

Yes, Folks, the misunderstanding that Adam and Eve had was that while God said, "Take and Eat of the Fruit of the tree of knowledge of Good and Waste, yes, Learn to Judge (Decide) right from wrong, as I Judge you, and that is to provide the alternative, then Forgive, Not Condemn, Reward, Not Punish, yes, Bless, Not Curse", "Do not Blame the other for your Misfortunes, and Strike at each other, but rather accept your own Blame and Forgive yourself and One-another as I Forgive you".

Yes, Folks, It is a Learning process from the Beginning and always will be World without End. And God created "Life in the Womb", Life on Earth, and "Life in Heaven" from the Beginning, And It will continue Forever and Ever (Eternally).

And So you see, Jesus was a "Saint" just like you and I, and he died a natural death and went to Heaven just like Adam and Eve and all of their Descendents of Present and the Future. Yes, Folks, God has no Past, just a Present and a Future, as we Recycle into and out of the Future.

Yes, this is what Adam and Eve were talking about and Jesus was one of the many who passed it on, and Each of us is a "Saint" as we pass on the Truth, and Cast-Out Illusion (The Shadow).

Thanks for Listening, as ever in, "The Spirit of Goodness",

"Saint Bill", (Coach)

Previews Institute of Universal Philosophy.

THE TRADITION OF "CHANGE FOR THE BETTER" IS BORN IN *"PREVIEWISM"*
www.previews-inc.com
Make 10 - 20 Copies per week and Pass It On. - God will be well Pleased.

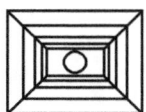

PREVIEWISM
Our World is Beautiful, Yes, Multi-Cultural

Dear Friends and Children of All ages:

Today we have a Story to tell you.

Once upon a Time there were a Hundred men with their wives sitting around a large Round table. They decided to each get a pen and paper to define what God is and does.

After all 200 had written out their definition they all put their paper in the centre of the Table. After a long process of reading each others definition they All agreed that all the definitions could stay in the middle of the Table.

Each of the 200 people had a First name and so they asked, which name shall we give to the definition of the Great God in the Centre of the Table.,

No one wanted to be Offended or left out, so they decided to give the God in the centre of the Table the name of: Jesus, Buddha, Confucius, Juda, Mohammed, Singh, Hindu, Zen, and a Few more.

As you know, folks, I was born into this world in the Minority and so I know Juda and Jesus the most. I found One was a Jew (a Barbarian) and One was a Gentile (a Gentleperson). But after much Meditation I found that only One of the above name was a Fictional character. Yes, you see Real characters seek to Glorify God, while a Fictional character seeks to Glorify Himself. And we all know whose characteristic that is, do we not,. Yes, the Liar. (A Hoity-Toity Selfrighteous Idiot)

As you know, all of the 200 people went their way, and after several Hundred years another Group of people were gathered around a Large round table. Amoung them were people with the name: Jesus, Buddha, Confucous, Juda, Mohammed, Singh, Hindu, Zen, and a Few more common Names including "Saint Bill".

All of these people decided to get a pen and paper to define what God is and Does. Dear Friends, I am running out of room on this page and so I can not give you all of the definitions (some of which were repititions) but I can give you one that caught my Eye. It was, quote, God the Real is "The Spirit of Goodness" and It has "A Free Spirit", "A Sense of Judgement", and "A Good Nature".

"The Spirit of Goodness" has many Children (Angels), the oldest being "The Spirit of Truth" and the youngest being "The Spirit of Enthusiasm", and of course there are many in between. (For further details on what It does see "The Compass" by "Saint Bill" and "The Sermons of Saint Bill" and "Object, Masters Degree, all suppliments to "The Compass" by Author: "Saint Bill".

Thanks for Listening, Folks, as ever in, "The Spirit of Goodness",

"Saint Bill".(Coach)

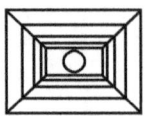

PREVIEWISM
Our World is Beautiful, Yes, Multi-Cultural

Dear Evelyn:

(Just a few words of Encouragement)

We at Previews have found that the Purpose of God in our Life is to make us Happy, Decent, Prosperous, and fill us with Peace of Mind.

And so in your travels in Life as you talk to people,. If you find they are Happy you say, Continue on your way. Because I am Happy too!!

And if you should find you are Unhappy sometime come to me and I will make you Happy. But if you find me Unhappy too, then find someone else to help you.

And so when you talk to people, and you find they are different than you, You ask, "Are you Happy?", and if they say, Yes, "You know what to say".

If they say they are Unhappy, You say, well, I am Happy, and from what you just told me, I would say, that I would have done it this way. What do you think?

If they agree, they will change their way.

If they do not agree, you say, well, all I can do is give you my opinion, because it makes me Happy. That is all I can do, but do not Despair because I am sure that God will Help you some time soon through your own experience or someone like me who is Happy.

That is it Evelyn,. "Start with, "Are you Happy"?. The rest will come as God wills It.

Thanks for Listening, as ever in,

"The Spirit of Goodness",

Good ole Dad, "Saint Bill".

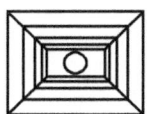

PREVIEWISM
Our World is Beautiful, Yes, Multi-Cultural

Dear Evelyn:

(Just a little further Insight)

According to (John 7, v.16-18)

The Real and True Nature of Humankind is to Glorify God (The Spirit of Goodness).

The Nature of God the Real is to Glorify Humankind.. (Yes, It considers Us all Saints) The Nature of God the Fraud is to Glorify Himself,, (By trying to Reduce Us to Animals) Therefore, In your travels of Life when you are talking to people, about the subject of God, you should always Glorify God by always referring to God the Real and not God the Fraud.,

Secondly, you should not mention what Religion you practice until someone asks you. Because if you push your Religion, you are Glorifying yourself and not God. Yes, let them hear what God has done in your Life and if they never ask what Religion you are, then so be It. But if they ask, Then you can add some Icing.

Yes, a Wise man once said, In God's territory their are many Mansions and their are always New ones being Built, The ones Built on a True Foundation will stand forever. The ones Built on a False Foundation will eventually Fall.

The Hindu Mansion is the predecessor of the Gentiles and is over 15,000 years old, and will stand forever. All related Mansions will stand with It.

The Juda Mansion is a decendent of the Pagan Mansion and the Pagan Mansion has long fallen, and the Juda Mansion is on Its last Breath. All related Mansions will fall with It, because It is the Foundation of Illusion (The Shadow)(Satan) Acts 26,v.16-18)

But All is not lost because the Chandeliers will be saved, and You arm one of Them. Chuckle, Chuckle, eh!!

Thanks for Listening, Evelyn, It was a pleasure.

Yours truly, as ever in, "The Spirit of Goodness",

Good ole Dad, "Saint Bill".

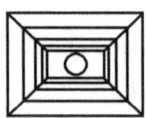

PREVIEWISM
Our World is Beautiful, Yes, Multi-Cultural

Dear Friends:

The following is the Cost of getting Fully-Involved:

1)	Buy "The COMPASS", (A New Bible, "The EverLast Testament")	$ 50.00
2)	Buy an Institutional "SIGN" to establish your "Summit" as your Home and Your Home as your "Summit", and Your Congregation as your Family, (Oh, Yes, and that Includes the whole Neighborhood)	$ 200.00
3)	Buy a Life-time Membership in "YOUR-E-MINISTRY" which allows you to "Edit" your Page once per week.	$2,000.00

Optional

    Enroll in a Program of Residual Income for your interest and effort of promoting "PREVIEWISM" being "The Objective of" God the Real, "The Spirit of Goodness", "The Spirit of Goodness" has three Characteristics, being, It has a "Free Spirit", "A Sense of Judgement", and "A Good Nature", "The Spirit of Goodness" has many Children (Angels), the oldest being, "The Spirit of Truth", and the youngest being "The Spirit of Enthusiasm", and of course there are many in between.

Yes, every "Previewlite" member will get his/her Just reward that will continue into Retirement and "Life Eternal".

Monthly Membership Fee is Two (2%) per cent of your monthly (Gross) income with a Minimum of $20.00 per month and a Maximum of $100.00 per month.

Thank you for your Interest. Now, Let us not Hesitate to say, "Let's Do It".

As ever in, "The Spirit of Goodness",

"Saint Bill" (Coach)

Previews Institute.

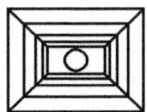

PREVIEWISM
Our World is Beautiful, Yes, Multi-Cultural

Dear Friends and Children of All ages:

We know that the "Rule" is:

"There is an Exception to every Rule".

Yes, there is an Exception to this Rule too!!

It goes like this: Our Rule at "Previews" is that we allow Everyone their Opinion and say, O.K., carry on.

But the Exception is when you are talking to a "Criminal". You find you Disagree!!

Yes, 1 in 400 is a Criminal, and when a Criminal voices his/her Opinion,. You say, Just hold it right There,. Our opinion Over-rules and we will carry on, but You must be Quiet until WE see life a little Different. Yes, Folks, to this there is no Exception.

Thanks for Listening Folks, It was a pleasure, as ever in,

"The Spirit of Goodness",

B.H., M.A., L.W. "Saint Bill" (Coach)

PROPHETIC WORLD COUNCIL OF TEMPLES

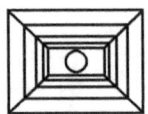

PREVIEWISM
Our World is Beautiful, Yes, Multi-Cultural

Dear Friends and Children of all ages:

Let us always remember that No Human being on Earth ever consciously knowingly chooses to do Wrong (Bad), but is always firstly Deceived to think it is Alright or O.K. and will do No harm. Yes, even after he/she has learned a lesson that says It is wrong, he/she is deceived again to think It is Alright, and after many Deceptions on the same point the Web of deception becomes so strong that the person becomes a Slave and Captive of the deception and is convinced that It is Right with God, and that Suffering makes you Strong.

Wrong, Suffering makes you a Sucker for more Suffering, and ultimately very Weak and Vain. Yes, It becomes pure Vanity in disguise as Goodness.

And so we must always Forgive our Neighbor for his/her Ignorance or Shortcomings. And not fall into the Trap of Condemning, Cursing, or Retaliating (Punishing). Because It causes a vicious Circle leading back to ourselves.

Yes, we must remember to not look at life through the Human Eye but rather always look at life through God's Eye. And without Exception for the Utmost results.

Yes, God the Real, "The Spirit of Goodness", is Everunderstanding, Everloving, and Everforgiving. Thank God, or we would be in Trouble.

Yes, Folks, we must remember that God's Love and Forgiveness is Unconditional without Exception, and if we remember that we are All created and born in God's image, we will overcome the unfulfilling influence of God the Fraud (The Shadow), and we will remember that we are all "Saints" in God's Eye.

And It is hoped that we will All be "Saints" in the Human Eye, One day Soon. Yes, in that Glorious day (Time) The Shadow will be totally deserted and left Crying in Its Beer. (Ha,HA,HA) Chuckle, Chuckle, eh!!

Thanks for Listening, as ever in, "The Spirit of Goodness",

"Saint Bill" (Coach)

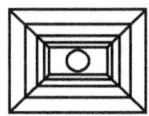

PREVIEWISM
Our World is Beautiful, Yes, Multi-Cultural

Tuff Love

Dear Friends and Children:

To begin today we have another question or two.

1) If someone said to you, "Do not Love you Neighbor" would this be a servant of God speaking or would this be a servant of "The Shadow" speaking?

Answer: Well, Let me tell you, It is obvious this is a servant of "The Shadow" speaking.

2)   If someone said to you, "Do not Judge"your Neighbor", would this be a servant of God speaking or would this be a servant of "The Shadow" speaking?

Answer: Well, Let me tell you, It is not so obvious, but this is a servant of "The Shadow" speaking.

Now, Let me explain: There are two kinds of Love,. Easy Love and Tuff Love. It is easy to love your Neighbor when you agree with him/her. But, It is Tuff to love your Neighbor when you Disagree with him/her.

Now, we know that "To Judge" is "To Decide" right from wrong, and we must do that to stay Sane.

And so when your Neighbor says or does something that you do not agree with, you must express your opinion or he/she will never Learn to see Oneself as others see him/her,. which means that he/she will never grow passed their Ignorance, and You will never grow passed your Ignorance.

Yes, folks, to Judge is to administer Tuff-Love because It takes an Effort to learn how to express your Opinion without Offending your Neighbor, but let me tell you, It can be done and must be done to make Progress,. And I assure you, It improves with practice.

Now, let me say, that when you express your Opinion (Judge) you should always begin by saying, that although you are expressing your Opinion (Judgeing), you are not Condemning him/her, but rather have already "Forgiven" him/her or you would not be talking, and just let him/her Suffer in his/her Ignorance.

Secondly, as you express your Opinion, you should remember to always give him/her Two Pats on the Back for every One kick in the Butt. In this way it becomes "Constructive Criticizm" which is positive and Good. And not a quick Tearing Down, which is negative and a Waste.

Yes, folks, If you remember this Formula you will find that your Neighbor is never (seldom,eh) Offended and will see your Opinion as a "Stepping Stone" and not a "Stumbling Block", and he/she will thank you for your Concern and Love. (Yes, Forever Real and Alive in "The Spirit of Goodness")

Thank you for Listening, and the Glory be to God,. as ever in, "The Spirit of Goodness",

"Saint Bill", (Coach) Previews Institute.

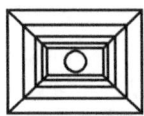

PREVIEWISM
Our World is Beautiful, Yes, Multi-Cultural

Dear Friends and Children of All ages:

Specifically, Rex, Vince, Evelyn & Greg. You know, you are very Fortunate to have known such a very Fortunate person. Yes, Wilhelm J. Handel, M.A., L.W.,. Alias, "Saint Bill". (Coach) Previews Institute of Universal Philosophy, Loc-001, H.O. .

You know, 1 in 10 is an Electrician, 1 in 10 is a Plumber, 1 in 10 is a Carpenter. 1 in 30 is a Salesperson, 1 in 100 is a Preacher, 1 in 100 is a Millionaire, I in 1000 writes a Book, and 1 in 20,000,000,000 writes a Bible.

Well, you know, "The COMPASS" is a New Bible, (The EverLast Testament). You know, when Paganism ran Its course, It changed Its name to Judaism, and when Judaism ran Its course, It changed Its name to Christianity, and when Christianity ran Its course, The Death knell was put to all of this Negative Psychology and replaced with True Positive Psychology, namely, PREVIEWISM. Yes, God the Real, "The Spirit of Goodness", is Positive, and God the Fraud, "Illusion" (The Shadow) is Negative. Yes, Positive is Truth, and Negative is Lie. And as we know, Truth is Reality, and Lie is Illusion.

You know, Jesus was a "Saint" just like you and I, and the Purpose of God in Jesus's life was to return us to our Original state. Yes, in Harmony and One with God in Spirit or Thought. Yes, Free of Guilt, Fear, Doubt, and Illusion,

"The Compass" re-introduces us to "The Spirit of God" or "The Spirit of Goodness". And "The Compass" was written for Jesus because He did not get a chance to write It because He was killed and Died prematurely.

The Mongrels and their Negative psychology that caused this Shame are now going to Die and The World will come back to Its Original State. Yes, we will all be able to walk in Peace with God on Earth and Recycle into and out of the Future, Spiritually, Eternally.

Thanks for Listening, as ever in the Spirit of Goodness,

"Saint Bill" (Coach)

Previews Institute.

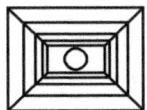

PREVIEWISM
Our World is Beautiful, Yes, Multi-Cultural

Dear Friends and Children of All ages:

Today we have a most wonderful Idea. You know, God the Real, "The Spirit of Goodness", lives in Heaven, in the World, and in your Heart, Mind, and Soul, from the Beginning (Conception).

God the Real, says, Love your Neighbor, but do not Worship him/her.

Because, Love comes from the Mind, while Worship comes from your Heart and Soul.

And so you see, I can say, I love Buddha, I love Singh, I love Jesus, I love Confucous, I love Mohamed, I love Hindu, I even love Juda a little bit.

Yes, I can say, I love all these "Lords" to some degree, but I do not Worship them.. I Worship God the Real, "The Spirit of Goodness", because Worship belongs to God, because God is Infallible, while Humans are Fallible.

Yes, "Lord" refers to Humans, while God refers to "The Spirit of Goodness"

Yes, God is My God, and God is my Salvation. I need no other.

Yes, Lords are not Gods, because Lords are like "The Shadow", they are always around with their hand out when the Sun shines, but when the Clouds come and the Rain falls, the times of need, they disappear, nowhere to be seen until the Sun shines again. Yes, they Fail you when the going gets Tuff.

God the Real, "The Spirit of Goodness", with all of Its angels (children) never fails you. Not in the Sunshine, Not in the Rain, and Not in the Hailstorms. God stays with you All the way, Yes, Infallible.

Yes, Worship comes from your Heart and Soul,. Love comes from your Mind. So Worship belongs to God. Love belongs to your Neighbor.

Thanks for Listening, as ever in, "The Spirit of Goodness",

B.H., M.A., L.W., "Saint Bill" (Coach)

Previews Institute

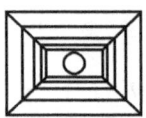

PREVIEWISM
Our World is Beautiful, Yes, Multi-Cultural

Dear Friends and Children of All ages: There are Three segments of people in Society. Two are Wrong, One is Right. Most of Society is in their Right frame of Mind most of the time. Some of Society are in their Right frame of Mind all of the time. Some of Society are in the Wrong frame on Mind all the time. It is those that provide us with the Biggest Challenge.

Yes, we must not give-up on the Insane, because they are just Living in Illusion and at any time they may See or Hear something that will bring them to Reality. And we know that Reality is God and God is Reality, Not Fantasy.

Some people think that God wants a Sacrifice, that is Illusion. Some people think that Illusion can become a Reality, that is Illusion. Illusion is Illusion, and Reality is Reality. Some people Act on Illusion and cause Pain and Suffering. Some people Act on Reality and cause Happiness, Decencey, Prosperity and Peace of Mind. Yes, nothing but Blessings. Thank God for Reality.

We know that God is the same Yesterday, Today, and Tommorrow, but at the same time Always making Progress and Improving Its Quality and Quantity of Goodness, knowing that It will Ultimately reach Its Goal of Heaven on Earth,. Imperfect as God is, but none the less, Heaven on Earth.

Some people think that God can become a Person, that is Illusion. Some people think that Illusion can become a Person, that is Illusion upon Illusion (Satan). Some people think that Satan lives in people, that is Illusion. Satan is Illusion and does not exist in any way, shape or form. It is just plain simple Illusion. Cast It Out. That is Right, Cast It Out of your Mind and let Reality which is God live in your Heart, Mind, and Soul. This brings you All the Blessings of God the Real, "The Spirit of Goodness", and all of Its children (angels), the Oldest being "The Spirit of Truth" and the Youngest being "The Spirit of Enthusiasm".

All of God's children have a "Sense of Judgement", a "Free Spirit", and a "Good Nature". Let them Flourish and God will be Glorified.

Once upon a time a certain group of people Killed a man because they thought He was Satan. After they Killed him, they came to Realize that he was Just a Man. And so to overcome their Shame they said they had seen him Rise from the Dead and ultimately Float up into the Clouds. They realized he had been serving God, so they said He was God on Earth, but gone to Heaven. Poor people, they further tried to Justify Murder by saying that God wanted a Sacrifice and that they had Served God. But they knew that God says, "Thou Shalt not Kill", but their Shame was so Great that they preferred to Justify Murder, and continued to preach their Lies and Illusions. Yes, the Lies and Illusions of the Dark ages.

Yes, folks, these people did not realize that God does not want a Sacrifice but that God wants Obedience to Its Good words. And that when God does not get Obedience, It says, Forgiven,. "Go, and Do it better next time, now that you have learned Reality from Illusion".

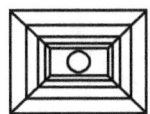

PREVIEWISM
Our World is Beautiful, Yes, Multi-Cultural

But this group of people has not learned a thing, because they would do the same thing over again if someone Confronted them with The Reality of God as "The Spirit of Goodness", and not the Illusion of Self-righteousness, Extortion, and Self-servance, and Perfection. Insanity.

Dear Friends, we think you got the Picture, so we will leave it at that.

Thanks for Listening, as ever in,

"The Spirit of Goodness"

Bill Handel, M.A., L.W. alias, "Saint Bill" (Head Coach)

Previews Institute

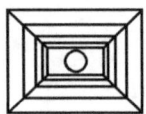

PREVIEWISM
Our World is Beautiful, Yes, Multi-Cultural

Dear Friend:

Our organization (Summit) is in the process of drawing Blue-prints for a "Shelter" for the Destitute, that we are going to Build in the Northeast sector of our great City of Calgary. The exact location has not been determined as yet, but we will do our Home-work and certainly find an Ideal location.

The Shelter (Summit) will provide a Sanctuary, a Cafeteria, and a place to Meditate on our Great God, "The Spirit of Goodness".

"The Spirit of Goodness" has a "Sense of Judgement", a "Free Spirit", and a "Good Nature", and most importantly a "Strong Work Ethic", and is very persistant and relentless in working toward Its Goal of "Heaven on Earth" for All of Us.

The Sanctuary and or Place of Meditation will provide an opportunity for the Destitute to come closer to God the Real, "The Spirit of Goodness", with all of Its angels (children), the oldest being "The Spirit of Truth" and the youngest being "The Spirit of Enthusiasm", and as we know there are many in between. We are gathering people who Support this Objective and hope you are one of them.

When you decide to Support this Financially, please visit our Website or come to our "Summit Loc-001, H.O." at the address shown below and we will make the neccessary arrangements to establish your personal "Summit Location number" and Life-time membership.

Trusting you are One who is first in line to improve our Nation's psychology, We hope to hear from you soon, remaining,

Yours truly, as ever in,

"The Spirit of Goodness",

W.J.(Bill) Handel, M.A., L.W. alias, "Saint Bill" (Head Coach)

Previews Institute of Universal Philosophy

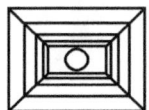

PREVIEWISM
Our World is Beautiful, Yes, Multi-Cultural

Dear Friends:

"Saint Jesus" together with "Saint Bill" and a whole host of other "Saints", represent God the Real, "The Spirit of Goodness", and not God the Fraud, "Illusion". Yes, today we are going to draw you a Picture. (Acts 26, vs. 16-18) (John 7,vs.16-18) (1 Jn.4, v.20) (2 Thes. 2, v.9-11)

In the Beginning there were three (3) entities. The first was God, the second was "The Messiah" and the third was "Adam and Eve". Yes, Adam and Eve are One. So there were three Entities.

God had a conversation with "Adam and Eve" first. Yes, God said, to Its Children, I want you to know that "Life is Eternal". Yes, we have "Life in the Womb", "Life on Earth", and "Life in Heaven", and each is Eternal unto Its own and are One as we recycle into and out of "The Future".

Now, I want to ask you a question, Children,. "Do you want to be a Slave, or do you want to be Free? And Adam and Eve said, "We want to be FREE!"

And God said, "Go, You are FREE".

Then "The Messiah" said, Wait, You must not use your "Sense of Judgement". Yes, Do not Judge, Do not Decide right from wrong, or you will Die.

Then God said, "You are a Liar", Stay out of My Sight... You illegit..

Then Adam and Eve asked, "Who should we Believe?" and God said, "You are Free", "Take your Choice"- Then Adam and Eve decided to Eat... and God said, God Bless you, Children, God Bless you!!

Yes, folks, most of us Use our "Sense of Judgement" to Judge (Decide) right from wrong, and make progress in Happiness, Decency, Prosperity, and Peace of Mind. And know without a Doubt that "Life is Eternal", knowing that Physical Death is just an Illusion trying to distract us from the Reality of Life Eternal.

A few of us are misled by Illusion (The Shadow), the Fear monger, Extortionist, Self-server, and Perfectionist,. and Live in Misery. But all is not lost because we are all God's children and God Forgives us our shortcomings and allows "Life Eternal" to continue,. Heaven on Earth without End.

Thank you, Dear God, Thank you.

Trusting you got It, we remain, as ever in, "The Spirit of Goodness",

"Saint Bill" (Coach)

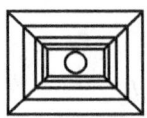

PREVIEWISM
Our World is Beautiful, Yes, Multi-Cultural

Dear Friend:

Do you Believe, that, "What you Sow, You Reap, Manifold"? If so, Do you contribute to "A Charity"?

If so, Do you contribute Money or Time and Energy?

If you contribute Time and Energy,. What do you Reap?

Answer: "Peace of Mind". (That is Good)

Who pays the Bills of "A Charity"?

Answer: The Bills are paid by those who contribute Money.

What do they Reap? Answer: In most cases, Nothing. (That is against the Law)

Well, we at "Previews Institute of Universal Philosophy" have created "A CHARITY" whereby we "Specialize in "Food for Thought"

Yes, MY-E-MINISTRY becomes YOUR-E-MINISTRY at www.previews-inc.com

and Every Member of our Congregation receives a "Pay-Day",

Yes, To Reap,.Manifold.

Here is How it Works.

1) Read page 2 of this package to become familiar with Your Objective.

Understand that we Need monthly paying Members to pay Operating Expenses.

Do unto others, as you would have them do unto You.

Become a Paying Member with Membership Fees between $20.00 to $100.00 (Monthly)

Become a Paid Volunteer Promoter and receive 50% of every Dollar you bring In.

Order Personal Business Cards to promote Your Website and Its Positive Message.

In the process of the Above, You are registered to receive 3 Levels of Residual Income of 50% and 10% and 5% respectively.

Obtain your Masters Degree in Psychology and Philosophy and Earn while you Learn to "Lead Your Own Ministry".

9) Yes, gain Happiness, Decency, Prosperity and Peace of Mind, by Introducing your Neighbors to God the Real, "The Spirit of Goodness", and all of Its Angels.

Thank you, as ever in, "The Spirit of Goodness",

(Head Coach) "Saint Bill".

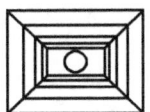

PREVIEWISM
Our World is Beautiful, Yes, Multi-Cultural

Dear Friends and Children of All ages:

Today we will see that Life is a Joke, Not a Yoke... Chuckle, Chuckle, Chuckle, Ha, Ha, Ha, Ha,.Chuckle Chuckle, eh!!

Here is Something to consider. AN IMPERFECT CREATION

1 in 900 is in Jail. (A Jailbird)

1 in 400 is a Retard. (A Jew) (A Barbarian) (Terminally Mentally ill.) (Condemning) (Ruthless Self-server) (Negative) Looking Down. Needs to be FORGIVEN for his/her Deformities. (Shortcomings)

1 in 100 is a Criminal on the Loose.

88% of people are "Saints" (Gentiles) (Gentle People) (Benevolent) (Forgiving) Understanding, Positive, Looking Up.

10% of people are "Sinners" (Confused) (Hypocrites) in Church with the Preacher.

God says, Go, you are FREE..., (Take your Choice) "You are what you Think".

Thanks for Listening, as ever in, "The Spirit of Goodness",

"Saint Bill." (Head Coach)

A Servant for God's sake.

(Acts 26, v. 16-18) Previews Institute, Loc-001, H.O.

P.S.: Remember, If you are not a Retard, You are not a Jew, You are probably an Isrealite,.. I am a Canadian. and there is no difference.

Also Remember, In God's Eye we are all "Saints", because God Forgives All, accepting us all into Heaven, Just as we are,

To Live Eternally with God and all of the other Saints.

Thanks again for Listening, as ever in, "The Spirit of Goodness",

(Saint Bill),

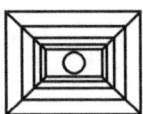

PREVIEWISM
Our World is Beautiful, Yes, Multi-Cultural

Dear Friends and Children of All ages:

Today we will reiterate that, Aggression is a Sin against Humanity.

Self-defense is an Act of God.

Now we know that God never Retaliates, But God does Defend Itself.

Question: What is the difference between Retaliation and Self-defense.

Answer: Retaliation wins and takes the Life of the Aggressor. Self-defense wins but Spares the Life of the Aggressor,

Question: Why does God never Retaliate, but only Self-defend?

Answer: Because God is EverForgiving and has FAITH that if you show Kindness, You will get Kindness back.

Yes, What you Sow, You Reap, Manifold.

Yes, Look Up, and Forgive one-another and Reap only Blessings, Barring the Weather, of course.

Thanks for Listening, as ever in,

"The Spirit of Goodness",

"Saint Bill" (Head Coach)

A Servant for God's sake, (

Acts 26, v. 16-18) (John 7, v. 16-18)

Previews Institute, Loc-001, H.0.   (1 Jn.4, v. 20)

PS.: Yes, Dwell on the Positive, Not the Negative.

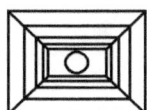

PREVIEWISM
Our World is Beautiful, Yes, Multi-Cultural

Dear Friends and Children of All ages:

Just a few more Questions:

1) What is God? Answer: God is a Spirit. Yes, The Spirit of Goodness".

    Answer: God is a Personal Ideal, that brings you Happiness, Decency, Prosperity, and Peace of Mind, and brings you to Peace and Harmony with your Neighbors.

    Answer: God is a selection of words arranged such that they form a psychology that bears a Good Fruit, that is agreeable and acceptable to All of Humankind.

P.S.: God the Real, "The Spirit of Goodness", has three Characteristics.

    1) "A Sense of Judgement" 2) "A Free Spirit" 3) "A Good Nature".

"The Spirit of Goodness" has many Children (angels), the oldest being "The Spirit of Truth" and the youngest being "The Spirit of Enthusiasm", with many in between. All of the Angels have the three characteristics of "The Spirit of Goodness".

2) What is God the Fraud? Answer: Illusion (The Shadow), Illusion (Satan), Illusion (The Devil), Illusion (The Scape-Goat). Yes, those who can not Face Reality (God) are with and in Illusion and this Illusion becomes their Scape-Goat, and so they become Self-righteous, Condemning Ruthless Self-servers. (Extortionists) (Murderers) anything to Try to prove they are Right or Real. Yes, they become Slaves to Illusion and Lie, "The Liar".

Poor People. They need to be FORGIVEN for their Deformity. (Shortcomings).

Thanks for Listening, as ever in,

"The Spirit of Goodness",

"Saint Bill"

A Servant for God's sake.

(Acts 26, v.16-18) (John 7, v.16-18) (1 Jn.4, v.20) (2 Thes.2, v.9-11)

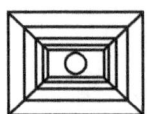

PREVIEWISM
Our World is Beautiful, Yes, Multi-Cultural

Dear Friends and Children of All ages:

Today we have another question.

Upon which scriptures do you base your Ministry?

If you take your scriptures out of the Old, You are in illusion.

If you take your scriptures out of the present, You are in Confusion. If you take your scriptures out of the New, You are in Reality.

Now we know that Life is of the Past, Present, and Future.

But we must Look to the Future to see what God has allowed to Recycle. Only the Future holds the Truth and Reality.

If you Look to the Present, You find Confusion and Illusion. If you Look only to the Past, You will go Insane.

So It is only Logical to conclude that to achieve the Highest degree of Truth one must try to always Look-Up and to the Future.

In This way we become Leaders, leading people to Happiness, Decency, Prosperity, and Peace of Mind. If we do otherwise we become the Blind leading the Blind, into Confusion and Illusion and ultimately into the Pits of Hell on Earth.

Yes, my Friends, Look to the Future as It holds only Truth and Reality, and you will find you are in Heaven on Earth, and you will find It a Joy to lead others to Heaven on Earth. Yes, the Finest Achievement, next to a Charity.

We at "Previews" have established a "Charity" and are now on our way of Leading people out of the "Pits of Hell On Earth" and into Heaven on Earth, where we find Happiness, Decency, Prosperity, and Peace of Mind, and the ability to deal in Peace and Harmony with our Neighbors.

Thanks for Listening, as ever in, "The Spirit of Goodness",

"Saint Bill" (Head Coach)

A Servant for God's sake.

(Acts 26,v.16-18)(John 7,v.16-18) Previews Institute, Loc-001, H.O.

(1 Jn.4,v.20)(2 Thes.2,v.9-11)

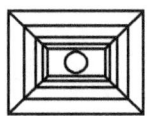

PREVIEWISM
Our World is Beautiful, Yes, Multi-Cultural

Dear Friends and Children of All ages:

Today we are going to talk about "Being Born Again". First let me explain that you can be Born Again into two Realms of Thought. One is Good and the Other is Waste.

Yes, you can be a born again "Messiah person". or You can be a born again "Jesus person".

This means you can be born again "Selfish and Ruthless" or

You can be born again "Benevolent and Forgiving".

You can be born again of "Illusion and Lie" or you can be born again of "Truth and Reality". Now we know that Illusion and Lie is the "Scape-goat". and we know that Truth and Reality is God as God is Reality, not Fantasy. Now that being said, Here is how you can be a born again "Godly Person".

You must go back to your Original state of Mind when you were Born into this world. You must throw out all the Garbage (Waste) and start over with "The Spirit of God", Yes, "The Spirit of Goodness" that was in you from Creation.

"The Spirit of Goodness" being "The Spirit of God" has a "Sense of Judgement", "A Free Spirit" and "A Good Nature"- You must from this day forward use your Sense of Judgement to control your Free Spirit to allow your Good Nature to grow.

Your Sense of Judgement is your ability to Judge (Decide) right from wrong, possible from impossible, reality from illusion. Yes, God the Real from God the Fraud.

Now as we know "The Spirit of Goodness" has many children (angels), the oldest being "The Spirit of Truth" and the youngest being "The Spirit of Enthusiasm, with many in between. As we Adopt one of these children (angels) each week

We will find that each has a "Sense of Judgement", a "Free Spirit", and a "Good Nature".

Yes, your Sense of Judgement will never let you down because It chooses Its children very wisely and very carefully, and you will soon have the whole Family of God in your Heart, Mind, and Soul.

Now, you can see, You will become a New person, looking to the Future with Enthusiasm as you learn something New everyday as you Re-organize a confused mess into a Clear picture of Truth and Reality, leading to Life with God in Heaven and Eternity.

Yes, folks, when you are "Born Again" in this way, you will become a "True Prophet", seeing only "Goodness" to come. And we need more "True Prophets" Yes, folks, as I see it now, we have 99 out of a 100 as "False Prophets" and only 1 out of a 100 as a "True Prophet".

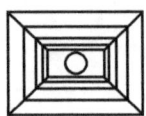

PREVIEWISM
Our World is Beautiful, Yes, Multi-Cultural

But do not despair, the ball is rolling and as I see it within 300 years we will have 99 out of 100 as "True Prophets" and only 1 out of 100 as "False Prophets".

Yes, we will have Heaven on Earth, Not Perfect, but indeed Heaven on Earth as God meant it to be. And then we will work from there to achieve 999 out of 1000 as "True Prophets and only 1 out of 1000 as "False Prophets".

Yes, Life will be Eternal in Heaven and on Earth and It will be Beautiful Bliss.

Thanks again for Listening, as ever in,

"The Spirit of Goodness",

"Saint Bill" (Head Coach) A Servant for God's sake.

(Acts 26, v.16-18)(John 7, v.16-18)(1 Jn.4, v.20)(2 Thes.2, v.9-11)

Previews Institute, Loc-001, H.0.

A Multicultural Proverb:

"The Spirit of Goodness" specializes in "Food For Thought".

So, when you eat of the words of "The Compass"

Remember the One who Planted them.

Previews Proverb.

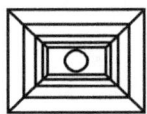

PREVIEWISM
Our World is Beautiful, Yes, Multi-Cultural

A Few Short Stories

WE

are Created, Conceived, and Born in the Image of God. We are Young and Ignorant while God is Old and Wise. We have much to Learn. But, We are considered Equal and One with God, and God is considered Equal and One with Us, always.

God the Real, "The Spirit of Goodness", with Its "Sense of Judgement, "Free Spirit", and "Good Nature", together with Its children (angels), the Oldest being "The Spirit of Truth" and the Youngest being "The Spirit of Enthusiasm", with many in between, Lives in Heaven, in the World, and in our Heart, Mind, and Soul. It never Dies, but Recycles into and out of the Future when our Bodies cease to function, and when we are Created.

WE

are FORGIVEN before we start our Day, and we are FORGIVEN after we end our Day, and while we Sleep we can do Nothing wrong. So we are always Saints.

WE

are IMMORTAL, Yes, once Created there is no looking back. Yes, Life in the Womb, Life on Earth, and Life in Heaven. GUARANTEED in writing by "The COMPASS", by Author: "Saint Bill", A Servant for God's sake.

The Seed, Instinctive Genius

The Roots, Acts 26, v.16-18) (John 7, v.16-18)   (1 Jn.4, v.20) (2 Thes.2, v.9-11)

The Tree, Love and Forgiveness

The Fruit, Happiness, Decency, Prosperity, and Peace of Mind.

Yes, Peace, Harmony, and Equality with your Neighbors and the World around you.

And Freedom from Guilt, Fear, Doubt and Illusion.

Thanks again for Listening, as ever in, "The Spirit of Goodness",

"Saint Bill" (Head Coach) A Servant for God's sake.

Acts 26, v.16-18) (John 7, v.16-18)   (1 Jn.4, v.20) (2 Thes.2, v.9-11)

Previews Institute "Summit Loc-001, H.O."

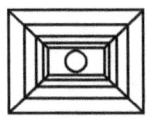

PREVIEWISM
Our World is Beautiful, Yes, Multi-Cultural

Dear Friend:

God is not the Liar. The Shadow (Satan) is the Liar when It says, we have Sinned against God, when in fact we have only Sinned against our Neighbor. God takes no Offence to anything, because It is Everunderstanding and as a result Everforgiving.

Our Neighbor takes Offence to some of our words or actions, because he/she does not have all the Facts in the circumstances. God does, so we have not Sinned against God, we have only Sinned against our Neighbor.

It is up to our neighbor to pass on the Love and Forgiveness that he/she has received from God for his/her shortcomings to us.

If he/she does not pass It on and Forgive us, then it is he/she who is carrying the Chips. We who understand this always forgive our neighbors for their short-comings, because it is us who Suffer if we do not.

It is obvious you need some lessons on the characteristics of a "Saint".

First you say, You are a Saint,. Then you say, You are a Sinner. You are obviously confused.

Jesus the man, said, You are either for God or You are against God, You can not be Both, unless you want to be a Hypocrite.

A Saint is a child of God, serving God. (Reality) (Truth)

A Sinner is a child of God, serving The Shadow (Satan) (Illusion) (Lie).

But God forgives us on the Spot for our Ignorance, so we are always Saints in God's Eye.. We Saints look at life through God's Eye, Not the Human Eye. And so we should never take Offence to anything but rather always forgive our neighbors. And always consider them Saints, as God does.

If we do otherwise, we are serving the Accuser (Satan), and this is what the Accuser wants because It causes much Pain, Suffering and Strife.

Yes, if we do not understand this we become "Suckers for Punishment" and think we are happy, as a Pig in a Mess. "Suckers for Punishment".

God is Knowledge and Understanding and It wants us to learn to Judge (Decide) right from wrong so that we can avoid the Pitfalls of life and not have to suffer needlessly.

The Shadow (Satan) wants us to Suffer, Suffer, Suffer, as "Suckers for Punishment" and so It says, "Do not Judge",. Do not Decide right from wrong and just walk around in circles like a useless Imbecile, hitting Pitfall after Pitfall.

And then The Shadow laughs away, saying God punishes. The Liar. We punish ourselves and It punishes Itself. All as a result of Illusion (Ignorance).

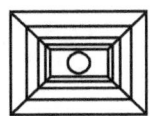

PREVIEWISM
Our World is Beautiful, Yes, Multi-Cultural

Then The Shadow says, Do not worry about it, Suffering makes you Strong. The Liar. Suffering makes you a "Sucker for more Punishement". (A Weak and Retarded person).

Yes, The Shadow is a Liar on every count. Go back to square One and start over with God the Real, "The Spirit of Goodness", with Its "Sense of Judgement", "Free Spirit", and "Good Nature", together with all of It children (angels), the oldest being ""The Spirit of Truth and the youngest being "The Spirit of Enthusiasm", and many in between.

Yes, in this way you will find Happiness, Decency, Prosperity, and Peace of Mind, and the ability to deal in Peace and Harmony with your Neighbors,

Thanks for Listening, as ever in,

"The Spirit of Goodness",

"Saint Bill" (Head Coach) A Servant for God's sake.

Previews Institute, "Summit Loa-001, H.O."

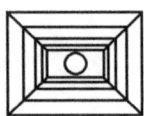

PREVIEWISM
Our World is Beautiful, Yes, Multi-Cultural

Dear Al. (My Equal) Chuckle, Chuckle, eh!!

God does not speak with words, God speaks with Actions, because Actions speak Louder than Words. Yes, You tell the Tree by the Fruit. (Results)

So, to have Justice, you have Perfection. And when we try to be Perfect the Results are Pain, Suffering, and Strife.

Equality is not Just and not Perfect. But when we do not try to be Perfect, but only try for Excellence (Acceptance of Reality) the Results are Happiness, Decency, Prosperity, and Peace of Mind, and the Ability to deal in Peace and Harmony with our Nieghbors. And this is the Goal that God wants Us to Achieve.

We have realized the difference between your appraoch to the problem and Our appraoch to the problem (Life).

Yours is in the most part a Theology, and ours is in the most part a Philosophy. A Theology is based on Theory, unproven, impractical Theory.

A Philosophy is based on Principals, proven, practical Principals.

Yes, We have to Accept the Reality of Today and work with It to achieve Excellence, and even Super Excellence, but not Perfection or Justice.

Because God is not Perfect or Just, God is considered Equal and One with Us, and We are considered Equal and One with God, always.

This approach Achieves the Goal, Yes, never ending Peace and Harmony on Earth. Thanks for Listening, as ever in, "The Spirit of Goodness",

"Saint Bill" (Head Coach) A Servant for God's sake.

(Acts 26, v.16-18) (John 7, v.16-18) (1 Jn.4, v.20) (2 Thes.2, v.9-11)

Previews Institute, "Summit Loc-001, H.O."

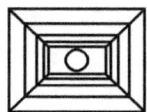

PREVIEWISM
Our World is Beautiful, Yes, Multi-Cultural

Remember: "The TIP", of the Iceberg
Give Someone a Smile, It is a Great Gift!!
Buy "The DESTITUTE" a Coffee, and A "FREE LUNCH", today,
Out of the "Goodness" of your Heart.
Remember It is Equally as BLESSED to GIVE, as It is to RECEIVE.

Thank you, Dear God, Thank you.
PREVIEWS INSTITUTE OF UNIVERSAL PHILOSOPHY
"A Non-Profit Charity" "Specializing in "Food for Thought"
www.previews-inc.com "SUMMIT"
Locations:
Sinclair's Diner - 5147-20 Ave. S.E., Calgary
4 Seas Restaurant - 3605-17 Ave. S.E., Calgary

"The One who Creates A CHARITY" and
The One who GIVES to A CHARITY
are Considered EQUAL Partners
FOUNDED By: "The Spirit of Goodness"

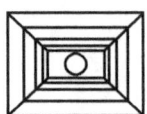

PREVIEWISM
Our World is Beautiful, Yes, Multi-Cultural

Dear Friends and Children of All ages:

Today we have another Question.

What is the Difference between a MARTYR and a SAINT.?

Answer: A Martyr dies for Its cause, and

A Saint lives for Its cause..

Yes, The Shadow (Illusion) (Satan) wants you to Die and so It offers you

Glory and Self-Righteousness as your reward for Killing yourself and Others.

God the Real, "The Spirit of Goodness" wants you to Live and so It lets you realize that God is Righteous but not Self-Righteous.

Yes, we should only Glorify God for all Goodness in the World and not Ourselves. And so It never becomes neccessary to Die for a Good cause.

One only needs to Die for a Bad (Wasteful) cause.

And this is Ludicrous when we use our "Sense of Judgement", and Judge (Decide) right from wrong, reality from illusion, God the Real from God the Fraud.

This is why The Shadow says, "Do not Judge". Yes, to render you an Imbecile or an Idiot, or a Lunatic, or a Hypocrite. Yes, a Shadow Worshipper.

Yes, Folks, we know that Aggression is a Sin against Humanity. Self-Defence is an Act of God.

But when Self-Defence Wins It spares the Life of the Aggressor.

If we do not Spare the Life of the Aggressor, It becomes Retaliation, and We know that God the Real does not Retaliate. Yes, It never takes Revenge, but rather always Forgives the Aggressor because God the Real has Faith that It will always Win. Yes, this we know, "Truth always Prevails".

Thanks for Listening, as ever in, "The Spirit of Goodness",

"Saint Bill" (Coach)

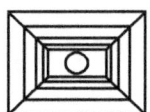

PREVIEWISM
Our World is Beautiful, Yes, Multi-Cultural

Dear Friends and Children of All ages:

Today we will talk about COMPROMISE.

The Shadow (Illusion) says, I am God, and God does not Compromise. This is two Lies in one sentence.

We wish to explain that God the Real, "The Spirit of Goodness", does Never talk to The Shadow (Illusion)(Satan). God totally ignores and does not acknowledge the existance of The Shadow because It is an Illusion, and so there is Never any opportunity or existence of Compromise between God and The Shadow.

God only talks to Its children from out of the Future and is continually compromising with Its children.

The Shadow, from out of the Past, is always suggesting things that have no relevance with the Present and the Future which is God. These suggestions are just plain simple Illusion that distracts us from the Reality of God in the Future.

In order for Us to progress to the Utmost, we must always look up and to the Future and never look down or back, and just Cast Out the Negative Suggestions of the Shadow, and pay attention to Reality which is God speaking with Actions. Yes, God speaks with Actions, not with words, because Actions speak Louder than words and to all of Humankind alike. So there is Never any contradictions.

All this is possible when we exercise our "Sense of Judgement" and Judge (Decide) right from wrong, possible from impossible, reality from Illusion, and God the Real, "The Spirit of Goodness" from God the Fraud, Illusion.

Yes, remember that God is very Compromising because It understands all our different circumstances and is by Nature Everloving and Everforgiving.

Thanks for Listening, as ever in,

"The Spirit of Goodness",

"Saint Bill" (Coach)

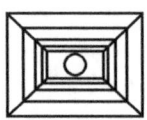

PREVIEWISM
Our World is Beautiful, Yes, Multi-Cultural

June 15/02/63 A.B.

Functions of "Previews Institute of Universal Philosophy"

"Summit Loc-001, H.O."

"Head Coach" Saint Bill.

1) Operate as a College or University of Religious Instruction.

2) Operate and Fund "Summit Locations" (Restaurants) for serving the Destitute with a "Free Lunch", Compliments of Previews.

3) Expose web-site address: www..previews-inc.com where-ever possible.

Objective:

1) Serve and Glorify our Neighbors and simultaneously Serve and Glorify God.

2) Always define God the Real, as "The Spirit of Goodness"

3) Train and Educate young people of different origin into "Previewism".

Method:

1) Carry on a Five Year instructional program leading to a "Masters Degree" in Psychology and Philosophy. Via a correspondence course carried out by E-mail conversations with the young Students.

2) Remember, We always Judge "For" our Neighbor and Not "Against" our Neighbor. Meaning, We never Condemn, but always Forgive. Never Punish, but always Reward. Yes, Never Curse, but always Bless.

3) Set up Collection Boxes in Fancy Restaurants to gather Funds to support the "Summit Location" restaurants. With any excess going toward other Charity, and or expenses.

Final Result:

Previews Institute, will become the Leader in "Prophetic World Council of Temples".

Creating Unity and Oneness of the "Good Spirits" in Heaven, in the World, and in "The Hearts, Minds, and Souls, of all of Humankind throughout the World.

Yes, "The Spirit of Goodness", is the God of the Future, and Not of the Past, because It has a "Sense of Judgement", a "Free Spirit", and a "Good Nature", and many children (angels), the oldest being "The Spirit of Truth" and the youngest being "The Spirit of Enthusiasm", with many in between.

Yes, "The Compass", "The Sermons of Saint Bill" and "Object, Masters Degree" by Author: "Saint Bill" will become the Predominant Books of Instruction in all Religious Institutions. Now, Let us not Hesitate to say, "Let's Do It".

(YOU will be Interested in Becoming a "FOUNDING PARTNER", when you Understand our Object)   "Call or Come in. Now!!!!"

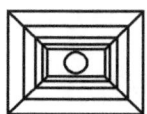

PREVIEWISM
Our World is Beautiful, Yes, Multi-Cultural

Dear Friends and Children of All ages:

In the Beginning there were small numbers of People on the Earth. There were Lush Forests and Gardens of Fruit and Vegatables. All lived in Peace and Harmony as there was a Surplus of everything. All Praised God the Real, "The Spirit of Goodness", as they Feared Nothing and they wanted for Nothing, as all their Needs were provided.

Then gradually the populations of various regions increased and gradually there became a neccessity to Save some Seeds and plant your own Garden..

Of course we know what happened, Some people were to Lazy to do some work and so they started to take from their Neighbor's Garden.

Then it became neccessary to make some Rules and Regulations to control the Free-Loaders. (the Parasites)

The Free-Loaders did not like this, so they got together and formed a Mafia. Yes, organized Crime. The Leader of the first Unit of organized Crime went by the Name of Juda. Juda had a Son called Abraham and so they together wrote out the terms of their Ideology. Their Ideology was called the "Master vs. Slave" Idea,

Otherwise called a Dictatorship. In it anyone who Joined their Organization was called a "Saint". And all of the Working Society were called "Sinners"

The First Rule that Juda and Abraham made was that they (the Mafia) made all of the Decisions, and all of the "Sinners" were Just their "Slaves" and not allowed to make any Decisions of their own or they would Die.

The Mafia declared themselves God's Children and their Ideology (Theology) the Law of God, and that according to the Law, they could Kill anyone who Disobeyed the First Law. Of course we know One thing led to another, and soon Extortion ran rampant, and "Society as a Whole" (The Workers, The True Saints) had a problem. Yes, How to control "The Mafia".(The Free-Loaders, The Dictators) (The Frauds)

Yes, "Society as a Whole" had to get Organized and form a Ideology (Philosophy) of their Own. They decided to call it a "Democracy".

Well, as we know, "Society as a Whole" (Democracy) has survived and thrived. And "Dictatorships" are losing the Battle. And "The Mafia" has been Isolated in a Small area in the Middle East, and surrounded by the Good-Guys (The Police); and "The Mafia" will die a Natural Death as the Old go to Heaven, and the Young are Converted to "Previewism", a Philosophy of Freedom of Thought for all and a Philosophy that says, "We are Masters of Our own Destiny".

Yes, We all know that God set us Free in the Beginning and allowed Us to make our own Rules and Regulations to achieve Peace, Harmony, and Equality for All of Humankind throughout the World.

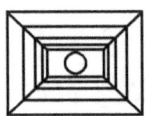

PREVIEWISM
Our World is Beautiful, Yes, Multi-Cultural

Yes, We are on the Road to Happiness, Decency, Prosperity, and Peace of Mind throughout the World within Three (3) Hundred years, as a Result of God the Real, "The Spirit of Goodness", revealing to "Saint Bill" the words of "THE COMPASS", (A New Bible) (The EverLast Testament) Yes, the True Covenant of God the Real.

"Thank you, Dear God, Thank you."

Thanks for Listening, as ever in,

"The Spirit of Goodness",

"Saint Bill" (Head Coach), A Servant for God's sake.

(Acts 26, v.16-18) (John 7, v.16-18) (1 Jn.4, v,20) (2 Thes.2, v.9-II) Previews Institute of Universal Philosophy.

Dear Friends and Children of all ages:

Previewism means "Previews of the Future", and

Previews of the Future means Happyism, and

Happyism means Multiculturalism, and

Multiculturalism means "The sum total of all the Parts", and

The sum total of all the Parts is Greater than any of the Parts.

This is where Previewism stand before God, and

God the Real is The Spirit of Goodness, with Its Sense of Judgement, Free Spirit, and Good Nature, together with Its Angels (characteristics), the oldest being The Spirit of Truth and the youngest being The Spirit of Enthusiasm, with many in between as we know.

Thank you, Dear God, Thank you for true Insight.
As ever in The Spirit of Goodness, Saint Bill, a Servant for God's sake.

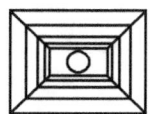

PREVIEWISM
Our World is Beautiful, Yes, Multi-Cultural

Dear Friends and Children of All ages:

In a Society Founded by God the Real, "The Spirit of Goodness", we are all Innocent until proven Guilty by the Law.

So the Innocent we call "Saints", and the Guilty we call "Sinners".

But since we are all Innocent until proven Guilty, where are the "Sinners"?

That is right, In Jail, where they belong until they turn themselves around.

And so you see, we are under No Illusion, we are all "Saints" in a Free World. This is the Positive Road, Yes, "The High Road", According to A Wise Person when It said, "You are Forgiven by God, Now go, and Sin No more.

Yes, Doubt No more. Simply have Faith. Dwell on The Spirit of God, which is "The Spirit of Goodness", and you shall Sin No more.

Thank you, Dear God, Thank you, for True Prophets. Yours truly, "Saint Bill".

Question: What is the difference between having God as your Salvation (Savior) And having A Lord as your Savior?

Answer: When God is your Savior (Salvation) the Verdict is in, You are Forgiven, and you are Accepted, Just as you are. Yes, You are Free to Go.

When A Lord is your Savior, the Verdict is just Postponed, and you are a Slave all your Life, Never having any true Faith in God.

A Statement of Faith by A Previewlite:

Dear Friends and Children of All ages:

Let us Worship God the Real, "The Spirit of Goodness", with Its Sense of Judgement, Free Spirit, and Good Nature, together with Its children (angels), the oldest being "The Spirit of Truth", and the youngest being "The Spirit of Enthusiasm", with many in between, as It lives in Heaven, in the World, and in Our Heart, Mind, and Soul. Let us Let It Flourish!!

Thank you, Dear God, Thank you,. Amen, Amen, and Amen.

P.S.: God says, You go and Serve your Neighbor First, No me, I have already looked after myself when I First Served you. So when you Serve your Nieghbor First, you will already have Served yourself and Me together, and we will All be Happy, Decent, and Prosperous, which will give Us All "Peace of Mind".

Thank you, as ever in, "The Spirit of Goodness",

"Saint Bill" (Coach)

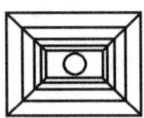

PREVIEWISM
Our World is Beautiful, Yes, Multi-Cultural

Dear Friends and Children of All ages:

The Question is: 1) What is Truth?

Answer: Truth is Reality Expressed.,

It starts with Light entering your Eyes, and you See Reality. You express Reality with words, and that is Truth.

If someone tells you something that you have not experienced, Do not Repeat It, until you have experienced It, because then It is Reality.

If you do not experience It, it could well be an Illusion.

And we should not express Illusions, because Illusion expressed is Lie. And we should not Lie, because Lie causes Punishment, Pain and Suffering.

So play It safe, and remember, Seeing is Believing., And Believe Nothing Else.

Thank you, Dear God, Thank you, for the Insight. as ever in,

"The Spirit of Goodness",

"Saint Bill", Head Coach, A Servant for God's sake

Question: What is the First Sin?
Answer: Expressing an Illusion.

What is the Second Sin?
Answer: Condemning your Neighbor for It.

What is the First Illusion?
Answer: There is not enough to go Around.

What is the First Punishment?
Answer: Someone Killed a Person for the Last Apple, instead of going out and Planting his own Garden, and Waiting for the Fruits.

To all this, God said, Look Up and Forgive One-Another and Reap only Blessings, Barring the Weather of course.

Thank you, Dear God, Thank you, for True Insight.

As ever in, "The Spirit of Goodness",

"Saint Bill"

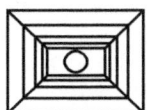

PREVIEWISM
Our World is Beautiful, Yes, Multi-Cultural

Dear Friends and Children of All ages:

Something just occurred to Us.

When "Saint Jesus" said, You must be born again, He was referring. to the Jews, and Not the Gentiles.

Yes, you see, 90% of Isrealites are born into this world with Condemnation and Curse on their Parents mind. And so they grow up Hard and Callous. And so they need to be born again.

However, 90% of Gentiles are born into this world with Love and Forgiveness on their Parents' mind. And so they do not need to be born again, because they were born Right the First time

10% of Isrealites do not need to be born again because they were born Right the First time.

10% of Gentiles (the Christians) need to be born again because they were Deceived into practicing Judaism by a Shrewd Jew called Saul. (2 Thes.2, v.9-11)

Thank you, Dear God, Thank you, for True Insight.

Dear Friends and Children of All ages:

"Saint Jesus" said, when The Spirit of God, Yes, The Spirit of Goodness is awakened in your Heart, Mind, and Soul, You will begin to recognize and appreciate the Beauty of Life on Earth, and develop Real Faith that there is a Spot reserved for you in Heaven.

Thank you, Dear God, Thank you, for Wise people.

Thanks for Listening, as ever in,

"The Spirit of Goodness",

"Saint Bill", Head Coach, A Servant for God's sake.

(Acts 26, v.16-18) (John 7, v.16-18) (1 Jn.4, v.20) (2 Thes.2, v.9-11)

Previews Institute, "Summit Loc-001, H.O.".

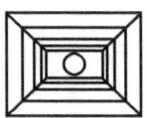

PREVIEWISM
Our World is Beautiful, Yes, Multi-Cultural

Dear Friends and Children of All ages:

We would suggest that you use your Sense of Judgement and recognize that we are all Created in the Image of God, Which is Sin Free, and with a Free Spirit and a Good Nature.

Yes, we have no Sin in God's Eye, because God does Never Condemn (Punish). It is only our Neighbor who condemns us, and our Neighbor is doing this out of Ignorance, not out of true knowledge. So you see, we should always Forgive our Neighbors for their Ignorance and Never respond with Condemnation. In this way the Tree of Condemnation never comes to Fruitation.

This is why a Wise man once said, Dear God, Forgive them for they know not what they Do or Say.

Oh, Yes, My Dear Friends, We have much in Common and it is Good to discuss this Simple subject called Religion.

Thanks for Listening, as ever in, "The Spirit of Goodness",

"Saint Bill" (Head Coach) Previews Institute.

Dear Friends:

No one knows the Absolute truth, So to say, I tell you the Absolute truth is a Lie.

The Absolute truth God does not tell us. It just asks us to have Faith that It is Good., This is why God set us Free, because It gave us a Sense of Judgement to use to guide us to the Truth within our Realm of existance. But Absolute truth is only a Leap of Faith because we know that God is Good.

This is why we have Freedom of Religion (Thought) because we must allow all others the same privilege that we have ourselves. But to try to force your opinion on others is against the Good Nature of God. And so you see, We have much in Common.

Now that you know the Truth within our Realm, you have a Choice. The Shadow is a Ruthless Dictator, God is a Freedom-Fighter.

One System is called a Dictatorship. The other is called a Democracy.

Which do you wish to Serve?

We are Canadian and so we choose to Serve God.

Thanks for Listening, as ever in, "The Spirit of Goodness",

"Saint Bill" (Head Coach) Previews Institute

Dear Friends: The Wisdom of God is so great and Far and Wide that it SEEMS It has no Bounds, but in fact It does. Yes, the Outer Limits of Light are God's Bounds. Beyond the reach of Light (Outer-darkness) God knows nothing because It has no darkness in It. God is in the Light and wants nothing to do with Darkness. That artificial knowledge is Cast Out (Kept Out). Yes, Reality is God, and God is Reality, Not Fantasy (Illusion).

Thanks for Listening, as ever in, "The Spirit of Goodness"

"Saint Bill" (Head Coach) Previews Institute.

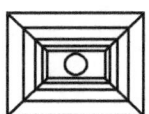

PREVIEWISM
Our World is Beautiful, Yes, Multi-Cultural

Dear Friends and Children of All ages:

We know there is No Sin against God, because God does never Condemn or take Offence, but rather always Forgives and says, Now Go, and do it better next time. Yes, we must seek Excellence, Not Perfection.

Seeking Perfection is Insanity, and this is why there is so much Sin against Humanity in the Minority (10%) of Society. Yes, these people call themselves Sinners, Only because they are Serving an Illusion (The Shadow) (False Instruction)

But the Majority (88%) of Society, seeking only Excellence, call themselves Saints, and rightly so, because God is EverLoving, EverForgiving, and EverUnderstanding. And of course we know, we should Act in the Likeness of God whenever possible.

Thanks for Listening, as ever in "The Spirit of Goodness",

"Saint Bill" (Head Coach) Previews Institute,

P.S.: Seeking Excellence creates a Great Success. (and Success Stories)
Seeking Perfection creates a Failure. (and Counterfeit Miracles)

God the Real, The Spirit of Goodness, tells you to Seek Excellence. (Blessed God)
God the Fraud, The Shadow, tells you to Seek Perfection. (Dirty Bastard)(Negative)

P.S.: We have made an Interesting observation.

According to Abraham there are only two types of people in the World. Jews and Gentiles,. One serving Satan, and One serving God.

The Messiah says, Wrong,. Both the Jews and the Gentiles are serving Satan.

Only Christians are serving God.. Yes, they are God's Chosen people.(Acts26,v.16-18) (Sounds familiar, eh!) Now we know, where there is Self-righteousness there is Illusion (The Shadow). Now the Question is, Of these three groups of people, which one is on the Right track.?

From the "Previewlite's" perspective it seems the Gentiles (88%) are doing the most Good and making the most Progress in the World as they Serve their Nieghbors, and subsequently live in Happiness, Decency, Prosperity, and Peace of Mind.

Thank you, Dear God, Thank you, for true Insight, Yours truly, as ever,

"Saint Bill" (Coach)

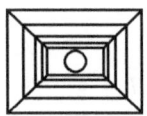

PREVIEWISM
Our World is Beautiful, Yes, Multi-Cultural

Dear Friends and Children of All ages:

Now for some interesting Statistics:

Here in Calgary, Alberta, Canada, 1 in every 1,500 people is a Preacher (Priest). Of these 1,500 people, 200 are in Church with the Preacher, and they call themselves Sinners including the Preacher, always complaining of their Misery. The balance, the 1,300 people are Saints out in the Free World serving their Neighbors, and Praising God for their Blessings, (In their Closet, of course).

The Question is: Who should we Follow.?

The Answer is: So obvious. (Chuckle, Chuckle, eh':)

As ever in, "The Spirit of Goodness",

"Saint Bill" Head Coach, Previews Institute.

Thank you, Dear God, Thank you, for true Insight.

Dear Friends:

According to our Understanding God's work was all done in 6 days, Six thousand years, after which God rested in Peace, Harmony, and Equality with Humankind. The Plan was finished, Yes, Life in the Womb, Life on Earth, and Life in Heaven. Guaranteed in writing by, the Gracious, Loving, Forgiving, and EverUnderstanding God of Goodness, according to "The Compass" by Author "Saint Bill". Yes, this we see as God the Real, "The Spirit of Goodness".

End of Story. Anything to the contrary is pure Fiction, Fantasy, and Illusion for the purpose of Extortion, Selfservance, and Self-righteousness by Lazy Ruthless Parisites. Yes, Illusion goes to any Extremes to try to prove that It is Real. But It is still simply Illusion (The Shadow) that leads us to Condemn, Punish, and cause Pain and Suffering. And then Lies and says, It is God's Will. Which is only to try to Justify Murder. What a Sadistic attempt to Glorify Evil. Garbage, Cast It Out,

So my Friends, Dwell on "The Spirit of Goodness" which is God the Real with Its Sense of Judgement, Free Spirit, and Good Nature together with Its children (angels), the oldest being The Spirit of Truth and the youngest being The Spirit of Enthusiasm, with many in between. Yes, Let them Flourish.

Thanks for Listening, as ever in, "The Spirit of Goodness",

"Saint Bill" (Coach).

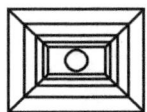

PREVIEWISM
Our World is Beautiful, Yes, Multi-Cultural

Dear Friends and Children of All ages:

The World or anyone in It can not put Stumbling Blocks in your path when you learn to Look Up and make them all Stepping Stones to a better way of Life.

A Wise man once representing God the Real pointed his finger into the Sky and said, Look to God the Real which is Upward and not to God the Fraud which is Downward.,

And so you see, we at Previews Look to God the Real, "The Spirit of Goodness", with Its Sense of Judgement, Free Spirit, and Good Nature, together with Its Angels (children), the oldest being The Spirit of Truth and the youngest being The Spirit of Enthusiasm, with many in between.

Yes, we Look Up and put The Shadow (Satan) behind us and walk on Its big fat Head. And every once in a while we put our Foot down Hard and say, Die, You Cocksucker, Die.

And so you See, when you look to God for your Strength It never Fails you.

But when you look to a Human Idol your Focus is off of God and the Idol is only there with Its hand out when the Sun shines, but when the Clouds come and the Rain falls, It is like The Shadow, It disappears, No where to be seen until the Sun shines again.

And so you see, when the Clouds come and the Rain falls, you are alone until you learn to Focus on God, and then you Realize that the Sun is still shining above the Clouds, and that God never Fails you, and then you have been Born again and Never look at or Trust a Human Idol again, because they represent God the Fraud.

And so you see, We say to you, Look Up and see Truth and Reality and become enthused by Opportunity, and Never Look Down again, because Looking Down is like Looking Back and God the Real Never Looks Back. Never, It may Look around but It Never looks Back.

Yes, remember, Your Sense of Judgement never fails you because your Decisions are based on Reality (Facts), and Not Illusion (Hearsay).

Thanks for Listening, as ever in,

"The Spirit of Goodness",

"Saint Bill" (Head Coach) A Servant for God's sake.

(Acts 26, v.16-18)(John 7, v.16-18)(1 Jn.4, v.20)(2 Thes.2, v.9-11)

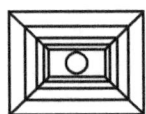

PREVIEWISM
Our World is Beautiful, Yes, Multi-Cultural

Dear Friends and Children of all ages:

The Shadow says, "I am God", My way is the Only way.

If you agree with It, you are being Self-righteous on The Shadow's behalf. God the Real says, The Tree of Life is Up-side down, so that Every way leads to God in Heaven and Life Eternal.

If you agree with It, you are being Righteous because You have set your Neighbor Free,

Yes, The Shadow has Its Roots in the Ground and It is Dark,

God has Its Roots above the Clouds and It is Bright out there.

Thank you, Dear God, Thank you, for true Insight. as ever in,

"The Spirit of Goodness",

"Saint Bill" (Head Coach) A Servant for God's sake.

Previews Institute, "Summit Loc-001, H.O."

Dear Friends:

God the Real, takes no Offence to anything we do or say, because It is EverUnderstanding, and where there is No Offence there is No Sin.

The Ignorant and Uninformed Human (Our Neighbors) take Offence to some of the things we say or do, and So it Seems they have Sinned against Us.

But we do not take Offence to anything You say or do. So where there is No Offence there is No Sin.

So beware of taking Offence to anything We say or do, But do Defend yourself.

Thank you, Dear God, Thank you, "We are All Saints".

as ever in, "The Spirit of Goodness",

"Saint Bill" (Head Coach)

Previews Institute.

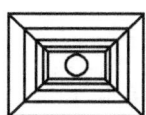

PREVIEWISM
Our World is Beautiful, Yes, Multi-Cultural

Dear Friends and Children of All ages:

A Wise person once said, Offensive words or actions are a Sin against Humanity.

Defensive words or actions are an Act of God.

So do not take Offence to any of your Neighbor's words or actions.

But if someone takes Offence to your words or actions, You Defend yourself. You just say, "We Forgive you for your Ignorance, Now be Gone, Out of My sight."

"You do your thing and I will do mine".

Thank you. Thank you, Dear God, Thank you, for true Insight.

"Saint Bill" (Head Coach) A servant for God's sake.

Previews Institute, "Summit Loc-001, H.O."

"The Body of God"

The Sun in the Centre is God's Heart.

The Light is God's Blood.

The Planets are God's Organs.

The Stars are God's Thoughts.

The Rain is God's Love.

And We are God's Children..

"Playing in the Mud"

"Creative, eh:` Chuckle, Chuckle, eh

Thank you, Dear God, Thank you,

"We are All SAINTS". Author: "Saint Bill" - Co-Authors: "Me & My Friends"

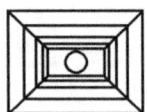

PREVIEWISM
Our World is Beautiful, Yes, Multi-Cultural

Dear Friends and Children of All ages:

God the Fraud, The Shadow, says, It gives you Freedom of Choice, but The Shadow is a Liar. God the Real, gives Us a "Sense of Judgement", and when We use our "Sense of Judgement", we base our Decisions on Facts (Reality), Not Hearsay (Illusion), and so the Truth is so obvious that there is No Choice, but to go with the Truth.

One would have to be a complete Retard (Barbarian)(Imbecile) to go for the Ridiculous Illusions of The Shadow.

So you see, when you Trust your "Sense of Judgement" you are Trusting God the Real, and the more you Do, the more Accurate your "Sense of Judgement" becomes.

And soon the unfulfilling influence of The Shadow is reduced to Less than a Speck of Dust, and in Reality reduced to Nothing, because Nothing is Perfect, and Less than a Speck of Dust is Good enough for God the Real, and in Fact just Super, Super Excellent.

And so you see, We are Free. Yes, We are Never outside God's Umbrella of Love. We can think, talk, and Do as we please while we Allow All others the same Privilege.

Oh, Yes, take No Offence to anything We say or do, because where there is No Offence there is No Sin.

Thank you, Dear God, Thank you,

"We are All SAINTS", Author: "Saint Bill" - Co-Authors: "Me & My Friends"

Dear Friends:

We should remember that "The Law" is our Neighbor's opinion. And when we respect our Neighbor's opinion, The Law serves God the Real, "The Spirit of Goodness", because the Majority Rules among the Wise.

If you think that "The Law" is God's opinion, then The Law serves Satan The Shadow (Illusion), because it becomes a Power-Struggle amoung Self-righteous Idiots.

Author: "Saint Bill" - Co-Authors: "Me & My Friends"

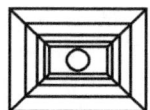

PREVIEWISM
Our World is Beautiful, Yes, Multi-Cultural

Dear Friends and Children the World over:

Some people take Offence to some of the things we say or do in Good Faith, and so we Forgive them for their ignorance in taking us the wrong way.

They have Tried to Sin, but we have not. And when we do not take Offence to their Offence they Failed to Sin and we have not Sinned.

Yes, you see, when we do not Retaliate in Word or Deed the other person has Failed in his/her attempt to Sin, and we have not Sinned. But many a time we have to Forgive the other for their Ignorance in attempting to make us Sin.

Yes, the Tree of Condemnation does not bear Fruit (Punishment) if we do not Retaliate in Word or Deed.

But this does not mean that we can not Defend ourselves against what Seems to be intentional Offence.

You see, Offensive words or actions (Aggression) is a Sin against Humanity. But Defensive words or actions (Self-Defence) is an Act of God.

So you see, only the Ignorant take Offence (Retaliate) and when there are Two that are Ignorant then there is what seems like Sin, But when One is Wise there is No Sin.

So, do not take Offence to anything your Neighbors Say or Do, because where there is No Offence there is No Sin.

Thank, you, Dear God, Thank you, "We are All SAINTS"',
Yours truly, as ever in, "The Spirit of Goodness",
"Saint Bill", Head Coach, A Servant for God's sake.

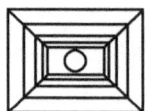

PREVIEWISM
Our World is Beautiful, Yes, Multi-Cultural

Dear Friends and Children the World over:

We have several, perhaps many, things in Common. The most important is that we are Brothers and Sisters. And we always Love our Brothers and Sisters regardless of the Difference in Opinions.

But we do know the Righteous serve their Neighbors and God and in that order.

The Self-righteous serves Satan and says, To Hell with your Neighbors unless they agree with Me and My God. (Luke 14, v.26).

Yes, the Self-righteous says, My way is the Only way, Do it My way or you are Dead, and that is serving Satan (The Shadow)(Illusion)(Lie).

The Righteous say, God's way is Everyone's way, and Everyone's way is God's way, because God set us Free, and gave us a Sense of Judgement to Use to Develop our Good Nature, which is to be Compromising.

Yes, Righteous, because God has promised Never to condemn us for our Differences. Yes, we are All Equal and One with God, and God is Equal and One with Us always.

And so the Tree of Condemnation Never bears Fruit (Punishment) among the Wise (Saints).

It only bears Fruit (Punishment) among the Ignorant (Sinners).

Saints know they are not Perfect. (Reality) (Serving "The Spirit of Goodness".

    Sinners think they are Perfect. (Illusion) (Serving God the Fraud, The Shadow).

So, do not take Offence to anything your Neighbors Say or Do, because where there is No Offence there is No Sin.

Thank you, Dear God, Thank you, "We are All SAINTS".

As ever in, "The Spirit of Goodness",

"Saint Bill" (Coach)

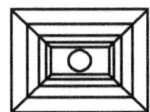

PREVIEWISM
Our World is Beautiful, Yes, Multi-Cultural

Dear Friends and Children the World over:

A Clarification of Faith For Us Previewlites:

We Love our God with All our Hearts, Minds, and Souls. Thank you. We Love our Neighbors as God Loves Us. Thank you.

We do not Sin because God set Us Free to Serve our Neighbors, and We serve our Neighbors as God serves Us. Thank you.

We will not Die, because we do not look at Physical death as the End, but only the Beginning. Yes, Physical death is just an Illusion trying to Distract Us from the Reality of Life Eternal.

We will Live Eternally with God in Heaven, in the World, and in the Hearts, Minds, and Souls of All generations of the Present and the Future, because God has No Past, only the Present and the Future. Thank you.

Thank you, Dear God, Thank you, for True Insight, Thank you, Dear God, Thank you, We are All SAINTS". For Now and Forever.

Thank you, Dear God, Thank you,

Author: "The Spirit of Goodness", by "Saint Bill".

A Note:

Life is a Tragedy for those who Feel, and A Comedy for those who Think. Thank you.

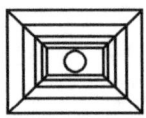

PREVIEWISM
Our World is Beautiful, Yes, Multi-Cultural

Dear Friends and Children the World over:

We "Previewlites realize that there is No Sin in the World, there is Only Some Ignorance.

So the Wise take No Offence, but rather Forgive their Neighbors for their Ignorance, and there is No Sin.

When there are Two that are Ignorant then there is sometimes Sin because it leads to Retaliation, which causes Pain and Suffering, which is an Offence against Humanity, which is Sin.

But We already know that 88% of people are Wise to this knowledge, and Only 10% of people are Ignorant to this knowledge, and Only 1% are out and out Criminals who Retaliate at almaost anything, and lastly only 1 in 400 is so many time Deceived that they think It is God's will to Retaliate and Enslave the world to themselves, the Shadow's servants. And because they are the most Ignorant and Deceived people on Earth they Serve The Shadow as they Lie and say we are All Sinners, and must Worship a Human Idol to be Redeemed or Forgiven.

Well, what a Ridiculous Scenario.

It is obvious the World is a Beautifull place to Live in, not withstanding the "Shadow Worshippers", and the Ignorant.

So, We Previewlites, representing Society as a Whole, being among the Wise will continue to Forgive our Neighbors for their Ignorance, and take No Offence to anything they Say or Do, and where there is No Offence there is No Sin.

Thank you, Dear God, Thank you, "We are All Saints" in your Eye and the Wise See life through God's Eye, and say "Be Gone" to The Shadow (A Dead Lord).

Thanks for Listening, as ever in, "The Spirit of Goodness",

"Saint Bill".

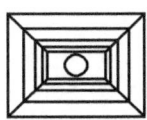

PREVIEWISM
Our World is Beautiful, Yes, Multi-Cultural

Dear Friends and Children of All ages:

A Poem - Step by Step to a Sin-Free Life

Where there is No Offence, There is No Sin,
Where there is No Sin, There is God.
Where there is God, There is Truth.
Where there is Truth, There is Love.
Where there is Love, There is No Punishment.
Where there is No Punishment, There is Understanding.
Where there is Understanding, There is Knowledge.
Where there is Knowledge, There is No Ignorance
Where there is No Ignorance, There is No Offence.
Where there is No Offence, There is No Pain,
Where there is No Pain, There is Bliss.
Where there is Bliss, There is Happiness.
Where there is Happiness and Bliss, There are "Saints".
Where there are "Saints", There are 88% of people.
Where there are "Hypocrites", There are 10% of people,
Where there are "Sinners", There are 1% of people.
Where there are "Retards", There are 1 in 400 people.
Where there are 1 in 400 as Retards, There is evidence that God is Not Perfect..
Where God is Not Perfect, There we have Peace.
Where God is Not Just, There we have Harmony.
Where God is Not Fair, There we have Equality.
Where we have Peace, Harmony, and Equality,
There we have Happiness, Decency, Prosperity, and Peace of Mind.
Where we have Happiness, Decency, Prosperity, and Peace of Mind,
There we have achieved the Purpose of God in our Life.
Where we have achieved the Purpose of God in our Life, There we have Eternal Life,
    in Body, Mind, and Spirit.
Where we have Eternal Life, We Need No More.
Where we Need No More, We Learn to Share.
Where we Learn to Share, We Learn to Love, and To Love is To Give
    without expecting a Return, But Thank God, we get a Lot of Thanks.

Thanks for Listening, as ever in, "The Spirit of Goodness",
"Saint Bill", Head Coach, "A Servant for God's sake"
Previews Institute, "Summit Loc-001, H.O."

The Tradition of "Change for the Better" is Born in *"PREVIEWISM"*
www.previews-inc.com
Make 10 - 20 Copies per week and Pass It On. - God will be well Pleased.

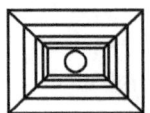

PREVIEWISM
Our World is Beautiful, Yes, Multi-Cultural

Dear Friends and Children of All ages:

Illusion is the Virus of a Mental disease called Schizophrenia (Insanity). In order for us to control this disease or to wipe It out, God gave us a Sense of Judgement to use to Judge (Decide) right from wrong (Reality from Illusion).

This is why Illusion (The Shadow) in Its struggle to survive instructs us "Not to Judge". Yes, So that we might fall into total Confusion and Illusion (Insanity).

A Criminal, we know, has a severe case of this Mental Disease as He/She will go to any extreme to try to achieve His/Her misguided objectives.

The Objectives being to get a "FreeRide" from Society and secondly to satisfy His/Her false-prided Ego. Yes, to Glorify Him/Her self as the Winner.

The segment of Society that promotes this Sick-psyche-Psychology is found in. the Doctrine of Judaism and Christianity.

Yes, Illusion is the Seed (Virus), Judaism is the Root (Doctrine) and Christainity is the Tree (Hypocricy), and a Crop of Negative, Sadistic, Lazy, Shameless, Self-righteous, Extortionist Parisites, Mentally ill and Distorted Idiots is the Fruit. Yes, Judaism hiding behind a Sheep-skin-Coat and the Mask of a Good man.

Thank God the Real, "The Spirit of Goodness" that "The Good People", "The Saints", always Prevail and win the war with Hands-down Intellect. Never resorting to Violence to win the War. This Positive-Psychology is a result of the three Gifts that God and All of Its Angels has given Us from Creation, Conception and Birth. Yes, "A Sense of Judgement", "A Free Spirit", and "A Good Nature".

Thanks again for Listening, Yours truly, as ever in, "The Spirit of Goodness",
"Saint Bill" (Head Coach) "A Servant for God's sake".

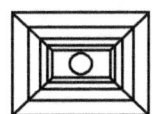

PREVIEWISM
Our World is Beautiful, Yes, Multi-Cultural

Dear Friends and Children of All ages:

In a Society founded by God the Real, "The Spirit of Goodness", when we are Children our Relatives say, You listen to your Father and Mother, and our Father and Mother say, You listen to the Preacher, and the Preacher says, You listen to the Lord.

Now, we have many Lords on this Earth, to mention just a few they include the likes of Buddha, Mohamed, Abraham, Confucous, Hindu, Singh, and Christ.

Now, A Good Lord says, Child, I am a Servant of God, but because I will one day Fail you,. You listen to God the Real, "The Spirit of Goodness", because It will Never fail you, because It gave you a Sense of Judgement, a Free Spirit, and a Good Nature. And when you use your Sense of Judgement you will learn how to avoid the Pitfalls of Life and not have to Suffer needlessly. Yes, My Dear Child, you will find Heaven on Earth when you follow God the Real, "The Spirit of Goodness", and all of Its angels, the oldest being The Spirit of Truth, and the youngest being The Spirit of Enthusiasm, with many in between. Yes, My Dear Child,, and do not worry about Heaven in Heaven because It is a Free Gift to us All because we were All Created, Conceived and Born in the Image of God, Yes, this Free Gift will come only too Soon, but It will be Beautiful, just as Heaven on Earth is Beautifull when you use your Sense of Judgement and Judge (Decide) right from wrong, truth from lie, Yes, Reality from Illusion.

Now, the Fraudulent Lord, and there is Really only One, says, Child, You listen to Me, I am God's Special Servant, all the others are Frauds, So you do as I say or you are Dead and that will be the End of you. Yes, there is only One way to Heaven, and that is to do as I say,. Now, Go walk accross the Ocean.

Chuckle, Chuckle, eh!, Folks,. Thanks for Listening,

"Saint Bill" (Coach)

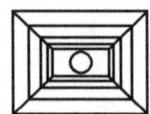

PREVIEWISM
Our World is Beautiful, Yes, Multi-Cultural

Dear Friends and Children of All ages:

We at "Previews" are setting a "New Standard" for the Charitable organization, whereby It is a "Good Provider", and not "A Parasite". Yes, Charity is Not Charity, Philanthropy is Not Philanthropy when the Founder(s) do not provide for their Personal Needs and the Overhead of the Organizational Facilities from their own Resources.

These Expenses (Personal and Corporate) are the Foundation of the "Eternal (Trust) Foundation" namely, WWW.PREVIEWS-INC.COM (Previews Inc.).

Twenty (20%) per cent of the Net, Net profit of the Organization is Donated to "Previews Institute of Universal Philosophy" for the Relief of Poverty, both Physical and Spiritual Poverty.

Previews Institute of Universal Philosophy does not and will not have Overhead Expenses (Personal or Corporate) that exceed the Twenty (20%) percent allocation from "Previews Inc.".... Never. Therefore, every Penny of every Dollar that the general public Donates to "Previews Institute of Universal Philosophy" goes to "The Relief of Poverty", both Physical and Spiritual Poverty. Yes, this is Philanthropy at Its best. Yes, a true Charity, and Not A Parasite.

You, the reader, and prospective Donor can review the other material on this subject and you will find that all supports this very Practical Principle.

We at "Previews" look forward to your participation with our Objective, being, "The Relief of Poverty", both Physical and Spiritual Poverty.

Thanks for Listening,
Yours truly, as ever in, "The Spirit of Goodness",
W.J. (Bill) Handel, M.A., L.W. Head Coach
Previews Institute, Summit Loc-001, H.O.

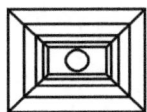

PREVIEWISM
Our World is Beautiful, Yes, Multi-Cultural

December 26/02/63 A.B.

Dear Friends and Children of All Ages:

Yes, It is a Season of Joy, and the Godly celebrate everyday of the Year. But of course, we are all Godly, while some have Great Joy, and others have Little Joy, but none the less, Joy throughout the Year.

When we are Joyous we reflect on the Goodness of Nature, and as such we come to realize that Nature is made up of "Solid, Liquid, and Gas", Yes, Body, Mind, and Spirit.

Now the Question is, Which was First,. Body, Mind, or Spirit.

Yes, that is Right, Spirit was First, Yes, It was All Gas, Hot Gas (Air), chuckle, chuckle, eh!!

Then It cooled off and became Liquid (Mind), and then It cooled some more to become Solid (Body).

And the Body contained Solid, Liquid, and Gas.

Then the Gas became Word, and the Word became Spirit, Yes, The Spirit of Goodness, which is God the Real, as we know It.

Yes, the Word is the Catalyst that brings us forward to the Beginning, and Beginning to Beginning. Yes, Into and Out of the Future, World without End.

Yes, the Definition of God is, "Life Eternal in The Spirit of Goodness", in Body, Mind, and Spirit, World without End.

And as we know that we were All Created, Conceived, and Born in the Image of God, we can be Assured of Life Eternal in Body, Mind, and Spirit.

Yes, My Dear Children, Heaven in Heaven is for All, and not just for the Hoity-Toity Self-righteous Idiots, Yes, the Ignorant and Uninformed Humans.

Yes, we all start out in Life a little Ignorant and so the Object of Life is to become Wise to the Good Nature of God, so that we can find Peace, Harmony, and Equality, and subsequently, Happiness, Decency, Prosperity, and Peace of Mind.

And where we have Happiness, Decency, Prosperity, and Peace of Mind, there we have Achieved the Purpose of God in our Life.

And where we have Achieved the Purpose of God in our Life, there we have "Eternal Life" in Body, Mind, and Spirit.

And where we have "Eternal Life", we Need No More. Where we Need No More, we Learn to Share.

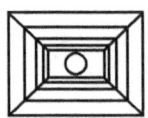

PREVIEWISM
Our World is Beautiful, Yes, Multi-Cultural

Where we Learn to Share, we Learn to Love, and To Love is To Give without expecting a Return. But thank God, We get a Lot of Thanks.

Thank you, Dear God, Thank you, for True Insight.

Thank you, Dear God, Thank you, "We are All Saints" in your Eye.

And what the Ignorant and Deceived "Shadow" thinks is of No Consequence when we do not take Offence to Its ridiculous suggestions.

Thanks for Listening, as ever in, "The Spirit of Goodness",

"Saint Bill", Head Coach, A Servant for God's sake.

Dear Friends and Children of all ages:

Today we have a Quiz.

What is the Shortest time it takes for God to Forgive you.?

Answer: The Blink of an eye.

What is the Longest time it takes for God to Forgive you.?

Answer: 24 hours, Less The Blink of an eye. (Eph. 4,vs.26)

Now, although God is more efficient than we are at the process of Forgiveness, we should always strive to stay within God's standard to the Best of our ability, and we will always receive God's Blessings.

Yes, Look Up and Forgive one-another and Reap only Blessings, barring the weather of course. (God's Law).

2) Looking after yourself is a Natural Instinct, but do not forget that to do this successfully you must always Dwell on your Neighbor's needs and Serve your Neighbor first and you will already have served yourself as you Reap what you Sow. (Man's Law).

Thank you, Dear God, Thank you, for true Insight.

Author: The Spirit of Goodness, by "Saint Bill", A Servant for God's sake.

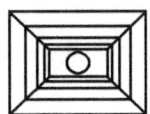

PREVIEWISM
Our World is Beautiful, Yes, Multi-Cultural

Dear Friends and Children of All ages:

"A Statement of Faith"

We believe in God the Real, "The Spirit of Goodness", and We thank God that We were All created, conceived, and Born in the Image of God, and that We will Never leave that state of Imperfection,. because Imperfection Drives Us to continue to make progress toward the Ultimate Purpose of God, which is to achieve Peace, Harmony, and Equality. Yes, Happiness, Decency, Prosperity and Peace of Mind for All of Humankind throughout the World. Our "Sense of Judgement", Free Spirit, and Good Nature together with All of God's Angels (children), the oldest being The Spirit of Truth and the youngest being The Spirit of Enthusiasm, with many in between, allows Us to be "Creative", "A Good Provider", and "A Staedfast Comfortor" to our Nieghbors.. And this Achieves the Purpose of God in Our Life. And where we have Achieved the Purpose of God in our Life, there we have Eternal Life, in Body, Mind, and Spirit.

Where we have Eternal Life, We Need No More. Where we Need No More, We Learn to Share. Where we Learn to Share, We Learn to Love, and

To Love is To Give without expecting a Return. But Thank God, We get a Lot of Thanks. Thank you, Dear God, Thank you, for True Insight. Thank you, Dear God, Thank you, "We are All Saints" in your eye. And what the Ignorant and Deceived "Shadow" thinks is of No Consequence when we do not take Offence to Its ridiculous suggestions.

Thanks for Listening, Folks, as ever in,

"The Spirit of Goodness",

"Saint Bill" (Head Coach) A Servant for God's sake.

Previews Institute, "Summit Loc-001, H.O."

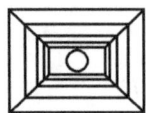

PREVIEWISM
Our World is Beautiful, Yes, Multi-Cultural

Dear Friends and Children of All ages:

Just a little further Insight

"Saint Jesus" said, that Christ means Messiah, and "Saint Jesus" said, that The Messiah is serving Satan (Acts 26, v.16-18)(2 Thes.2, v.9-11)

In fact "Saint Jesus" went a step further and said, that The Messiah is Satan, because The Messiah is a Fictional character just like Satan. And the Fictional Character resides in a Fictional place called Hell. Yes, The Messiah is still in Hell, and "Saint Jesus" went to Heaven just like we all do when our Bodies cease to Function.

But The Messiah is the Deceiver of Deceivers and so Its servant Mr. Paul came up with the Illusion that The Messiah had risen from the Dead, and that Its name was "Jesus the Christ", and Mr. Paul took this story to the Gentiles and said, that Jesus the Christ was the Only Son of God, and that if they would Worship this Character they would be the Only true Children of God, Yes, "The Chosen Ones". (Sounds familiar, eh!)

Yes, they could continue to Preach the Lies and Illusions of the Dark ages, and Pretend that they were Better than others. Yes, Special children of God called "Sinners". Yes, Servants of Satan, but Forgiven.

How ridiculous can you get. Folks? World wide, 1 in 900 is Insane, 1 in 400 follow Judaism, 1 in 100 is a Criminal on the Loose, 1 in 10 is a "Shadow Worshipper", and 88% of people are Gentiles (Gentle People) (Saints) out in the Free World serving their Neighbors, and Praising God the Real, "The Spirit of Goodness", for their Blessings. (In their Closet of Course). Yes, Truth always Prevails.

Thank you, Dear God, Thank you, for True Insight,

As ever in, "The Spirit of Goodness",

Saint Bill, "A Servant for God's sake".

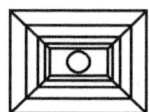

PREVIEWISM
Our World is Beautiful, Yes, Multi-Cultural

Dear Friends and Children of All ages:

The other day I asked a Stranger, What Religion He considered He belonged to.

And He said, He considered himself a "Christian". And I said, I think you are a "Previewlite". And He said, I think you are a "Christian". And I said, that is Good, that means we have something in Common. Yes, that means We are both going to Heaven.

And the Stranger said, Well, It means we both think we are going to Heaven. And I said, Well, I think you are a "Previewlite" because I know you are going to Heaven. Then I said, Why do you think that I am a "Christian".

Well, He said, I am not quite sure. Because to be a Christian, you must bow down and Worship "Christ" or you are Dead, and go to Hell.

Then I said: Tell me, Who wants me out of Heaven, Satan or God.?

And He said, I guess Satan wants you out of Heaven, Because God certainly does Not.

Then I said, So who are these Christians serving, Satan or God.?

And He said, Well, It is obvious they are serving Satan, because they are Self-righteous Idiots just like Satan, who wants to Glorify Himself above God.

And I said, that is Right, So now that you understand the Truth, You go and tell the World that "Jesus" was a "Previewlite" (Gentile) (Gentle Person) (Saint) , and "Christ" was a "Jew" (A Self-righteous Idiot) called a "Sinner". Yes, a Negative, Sadistic, Mean, Lazy, Shameless Parasite, who goes to any extreme to try to prove that Satan is better than God, or that He is better than you.

And the Stranger said, Who are you, anyway, and I said, My name is "Saint Bill" brother of You and "Saint Jesus", who worshipped God the Real, "The Spirit of Goodness", with Its Sense of Judgement, Free Spirit, and Good Nature, together with Its angels (children), the

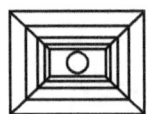

PREVIEWISM
Our World is Beautiful, Yes, Multi-Cultural

oldest being The Spirit of Truth, and the youngest being The Spirit of Enthusiasm, with many in between, as they Live in Heaven, in the World, and in Our Heart, Mind, and Soul. (John 7, v.16-18) They Never Die, but recycle into and out of the Future when our Bodies cease to Function and when we are Created, Conceived and Born in the Image of God.

Yes, My Friend, The Wise person says, "We are One", and that makes Us equal, and when we are equal with God and One-Another, We live in Peace, and Harmony because We are Living in Reality and Freedom of Thought.

The Idiot says, "I am It", I am better than you,., Ya, I am Perfect. So you must be My Slave,. So you do as I say or you are Dead.. Now, Go walk accross the Ocean... This causes much Pain and Suffering because It is Living in Illusion and Mental Slavery.

So My Friend, Cast this Type of Garbage Out, and Go your way, Dwelling on God the Real, "The Spirit of Goodness", as you now Know It.

Thanks for Listening, as ever in, "The Spirit of Goodness"

"Saint Bill", Head Coach, A Servant for God's sake.

Previews Institute, "Summit Loc-001, H.O."

Thank you, Dear God, Thank you.

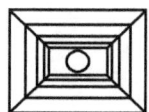

PREVIEWISM
Our World is Beautiful, Yes, Multi-Cultural

MORE
PROVERBS
BY
"Saint Bill"

Supplement To: "THE COMPASS"

The EverLast Testament

A misconception of Old is the Saying, that the Road of Life is Long, Straight, and Narrow. Wrong. The Road of Life is Short, Straight, and 26 Lanes,.... "All One-Way"   a n d there is No Speed Limit... But do not despair,... When you Do a Shoulder-Check before you Switch Lanes, You will do just Fine.

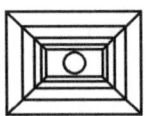

PREVIEWISM
Our World is Beautiful, Yes, Multi-Cultural

Dear Friends and Children of All ages:

When we look at Life It presents a "Big Picture", and It is a Puzzle, and in Fact It has 46,656 pieces of Puzzle, The other day, I asked a young boy how many of these pieces of Puzzle He thought He had in place as His foundation of Life that He could walk on. This young Boy thought for a moment, and said, that He probably had about 1002 pieces in Place around Him, I said, that is Good, Son, you keep building

and as you build, try to build the Picture in a Circle, and as It gets Bigger and Bigger, Do not worry about a few Holes that will develop. Because you can always walk around the Holes and as you keep building on the Big Picture, every time you have to walk around a Hole, You Ask a Question, and you will find that the Answer is in the Question. And when you find the Answer to the Questions the Holes will disappear, or form a Lake, that you have to walk around. But do not despair, because the Scenery is very Beautiful around a Lake.

The young Boy thought for a moment, and asked, Sir, How many pieces of Puzzle do you have in Place around you? And I said, Son, I have 43,560 pieces of Puzzle in Place around me and the Picture is from Horizon to Horizon, to and Beyond the Outermost reaches of the Earth. There are many Lakes and Valleys but No Holes. Because, right now, I am on the Plateau of Mount Everest, and It is Now Level.

When I arrived on the Plateau of Mount Everest, I found a Big Boulder in the middle of It. So with One Big Leap of Faith, I jumped upon the Boulder, Stood Up, Looked Up and put My Foot Down Hard, and It went to Slitherines, and I rubbed with my Rubber Rubber Heel until there was Nothing left but Dust. Then I said, to the other Four Gentlemen around me, Bow, you Gentlemen, Bow,. Knees and All, you Gentlemen Bow.. Chuckle, Chuckle, eh! , My Son,. I am running out of paper, So I will tell you more about that later,. Bye, for Now

As ever in, "The Spirit of Goodness",

"Saint Bill", "A Servant for God's sake".

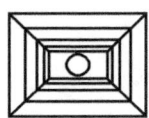

PREVIEWISM
Our World is Beautiful, Yes, Multi-Cultural

Dear Friend,

It is known that the wise person represents God the Real, "The Spirit of Goodness", and so the wise person says, "We are One", that makes us equal, and when we are equal with God and one-another, we live in Peace and Harmony because we are living in Reality and Freedom of Thought.

The idiot represents God the Fraud, "Illusion", and so the idiot says, "I am It", I am better than you. Ya, I am perfect. So you must be my slave. So you do as I say or you are Dead.. Now, Go walk accross the Ocean. This causes much pain and suffering because it is living in Illusion and mental slavery.

We trust you are the type of individual first in line to help improve our Nation's psychology. As such you will be interested in becoming one of our Founding Partners.

We have a Vision. A vision of Happiness, Decency, Prosperity, and Peace of Mind throughout the world within three hundred years. Therefore, we have established "An Eternal (Trust) Foundation". The object of the (Trust) is: To relieve poverty. (Both physical and spiritual poverty). This is a long standing need in Humanity that needs to be filled by someone. But since any one person can not do it by his/her own resources, be it financial, physical, or spiritual, we are calling on you to contribute your share toward the Burden.

"Saint Bill", the Founder of the (Trust), has contributed $100,000.00 financially, many hours of labor physically, and a new bible, "The Compass", spiritually as a track to run on.

The "Eternal (Trust) Foundation" operating under the name of "Previews Inc." is designed to produce fruit (Revenue) and this revenue will grow and grow, just as the (Trust) will grow and grow.

Now the Net Net revenue of the (Trust) will be allocated in the following manner.

1) 20% to Charity (To relieve poverty) (Both physical and spiritual poverty)
2) 25% to Class-B-Voting shareholders. (The descendants of the Founder and the Founding partners.)
3) 40% to re-investment so that the (Trust) will grow and grow, in order to fullfill its mandate.
4) 15% to the Class-A-Voting shareholder (Executor) for administration expenses and services.

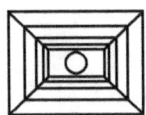

PREVIEWISM
Our World is Beautiful, Yes, Multi-Cultural

In order for the "Eternal (Trust) Foundation" to reach self-sufficiency It must be valued at $12,215,908.00 . Therefore, "Saint Bill", the Founder of the (Trust) is appealing to you to become a "Founding Partner".

"Saint Bill" has contributed $100,000.00 to the (Trust), and we shall call him a "One Star General". If you will contribute $500,000.00 to the (Trust), we will call you a "Five Star General". And if you will contribute $2,600,000.00 to the (Trust), we will call you a "Twenty-Six Star General".

This is the maximum we will accept because Charity is Love and to love is to give without expecting a Return, and we do not want you to expect a return other than the personal satisfaction of helping your Descendants in perpetuity.

In addition, All founding partners will be eternally recorded along with "Saint Bill" in the book of life, "The Compass", (The EverLast Testament).

Please give this your optimistic consideration and do not hesitate to say, "Lets Do It".

Remaining, Yours truly,

as ever in, "The Spirit of Goodness",

W.J. (Bill) Handel, M.A., L.W. (Executor)

Previews Inc. "Eternal (Trust) Foundation"

Note: We have Privates at $10,000.00, Corporals at $25,000.00, Sergeants at $50,000.00 and Lieutenants at $75,000.00

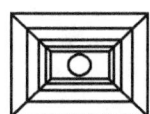

PREVIEWISM
Our World is Beautiful, Yes, Multi-Cultural

Dear Friends and Children of All ages:

You know, You are what you Think, and also,

It takes One to see One.

So when I say, I think you are a Saint, It means I am one. If you say, You think I am a Sinner, It means you are one. But I do not believe you are a Sinner. No way, I see no evidence. So I think you are a Saint.

Yes, I Love you, and so I Forgive you, and there is No Sin. And where there is No Sin, there is God.

When I say, You are going to Heaven, It means I am.

If you say, I am going to Hell, It means you are.

Oh yes, You reap what you sow,

But I do not believe you are going to Hell.

Because God will not have it.

No, not one has fallen short of the Grace of God.

A Wise man once said,

> Say unto others as you would want them to say unto you. Yes, what you wish for others, You receive for yourself,

Thank you, Dear God, Thank you, for true Insight.

Thank you, Dear God, Thank you, "We are All Saints" in God's eye, and We look at Life through God's eye.

As ever in, "The Spirit of Goodness",

"Saint Bill", A Servant for God's sake.

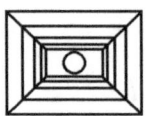

PREVIEWISM
Our World is Beautiful, Yes, Multi-Cultural

Dear Friends and Children of All ages:

We must always remember and Realize that there is only "One Voice of God", but that there are two kinds of people on Earth who Interpret what God says. (Now remember, God speaks with Actions)

One kind of people are Positive, Creative, Good Providers, and Steadfast Comfortors using their "Sense of Judgement". (These people are Looking Up to Reality which is God)

The Other kind of people are Negative, Sadistic, Mean, Lazy, Shameless, Extortionist Parasites that go to any extreme to try to get a "Free Ride" from Society. All the while claiming they are Better than the Positive ones. This causes nothing but Dissension, Pain and Suffering. And then they say, Pain and Suffering makes you Strong. This adds up to "Sadism". Yes, Living in the Pits, while they Condemn the other for their Misery. (These people are Looking Down to the Shadow which is Illusion.)

The Positive are practicing "Happyism" and are living in Heaven on Earth, while they Forgive the Ignorance of the other.

Which do you think is God's Will?

P.S.:   Jesus was One kind of person, and
                    The Shadow is the other kind of person

Thank you, Dear God, Thank you, for true Insight.

Thank you, Dear God, Thank you, "We are All Saints" in God's eye, and We look at Life through God's eye.

Note: 88% of people are Positive, and to some degree negative.
                    12% of people are Negative, and to some degree positive.

And the Majority Rules among the Wise. (Yes, a Democracy works Best.)

Thanks for Listening, as ever in, "The Spirit of Goodness"

"Saint Bill", A Servant for God's sake.

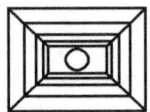

PREVIEWISM
Our World is Beautiful, Yes, Multi-Cultural

Dear Friends and Children of All ages:

The Reality of Life is that It is Eternal in Body, Mind, and Spirit. Yes, Into and Out of the Future, world without End. Yes, the Circle (Cycle) of Life is very Large, so Large that we think we are traveling in a Straight Line, but It is a Long Curve that forms a Circle, and so It is Never Ending.

When we are Conceived, the Spirit becomes Body (Life in the Womb), then the Body becomes Word (Life on Earth), then the Word becomes Spirit (Life in Heaven). Yes, from Beginning to Present, and from Present to Beginning, and from Beginning to Beginning, and from Beginning to Present, and so on and on, World without End.

The Complete Cycle spans approximately 300 years from Birth to Re-Conception. That is approximately 100 years on Earth (seldom over 111), and approximately 200 years in Heaven (seldom over 222), then It is back to Body. This spells "Eternal Life", and a Life of Bliss. All else is a story of The Shadow, pure Bad Fiction (Illusion). Yes, there is No longer any Curse. (Rev.22, v.3)

And so you See, Folks, the World is a Beautifull place to Live in, but The Shadow (Illusion) (Satan) says, The World is Bad, and Its Institution is Good. But we know that Satan (The Shadow) is a Liar. Its Institution is trying to Rule the world by using "Fear Tactic", and NEGATIVE, Sadistic, Mean, Lazy, Shameless, Self-righteous, Extortionist, Parasitic psychology called "Sadism"

But God will not allow it, because God has given the World a "Sense of Judgement", a "Free Spirit", and a "Good Nature", and many POSITIVE characteristics (angels), the oldest being The Spirit of Truth, and the youngest being The Spirit of Enthusiasm, with many in between that results in "Happyism", and this keeps the Unfullfilling Influence of The Shadow (Satan) (Illusion) under control and reduced to Less than a Speck of Dust, for 88% of the World's population.

So you see, God rules the World, and the Self-righteous Idiots can Lie all they want, and gain nothing but Pain and Suffering for themselves. Yes, The Shadow Worshippers.

But, God being in control, Forgives even The Shadow Worshippers, and allows Life to continue, Heaven on Earth, World without End.

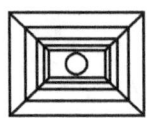

PREVIEWISM
Our World is Beautiful, Yes, Multi-Cultural

Oh, Yes, We have herein a "New Psychology" according to "The Spirit of Goodness" God the Real, as manifested in and by "The Compass", a New Bible, The EverLast Testament, by Author: "Saint Bill", and in approximately 260 years I will be back to enjoy the Fruits of our Labor. Chuckle, Chuckle, eh!! (And to ask God to renew our mandate, and it will renew, into Eternity).

Thank you, Dear God, Thank you, for true Insight.

Thank you, Dear God, Thank you, "We are All Saints" in God's eye, and We Look at Life through God's eye.

Thanks for Listening, Folks, It was a Pleasure,

As ever in, "The Spirit of Goodness",

"Saint Bill", A Servant for God's sake.

Note: 88% of people are Positive, and to some degree negative.
12% of people are Negative, and to some degree positive.

And the Majority Rules among the Wise. (Yes, a Democracy works Best)

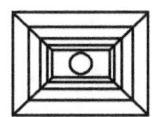

PREVIEWISM
Our World is Beautiful, Yes, Multi-Cultural

Dear Friends,

We at "Previews" turn Stumbling blocks into Stepping Stones. But, we are not born with Stumbling blocks, we are born with Stepping Stones.

Oh, Yes, My Friends, Stumbling blocks come from Ignorant people around us, and when we learn to Forgive people for their Ignorance and not Condemn (Punish) them, the Stumbling block fails to accomplish Its mission. And we continue on our way on our Stepping Stones.

Oh, Yes, My Friends, the One who Condemns is The Shadow (Illusion) (Satan). Yes, a Self-Damned Fool, who thinks he is born with Stumbling blocks.

Yes, My Friends, Negative, Sadistic, Mean, Lazy, Shameless, Self-righteous, Extortionist, Parasitic psychology called "Sadism".

We at "Previews" are Positive, Creative, Good Providers, and Steadfast Comfortors, as a result of following God the Real, "The Spirit of Goodness", which tell us to use our "Sense of Judgement", Free Spirit, and Good Nature, along with Its angels (Characteristics), the oldest being the Spirit of Truth and the youngest being the Spirit of Enthusiasm, with many in between, and this spells a psychology called "Happyism".

Yes, the Purpose of God in our Lives is to make us Happy, and Free us of Guilt, Fear, Doubt and Illusion.

Yes, One psychology is called "Sadism" and One psychology is called "Happyism", and we would rather be Born Happy than Sad.

The Shadow (Satan)(Illusion) is a Sadist but is a Liar and says, He is Happy because He does not Face God, and then He says, follow me and I will make you Happy, and then He gives you nothing but False instruction and you become a Sadist. And then He says, Do not worry, Suffering makes you Strong. Yes, a Sucker for Punishment. And then He says, He is Happy. Yes, Happy as a Pig in a Mess. What a "xxxx" pile of Garbage that Bastard feeds Us.

Thank God the Real, "The Spirit of Goodness", that we do not have to Listen to that Garbage anymore. Yes, we can now say, Shuv It, because we now have an Alternative.

Dear Friends, One day soon you will see the Light, and you will change the Name of your Church to "Previews Institute of Universal Philosophy" "Summit Loc-031". Yes, and then soon, we will have "Summit Loc-999", Chuckle, Chuckle, eh!!

Author: The Spirit of Goodness by Saint Bill, a servant for God's sake.

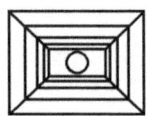

PREVIEWISM
Our World is Beautiful, Yes, Multi-Cultural

Dear Friends and Children of All ages:

Saints are children of God, serving God to the Best of their ability, given their Experiences.

Sinners are children of God, serving Satan. In which group do you Stand.?

"We are All Saints" in God's eye, and We look at Life through God's eye. Through which Eye do you Look at Life.?

Some, 88% of people look at Life through God's eye, the eye of Reality, and know they are Saints (Winners) (Positive).

Some, 2% of people look at Life through the Human eye, the eye of Illusion, and think they are Sinners (Loosers) (Negative)

Some, 10% of people look at Life through Both eyes, and are obviously Confused Hypocrites.

The Doctrine of The Shadow (Satan) (Illusion) is Dictatorship. The Doctrine of Wise people (God's people) is Democracy.

The Doctrine of Satan (The Shadow) (Illusion) is passing away, and within 300 years will be reduced to less than a Speck of Dust, Because Its Servants are Now operating a Democracy.

Dictators (Barbarians) are careless and usually Strike the First Blow. Wise people (Gentiles) (Gentle people) (Saints) Never Strike the First Blow.

Oh, Yes, My Friends, The New Psychology (Doctrine), PREVIEWISM as defined by The Spirit of Goodness, in and by "The Compass" by author: "Saint Bill", will be Predominant throughout the World within Three Hundred 300 years and All will live in Peace, Harmony, and Equality, Yes, Happiness, Decency, Prosperity, and Peace of Mind, as All the Countries of the World will operate a Democracy, and the "United Nations" (U.N.) will be a Democracy of Democracies. Ah, Yes, Satan (The Shadow) (Illusion) Lost the Battle.

We are Now in the process of Cleaning-Up the Mess after the Battle, and Re-Building according to the Will of God the Real, "The Spirit of Goodness", with Its "Sense of Judgement", "Free Spirit", and Good Nature, together with Its angels (characteristics), the oldest being The Spirit of Truth, and the youngest being The Spirit of Enthusiasm, Ah, Yes

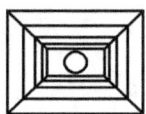

PREVIEWISM
Our World is Beautiful, Yes, Multi-Cultural

My Friends, the Purpose of God has always been to make Us Happy, and Free Us of Guilt, Fear, Doubt, and Illusion. Yes, To achieve Heaven on Earth so that we can become accustomed to conditions in Heaven in Heaven, Chuckle, Chuckle, eh!!

Thanks for Listening, Folks, It was a Pleasure,

as ever in, "The Spirit of Goodness",

"Saint Bill", (Head Coach) A Servant for God's sake

And Now a Question.

Dear Friends and Children of all ages:

Are you a Leader or are you a Follower.?

Well, let me tell you, God wants you to be a Leader, because a Leader walks with God.

A Follower walks with a Lord, and a Lord can lead you astray.

God will never lead you astray, because when you walk with God, you use your Sense of Judgement to Judge (Decide) right from wrong and you come closer and closer to God at every turn, and God gives you Its Blessings and considers you a Saint, Yes, a Child of God.

When you walk with The Lord, he says, Do not Judge, Do not Decide right from wrong or you will Die.

Just follow me and I will take you to Heaven, and then he takes you to Hell the long way around, right here on Earth, as he continually calls you a Sinner, Yes, an Idiot, Yes, a Lost Sheep.

Thank you, Dear God, Thank you, for an obvious and easy choice.

Author: The Spirit of Goodness, by, Saint Bill, a Servant for God's sake.

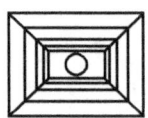

PREVIEWISM
Our World is Beautiful, Yes, Multi-Cultural

Dear Friends and Children of All ages:

Question: What is Sin.?

Answer: Sin is Pain and Suffering. And the cause of It is Lie., another Sin.

And so if you live under the Influence of a Lie, you act accordingly and cause yourself and others Pain and Suffering, and become a "Sadist", practicing Negative, Sadistic, Mean, Lazy, Shameless, Self-righteous, Extortionist, Parasitic psychology called "Sadism".

But when we do not Believe the Big Lie, then we act according to the Good Nature of God within us, and we have No Sin (No Pain and Suffering), and this causes Us to be Happy, Decent, Prosperous people, Filled with Peace of Mind, practicing a Positive, Healthy psychology called "Happyism".

Thank you, Dear God, Thank you, for an Obvious and Easy choice.

Thank you, Dear God, Thank you, for true Insight.,

As ever in, "The Spirit of Goodness",

"Saint Bill", A Servant for God's sake

(Acts 26, v.16-18)(John 7, v.16-18)(I Jn.4, v.20 (2 Thes.2, v.9-11) Previews Institute.

P.S.: Poverty is a Reality to Some. Misery is an Illusion to Most.

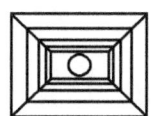

PREVIEWISM
Our World is Beautiful, Yes, Multi-Cultural

Dear Friend:

We all know that: Sin is Lie, and Lie is Sin.

Therefore, A Sinner is a Liar, and a Liar is a Sinner.

Therefore, It is obvious that We have proved that you are a Liar when you say, You are a Sinner. And you are a Liar when you say, Your people are Sinners. Because they are Children of God, serving God to the Best of their ability, and that is Good enough for God, and so God considers them "Saints".

Beautiful Godly people, Yes, Saints. Never once Condemned or Accused of Wrong Doing, but rather always Loved.

So you see, We do not believe you are a Sinner, because No-one ever consciously Lies. They have to be Deceived first. So we can always Forgive you, and Love you.

And so Now that you Understand that you are a Liar when you say, You think you are a Sinner, when in Fact, You know you are a Saint, You can now make an About Turn and start Practicing Previewism. Yes, Preach the Positive message of "Happyism". And Stop serving Illusion (The Shadow) (Satan) (The Liar) (The Sadist)

Yes, you are now at the Point where you Should change the Name of your Church to: Previews Institute of Universal Philosophy, "Summit Loc-031"

Coach: Saint Gordon.

Chuckle, chuckle, eh, Folks,. Thanks for Listening, Thank you, Dear God, Thank you, for true Insight.

"We are All Saints" in God's eye, and

We look at Life through God's eye.

As ever in, "The Spirit of Goodness",

"Saint Bill" (Head Coach) A Servant for God's sake.

Previews Institute, "Summit Loc-001, H.O." .

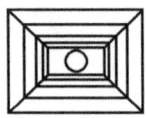

PREVIEWISM
Our World is Beautiful, Yes, Multi-Cultural

My Dear Friends,

"The Shadow Worshippers", chuckle, chuckle, eh !! We all know that: Sin is Lie, and Lie is Sin.

But when One does not Believe the Lie, There is No Sin.

And when One does not Repeat the Lie, There is No Sin.

So you see, We at "Previews" have No Sin.

And as a Result, No Pain and Suffering.

So you see, If you are so Burdened with Lie (Sin), Pain and Suffering, Why do you not Look-Up, to God the Real, "The Spirit of Goodness", With Its "Sense of Judgement", "Free Spirit", and Good Nature, Which relieves you of Lie (Sin), and Pain and Suffering.

Oh, Yes, My Friends, We at "Previews" recognize the Original Sin (Lie), And we do not Repeat It, any more and Never will again, because We now know It for what It is, Yes, the cause of Pain and Suffering.

The Original Sin (Lie) was when Abraham expressed the Illusion that You are Separated from God. Wrong. You are Never Separated from God, No matter if you are Insane, a Retard, a Barbarian, or a Criminal, or a Shadow Worshipper. No matter, God is with you, Always.

The bigger problem was that Abraham said this to his Neighbor, and Not Himself. Yes, He was a Self-righteous Idiot, All because He was Lazy, and wanted a "Free Ride" from Society. And so he resorted to Extortion, and Parasitic psychology called "Sadism".

And we all know that "Sadism" goes to any extreme to try to get a "Free Ride". Yes, to any extreme including Suicide.

So you see, My Friends, This is why We practice "Happyism", which is found in the Doctrine of "Previewism" as manifested by "The Spirit of Goodness", God the Real, in and by "The COMPASS", a New Bible, The EverLast Testament, by Author: "Saint Bill".

Yes, We are All Saints, in God's eye, and We look at Life through God's eye.

Thanks for Listening, as ever in, "The Spirit of Goodness",

"Saint Bill" (Head Coach)

THE TRADITION OF "CHANGE FOR THE BETTER" IS BORN IN *"PREVIEWISM"*
www.previews-inc.com
Make 10 - 20 Copies per week and Pass It On. - God will be well Pleased.

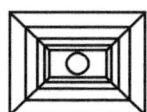

PREVIEWISM
Our World is Beautiful, Yes, Multi-Cultural

Dear Friends and Children of All ages:

All understood and Summarized, We find there are two Forces in the World.

Yes, the Positive force, and the Negative force.

The Positive force is God the Real, "The Spirit of Goodness" , and

The Negative force is God the Fraud, "Illusion"

The Positive force, being Reality, Ultimately leads to a Life of Bliss and Happiness.

The Negative force, being Illusion, Ultimately leads to Depression and Suicide.

The Solution for those who fall into Illusion is to Look-Up to and Above the Horizon, and they will Instinctively gain Trust in God the Real, "The Spirit of Goodness" and then they should Never Look-Down or Back again, but rather just Dwell on "The Spirit of Goodness", God the Real, and just walk on (Stomp-on) The Shadow with each Step ahead, saying, Die you Cocksucker, Die.

And It will Die, because It is Illusion that Lost the Battle, when You Looked-Up.

Thank you, Dear God, Thank you, for true Insight.

"We are All Saints", in God's eye, and

We look at Life through God's eye, The Eye of Reality.

Thanks for Listening, as ever in, "The Spirit of Goodness",

Saint Bill, Head Coach, A Servant for God's sake.

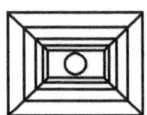

PREVIEWISM
Our World is Beautiful, Yes, Multi-Cultural

Dear Friends and Children of All ages:

Illusion expressed is Lie and Lie is Sin. Sin is Spiritual Pain and Suffering, All Sin is a Result of Lie.

Therefore, When you Eliminate Lie, you eliminate Sin.

To eliminate Lie, you must Cast Out Illusion.

To Cast Out Illusion, you must always face Reality which is God.

God gave Us a "Sense of Judgement" to use to Judge (Decide) right from wrong. So we must always base our Decisions on Reality and not Illusion. That is to say, we must base our Decisions on Facts, and not Hear-say. Yes, Seeing is Believing, and Believe nothing else.

When you follow this formula to a High degree, you eliminate Sin to a great degree. And in Fact the Unfullfilling Influence of The Shadow is reduced to next to Nil and you can then avoid all Sin, and Live Sin Free.

Yes, in Happiness, Decency, Prosperity, and Peace of Mind, and in Peace, Harmony, and Equality with your Neighbors and the World around you.

Yes, Sin is like The Shadow, It seems Real, but It is not Real, but just an Illusion Expressed. Yes, Sin is Lie, and Lie is Sin, Yes, Illusion Expressed.

Therefore, the Original Sin was the Original Lie, and the Original Lie was the Original Illusion, and the Original Illusion was that You are separated from God. Wrong. You are Never Separated from God. God is always with You.

You may be Distracted from God by The Shadow of God, but You are Never separated from God. God Never leaves you, Not in the Sunshine, Not in the Rain, and Not in the Hailstorms. God Never leaves you. Yes, God is with you Always.

Thanks for Listening, as ever in, "The Spirit of Goodness",

"Saint Bill" (Head Coach) A Servant for God's sake.

"Previews Institute."

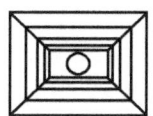

PREVIEWISM
Our World is Beautiful, Yes, Multi-Cultural

con't....

And so you see, Folks, The Original Illusion was the Seed of Illusion that grew into a Pile of Mess. But now that we have Identified the Seed of Illusion You simply need to Eliminate and Destroy the Seed, and the Mess will gradually wither and disappear. And you will come to Live Sin Free. Yes, without Guilt, Fear, Doubt or Illusion. Yes, in Happiness, Decency, Prosperity, and Peace of Mind. Yes, in Peace, Harmony, and Equality with your Neighbors, and the World around you.

Thank you, Dear God, Thank you, for true Insight.

Now remember,   We are All Saints, in God's eye, and

    We look at life through God's eye.

Thanks for Listening, as ever in, "The Spirit of Goodness",

"Saint Bill" (Head Coach) A Servant for God's sake.

Previews Institute,

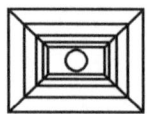

PREVIEWISM
Our World is Beautiful, Yes, Multi-Cultural

Dear Friends and Children of All ages:

As children of God, we all grow closer and closer to God, and a better and better Understanding of Truth and Love. This is a Daily process and so the Newness of Life keeps us Forever Enthused.

Today we have a question for you: Are we all born Saints, Are we all born Sinners, or are we all born Hypocrites? Which of the three do you think it is.?

The answer is that, We are All conceived as Hypocrites, and we are All born as Saints, and we All live as Saints, and we all go to Heaven as Saints.

This is So, because God will not recognize or acknowledge Illusion or Negative thinking, but rather just keeps It Cast Out, Yes, God Casts Illusion out into outer darkness, beyond the reach of Light. Yes, out of Sight, out of Mind, and Out of Mind, Out of Existence.... Yes, there is no Death in God's world, but rather Life Eternal in Body, Mind, and Spirit.... Yes, into and out of the Future, World without End. Yes, It is a big Circle that is Never Ending.

When we are Conceived the Spirit becomes Body, and so It is from Light to Darkness, Yes, Hypocrite. When we are Born the Body becomes Word, as the Light shines, and the Wise look Up to God, and follow God, and as such are Considered Saints by God, and those who look at Life through God's eye, Yes, Creative people, Good Providers, and Steadfast Comforters,. Yes, these are God's people.

And after some time the Word becomes Spirit as we re-enter Heaven with God.

And then after some time the Spirit becomes Body again as we return to enjoy the Fruits of our Labor, from the previous time Round.

Oh, Yes, My Friends, this Spells Eternal Life in Body, Mind, and Spirit, and a Life of Happiness and Bliss. Not to mention Prosperity, and Peace of Mind.

Thanks for Listening, Folks, It was a Pleasure, as ever with God,

"Saint Bill" (Coach)

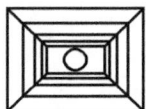

PREVIEWISM
Our World is Beautiful, Yes, Multi-Cultural

Dear Friends and Children of All ages:

Now for some Definitions.

1) God the Real, is "The Spirit of Goodness", and is a Positive Force. This is Good.

2) God the Fraud, The Shadow, is "Illuison", and is a Negative Force. This is Waste.

3) A Previewlite is a person who knows that he/she is considered equal to his/her Neighbor. Therefore, a Previewlite is a "Saint", yes, a Child of God, serving God to the Best of his/her ability, given his/her experiences. This brings about Peace, Harmony, and Equality and subsequently Happiness, Decency, Prosperity and Peace of Mind.

4) A Jew is a person who thinks he/she is Better than his/her Nieghbor, and so he/she thinks he/she can tell his/her Neighbor what to do and how to Live. This brings about Strife, Disharmony, and Confusion in War, and subsequently Suicide.

5) The Third type of person is a Hypocrite and a Liar that says he/she is equal to others, but Thinks he/she is Better than others, Yes, A Christian. This brings about Strife, Disharmony, and Confusion in War, and subsequently Suicide.

Which of these Two types of people do you know you are?

Thanks for Listening, Folks, It was a pleasure. As ever in, "The Spirit of Goodness",

"Saint Bill", *A Servant for God's sake.*

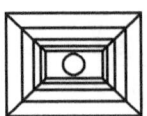

PREVIEWISM
Our World is Beautiful, Yes, Multi-Cultural

Dear Friend,

Our Church is Our Home and Our Home Is Our Church,

and

Our Congregation is Our Family, Oh, Yes, and That includes You.

My name is Bill Handel, that makes me a Previewlite, and I consider You my Brother, so that makes you a Previewlite.

Can you say the Same, about who you are?

If not, you have False Pride, and are a Self-righteous Idiot.

If you can say the Same, You are a Good Man or Woman.

Thank you, Dear God, Thank you, for true Insight.

"Saint Bill", A Servant for God's sake.

Dear Friend:

There are as many Ways to Heaven as there are People on the Earth. The difference is that Some people know It, and Some people do not know It. When you Decide you want to go to Heaven, the Way becomes apparent, and You know you are going to Heaven.

If you do not Decide you want to go to Heaven, You are going to Heaven, but You do not know It.

So do not let anyone tell you that His/Her Way is the Only Way, because they are Liars. Your Way is Unique to you when you Decide to go to Heaven.

Thank you, Dear God, Thank you, for true Insight. Now remember, We are All Saints, in God's eye, and

We look at life through God's eye, the eye of Reality.

Thanks for Listening, as ever in, "The Spirit of Goodness",

"Saint Bill" (Coach)

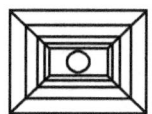

PREVIEWISM
Our World is Beautiful, Yes, Multi-Cultural

Dear Friends and Children of All ages:

Today we are going to talk about the Living and the Dead.

The Living we can and should Forgive, to let them Live to be Reconceived. The Dead we can not Forgive because It has not done anything Right.

All Living things and beings have done something Right, So we can Forgive. God the Real, "The Spirit of Goodness" is a Living being, So we should always Forgive It, and Love It with All our Heart, Mind, and Soul.

God the Fraud, The Shadow (Illusion) is Dead, So we can Never Forgive It, because if we did it would be Pure Vanity (Insanity).

Since God the Real, works through people, we should always Serve our Neighbor first and simultaneously serve God. If we serve God first, we are serving ourselves, which is Pure Vanity (Insanity).

The above is without exception because It is the exception to the Rule that there is an exception to every Rule.

Thanks for Listening, as ever in, "The Spirit of Goodness",

"Saint Bill" (Head Coach) A Servant for God's sake.

Previews Institute

PS: The Shadow says, All for One and One for All, because It causes
        Dissension, Strife and War.

   God says, Each unto His/Her Own, as It brings about Peace, Harmony
        and Equality. Yes, Happiness, Decency, Prosperity, and Peace of Mind.

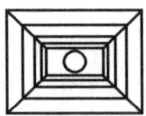

PREVIEWISM
Our World is Beautiful, Yes, Multi-Cultural

Dear Friends and Children of All ages:

Just as "Saint Jesus" Proved that the Jews are Serving (Worshipping) Satan (The Messiah). (Acts 26, vs. 16-18) Yes, the "I", "I", "I" guy.

So We have Proved that the Christians are Serving (Worshipping) Satan (The Messiah) (The Christ) (The Shadow) (The Illusion of God). (2 Thes.2, vs,9-11).

All the Rest including "Previewlites" say, We are One, that makes Us equal, and when We are equal with God and One-another, we are living in Reality (God), and Freedom of Thought. This brings about Peace and Harmony, and subsequently Happiness, Decency, Prosperity, and Peace of Mind.

Yes, God the Real is "The Spirit of Goodness", and It has many Angels,(Children) (Characteristics), the oldest being The Spirit of Truth, and the youngest being The Spirit of Enthusiasm, with many in between, and they together Live in Heaven, in the World, and in Your Heart, Mind, and Soul, from creation, conception, and Birth. Yes, God is with Us always.

Thank you, Dear God, Thank you, for true Insight.

Now remember:

We are All Saints, in God's eye, and

We look at Life through God's eye, the eye of Reality.

Thanks for Listening, as ever in,

"The Spirit of Goodness",

"Saint Bill", Head Coach, A Servant for God's sake.

(Acts 26, v. 16-18)(John 7, v.16-18)(1 Jn.4, v. 20)(2 Thes.2, v. 9-11)

Previews Institute of Universal Philosophy, "Summit Loc-001, H.O."

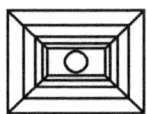

PREVIEWISM
Our World is Beautiful, Yes, Multi-Cultural

Dear Friends and Children of All ages:

A Poem

The Ultimate State of Mind

Life is Eternal in Body, Mind, and Spirit.

Yes, Life in the Womb, Life on Earth, and Life in Heaven.

Yes, Into and Out of the Future, World without End.

Yes, It is a Big Circle.

When we are Conceived, the Spirit becomes Body, Life in the Womb.

When we are Born, the Body becomes Word, Life on Earth.

When we Pass-On to Better things, the Word becomes Spirit.

Yes, Life in Heaven.

And some time Later, we are Conceived again, Yes, back to Body.

Yes, from Beginning to Present, and from Present to Beginning, And from Beginning to Beginning, and from Beginning to Present.

Yes, Life without End, World without End, Heaven without End. Yes, Into and Out of the Future, World without End.

Thank you, Dear God, Thank you, for true Insight.

Author: God the Real, "The Spirit of Goodness", As manifested in and by "The Compass",

A New Bible, by Author: "Saint Bill".

Co-Authors: "Me and My Friends"

And there are Many "Servants for God's sake" Yes, Indeed, The World.

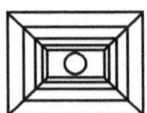

PREVIEWISM
Our World is Beautiful, Yes, Multi-Cultural

Dear Friends and Children of All ages:

Our Summit is our Home and Our Home is our Summit and Our Congregation is our Family, Oh, Yes, and that includes You.!!

Previewism being Multicultural represents "Society as a Whole", and thereby God the Real, "The Spirit of Goodness", with Its "Sense of Judgement", "Free Spirit", and "Good Nature", together with Its Angels (Children) (Characteristics), the oldest being The Spirit of Truth, and the youngest being The Spirit of Enthusiasm, with many in between, and they together Live in Heaven, in the World, and in Your Heart, Mind, and Soul, from creation, conception, and Birth. Yes, God is with You always.

The Wise person represents God the Real, and so the Wise person says,

"We are One", and that makes Us equal, and when we are equal with God and One-another we live in Peace and Harmony, because we are Living in Reality and Freedom of Thought.

The Idiot represents God the Fraud, and so the Idiot says, "I am It", I am better than you, Ya, I am Perfect. So you must be my Slave. So you do as I say, or you are Dead. Now, Go walk accross the Ocean. This causes much Pain and Suffering because It is Living in Illusion and Mental Slavery.

Thanks for Listening Folks, It was a Pleasure.

As ever in, "The Spirit of Goodness",

"Saint Bill", Head Coach, A Servant for God's sake

(Acts 26, v.16-18) (John 7, v.16-18) (1Jn.4, v.20) (2Thes.2, v.9-11) Previews Institute.

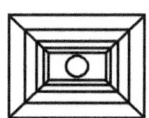

PREVIEWISM
Our World is Beautiful, Yes, Multi-Cultural

Dear Friends and Children of All ages:

Yes, It is a Great day, as we Previewlites realize that God has Never Once condemned us, but rather has and does Judge us every day, and chooses to Forgive us all our Shortcomings, and continues to LOVE and BLESS us, Just as we are.

Yes, Forever and Ever Faithful' to Its Good Nature, so that It will never Loose any One of us. Yes, God has a place reserved in Heaven for All of us, and It will be taken One day by each of us, without a Doubt.

Thank you, Dear God, Thank you, for true Insight.

Now remember, We are all Saints, in God's eye, and

We look at life through God's eye, the eye of Reality.

As ever in, "The Spirit of Goodness",

"Saint Bill", Head Coach, A Servant for God's sake.

Previews Institute, "Summit Loc-001,

Dear Friends:

We at Previews (Previewlites) worship "The Spirit of Goodness", and not a "Human Idol", because God the Real, "The Spirit of Goodness" is Far, Far, Far, Far ahead of Us in Learning and Experience and so is Worthy of our Trust in It. Yes, we consider "The Spirit of Goodness" with Its "Sense of Judgement", Free Spirit, and Good Nature, together with Its Angels (Children) (Characteristics) Infallible.

Any "Human Idol" that suggests He/She is Infallible is a Confused Idiot and a Fraud who has been Deceived by The Shadow (Illusion).

To this there is No Exception.

Yes, God is God, and God is our Salvation, We need No other.

Thanks for Listening, Folks, It was a Pleasure,

As ever in, "The Spirit of Goodness",

Saint Bill, "A Servant for God's sake"

Previews Institute.

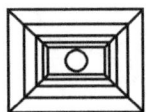

PREVIEWISM
Our World is Beautiful, Yes, Multi-Cultural

Dear Friends and Children of All ages:

God the Fraud, The Shadow, says, Give God what is Right,. Not what is Left. Then The Shadow says, Now, Do not Judge,.. I will be the Judge. Then the Shadow says, Give me your Last One Hundred Thousand dollars, or your Last Three pennies, either way I will take It.

God the Real, The Spirit of Goodness, says, Give God Nothing, but Thanks, and you will be Forever Blessed, as you develop a Sincerily Charitable Heart. Yes, Give some to your Needy Neighbor. Yes, Give some to Charity.

God Ordained,. God Sustained.

The Staircase to Heaven on Earth

Take the First Step ON

The Road of Success

Yes, Set your Goal, then Plan your Work, and Work your Plan,. Until your Plan Works,

Yes, Sincerity, Organization, Perserverance, and Enthusiasm.

GUARANTEED in Writing by "The Spirit of Goodness" as manifested in and by "The COMPASS", a New Bible, by Author: "Saint Bill".

Thank you, Dear God, Thank you, for true Insight.

As ever in, "The Spirit of Goodness",

Saint Bill, "A Servant for God's sake"

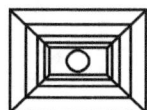

PREVIEWISM
Our World is Beautiful, Yes, Multi-Cultural

Dear Friends and Children of All ages:

Another Version of our Prayer

Dear God, My Dear God in Heaven, "The Spirit of Goodness",..

with Its "Sense of Judgement", Free Spirit", and "Good Nature",... together with Its Angels (children) (characteristics), the oldest being The Spirit of Truth, and the youngest being The Spirit of Enthusiasm, with many in between, Lives in Heaven, in the World, and in My Heart, Mind, and Soul, from creation, conception, and Birth.

Yes, God is with You Always,. And I thank you for Letting me remember to Look Up in my Daily activities, to see Truth and Reality, and take advantage of Opportunity.

Dear God, Thank you for letting me remember to Forgive one another, as thou hast Forgiven Us, Unconditionally.

Thank you, for letting me remember to everyday more and more, Please you, for It is to my advantage,....

Thank you for My Daily Bread, It is Good

Thank you for My Health and Well Being, in Spirit, Body, and Mind.. That is number One, Health and Well being in Spirit, Body, and Mind. Thank you for All my Blessings...etc. etc. etc.,- and finally

Thank you for "The Compass" and all related material, for Thy Kingdom has come by It all, and Thy Will is now done on Earth, as It is in Heaven, Eternally.

Thank you, Dear God, Thank you,. Amen, Amen., and Amen..

Note: Prepared by: "Saint Bill". Alias: Wilhelm J. Handel, M.A.,L.W.

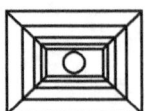

PREVIEWISM
Our World is Beautiful, Yes, Multi-Cultural

Dear Friends and Children of all ages:

"Saint Bill" has known the Christian-Jewish version of Joy and Peace for 40 years, Yes, Happiness as a Pig in a Mess. Yes, a Poor miserable Sinner, Yes, a servant of Satan (Illusion).

Then I became Born again of The Spirit of God, Yes, The Spirit of Goodness, and became a servant of God (Reality), and have now found true Joy and Peace of Heart, Mind, and Soul. Overwhelming Happiness as a Saint in Bliss. Yes, even Heaven on Earth.

God the Real, The Spirit of Goodness, told Saint Bill to write down every Twist and Turn needed to Unravel the Web of Satan (Illusion) in the Old Books of knowledge, and in doing so Saint Bill has written the Final Testament for Eternity. All is found in The Compass, a New Bible, The EverLast Testament, revealing to the World the true meaning of Life according to True Prophets.

Prophecies being Previews of the Future, led Saint Bill to name the Universal Philosophy, "Previewism" as manifested by The Spirit of Goodness, God the Real.

Being born again of the True meaninig of life, Saint Bill and his followers are now in the process of Teaching the world how to achieve Heaven on Earth for their Neighbors and Themselves.

This is an Eternal process because Life is Eternal in Body, Mind, and Spirit. Yes, we have Life in the Womb, Life on Earth, and Life in Heaven, as each is Eternal unto Its own, and are One as we Recycle into and out of the Future, World without End. Yes, there is No Death in God's world. Only Life Eternal. Is that not Wonderful. Yeh, that is Wonderful.

P R E V I E W I S M is so Far ahead of the present Psychology of Society that it seems It is coming from Behind. But Its followers know that Truth always prevails, and so within 300 years Previewism will be the Predominant psychology throughout the World, and All will live in Peace, Harmony, and Equality. Yes, in Happiness, Decency, Prosperity, and Peace of Mind.

Glory, Glory Hallelujah, and Praise be to God the Real, The Spirit of Goodness, with Its Sense of Judgement, Free Spirit, and Good Nature, together with all of Its angels (children)

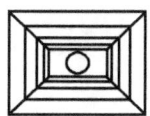

PREVIEWISM
Our World is Beautiful, Yes, Multi-Cultural

(characteristics), the oldest being The Spirit of Truth and the youngest being The Spirit of Enthusiasm, with many in between, as they together live in Heaven, in the World, and in Your Heart, Mind and Soul, from creation, conception, and Birth. Yes, God is with you, Always.

Thank you, Dear God, Thank you, for true Insight.

Now remember,

We are All Saints in God's eye, and

We look at Life through God's eye, the eye of Reality.

Thanks again for Listening, folks, as ever in, The Spirit of Goodness,

"Saint Bill" (Head Coach) A Servant for God's sake.

(Acts 26, v.16-18) (John 7, v.16-18) (1 Jn,4, V. 20) (2Thes.2, v.9-II)

Previews Institute, "Summit Loc-001, H.O."

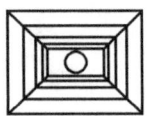

PREVIEWISM
Our World is Beautiful, Yes, Multi-Cultural

Dear Friends and Children of All ages:

A Wise man once said, You are either For God or You are Against God,. You can not be Both unless you are a confused Hypocrite. And so we must remember:

"Saints" are children of God, serving God, "The Spirit of Goodness" (Reality).
"Sinners" are children of God, serving Satan, "The Shadow" (Illusion).

In which Group do you Stand? Well, we find that, 88% of people are Saints.

10% of people are Hypocrites.

1% of people are Criminals (Sinners) In the Human eye. 1/400 are Retarded people.

1/900 are either Insane or in Jail.

1/1500 people is a Preacher (a Parasite).

All of these people know where they Stand, except the Hypocrites.

The Hypocrites do not know where they Stand, and so they say, they are Both Sinner and Saint at the Same time. Yes, they are Sitting on the Fence with

One Foot on one side of the Fence and One Foot on the other Side of the Fence. And the Fence is Up the Middle, causing them nothing but Pain and Suffering. And so they are Bleeding Hearts, always Crying in their Beer, and blaming the World for their Misery. Yes, the Poor Miserable people.

But their God, The Shadow, says, Do not Judge, Do not Decide right from wrong, or You will Die. Then The Shadow says, Now follow Me and I will take you to Heaven, and do not Worry, Suffering makes you Strong, and together We will Rule the World., by the way of Extortion, Yes, a Dictatorship.

But We know Better, The Wise people, the Saints, Rule the World by way of a ...Democracy. This is why there is a Lot more Good in the World than there is Bad.

Yes, the Wise people, The Saints, look at life through God's eye,

the eye of Reality, and have Learned to Love and Forgive one-another.

The Sinners, the Criminals, look at life through the Human eye,

the eye of Illusion, and do not realize that they Hate themselves more than Others.

THE TRADITION OF "CHANGE FOR THE BETTER" IS BORN IN *"PREVIEWISM"*
www.previews-inc.com
Make 10 - 20 Copies per week and Pass It On. - God will be well Pleased.

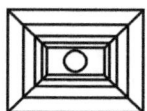

PREVIEWISM
Our World is Beautiful, Yes, Multi-Cultural

The Hypocrites, the Ones of the Fence, look at life through Both eyes,

and Blame the World for their Troubles, while they think they are Perfect. Yes, the poor, confused, Miserable people.

But do not despair, God the Real, The Spirit of Goodness, is EverUnderstanding, Loving, Forgiving, and above all True to Its word, and so accepts us All,

Just as we are. Yes, God always get the Last Word, and the Last word is..Forgiven.

Thank you, Dear God, Thank you, for true Insight

Now remember,

>We are All Saints, in God's eye, and

>We look at life through God's eye, the eye of Reality.

Thanks for Listening, Folks, It was a pleasure, As ever in, "The Spirit of Goodness",

"Saint Bill" (Head Coach) A Servant for God's sake.

Previews Institute, "Summit Loc-001, H.O."

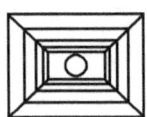

PREVIEWISM
Our World is Beautiful, Yes, Multi-Cultural

Dear Friends and Children of All ages:

Is God your God, or is A Lord your God?

If God is your God, you are on the Right Track.

If A Lord is your God, you are worshipping a Human Idol.

Because Lord refers to a Human, while God refers to a Spirit.

Yes, the Good One, Yes, The Spirit of Goodness, with Its Sense of Judgement, Free Spirit, and Good Nature, together with Its angels (children) (characteristics) the oldest being The Spirit of Truth, and the youngest being The Spirit of Enthusiasm, with many in between, and they together live in Heaven, in the World, and in your Heart, Mind, and Soul, from creation, conception, and Birth.

Yes, God is with you. Always.

A Lord is only there with Its hand out when the Sun shines, but when the Clouds come and the Rain falls, the times of need, He/She is like The Shadow, He/She disappears, no where to be seen, until the Sun shines again.

Yes, God the Real, The Spirit of Goodness, has one face, and one face only.

Thee Lord has two faces, and sometimes many more. Yes, a confused Hypocrite, saying one thing and doing another,

Yes, Thee Lord is like The Shadow, It says. If you do not worship me, you are going to Hell. But It is a Liar. If we do not worship It, we will find Heaven on Earth as God wants it to be.

And Heaven in Heaven is assured to us because God Forgives, as guaranteed in writing by The Spirit of Goodness, in and by "The Compass", a New Bible, The EverLast Testament, by Author; "Saint Bill".

Chuckle, Chuckle, eh, Folks!!

Thanks for Listening, as ever in, TheSpirit of Goodness,

"Saint Bill" (Head Coach) A Servant for God's sake.

(Acts 26, v.16-18)(John 7, v.16-18)(1 Jn.4, v.20)(2 Thes.2, v.9-11)

Previews Institute, "Summit Loc-001, H.O."

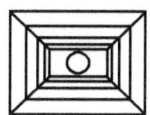

PREVIEWISM
Our World is Beautiful, Yes, Multi-Cultural

Good Friday

Dear Friends the World over:

We are to look to the Future, because It inspires us to do Good, because of the Promise of Goodness to come.

But we are only Human, and so we sometimes reflect on the Past. And so today is "Good Friday", and so today we are going to reflect on what happenned that day.

Society in a certain region of the World was in turmoil, just as It is today, and a certain man whom we now call "Saint Jesus" was in protest of his people.

He said to his people that they were serving Satan (Messiah) (The Shadow) (Illusion), Acts 26,v.16-18) and so his people decided that He was Satan, and Crucified him.

After they killed him they realized that he was just a Man, and then they remembered that God says. Thou shalt not kill, and so to overcome their shame they said that He was the Messiah, Their God, Yes, they put the Mask of a Good man on the Head of Satan, and clothed It with a Sheep-skin-coat, and continued to preach the Lies and Illusions of the Dark ages.

And then to further try to justify their shame (Actions), their story became quite elaborate and filled with Counterfeit Miracles. (2 Thes".2, v.9-11), and in doing so they deceived a few Gentiles into practicing Judaism while they called them Christians.

But do not despair, because God is still God, the Spirit of Goodness, (Truth and Reality), and Satan (The Messiah) (The Shadow) is still Satan (The Messiah) (The Shadow), Yes, Illusion and Lie.

Yes, Saint Jesus said, that God is a Spirit and not a Man or a Lord, and when we talk about The Spirit of God, we are talking about The Spirit of Goodness, with Its Sense of Judgement, Free Spirit, and Good Nature, together with all of Its angels (children)(characteristics), the oldest being The Spirit of Truth, and the youngest being The Spirit of Enthusiasm, with many in between.

Yes, The Spirit of Truth is related to our Sense of Judgement and our Sense of Judgement leads us to the Truth, and the Truth is that Life is Eternal, in Body, Mind, and Spirit. Yes, Life in the Womb, Life on Earth, and Life in Heaven, as each is Eternal unto Its own and are One as we Recycle into and out of the Future, world without End.

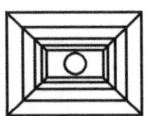

PREVIEWISM
Our World is Beautiful, Yes, Multi-Cultural

Yes, My Friends, we are all born Ignorant, and we all become wise to different degrees depending on the circumstances and the environment we live in.

But we are a Free people, and we all have a "Good Nature", and so we travel from region to region Promoting God's principals as we see them.

But it is obvious that some people are Less Deceived than others and subsequently find Happiness, Decency, Prosperity, and Peace of Mind.

And since we are All God's children, we are not to condemn one-another because God does not condemn. Yes, we are to Forgive one-another for our Ignorance (Shortcomings), because God always Forgives and does not Punish, but rather says, Go and do it better next time, now that you have learned Reality from Illusion.

Yes, Folks, It is a Fading story, but Thank God the Real, The Spirit of Goodness, things are improving, and always will, and someday soon we will have (reach) Heaven on Earth as God wants It to be, as it was in the beginning before Lazyness set in and caused some people to think they can get a Free ride from Society at any cost to their Neighbors.

In the meantime, The Wise will keep Looking Up and to the future which is above the Horizon to see the Pitfalls of Life and avoid them, so as not to have to Suffer needlessly.

Thanks for Listening, Folks, It was a pleasure,

As ever in. The Spirit of Goodness,

"Saint Bill", A Servant for God's sake.

Previews Institute, "Summit Loc-001, H..Q."

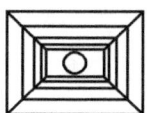

PREVIEWISM
Our World is Beautiful, Yes, Multi-Cultural

Judge

Dear Friends and Children of All ages:

To Repent is to Judge (Decide) right from wrong, and Act on the Right.

To Judge is to gather the Facts, weigh them. Decide right from wrong, and Act on the Right.

Without Action there is no Judgement and no Repentance, but just Wishful thinking.

Like many people, I caught my God in a Lie one day.

I gathered the Facts, weighed them, and Decided right from wrong.

I Decided that God does not Lie, therefore I must be serving Satan, and so I "Cast him Out".

Then I said. Hey, where there is One Lie, there are a hundred, and so I started to ask some questions.

Well, the story got so confusing that it was obvious that it was All based on Lie and Illusion.

Yes, there were no Answers, and so I had to Find the answers by My-self, by using my Sense of Judgement, Free Spirit, and Good Nature, along with all of God's angels (children)(characteristics), the oldest being The Spirit of Truth, and the youngest being The Spirit of Enthusiasm, with many in between as you know.

Yes, the Free Gifts that our Dear God gives us upon Creation, conception, and Birth, always lead us to the Truth.. And as we know, the Truth always prevails.

Thank God the Real, The Spirit of Goodness, for our Natural Good Instincts, that keep us truly Free from Guilt, Fear, Doubt, and Illusion.

Yes, My Friends, when you'learn to Judge in God's fashion, you will come to the Truth as well.

And to Judge in God's fashion is to always Forgive, Not Condemn, Bless, Not Curse, yes. Reward, Not Punish.

But remember, we can not Forgive Satan (The Shadow) (Illusion), because It does not Repent (Judge) (Decide) right from wrong, and asks us to follow Its instruction, and walk around like useless Imbeciles, hitting Pitfall after Pitfall, and then says. Do not worry. Suffering make you Strong.

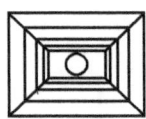

PREVIEWISM
Our World is Beautiful, Yes, Multi-Cultural

Yes, My Friends, False instruction upon False instruction.

Now remember,

We are All Saints in God's eye, and

We look at life through God's eye, the eye of Reality.

Through which eye do you look at life?

Thanks for Listening, Folks, It was a pleasure,

As ever in The Spirit of Goodness,

"Saint Bill", Head Coach, "Summit Loc-001, H..O."

Previews Institute.

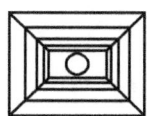

PREVIEWISM
Our World is Beautiful, Yes, Multi-Cultural

Dear Friends and Children of all ages:

We understand that to Judge is to gather the Facts, weigh them. Decide right from wrong, and Act on the Right.

In short, to judge is to Decide right from wrong for ourselves and allow all others the same Privelege.

Yes, take and Eat of the Fruit of the Tree of the Knowledge of Good and Waste, and you shall become Wise and aware of your maker, and you shall then know that you have Eternal Life with God, and as a result you will live abundantly in the physical, material, and spiritual sense.

Question 1) What is a person that does not Judge?

Answer: A misguided person walking around in circles hitting Pitfall after Pitfall, all the while believing, you need not worry. Suffering makes you Strong.

P.S.: So do not obey that which says, "Do not Judge". That is false instruction with an ulterior and insidious motive.,

Question 2) What is a person who "Tries to be Perfect."?

Answer: A Hypocrite, saying one thing and doing another, and a frustrated person, and ultimately a negative Failure.

P.S.: So do not obey that which says, "Go and be Perfect". That is false instruction, with an ulterior and insidious motive.

Question 3) What is the purpose of a counterfeit Miracle.?

Answer: To disintegrate your Sense of Judgement, so that you do not know right from wrong. Good from Waste, Reality from Illusion, or God the Real from God the Fraud.

P.S.: So discard Counterfeit Miracles for what they are. Pure Fantasy, Illusion.

......And have faith in your Sense of Judgement, It is God's Gift to you. Use it.

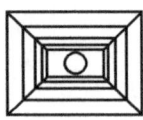

PREVIEWISM
Our World is Beautiful, Yes, Multi-Cultural

Question 4)   In which Image did God create you?

Answer: In God's image.

    P.S.: Therefore, the creation not being Perfect, means that God is not Perfect. This is why God the Real can always Forgive us, because It knows we have room for Error, just like It has. But God the Real has Billions of years of experience so there is not much room for Error in God. But there is one bit of Waste that keeps hanging around, since the beginning, and that is "The Shadow", Illusion.

    But God allowed that to be, because It knew that "Illusion" can be overcome when we use our Sense of Judgement, Free Spirit, and Good Nature, along with all of God's angels (children) (characteristics), the oldest being The Spirit of Truth, and the youngest being The Spirit of Enthusiasm, with many in between, as we know. Thank God for being very Wise, Brave and Steadfast.

Question 5)   Does anyone ever choose to be Evil.?

Answer: No, they have to be Deceived first, by Illusion (The Shadow).

This is why we can always forgive them for their Ignaoance, for they know not what they do.

So use your Sense of Judgement and progress!!

Note: When you learn to Judge, you will quickly realize how to avoid Man's Law of "You reap what you Sow", and then quickly learn to live by God's Law that says, "Look-Up, and Forgive one-another and reap only Blessings, barring the weather of course".

Yes, you will quickly learn to Judge in God's fashion, which is to always provide the alternative, then Forgive, Not condemn. Bless, Not curse. Yes,

Reward, Not Punish.

Yes, your days of Pain and Suffering will be over and gone when you understand

Previewism. And The Shadow will be left Crying in Its Beer, out in outer Darkness beyond the reach of Light, as it was in the beginning.

Have a great day folks and remember God Loves you.

Author: The Spirit of Goodness, by "Saint BIll", A servant for God's sake.

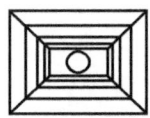

PREVIEWISM
Our World is Beautiful, Yes, Multi-Cultural

A Few more Basics

Dear Friends and Children of all ages:

We are all Born Sin-Free.

and

Because God Loves us Unconditionally, It Forgives us all our Shortcomings and misconceptions at every Instance to keep us Spotless, Yes, Sin-Free, Fit to take our place in Heaven any time, any day, Just as we are.

Naturally, we have to use our Sense of Judgement to Judge (Decide) right from wrong for ourselves and allow all others the same privelege in order for us to learn and grow in Understanding and Love of God's kind.

Any story to the contrary is simply Illusion (Lie)(Fear Tactic) for the purpose of Extortion by Lazy, Selfrighteous, Fearmonging Extortionist parasites wanting a Free ride from Society at any cost to their Neighbors.

Thank you, Dear God, Thank you, for true Insight.

Now, Let us face Reality.

The Messiah (Christ) (The Shadow) is Dead.

and

Its Holy Ghost (Illusion) is Dieing.

and

Within 300 years will be out of Existance.

Yes, Out of Mind, Out of Existance.

as

God the Real, The Spirit of Goodness, Lives on.

and

All will live in Peace, Harmony, and Equality with their Neighbors and the world around them.

Thank you, Dear God, Thank you, for true Insight.

Author: The Spirit of Goodness, by "Saint Bill", A Servant for God's sake.

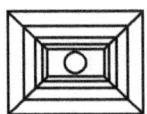

PREVIEWISM
Our World is Beautiful, Yes, Multi-Cultural

Dear Friends and Children of all ages:

Do you know why I know that I am going to Heaven.?

It is because My Beloved God, The Spirit of Goodness, created me Eternal, in Body, Mind, and Spirit. Yes, life in the Womb, life on Earth, and life in Heaven, as each is Eternal unto Its own, and are One as we Recycle into and out of the Future, World without End.

When God created the Heavens and the Earth there were 26,000,000,000. Human Souls divided between life in the Womb (Body), life on Earth (Mind), and life in Heaven (Spirit). And there are 26,000,000,000. Human Souls divided between the three Stages of life in the Heavens and the Earth today.

All that changes is the Ratios, which, depend on the Supply and Demand of life according to the means of the Support that all of Nature provides.

All of the Species of life have their own Ratios and their own Space in life, and are Eternaly alive in One of the three Stages of life. Just as We are.

This is as close to the Absolute Truth that we can get. Anything further to this is pure Speculation, and not worthy of the written word.

Yes, The COMPASS by "Saint Bill" together with all of the related material on the Subject by "Saint Bill" is truly the Last Word and The EverLast Testament revealed by The Spirit of God, The Spirit of Goodness, for Eternity.

Thanks for Listening Folks, It was a pleasure,

As ever in The Spirit of Goodness,

"Saint Bill" (Head Coach) A Servant for God's sake

Previews Institute, Summit Loc-001, H.O.

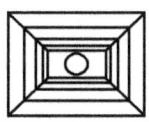

PREVIEWISM
Our World is Beautiful, Yes, Multi-Cultural

August 20/04/65 A.B.

To My Dear Successor:

God is not in a Hurry.

God has lots of Time.

Easy, Safe, and Steady does it every time.

The Plan is over 12 generations of 25 years each for a total of 300 years.

We start with $100,000.00 and we double the principal every 25 years.

We never spend the Principal, we just spend the Interest.

As God says. You do not eat the Tree, You eat the Fruit.

Now, if you take 2 to the second power it equals 4 and to the 3rd power it equals 8, and to the 4th power it equals 16, and so on to the 12th power. It equals 4096.

Therefore, If we start with $100,000.00 and double It every 25 years 12 times (to the 12th power) the Principal will equal $409,600,000.00

All during this time we will be spending the Interest as we go along on Charity for the Ones who have fallen through the Cracks.

Yes, Previews Institute, is and will Be an Eternal Foundation always

Looking to the Future and Newness of Life always promoting Positive psychology according to "P R E V I E W I S M" as manifested in and by The COMPASS according to "The Spirit of Goodness", God the Real, with Its Sense of Judgement, Free Spirit, and Good Nature, along with all of Its Angels (characteristics), the oldest being The Spirit of Truth and the youngest being The Spirit of Enthusiasm. (Oh, yes. Enthusiasm)

Now, Go and carry Our Torch!! Thank you. As ever in The Spirit of Goodness,

"Saint Bill" (Head Coach) Previews Institute.

"We are All Servants for God*s sake."

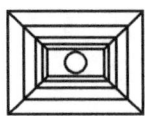

PREVIEWISM
Our World is Beautiful, Yes, Multi-Cultural

Subject: A Business Opportunity !'

Hi, My Dear Bob: Just a little further Insight.

The purpose of God the Real. The Spirit of Goodness, in our lives is to make us Happy, and Free us of Guilt, Fear, Doubt and Illusion, and in doing so It exposes the truth about Christianity.

Yes. "Saint Jesus" said, The Jews (Judaism) is serving Satan (Illusion) (The Shadow) (The Messiah), a Lord God or a Human Idol.

"Saint Jesus" said that God is a Spirit, the Good one. yes, The Spirit of Goodness, and It is the Creator. The Good Provider, and The Steadfast Comforter.

Satan (Illusion) (The Shadow) (The Messiah) said, Both the Jews and the Gentiles are serving Illusion, only My followers are serving God, because I am God, yes, the choosen one.(Acts 26 vs 16-18)

Saint Jesus said. the Gentiles are doing just fine, because Saint Jesus said. that those that know nothing about It will be treated better in Heaven than those that do know something about It.

So you see. It is not the Gentiles we need to worry about. It is the deceived Jews and Shadow worshippers that we have to help out of their Guilt, Fear, Doubt and Illusion, and subsequently make them happy as a Saint in Bliss, and not happy as a Pig in a Mess.

Yes. Saint Jesus said. the Jews are serving Satan and so Its servant Mr. Paul changed the word Messiah to Christ, put on a sheepskin coat and the Mask of a Good man and continued to preach the Lies and Illusions of the Dark ages.

And in doing so He deceived a few Gentiles into practicing Judaism while He called them Christians. The Chosen ones.

Yes the "I", "I". "I" guy is still at play with the Ignorant as He says. Do not Judge (Do not Decide right from wrong or you will Die).

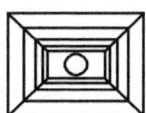

PREVIEWISM
Our World is Beautiful, Yes, Multi-Cultural

Yes, nothing but Fear tactic, as the wise know that Death is just an Illusion trying to distract us from the Reality of Life Eternal in Body Mind and Spirit. Yes, Life in the Womb, Life on Earth, and Life in Heaven, as each is Eternal unto Its own and are One as we Recycle into and out of the Future, World without End.

Yes, My Friend, the Bad guy. the "I", "I", "I" guy must be reduced to less than a speck of Dust. and put out of Sight out of Mind, and out of Mind out of Existence, in order for you to find true Happiness and Freedom from Guilt, Fear, Doubt, and Illusion.

Yes. My Friend, Previewism is where It is at and we are now on the road to Happiness, Decency. Prosperity, and Peace of Mind.

Yes, this is the purpose of God in our Lives and we at Previews have now achieved our Purpose.

If you live in or near Calgary, AB., Canada, and would like to be the Successor to the Founder of this Philosophy and Psychology and become a Servant of God, while assuming the Administration of the Assets of the Foundation, please contact us by return email or by phone at the number shown below.

Thanks for Listening, as ever in, 'The Spirit of Goodness",

"Saint Bill" (Head Coach) A Servant for God's sake.

(Acts 26. v.16-18) (John 7, v.16-18) (1 Jn.4, v.20) (2 Thes.2. v.9-11)

Previews Institute. "Summit Loc-001. H.O."

www. previews-inc.conn

1-403-273-9182

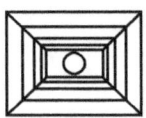

PREVIEWISM
Our World is Beautiful, Yes, Multi-Cultural

Dear Friends and Children of All ages:

Just a little further Insight

We are lucky that God considers us All Saints. (Because)

God Loves Saints.

God does not Love Sinners.

God Tolerates Sinners.

So you see,

God the Real Loves Saints.

God the Fraud Loves Sinners-

God the Real Tolerates Sinners, and

Forgives them to end the Pain and Suffering.

God the Fraud says It forgives Sinners, but

tells them not to Judge so that they continue to Sin (Walk in Illusion).

And then says. Bow and Pay, Bow and Pay, Bow and Pay.

"Saint Bill" says, to Hell with the Earthworm (The Shadow).

Out into outer darkness, beyond the reach of Light, and

Stay there, we need you there for reference.

Thank you. Dear God, Thank you, for true Insight.

As ever in The Spirit of Goodness,

"Saint Bill", A Servant for God's sake.

Previews Institute.

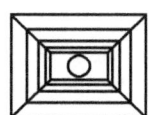

PREVIEWISM
Our World is Beautiful, Yes, Multi-Cultural

Dear Friends and Children of All ages:

There are many ways to motivate our Nieghbors to do Good, but they all fall into two catagories.

1) Motivation by Promise of Goodness to come or Promise of Gain.

2) Motivation by "Fear Tactic" or Fear of Consequences or Fear of Loss.

Previewlites (Gentiles) (Gentle people) (Saints) choose No. 1 because God the Real, The Spirit of Goodness, never hands out Consequences. Yes, there is No Fear in God.

Shadow Worshippers (Mean, Lazy, Fearmonging, Extortionist Parasites) choose No. 2, because they know they have Nothing to Loose, but only to Gain, because they know that God does not hand out Consequences. And so they have to Hand out their own consequences, and so they create a Vicious circle, but they do not mind because they are Suckers for Punishment just like The Shadow that they worship. Yes, The Shadow says, Do not worry, Suffering makes you Strong and together we will rule the World by Fear Tactic and Extortion or what ever else is neccessary to get a Free Ride from Society.

Then The Shadow says, Do not Judge, Do not Decide right from wrong or you will Die. Yes, My Henchmen will Kill you. Ah, pardon me, they will put you to Sleep, and you will go to Heaven as I promised you. Yes, You know what I mean by Heaven, Yes, that Spot that I reserved for you upon your Birth. Yes, from Ashes to Ashes, and Dust to Dust. Then The Shadow says, Do not worry, this is True Hope for the Future. Really It is. I would not Lie to you would I? If It were not so, I would tell you, right. Yes, The Shadow goes on and on with Its Garbage. And the Lazy Preachers just Lap it up. Chuckle, chuckle, eh, Folks.

Thanks for Listening, as ever in, The Spirit of Goodness,

"Saint Bill" (Head Coach) A Servant for God's sake,

at Previews Institute.

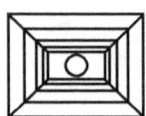

PREVIEWISM
Our World is Beautiful, Yes, Multi-Cultural

Dear Friends and Children of All ages:

Just a Few more Proverbs

1) When you start on Easy Street, It leads to The Hard Road.
   When you start on The Hard Road, It leads to Easy Street.

2) A Wise person once said, "Always Expect the Best, and make the Best of what you Get, and You will never have a Bad Day."

3) A Fool is a Person who Initiates physical violence.
   Verbal violence is Simply Self-Defence.
   And Self-Defence is an Act of God.

4) Misery is an Illusion to Most. Poverty is a Reality to Some.

   The farther you are from Perfection, The Closer you are to God.
   Because Perfection is looking Back to Death.

   God is looking Forward to the Future Life.

5) A Sinner is a Person who Thinks he/she is Condemned by God.
   And so a Sinner is a Person who has been Deceived. And a Deceived person is a Fool.

   And a Fool is always... Forgiven.

Thank you, Dear God, Thank you, for true Insight.

As ever in, The Spirit of Goodness,

"Saint Bill" (Head Coach) A Servant for God's sake.

Previews Institute, "Summit Loc-001, H.O.".

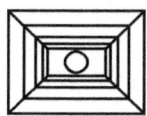

PREVIEWISM
Our World is Beautiful, Yes, Multi-Cultural

Dear Friends and Children of All ages:

Just a little further Insight

Satan is only Satan while we are Ignorant. (And so It seems It is Real).

When we become Wise Satan is Illusion, Yes, The Shadow, (Illusion).

While we think Satan is Real, It has power over Us.

When we know Satan is Illusion, It has No power over Us, because We Cast It out into Outer Darkness, beyond the reach of Light.

And say, Stay there, We need you there for Reference.

Yes, The Shadow of God is a Fictional character, because beyond the reach of Light, there is Nothing but Vacuum.

And so you See, Behind the Sun, It is Dark. Yes, All things Real are in the Light, and All things of Illusion are in the Dark.

This is why God has only One eye, the eye of Reality, and The Shadow has only One eye, the eye of Illusion.

So Cast-It-Out, and Dwell on the Positive, Yes, The Future.

Yes, God has no Past, only the Present and the Future.

Yes, from Beginning to Present and from Present to beginning and

from Beginning to Beginning and from Beginning to Present, and

so on and on, World without End.

Yes, Life in the Womb, Life on Earth, and Life in Heaven,

as we Recycle into and out of the Future, World without End.

Thanks for Listening, Folks, It was a Pleasure, as ever in, "The Spirit of Goodness",

"Saint Bill" (Head Coach) A Servant for God's sake.

Previews Institute, "Summit Loc-001, H.O."

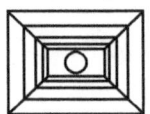

PREVIEWISM
Our World is Beautiful, Yes, Multi-Cultural

Dear Friends the World over:

Just a little further Insight

According to "Abraham" there are only two types of people in the World, Yes, Jews and Gentiles.

According to "The Christ" there are three types of people in the World, Yes, Jews, Gentiles, and Christians. (Acts 26, v.16-18) (2Thes.2, v.9-11) According to "A Previewlite" (Saint Bill and his followers) there is only One kind of people in the World, Yes, Previewlites,

Who do you think is Right.?

Well, by definition, "Previewlites" are children of God, serving God to the Best of their ability, given their experiences, and this is Good enough for God, so God considers us All "Saints", as God accepts us all, Just as we are, and Yes, We are all Saints in God's eye, and We look at life through God's eye, the eye of Reality. Through which eye do you look at life?

Furthermore: Saints are children of God, serving God the Real, "The Spirit of Goodness" (Reality)

Sinners are children of God, serving Satan, The Shadow (Illusion).

In which Group do you Stand?

Now, remember, "Saint Jesus" said, You are either For God, or you are Against God, You can not be Both, unless you are a confused Hypocrite, sitting on the Fence, with one foot on one side of the Fence, and one foot on the other side of the Fence, and the Fence is up the middle, causing you nothing but Pain and Suffering , and so you are Bleeding Hearts, always Crying in your Beer.

And I, Saint Bill, say, Yeh,. Hurrah for "Saint Jesus". Chuckle, chuckle, chuckle, eh!

Yes, Folks, there are only One kind of people in the World. We are All born Ignorant, and We All become Wise to different degrees, depending on the circumstances and the environment. Yes, given our experiences.

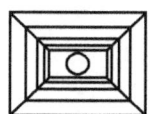

PREVIEWISM
Our World is Beautiful, Yes, Multi-Cultural

Yes, Experience is the best Teacher, because God speaks with Actions, not with Words,. Yes, Actions speak louder than Words,. Empty words and Counterfeit Miracles.

And so you see, Folks, there are 5.7 Billion people in the World today, and we all see life just a little different. But God being EverUnderstanding because It knows the circimstances and environment we came from,. accepts us All, just

as we are. Yes, "Previewlites", where we are All considered Equal and One with God, and where God is considered Equal and One with Us, Always.

Yes, Peace, Harmony, and Equality, and Happiness, Decency, Prosperity, and Peace of Mind,. Yes, to stay Free of Guilt, Fear, Doubt and Illusion.

These are the Objects of God in our Life, and we are now on the Right Road to achieve them.

Thank you, Dear God, Thank you, for true Insight.

Thanks for Listening, folks, It was a pleasure,

As ever in, "The Spirit of Goodness",

"Saint Bill" (Head Coach)

"Summit Loc-OO1, H.O." Previews Institute of Universal Philosophy.

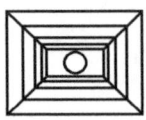

PREVIEWISM
Our World is Beautiful, Yes, Multi-Cultural

Dear Friends and Children of All ages:

Just a little further Insight

When you (a Previewlite) discuss Religion with a "Shadow Worshipper", he/she loses the discussion at every turn because You (a Previewlite) use your sense of Judgement and base your arguement on Reality (Facts), while the "Shadow Worshipper bases his/her arguement on Illusion (Hearsay).

And so the "Shadow Worshipper" ultimately says, If you are Right, I have nothing to lose because we all go to Heaven. But If I am Right, You are in Trouble.

And then you have two Responses at your service.

1) You say to the Shadow Worshipper,. Yes, you think you have nothing to lose for being a Sinner because you know you are going to Heaven, but you are wrong because you lose the opportunity to Live in the Kingdom of Heaven on Earth. As all those who know they are Saints come to enter the Kingdom of Heaven on Earth. And they know that Heaven in Heaven is their God given Birthright.

2) You say to the Shadow Worshipper. Yes, and who do you hope is Right.? (If he/she is wise, he/she will say, I hope you are Right.

(If he/she is according to his/her Ignorance, he/she will say, I hope I am Right. Then You say, You believe You Reap what you Sow. Therefore, What you wish for others, You receive for yourself.. So if you say, I am going to Hell, it means You are. And if I say, You are going to Heaven, it means I am.

Oh, Yes, You Reap what you Sow.

And the Shadow Worshipper is left Crying in his/her Beer. (Chuckle, Chuckle, eh)

Thanks for Listneing, Folks, It was a Pleasure.

As ever in, "The Spirit of Goodness"

"Saint Bill", Head Coach, A Servant for God's sake

Previews Institute.

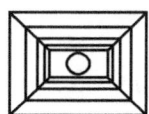

PREVIEWISM
Our World is Beautiful, Yes, Multi-Cultural

Previewism being Multicultural represents "Society as a Whole" and thereby God the Real, "The Spirit of Goodness", with Its Sense of Judgement, Free Spirit, and Good Nature, together with all of Its angels (children) (characteristics), the oldest being The Spirit of Truth, and the youngest being The Spirit of Enthusiasm, with many in between, and they together Live in Heaven, in the World, and in your Heart, Mind, and Soul, from creation, conception, and Birth. Yes, God is with you, Always.

By Definition

1) A Previewlite is a Child of God, serving God to the best of his/her ability, given his her experiences.

2) A Saint is a Child of God, serving God to the best of his/her ability, given his/her experiences.

3) God the Real is "The Spirit of Goodness",

4) God the Fraud is "Illusion", Yes, The Shadow.

Note: Any deviation to this is just a Distorted Echo.

And so you see, We are all Servants for the sake of God the Real, The Spirit of Goodness, "Specializing in "Food for Thought",.

And

Our Object is to make our Neighbors Happy, and Free them from Guilt, Fear, Doubt, and Illusion. Yes to advance All of Humankind in the Spiritual Sense, because Spiritual Success leads to Material Success. Yes, this is the Relief of Poverty, both Physical and Spiritual Poverty. Yes, a Charity, Philanthropy at Its Best.

Furthermore, God the Real, The Spirit of Goodness, reveals to us that Life is Eternal, in Body, Mind, and Spirit. Yes, Life in the Womb, Life on Earth, and Life in Heaven, as each is Eternal unto Its own, and are One as we Recycle into and out of the Future, World without End. When we are Conceived, the Spirit becomes Body, Life in the Womb. When we are Born, the Body becomes Word, Life on Earth. When we go on to better things, the Word becomes Spirit, Life in Heaven. After sometime we are Re-concieved again, to come again to Live and enjoy the Fruits of our Labor from the previous time round. Yes, from beginning

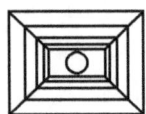

PREVIEWISM
Our World is Beautiful, Yes, Multi-Cultural

to present, and from present to beginning, and from beginning to beginning, and from beginning to present, and so on World without End.

This spells Eternal Life, and a Life of Bliss. All else is a Story of The Shadow, that we "Cast-Out" as Pure Bad Fiction.

Yes, there is no longer any Doubt, as God is with you, Always.

Thank you, Dear God, Thank you, for true Insight.

Now remember,

We are all Saints in God's eye, and

We look at life through God's eye, the eye of Reality.

Thanks for Listening, Folks,

As ever in, The Spirit of Goodness,

"Saint Bill" (Head Coach) A Servant for God's sake.

Previews Institute, "Summit Loc-001, H.O."

P.S.: The above knowledge comes to us as a result of Truth and Love, and gives us a Purpose in Earthly Life in unity with a philosophy of Happyism.

Some people think that Death is Final and just pay Lip-service to Eternal Life, as into Oblivion. This comes to them as a result of Lie, Fear, and Hate, resulting in Self-punishment, Yes, Sadism.

The Wise know that Truth is always an obvious and easy choice. Thank you, Dear God, Thank you, for true Insight.

As ever, "Saint Bill", A Servant for God's sake.

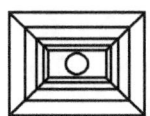

PREVIEWISM
Our World is Beautiful, Yes, Multi-Cultural

Dear Friends and Children of All ages:

1) To be Righteous is to give God the Glory.

   To be Self-righteous is to give Yourself the Glory.

   Self-Esteem based on righteousness is Good.

   Self-Esteem based on self-righteousnes is Arrogance. Self-Esteem based on Results is Good.

   Self-Esteem based on Words only is Arrogance.

2) The Law is My Neighbor's opinion.

   Sometimes I agree with It,

   And Sometimes I do not,

   But the Majority Rules,

   And that is "The Law".

So you see, I always go with the Majority.

Yes, A Democracy works Best.

3) We must Learn to Judge. (There are Four steps to Judgement)

   i) Gather the Facts.

   ii) Weigh them (Pro or Con)

   iii) Decide (Right or Wrong)

   iv) Take Action on the Right.

Without Action there is No Judgement and No Decision, But just Wishful thinking.

Thanks for Listening, in,

The Spirit of Goodness,

Prepared by: "Saint Bill" (A Servant for God's sake.)

THE TRADITION OF "CHANGE FOR THE BETTER" IS BORN IN *"PREVIEWISM"*
www.previews-inc.com
Make 10 - 20 Copies per week and Pass It On. - God will be well Pleased.

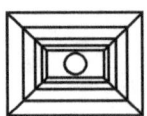

PREVIEWISM
Our World is Beautiful, Yes, Multi-Cultural

Dear Friends and Children of All ages:

The greatest story ever told was a Fictional story, and a complete Illusion. It was a story about how "The Shadow" (Satan) (Illusion) had become a Man.

But (Satan) being a Liar, said that God had become a Man, and that He was God. This left Women without a voice in things, and the World in Turmoil.

But we know that God is not a Man, God is a Spirit, the Good one,

Yes, The Spirit of Goodness, and It speaks for Men as well as Women, and

It speaks in Truth and Reality, Not in Illusion and Lie. Thank God the Real, for Women who keep us in Line. Chuckle, Chuckle, eh.!!

Yes, God the Real, The Spirit of Goodness, lives in Heaven, in the World, and in your Heart, Mind, and Soul, from creation, conception, and Birth. It never leaves you, but Recycles into and out of the Future when our Bodies cease to function and when we are created. World without End.

Yes, God is with you always.

Thank you, Dear God, Thank you, for true Insight.

Now remember:

> We are All Saints in God's eye, and
>
> We look at life through God's eye, the eye of Reality.

Through which eye do you look at life?

Furthermore:

Saints are Children of God, serving God. Sinners are Children of God, serving Satan.

In which group do you Stand?

Now remember:

A wise man once said, You are either for God, or you are against God.

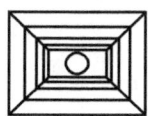

PREVIEWISM
Our World is Beautiful, Yes, Multi-Cultural

You can not be Both unless you are a confused Hypocrite, sitting on the Fence, with one foot on one side of the Fence, and one foot on the other side of the Fence, and the Fence is up the middle, causing you nothing but Pain, and Suffering, which leads to Sadism. And so you are Bleeding Hearts always Crying in your Beer.

Chuckle, Chuckle, eh, Folks.

Hurrah for a Wise man. Yes, "Saint Jesus".

Thanks for Listening, It was a pleasure.

"Saint Bill" (Head Coach) A Servant for God's sake.

Previews Institute of Universal Philosophy.

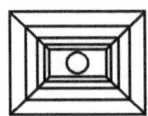

PREVIEWISM
Our World is Beautiful, Yes, Multi-Cultural

Dear Friends and Children of All ages:

"Truth always Prevails".

This is why there is a lot more Good in the World than there is Bad. Yes, 1 in 1,500 people is a Parasite, Yes, a mean, lazy, shameless, Fearmonging extortionist Parasite promoting a sick psychology called Sadism, the seed of which is Illusion, Yes, The Shadow, Yes, in disguise as Goodness.

1 in 900 people is either Insane or in Jail.

1 in 400 people is a Retard.

1 in 100 people is a Criminal on the loose.

1 in 10 people is a Shadow Worshipper, Yes, a Hypocrite, saying one thing and doing another.

That leaves 88% of people who are Gentiles (Gentle people)(Saints) in the Human eye, out in the Free World serving their neighbors, and praising God the Real, "The Spirit of Goodness", for their Blessings. In their Closet of course.

But, being Saints, they realize that in God's eye we are All Saints because God Forgives and accepts us All into Heaven, Just as we are.

So The Shadow (Devil) can go to Hell by Itself, when It says we are All Bad. Not One has fallen short of the Grace of God, because God Loves and Forgives, "Unconditionally".

The Devil (Shadow) says, there are conditions, but It is a Liar, trying to get Its foot, in the door. Once in It makes you a Slave to Its conditions.

God wants you to stay Free, so It makes Its love and forgiveness "Unconditional".

So remember, Reality is God, and God is Reality, Not Fantasy.

Yes, Folks, It is a Big and Beautiful' world we live in when we Dwell on the Positive, and not allow The Shadow to instill Fear, Guilt, Doubt, and Illusion in our Heart and Mind with Its Negative psychology.

Yes, Folks, always remember that the purpose of God the Real, The Spirit of Goodness, in our lives is to make us Happy, and Free us of Guilt, Fear, Doubt and Illusion by reminding us that Its love and forgiveness is Unconditional, and that It accepts us, Just as we are, any time, any day.

Thanks for Listening, as ever in, The Spirit of Goodness,

"Saint Bill" (Head Coach) A Servant for God's sake.

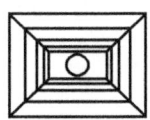

PREVIEWISM
Our World is Beautiful, Yes, Multi-Cultural

Dear Friends and Children of all ages:

Just a little further Insight

To take Offence is a Sin against Humanity.
To react in Self Defence is an Act of God.
Therefore, where there is No Offence, there is no Sin.
Where there is Self Defence, there is God.
Oh, yes, we must decide right from wrong for ourselves, and allow all others the
    same privilege, in order for us to learn and grow in Understanding and Love.
Yes, we must learn to Judge one-another as God Judges us, and that is to always
    provide the alternative, then Forgive, Not Condemn, Bless, Not Curse, Yes,
Reward, Not Punish.
Oh, yes, we all Act according to our Understanding, which is Self Defence, and not
meant as Offence because we have a Good Nature.
When it seems that one has taken deliberate Offence, we must Forgive them
    for their Ignorance and Illusion (Lie) they are living in.
And so you see, we who understand this Live Sin-Free, and are called Saints, or
Previewlites. and since our Neighbors are always Forgiven, we consider them
    Saints too.
Yes, Saints are Saints, and in the remainder some are less deceived than others, and
    as you know we always
Forgive the Deceived for they know not what they do or say.
And we realize that when we set the example the Deceived will one day become
Wise and Forgive to live Sin-Free.
Is that not wonderful, the opportunity to live Sin-Free is at your step.
All you have to do is learn to Judge in God's fashion, and that is to always provide
    the alternative, then Forgive, Not Condemn, Bless, Not Curse,
Yes, Reward, Not Punish.
Now do not turn to walk away because when you have no alternative, just keep
    your Mouth shut, and
Forgive, Not Condemn, Bless, Not Curse, Yes, Reward, Not Punish.
And you are still Sin-Free. So do not hesitate to say, "Let's do It"
Thank you, Dear God, Thank you, for true Insight.

PS: There is No Death, when you are Sin-Free.
PS: When there are Two that are Ignorant, there is sometimes, what seems like Sin.
But when One is Wise, there is no Sin.

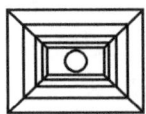

PREVIEWISM
Our World is Beautiful, Yes, Multi-Cultural

Dear Friends and Children of all ages:

Sin seems to be Something that seperates us from God But such a something does not exist and is just an Illusion, because God is always with you, and God is with you Always.

When you are following God. God faces the Future, and you face God's Back, and you walk in Light. If you turn to walk away from God, God turns to follow you and is still with you, as you walk in Darkness. And God says. My poor Innocent child, Not Guilty by reason of Insanity.

And so you see. when you look Up and to the Future, you are following God (Reality). When you look Down and to the Past you are following The Shadow (Illusion).

Now, Illusion is not Sin, and Sin is not Illusion. Sin is Illusion Expressed. And Illusion expressed is Lie, and Lie is Sin, and Sin is Lie. And Actions based on Lie cause Pain and Suffering, and Pain and Suffering leads to Sadism, and ultimately Suicide.

So you look Up and see Truth and Reality, which is God, because Actions based on Truth and Reality brings Happiness, Decency, Prosperity, and Peace of Mind, allowing you to live in Peace, Harmony, and Equality with your Neighbors and the world around you, and this we call Happyism, which leads you to know that Life is Eternal in Body, Mind. and Spirit.

Yes. Life in the Womb. Life on Earth, and Life in Heaven, as each is Eternal unto Its own, and are One as we recycle into and out of the Future, world without End.

Thank you, Dear God, Thank you, for true Insight.

Thanks for Listening, as ever in, 'The Spirit of Goodness",

"Saint Bill" (Head Coach) A Servant for God's sake.

(Acts 26. v.16-18) (John 7. v.16-18) (1 Jn.4. v.20) (2 Thes.2. v.9-11)

Previews Institute, "Summit Loc-001, H.O."

www. previews-inc.com

1-403-273-9182

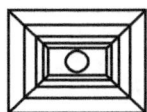

PREVIEWISM
Our World is Beautiful, Yes, Multi-Cultural

Dear Friends and Children of all ages:

To Judge is to Decide right from wrong and Act on the Right, Yes, provide the Alternative, then Forgive, Not Condemn, Bless, Not Curse, Yes, Reward, Not Punish, and allow all others the same privilege in order for us to learn and grow in Understanding and Love.

Those that Do not Judge, walk around like useless Imbeciles hitting Pitfall after Pitfall and live in Sin, which is Pain and Suffering, and Pain and Suffering leads to Sadism and Ultimately Suicide. All the while The Shadow (The Sadist) says, Do not worry, Suffering makes you Strong, So bear with me, and I will make you Rich beyond your wildest dreams. And finally The Shadow says, please bear with me, and I will prepare a table for you in Heaven.

Those that learn to Judge, learn to look ahead and see the Pitfalls coming and avoid them to live Sin-Free. This leads to Happyism which leads you to know that Life is Eternal in Body, Mind, and Spirit. Yes, Life in the Womb, Life on Earth, and Life in Heaven, as each is Eternal unto Its own, and are One as we recycle into and out of the Future, World without End.

Yes, they learn to live in Heaven on Earth and realize that Heaven in Heaven will come only to Soon, but It will be Beautifull just as Heaven on Earth is Beautifull when we use our Sense of Judgement, and Judge one-another as God Judges us, Daily. And that is to Always provide the Alternative, then Forgive, Not Condemn, Bless, Not Curse, Yes, Reward, Not Punish.

Thank you, Dear God, Thank you, for true Insight.

Thanks for Listening, as ever in, "The Spirit of Goodness",

"Saint Bill" (Head Coach) A Servant for God's sake.

(Acts 26, v.16-18) (John 7, v.16-18) (1 Jn.4, v.20) (2 Thes.2, v.9-11)

Previews Institute, "Summit Loc-001, H.O."

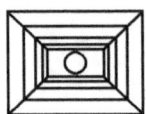

PREVIEWISM
Our World is Beautiful, Yes, Multi-Cultural

Hi, My Dear Evelyn and Tim: Tell me, what is the Latest.

As you know, I am a retired Real Estate Broker, and when I retired 15 years ago, I took up a Hobby, which was writing on the subject of Psychology and Philosophy.

Well it took me 9 years to write "The Compass" and It has 342 pages. Then it took me 6 years to write "Object, Masters Degree" and It has 325 pages.

The Last Two pages were written about 10 days ago and I have now decided that My writing is complete (Finished).

I used to divide my time between writing and Practicing, but now that my writing is done, I am now a Full time "Spiritual Practitioner". Yes, I do not Preach, I Practice, and as you know, Practice make Excellence, Not Perfect, but Super Excellence, Every day a little improvement upon yesterday, and It is never ending because we look to the Future and not the Past.

We are enjoying Life to the Fullest because we are making People Happy, and Freeing them of Guilt, Fear, Doubt and Illusion, which allows them to live in Peace, Harmony, and Equality with their Neighbors and the world around them.

As a Practitioner, we are curious to know how we can help you improve upon an already acceptable Life style, because Improvement is the Spice of Life.

And so we have a question for you,

Do you live Sin-Free?
> If so, let us know. If not, let us know.
>> Either way It will be helpfull to come to understand you better.

Waiting to hear from you soon,

We remain, Yours truly,
> as ever in The Spirit of Goodness,

Good ole Dad.

Thanks for Listening, as ever in, "The Spirit of Goodness",

"Saint Bill" (Head Coach) A Servant for God's sake.

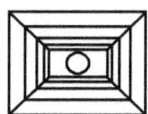

PREVIEWISM
Our World is Beautiful, Yes, Multi-Cultural

Hi, Andrew,... How are you today.? Just Fine, we assume...

We here at "Previews" just wanted you to know that we think you are a "Saint".

The reason why we think you are a Saint, is because we think you live Sin-Free.

The reason why we think you live Sin-Free is because a Sin is only a Sin while it is not Forgiven.

Once Forgiven, it is gone and no longer exists.

And since you were Forgiven before you were conceived, you will now realize that you have been Sin-Free all your life and did not know it because The Shadow's servants had you believe that you are seperated from God, and that you have to follow them to be re-united. (Hogwash).

Because we know that God is always with us, and God is with us, Always. Whether we are walking frontward or backward, God is with us Always, and continues to Forgive us for our Shortcomings, and misconceptions.

So you see, We are always Sin-Free.

And the Glory be to God the Real, and not to God the Fraud.

Thanks for Listening,

as ever in, "The Spirit of Goodness",

"Saint Bill" (Head Coach) A Servant for God's sake.

(Acts 26, v.16-18)(John 7, v.16-18)(1 Jn.4, v.20)(2 Thes.2, v.9-11) Previews Institute,

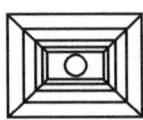

PREVIEWISM
Our World is Beautiful, Yes, Multi-Cultural

Hi, My Dear Rex and Wendy:

The Christ (The Messiah) trys to put Itself above the Angels.

But God is an Angel amoung the Angels and they are All equal partners. This is why God kicked The Christ (The Messiah) out of Heaven, and into Hell. And The Christ (The Messiah) is still in Hell,

and Saint Jesus went to Heaven just like we all do when our Bodies cease to function.

Yes, there is no struggle for Supremacy in Heaven, but rather Peace, Harmony, and Equality amoung all of the Angels including the Oldest one (God).

There is only a struggle for Supremacy here on Earth because of The Christ (The Messiah) (The Shadow) Illusion.

The Shadow (The Christ) (The Messiah) says It rules the World, but It is a Liar,

God the Real (The Spirit of Goodness) rules the world, this is why there is a lot more Good in the world than there is Bad.

Yes, only 1 in 1500 people is a Parasite, yes, a Mean, Lazy, Shameless, Fearmonging, Extortionist Parasite trying to get a Free ride from Society, while promoting a sick psychology called Sadism, the Seed of which is Illusion, yes, The Shadow, yes, In disguise as Goodness.

1 in 900 people is either Insane or in Jail.

1 in 400 people is Retarded.

1 in 100 people is a Criminal on the Loose.

1 in 10 people is a Shadow Worshipper, yes, a Hypocrite saying one thing and doing another.

That leaves 88% of people who are Gentiles (Gentle people) (Saints) in the Human eye out in the Free world serving there Neighbors, and praising God the Real (The Spirit of Goodness) for their Blessings, in their Closet of course.

Oh, Yes, my Children, we must cast out the "I", "I", "I" guy from our Heart and Mind for us to find true Happiness, Decency, Prosperity, and Peace of Mind, which will allow us to live in Peace, Harmony, and Equality with our Neighbors and the world around us.

This is the Purpose of God in our lives, to bring Heaven to Earth, so that we can be Happy, and be Free of Guilt, Fear, Doubt, and Illusion.

Thanks for Listening, as ever in, "The Spirit of Goodness",

"Saint Bill" (Head Coach) A Servant for God's sake.

(Acts 26, v.16-18)(John 7, v.16-18)(1 Jn.4, v.20)(2 Thes.2 v.9-11)

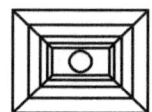

PREVIEWISM
Our World is Beautiful, Yes, Multi-Cultural

Dear Saint Ron:

Your Bible is different than my bible, In my bible it says that Paul is to turn the Jewish people from the Kingdom of Satan, and to the Kingdom of God.

In my bible it says that the Old word shall pass away and the New Word shall come to be. The old word was Condemnation and Curse.

The New word is Forgiveness and Blessings.

Saint Jesus was a young man in the beginning of his ministry and had he lived to a natural death he would have written the New Word himself. But the opportunity was taken from him by the Servants of Satan.

And then the writing was left to a Confused Jew call Saul.

Saul changed his name to Paul, and changed the word Messiah to Christ, put on a Sheepskin coat and the mask of a Good man and continued to preach the Lies and Illusions of the Dark ages.

And in doing so he deceived a few Gentiles into practicing Judaism while he called them Christians.

Yes, a Christian is a Gentile converted to Judaism, with a different name. Just like Lucifer changed his name to Satan.

It is obvious that the Foundation of your Faith is based on a Lie.

And the Lie is the statement that we have been seperated from God. (Hogwash). We are never seperated from God. God is always with us, and God is with us Always. No matter whether we are walking frontward or backward, God is with us always, and continues to Forgives us for our Shortcomings and Misconceptions.

So you see, we are always Sin-Free.

And the Glory be to God the Real, and not to God the Fraud.

So you see, what we at Previews have done is written "The Compass" for Saint Jesus, the Job he left undone.

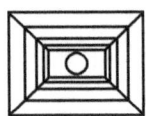

PREVIEWISM
Our World is Beautiful, Yes, Multi-Cultural

The Compass was written on the basis that we are all created, conceived, and Born in the Image of God, and as such we are All Saints, in the likeness of God. And thank God we never leave that state of Imperfection, because It is Eternally alive in Body, Mind, and Spirit, and continues to increase and improve in Its quality and quantity of Goodness, until we reach our Goal of Happiness, Decency, Prosperity and Peace of Mind for all of Humankind, in order for Us to live in Peace, Harmony, and EQUALITY with our Neighbors and the world around us, as It was in the Beginning, before Lazyness set in and led some people to Try to get a Free ride from Society at any Cost, Barring Nothing, including Suicide.

So you see, My Dear Friend,

Would you rather be a Saint and work for God (Reality) or Would you rather be a Sinner and work for Satan (Illusion)

Please answer this question, to continue.

Thanks for Listening, as ever in, "The Spirit of Goodness",

"Saint Bill" (Head Coach) A Servant for God's sake.

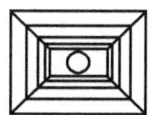

PREVIEWISM
Our World is Beautiful, Yes, Multi-Cultural

Dear Saint Ron: You are worshipping a Human Idol, just like the Pagan did.

But the Pagan passed away, just as Its descendant Judaism was passing away, when Mr. Saul came on the scene. Mr. Saul changed his name to Mr. Paul, changed the word Messiah to Christ, changed Lucifer to Satan, put on a sheepskin coat, and the Mask of a Good man, and continued to have the people worship a Human Idol.

But all this will pass away, just as the Pagan passed away, because now we have a New Bible, The EverLast Testament, Yes, The Compass, by author Saint Bill, who has revealed that God the Real is The Spirit of Goodness, and that God the Fraud is illusion (The Shadow), and God the Human is a Hypocrite not worthy of any praise at all. He just tries to steal the Glory for what God the Real has done. Secondly Human idols always fail you when the going gets tuff. They are always there with their hand out when the sun shines, but when the clouds come and the rain falls, the times of need, they are like The Shadow, they disappear, nowhere to be seen until the Sun shines again.

So you see, My Dear Saint Ron, you are following a dying God.

We at Previews are following the Everlasting and Eternal God, Yes, The Spirit of Goodness, with Its Sense of Judgement, Free Spirit, and Good Nature, together with all of Its angels (children)(characteristics), the oldest being The Spirit of Truth, and the youngest being The Spirit of Enthusiasm, with many in between, and they together live in Heaven, in the World, and in your Heart, Mind, and Soul, from creation, conception, and Birth, And your Soul never Dies, but recycles into and out of the Future, world without End.

Yes, My Friend, you are a Previewlite just as you are, but do not realize it until now.

But now that you do, It is time to Preach the Truth, and put the Lies, Illusions, and Counterfeit Miracles behind you, and never look back again. Yes, My Friend, Look Up and to the Future, because It has only Goodness to Bring.

Thank you, Dear God, Thank you, for true Insight.

Thanks for Listening, as ever in, "The Spirit of Goodness",

"Saint Bill" (Head Coach) A Servant for God's sake.

(Acts 26, v.16-18) (John 7, v.16-18) (1 Jn.4, v.20) (2 Thes.2, v.9-11) Previews Institute, "Summit Loc-001, H.O."

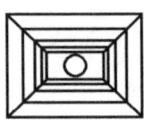

PREVIEWISM
Our World is Beautiful, Yes, Multi-Cultural

Dear Friends:

In the Spiritual Realm there are Tons of knowledge that we acquire during our walk with God the Real, The Spirit of Goodness. But we must not loose sight of the Basics, Yes, the Foundation.

The Foundation, The Basics we should keep in Front of us, and the Tons of knowledge behind us. In this way we always stay on track, and not confused.

The Basics of our Faith are as follows:

1) We are all created, conceived, and Born in the Image of God, and are therefore Saints, in the likeness of God, The Spirit of Goodness.

2) God is Omnipresent, and therefore we are Never Seperated from God. God is with us Always, and God is Always with us, whether we are walking frontward or backward, God is with us Always, and continues to Forgive us for our Shortcomings and misconceptions. Therefore we are always Sin-Free.

3) To take Offence is a Sin against Humanity.

    To react in Self-Defence is an Act of God.

    Therefore, where there is no Offence, there is no Sin.
    Where there is Self-Defence, there is God.

4) So Let us talk from the Heart, with our Sense of Judgement, Free Spirit, and Good Nature.

Thank you, Dear God, Thank you, for true Insight.

Hoping to hear from you soon, we remain,

Your truly, W.J. (Bill) Handel, M.A., L.W. (An Ordained Minister)

Yes, God Ordained,... God Sustained. Is that not wonderful,.. Yeh, that is wonderful. And we say, Thank you, Dear God, Thank you.

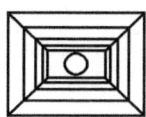

PREVIEWISM
Our World is Beautiful, Yes, Multi-Cultural

1/20/05

Now remember,

We are All Saints in God's eye, and

We look at life through God's eye, the eye of Reality.

And now we are ready to Invite you to Join "Our-E-Ministry"

and make It "Your-E-Ministry" to serve Humanity with the Object

being to gain your "Masters Degree" in psychology and philosophy, and become "God Ordained",... "God Sustained".

When you go to the address: www.previews-inc.com

You will be introduced to the opportunity and you will be delighted.

Now, Do not hesitate to say, "Let's Do It".

Thank you. (Cheers)

Thanks for Listening, as ever in, "The Spirit of Goodness",

"Saint Bill" (Head Coach) A Servant for God's sake.

(Acts 26, v.16-I 8) (John 7, v.16-18) (1 Jn.4, v.20) (2 Thes.2, v. 9-11)

Previews Institute, "Summit Loc-001, H.O."

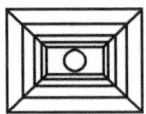

PREVIEWISM
Our World is Beautiful, Yes, Multi-Cultural

Dear Friends and Children of All ages:

Heaven on Earth is for All who use their Sense of Judgement to Judge (Decide) right from wrong and Act on the Right.

Hell on Earth is for those who do not use their Sense of Judgement and Do not Judge (Decide) right from wrong and continue to wallow in the Mud.

All of us use our Sense of Judgement to different degrees and subsequently find different degrees of Happiness, Decency, Prosperity and Peace of Mind.

God the Real, The Spirit of Goodness, being EverUnderstanding, Loving, and Forgiving does not Forget any Goodness you have done in your Life here on Earth, and therefore not one has fallen short of the Grace of God, and is accepted into Heaven in Heaven, Just as you are when you go on to Better things.

Therefore, we can assume that Some of us enter Heaven as Children of different ages, and Some of us enter Heaven as Adults of different ages.

And the Wise then teach the New comers the Ropes is Heaven.

After some time It comes time to be Re-conceived again, Back to Body, to come again to live and enjoy the fruits of our Labor from the previous time round. Chuckle, chuckle, eh !!

So look to the Future, and Prepare.

Thank you, Dear God, Thank you, for true Insight.

Thanks for Listening,

as ever in, "The Spirit of Goodness",

"Saint Bill" (Head Coach) A Servant for God's sake.

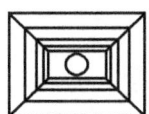

PREVIEWISM
Our World is Beautiful, Yes, Multi-Cultural

Dear Friends and Children of All ages:

Who was the wiser man, Juda or Abraham?

You may ask, who is Juda.? Well, Juda was Abraham's Father. Juda was a Pagan Indian, Lazy, Illiterate, a Criminal, Yes, a Fearmongering Parasite and a Murderer, and Insane by most standards. Abraham being the youngest in the Family was educated and not a Murderer, but none the less a member of the Family.

Abraham was afraid of his Father because he was a Murderer, and so Abraham was Loyal to his Father when they decided to write out the terms of their Ideology. Their Ideology was called the Master vs Slave idea. Otherwise called a Dictatorship.

Although Abraham was Loyal to his Father, Abraham had doubts about the Future of their organization. And so Abraham sublimely predicted an end to the Insanity of it all. Oh, yes, Abraham knew that you cannot forever justify Murder, Never. Murder can be forgiven and forgotten, but never justified. Only the ignorant and deceived try to justify Murder,. Ultimately with a twisted motive for a story of Suicide and the Raising of the Dead. Yes, pure fantasy and Illusion of the Deceived and Insane. (2 Thes.2, v.9-11.)

Well, the End is now here, because we now have a New Bible, The EverLast Testament. Yes, The Compass, manifested by The Spirit of Goodness, by, Saint Bill, alias, Wilhelm J. Handel, M.A., L.W. (An Ordained Minister) from a Family of Hard working Farmers. Pioneers yet, in a country governed by way of Democracy, the philosophy of Wise Sane people.

Thank God the Real, The Spirit of Goodness, for being very Wise, Brave, and Steadfast in guiding "Saint Bill" with every word written in "The Compass" and all of the related material.

We now have true Hope for the Future and a Promise of Happiness, Decency, Prosperity, and Peace of Mind for all of Humankind throughout the World, so that we can live in Peace, Harmony, and EQUALITY.

Yes, the "I", "I", "I" guy is Dying and within 300 years will be reduced to less than a speck of Dust. Yes, out of Sight out of Mind, and out of Mind out of Existence.

Thank you, Dear God, Thank you, for true Insight.

Thanks for Listening, as ever in, "The Spirit of Goodness",

"Saint Bill" (Head Coach) A Servant for God's sake.

(Acts 26, v.16-18) (John 7, v.16-18) (1 Jn.4, v.20) (2 Thes.2, v.9-11) Previews Institute,

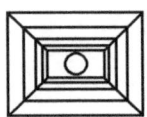

PREVIEWISM
Our World is Beautiful, Yes, Multi-Cultural

Dear Friends and Children of all ages:

Just another Proverb and what It means.

A Fool thinks It is better than you.

But when It speaks, We find that We are equal

The Fool has a God, which is Satan, and Satan is a Liar, and a Lie is an Illusion expressed. Therefore Satan is an illusion.

Yes, an illusion expressed, and so It seems Real, But It is not.

When Satan thought It was better than God, God kicked It out into outer darkness, beyond the reach of Light, and said, Stay there,.. We need you there for Reference.

Yes, Folks, when a Fool speaks, the Listener then knows what the Fool knows and so they are equal. This is the Reality, and all know that Reality is God, and God is Reality, Not Fantasy.

Thank you, Dear God, Thank you, for true Insight.

Thanks for Listening, as ever in, 'The Spirit of Goodness",

"Saint Bill" (Head Coach) A Servant for God's sake.

(Acts 26, v.16-18) (John 7, v.16-18) (1 Jn.4, v20) (2 Thes.2, v.9-11)

Previews Institute, "Summit Lod l, H.O."

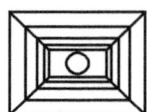

PREVIEWISM
Our World is Beautiful, Yes, Multi-Cultural

The Big Lie comes Three Fold,
with many Branches and Twigs.
But when you Uproot the Basics,
The Branches and Twigs will wither and Die.

Dear Friends and Children of all ages:

Saint Jesus said, the Jews (Judaism) are serving Satan (Illusion). Acts 26, vs 16-18.

Then in the next breath Saint Jesus said, To enter the Kingdom of Heaven on Earth, you must be Born again.

Now since Saint Jesus said that the Jews are serving Satan, and we know that Satan is a Liar, what are the Basic Lies of the Old Testament.

If you do not recognize the basic Lies of The Old Testament, you are not Born again, and are in effect promoting Judaism. The Kingdom of Satan. (Yes, The Kingdom of Hell on Earth)

When you recognize the basic Lies of the Old Testament, you are born again into a New World, where you use the Natural Gifts that God gave you upon Creation, Conception and Birth, and you begin to unravel a Twisted Web of Lies, as you simultaneously Cast Out the Illusions of the Past, as the Reality of God the Real, The Spirit of Goodness, becomes clearer and clearer in Front of you. Yes, Reality is God, and God is Reality, Not Fantasy.

The Natural Gifts (Instincts) that God gave you upon creation, conception, and Birth, are your Sense of Judgement, Free Spirit, and Good Nature.

When you use your Sense of Judgement to Judge (Decide) right from wrong you gradually come closer and closer to God the Real, The Spirit of Goodness, far in front of you, and God the Fraud, Satan (Illusion) (The Shadow) fades farther and farther into the distance behind you, until one day It gives up the battle and leaves you alone with God. And then you find Peace, Harmony, and Equality with your Neighbors and the world around you.

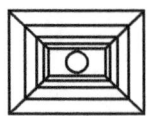

PREVIEWISM
Our World is Beautiful, Yes, Multi-Cultural

The first Lie of the Old Testament was when Abraham expressed the Illusion that you are Separated from God, and that you have to follow His instructions to be re-united with God. (Hogwash).

We are Never separated from God, God is Omnipresent, and so God is always with us, and God is with us Always, whether we are walking Frontward or Backward, God is with us Always, and continues to Forgive us for our Shortcomings and misconceptions. Therefore, we are always Sin-Free.

The second Lie that Abraham told was in the story of Adam and Eve, where he expressed the Illusion that God had condemned us to Death, for doing what comes Naturally. (Hogwash).

God the Real, The Spirit of Goodness, Blessed us with Life Eternal in Body, Mind and Spirit from the Beginning and It is still so today. Yes, Life in the Womb, Life on Earth, and Life in Heaven, as each is Eternal unto Its own, and are One as we Recycle into and out of the Future, world without End.

The third Lie of the Old Testament was when Mr. Saul (Paul) wrote that "Saint Jesus" was The Christ (Satan) (Illusion) (The Shadow) (The Messiah),.. Wrong,.. Saint Jesus was a man like you and I, who used his Sense of Judgement to Judge (Decide) right from wrong for himself and allowed all others the same Privilege. Which is against the wish of Satan (Illusion) (The Shadow).

(The Messiah), which says, Do not Judge (Decide) right from wrong, Do not eat of the Fruit of the Tree of the knowledge of Good and Evil,.. Do not question me, just Believe me, pleease, I love you, I would not Lie to you, would I,.. If it were not so I would tell you, right.

Well, Folks, you can see the Pit in that one.

Thank God the Real, The Spirit of Goodness, for our Natural Good Instincts that lead us to the Truth and keep us truly Free from Guilt, Fear, Doubt, and Illusion, in order that we might find Peace, Harmony, and Equality with our Neighbors and the world around us, and subsequently find Happiness, Decency, Prosperity and Peace of Mind.

Thank you, Dear God, Thank you, for true Insight.

Thanks for Listening, as ever in, "The Spirit of Goodness",

"Saint Bill" (Head Coach) A Servant for God's sake.

(Acts 26, v.16-18) (John 7, v.16-18) (1 Jn.4, v.20) (2 Thes.2, v.9-11) Previews Institute

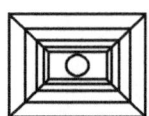

PREVIEWISM
Our World is Beautiful, Yes, Multi-Cultural

An Ounce of Prevention is preferred to a Pound of Cure

Dear Friends and Children of all ages:

Saint Jesus said, we did not come to Cure the Healthy,. we came to cure the Sick.

So we at Previews want you to know that we think you are all very Healthy and doing just Fine.

But the Negative influence of The Shadow (Illusion) is an Eternal threat to our Positive Mental Health.

And so we have an Ounce of Prevention for you today, which is preferred to a Pound of Cure.

Today we have another question for you.

What is the Difference between a Martyr and a Saint?

Answer: A Martyr dies for Its cause, and a Saint Lives for Its cause. Yes, Satan (Illusion)(The Shadow) convinces a person to commit Suicide for a cause with the Promise that It will be Glorified as a Martyr.

While God the Real, suggests that a person Live for a cause because God needs you to Live to carry out the cause, regardless of the circumstances.

Now we know that God does not want us to Kill, especially not Ourselves.

So you see, a Martyr is serving Satan (Illusion), while a Saint is serving God, The Spirit of Goodness.

Thank you, Dear God, Thank you, for true Insight.

Thanks for Listening, as ever in, 'The Spirit of Goodness",

"Saint Bill" (Head Coach) A Servant for God's sake.

(Acts 26, v.16-18) (John 7, v.16-18) (1 Jn.4, v.20) (2 Thes.2, v.9-11) Previews Institute,

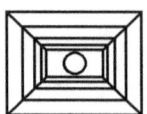

PREVIEWISM
Our World is Beautiful, Yes, Multi-Cultural

Dear Friends and Children of All ages:

God the Real, The Spirit of Goodness, is multicultural and therefore very Wise, it knows and understands what is written in every Book in every Library in the World. Yes, beyond Human comprehension, but none the less, Finite.

God the Fraud, Satan (illusion) The Shadow) is the "1", "I", "I"   guy and is very limited by Its idiosyncracies because It is Illiterate, and therefore no wiser than the foolish person that serves It. But Satan (Illusion) being a Liar, says Its kwoledge is Infinite. What a Fat Head, eh !! chuckle, chuckle, eh !!

Dear Friends, God the Real, The Spirit of Goodness, created us with a Sense of *Judgement, a Free Spirit, and a Good Nature, in Its Likeness.* These are our Instincts, and then we adopt all of God's angels children characteristics, the Oldest being The Spirit of Truth, and the youngest being The Spirit of Enthusiasm, with many in between. When we use our Sense of Judgement to Judge (Decide) right from wrong with one another, Our Sense of Judgement leads us to the Truth, and as we respect our neighbor's opinion, we gain a *very* Broad understanding of Humanity and God, so that we come to live in Peace, Harmony, and Equality with one-another, and subsequently find Happiness, Decency, Prosperity, and Peace of Mind. This is the purpose of God in our Lives.

Thank you, Dear God, Thank you, for true Insight.

P. S.: We welcome your Interpretations and or questions.

Thanks for Listening, as ever in, 'The Spirit of Goodness",

"Saint Bill" (Head Coach) A Servant for God's sake_

(Acts 26, v.16-18) (John 7, v.16-18) (l Jn.4, v.20) (2 Thes.2, v,9-11)

Previews Institute

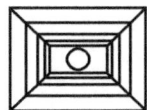

PREVIEWISM
Our World is Beautiful, Yes, Multi-Cultural

Dear Friends and Children of All ages:

According to the record "Saint Jesus" was made out to be quite a Wise man in speaking out against the Jews (Judaism), and became an Outlaw in his time, and hunted by the Authorities.

When he was turned in by his own men the Authorities made him out to be a complete Lunatic and an Accomplice to Murder.

Yes, they said he fell for Satan's promise of Glory if he would commit Suicide to become a Martyr.

And according to the record "Saint Jesus" refused to defend himself in court to allow the Authorities to kill him for the sake of Glory, and to try to Justify murder. All as though it were God's Plan.

What an Insane society this poor man lived in at the Time, to suggest that God is a premeditated murderer. It is obvious these people and all who support them were and still are Insane.

Yes, in God's eye there is Never any Justification for murder or Suicide. But we can say, Forgiven and Not Guilty by reason of Insanity.

Thank you, Dear God, Thank you, for true Insight.

Thanks for Listening, as ever in, The Spirit of Goodness",

"Saint Bill" (Head Coach) A Servant for God's sake.

(Acts 26, v.16-18) (John 7, v.16-18) (1 Jn.4, v.20) (2 Thes.2, v.9-11)

Previews Institute, "Summit Loc-001, H.O."

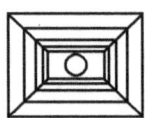

PREVIEWISM
Our World is Beautiful, Yes, Multi-Cultural

Dear Friends and Children of all ages:

What does it mean, To be Born again"?

To be born again, you must go back to square one, as though you were born yesterday, and begin a process of Re-Evaluation of all Preconceived ideas or valuations in your Heart and Mind.

You begin by addressing God in the following manner:

Dear God, please Awaken the Spirit of God, Yes, The Spirit of Goodness, within me and allow Its Sense of Judgement, Free Spirit, and Good Nature to Learn and grow in Understanding and Love of your kind.

Thus begins a process of Questions and Answers according to your Sense of Judgement, Free Spirit, and Good Nature, along with all of God's angels (children)(characteristics), the oldest being The Spirit of Truth, and the youngest being The Spirit of Enthusiasm, with many in between, as they along with your Instincts live in Heaven, in the World, and in your Heart, Mind, and Soul, from creation, conception, and Birth. Yes, remember, God is with you Always.

Also remember, that God's kind of Love is the kind that Gives without expecting a return. Yes, Pure and Unconditional, and Eternal.

Now, remember, Knowledge comes from Three sources,

1) Talking to Wise people, and that means Everyone.
2) Reading a Good Book. (You, may start with "The COMPASS", as manifested by "The Spirit of Goodness" by Author: Saint Bill.
3) Personal Experience. This is the most accurate source of Knowledge. It along with your Sense of Judgement will lead you to the Truth, and the Truth will set you Free from Guilt, Fear, Doubt, and Illusion, and thus Free in Spirit, Body, and Mind.

Thank you, Dear God, Thank you, for true Insight.

Thanks for Listening, as ever in,

"The Spirit of Goodness",

"Saint Bill" (Head Coach) A Servant for God's sake.

(Acts 26, v.16-18) (John 7, v.16-18) (1 k.4, v.20) (2 Thes.2, v.9-11)

Previews Institute, "Summit Loc-001, H.O."

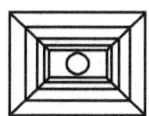

PREVIEWISM
Our World is Beautiful, Yes, Multi-Cultural

Dear Friends and Children of All ages:

Satan being Illusion means that Satan in Reality is a Human Idol. And we all know that we should not worship Human Idols.

Because Human Idols fail you when the going gets Tuff.

We should worship The Spirit of God, Yes, The Spirit of Goodness. Because The Spirit of Goodness never fails you, not in the Sunshine, not in the Rain, and not in the Hailstorms. The Spirit of God stays with you all the way.

A Human Idol is a Lord God, and there are two kinds of those.

A Bad Lord God, and a Good Lord God, but they have one thing in common, they are both Human, and that makes them both Fallible. This is why we should not worship Human Idols.

The Jews are said to have a Bad Lord God, and the Christians are said to have a Good Lord God, but the problem is that they are both said to be The Christ (The Messiah), and this is False because Saint Jesus said The Messiah is Satan (Illusion) the God of the Jews. (Acts 26, vs. 16-18)

Therefore, Saint Jesus was not the Christ (Messiah). Jesus was a man like you and I that used his Sense of Judgement to Judge (Decide) right from wrong to come closer and closer to God the Real, The Spirit of Goodness, with Its Sense of Judgement, Free Spirit, and Good Nature, together with all of Its angels (children) (characteristics), the oldest being The Spirit of Truth and the youngest being The Spirit of Enthusiasm, with many in between as we know.

Yes, indeed, we all come closer and closer to God the Real, when we use our Sense of Judgement and Judge (Decide) right from wrong for ourselves, and allow all others the same privilege, and God the Fraud, Satan (Illusion) fades away as the Illusions are Cast out.

As Truth and Reality prevails, It brings you closer to God, because Reality is God, and God is Reality, Not Fantasy.

The Bad Lord God was named Juda, who was Abraham's Father. The Good Lord God was named Jesus, who was Joseph's Son. The Bad Lord God was made out to be an Insane Murderer.

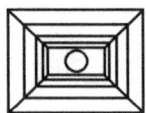

PREVIEWISM
Our World is Beautiful, Yes, Multi-Cultural

The Good Lord God was made out to be Perfect, but we know that Nothing is Perfect, and so they are Both Frauds. Yes, Human Idols.

And so you see folks, Look Up and see Truth and Reality, and say, to Hell with The Shadow (Satan)(Illusion), and never look down or back again because God the Real, The Spirit of Goodness, is the God of the Future, and It lives in Heaven, in the World, and in your Heart, Mind, and Soul, from creation, conception, and Birth, Yes, God is with you Always. And It leads you to know that Life is Eternal in Body, Mind, and Spirit. Yes, Life in the Womb, Life on Earth, and Life in Heaven, as each is Eternal unto Its own, and are One as we Recycle into and out of the Future, World without End.

When we are conceived, the Spirit becomes Body, Life in the Womb. when we are Born, the Body becomes Word, Life on Earth. when we go on to better things, the Word becomes Spirit, Life in Heaven. After some time we are Re-conceived again to come again to Live and enjoy the Fruits of our Labor from the previous time round. Yes, from beginning to present, and from present to beginning, and from beginning to beginning, and from beginning to present, world without end. This spells Eternal Life, and a Life of Bliss. All else is a Story of The Shadow that we Cast-out as pure Bad Fiction. Yes, there is no longer any curse. (Rev.22, vs.3).

Thank you, Dear God, Thank you, for true Insight.

Thanks for Listening,

as ever in, 'The Spirit of Goodness",

"Saint Bill" (Head Coach) A Servant for God's sake.

(Acts 26, v.16-18) (John 7, v.16-18) (1 Jn.4, v.20) (2 Thes.2, v.9-II)

Previews Institute, "Summit Loc-001, H.O."

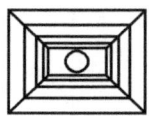

PREVIEWISM
Our World is Beautiful, Yes, Multi-Cultural

Dear Friends and children of all ages:

Today we have a Miscellaneous proverb for you.

1) A Wise person does not come to Talk. A Wise person comes to Listen.

   Oh, Yes, A Wise person does not speak First. A Wise person speaks Last, and

   The Last word is,.... Forgiven.

Chuckle, chuckle, eh, Folks.

Yes, Life is a Joke, not a Yoke.

Cheers

and a Question:

What do "Previewlites" do to get to Heaven.?

Answer:

Nothing, except Respect their Neighbor's opinion, and Praise God for their Blessings.

Because their Neighbor's opinion is the Law. Yes, the majority rules amoung the Wise. Yes, the Wise run a Democracy.

The Idiots, The Shadow's Servants, try to run a Dictatorship.

Yes, when you respect your Neighbor's opinion, the Law serves God, cause the majority rules among the Wise.

If you think the Law is God's opinion, the Law serves Satan (The Shadow) (Illusion), because It becomes a power struggle among Self-righteous Idiots.

Thank you, Dear God, Thank you, for true Insight.

Thanks for Listening,

as ever in, "The Spirit of Goodness'",

"Saint Bill" (Head Coach) A Servant for God's sake.

(Acts 26, v.16-18) (John 7, v.16-18) (1 Jn.4, v.20) (2 Thes.2, v.9-11) Previews Institute, "Summit Lac-001, H.O."

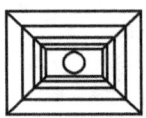

PREVIEWISM
Our World is Beautiful, Yes, Multi-Cultural

Dear Friends and Children of All ages:

God the Real, The Spirit of Goodness, creates in the order of Spirit, Body, and Mind, almost simultaneously, with a Sense of Judgement, Free Spirit, and Good Nature, and they are Inseparable.

Yes, God is a Spirit of Action because Actions speak louder than words. And our Actions together with our Sense of Judgement lead us to the Truth through the Reality of God all around us.

And the expression of Reality with words is what we call Truth.

Yes, God is not Perfect, just as we are not Perfect. Because to be Perfect is to be Dead, or without further room for Improvement.

God is not Dead, God is Alive, and always has room for Improvement.

And we are not Dead, because Life is Eternal in Body, Mind and Spirit. Yes, Life in the Womb, Life on Earth, and Life in Heaven, as each is Eternal unto Its own, and are One as we recycle into and out of the Future, World without End.

Yes, God the Real, The Spirit of Goodness, has a Sense of Judgement, Free Spirit, and Good Nature, so use your Sense of Judgement to Judge (Decide) right from wrong for yourself and allow all others the same Privilege, to allow your Good Nature to learn and grow in Understanding and Love of God's kind.

And God's kind of Love is the kind that Gives without expecting a return. Yes, Pure and Unconditional and Eternal.

Now remember: We are all Saints in God's eye, because we are always Loved and Forgiven, and accepted Just as we are, any time, any Day. And We look at life through God's eye, the eye of Reality.

Thank you, Dear God, Thank you, for true Insight.

Thanks for Listening, as ever in, "The Spirit of Goodness",

"Saint Bill" (Head Coach) A Servant for God's sake.

(Acts 26, v.16-18) (John 7, v.16-18) (1 Jn.4, v.20) (2 Thes.2, v.9-11)

Previews Institute

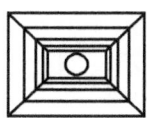

PREVIEWISM
Our World is Beautiful, Yes, Multi-Cultural

Dear Friends and Children of all ages:

(1) An Old Sick Satanic mind needs a Pound of Cure (Expensive)

A Young Healthy Godly mind needs an Ounce of Prevention (Free)

To the Old, "The Compass", a New Bible is a Pound of Cure.

To the Young a Page, daily, is an Ounce of Prevention.

It is time to invest in the Future of our Children.

(2) A person who says that we all go to Heaven is a very Humble person.

And living in Heaven on Earth. Yes, a Saint.

A person who says that only Me and my followers go to Heaven is a Self-righteous Insane Idiot and Its followers are a bit confused and Deceived, walking through the Pits of Hell on Earth.

And they think they are Sinners and want us to follow them.

Fact is that when they kick the "I", "1", "1" guy out of their Heart and Mind they become Saints walking in Heaven on Earth.

(3) A Sinner is a Person who Initiates physical violence.

Verbal violence is Simply Self-Defence.

And Self-Defence is an Act of God.

(4) When you start on Easy Street, It leads to The Hard Road.

When you start on The Hard Road, It leads to Easy Street.

Thanks for Listening, as ever in, "The Spirit of Goodness",

"Saint Bill" (Head Coach) A Servant for God's sake.

(Acts 26, v.16-18) (John 7, v.16-18) (1 Jn.4, v.20) (2 Thes.2, v.9-11)

Previews Institute, "Summit Loc-001, H.O."

A Servant for God's sake.

THE TRADITION OF "CHANGE FOR THE BETTER" IS BORN IN *"PREVIEWISM"*
www.previews-inc.com
Make 10 - 20 Copies per week and Pass It On. - God will be well Pleased.

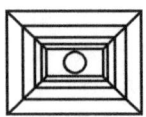

PREVIEWISM
Our World is Beautiful, Yes, Multi-Cultural

Dear Friends and Children of All ages, the World over:

We, here at Previews, do not consider you a member of any other religion except Previewism. Because by Definition a Previewlite is a child of God, serving God to the best of his/her ability given his/her experiences. And we know that you all Fit that Armor. And you can be Proud because you are a Saint, yes, a child of God, serving God to the best of your ability given your experiences. And that is Good enough for God because God accepts you, Just as you are. Any time, any Day.

Secondly, we all know that God is a Spirit, yes, the Good one, Yes, The Spirit of Goodness, and we all understand what "The Spirit of Goodness" means. Yes, Our Good Nature, Free Spirit, and Sense of Judgement, in the Image of God. Yes, these are the instincts that we inherit from God. And since we all adopt different angels (characteristics) of God, the oldest being The Spirit of Truth and the youngest being The Spirit of Enthusiasm, with many in between, and to different degrees, we are all unique individuals that hold a special place in God's Heart, Mind, and Soul, so that we can be assured that we are all Loved Equally from the beginning of Day to the End of Day, new Day after new Day.

Thirdly, we all know that God the Fraud is Illusion, Yes, The Shadow. And The Shadow of God, as with any other Shadow is just an Illusion, and an Illusion expressed is Lie and so The Shadow is a Liar, by nature disguised as goodness.

This is why God the Real, The Spirit of Goodness, gave you a Sense of Judgement to use to Judge (Decide) right from wrong, true from false, Yes, Reality from Illusion, so that you might enjoy your Blessings from God, and find Happiness, Decency, Prosperity, and Peace of Mind, and Freedom from Guilt, Fear, Doubt and Illusion.

Yes, my Children and Friends, this is the purpose of God in our lives, and we at "Previews" have now achieved our Purpose.

Thank you, Dear God, Thank you, for true Insight.

Thanks for Listening,

as ever in, "The Spirit of Goodness",

"Saint Bill" (Head Coach)

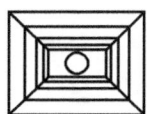

PREVIEWISM
Our World is Beautiful, Yes, Multi-Cultural

Dear Friends and Children of all ages:

We, at Previews, have Faith in God the Real, The Spirit of Goodness, because It is Ever Understanding, Loving, and Forgiving. And does always Forgive, Not condemn, Bless, Not Curse, Yes, Reward, Not Punish. And we know that when we do likewise toward our Neighbors we will reap the Blessings of God. That is right, No Doubt in our Minds. And as a result we live as Saints. Yes, in Heaven on Earth.

The Shadow worshippers are Lazy parasites and have been deceived into thinking that they can get a Free-ride from Society.

And will go to any extreme to try to prove it. Yes, they will break all of Man's laws, including Extortion, to try to get a Free-ride.

And so they Connived Hell and Damnation and Fear Tactic of every kind, including Death if you do not bow to their demands.

And so they bring It all upon themselves and live as Poor Miserable Sinners because they believe that Suffering makes you strong. Yes, in Hell on Earth because they do not realize that The Shadow is a Liar.

All they have to do is Look Up and to the Future to change their attitudes and they will begin to live as Saints as God wants them to.

PS.:   An Old Sick Satanic (Sadistic) mind needs a Pound a Cure, (Expensive).

        A "Young Healthy Godly (Happy) mind needs an Ounce of Prevention. (Free).

        To the Old, The Compass, a New Bible, is a Pound of Cure.

        To the Young, a Page, daily, is an Ounce of Prevention.

        It is time to invest in the *Future of our Children.*

Thanks for Listening, as ever in, 'The Spirit of Goodness",

"Saint Bill" (Head Coach) A servant for God's sake.

(Acts 26, v.16-18) (John 7, v.16-18) (1 Jn.4, v.20) (2 Thes. 2, v.9-11)

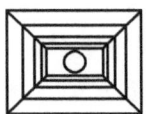

PREVIEWISM
Our World is Beautiful, Yes, Multi-Cultural

Dear Friends and Children of all ages:

A Personal Investment plan or Strategy.

1)   25% of Net worth should be in Cash on Hand.

       25% of Real property should be in Equity.

2)   Your Real property should grow at 10% per year, Including Cash Flow, Inflation, and Mortgage reduction.

3)   Your Employment should pay for your Living expenses, and allow for some 10% of Net income, in Savings per year.

The Young and wise who follow this formula become wealthy, and The Careless remain slaves to a Career.

Thanks for Listening, as ever in, The Spirit of Goodness",

"Saint Bill" (Head Coach) A Servant for God's sake.

(Acts 26, v.16-18) (John 7, v.16-18) (1 Jn.4, v.20) (2 Thes.2, v.9-11)

Previews Institute, "Summit Locl , H.O."

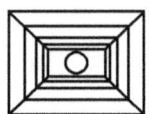

PREVIEWISM
Our World is Beautiful, Yes, Multi-Cultural

Dear Friends and Children of all ages:

There are Two kinds of Religion. Good Religion and Evil Religion.

A Good religion provides a Service to Society as a whole, whereby It brings about a Good healthy Mind, Love and Hope to the Heart, and Peace to the Soul.

Because these benifits are all Gifts from God, they come Free of charge when the Leaders simply reveal the Truth about God the Real, The Spirit of Goodness, with Its Sense of Judgement, Free Spirit, and Good Nature. Yes, these are the Instincts that we Inherit from God. Our Free Spirit makes us Creative, Our Good Nature makes us Good Providers, and Our Sense of Judgement makes us Steadfast Comfortors. Thank God the Real for Truth and Reality.

Now the Evil religion is a Parasite upon the Ignorant, whereby the Leaders resort to Hell and Damnation and Fear Tactic of every kind, including Death if one does not Bow to their Demands. Yes, pure and simply Extortion.... Extortion first of Money and secondly Extortion of Praise and Glory.

These people we call "Shadow Worshippers" and are the biggest Hypocrites that live on Earth because they seem to know what they are doing, but they do not, and so they continue in their Decieved state of Mind.

Thank God the Real, they are in the Minority, because It would be difficult to continually Forgive them for their Ignorance if they were in the Majority.

In the Regions where they are in the Majority, It is obvious they are living in the Kingdom of Hell on Earth. (Acts 26, v.16-18)

So, Folks, Let us continue to Look Up and to the Future, as It holds only Goodness to come. Yes, we will continue to work toward Freedom from Guilt, Fear, Doubt, and Illusion, to achieve Peace, Harmony, and Equality with our Neighbors and the world around us, and subsequently find Happiness, Decency, Prosperity and Peace of Mind for all of Humankind throughout the world. This is the Purpose of God in our Lives. Yes, to bring about

Heaven on Earth for All, according to The Compass, a New Bible. Yes, The EverLast Testament, as manifested by The Spirit of Goodness, by Author: Saint Bill, alias: Wilhelm J. Handel.

Thank you, Dear God, Thank you, for true Insight.

Thanks for Listening, as ever in, "The Spirit of Goodness",

"Saint Bill" (Head Coach) A Servant for God's sake.

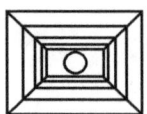

PREVIEWISM
Our World is Beautiful, Yes, Multi-Cultural

Dear Friends and Children of all ages:

In the Religion (World) of Previewism a Leader is called a Coach. All Coaches are Self-supporting businesspeople. They do not rely on income from the Membership for their daily needs of Food, Shelter, and Clothing.

Any and All monies donated by the Membership goes toward the Relief of Poverty with the ones who have fallen through the cracks.

All Coaches lead their Ministry according to the Principles of "The Compass" and the related material, "Object, Masters Degree", as manifested by "The Spirit of Goodness" by Author: Saint Bill, alias: Wilhelm J. Handel.

Thank you, Dear God, Thank you, for true Insight.

Thanks for Listening,

as ever in, "The Spirit of Goodness",

"Saint Bill" (Head Coach) A Servant for God's sake.

(Acts 26, v.16-18) (John 7, v.16-18) (1 Jn.4, v.20) (2 Thes.2, v.9-11)

Previews Institute, "Summit Loc-001, H.O."

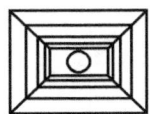

PREVIEWISM
Our World is Beautiful, Yes, Multi-Cultural

Dear Friends and Children of all ages:

We are not to Separate, we are to Co-exist.

God the Real, The Spirit of Goodness, is the Creator, the Good Provider, and the Steadfast Comfortor of one big Family called the Human Race. Yes, we are One with God, and God is One with Us, always.

We are to work together in the Spirit of God, The Spirit of Goodness, through thick or thin, and never give up on the Object of Oneness in the Spirit of God, The Spirit of Goodness.

If we give up, as a certain group of people once did, and separate from the Family of God, we are decieved into thinking that we can create a better plan than God has for us, in Oneness, and we bring Pain and Suffering upon ourselves, Just as the people did that once separated themselves from God's Family, the Human Race.

People that separate themselves from the Human Race are called Shadow Worshippers, and they become Self-Righteous, Lazy, and Insane by the standards of God's Family.

But the members of God's Family realize that these people have been deceived by Illusion (The Shadow), and thus Forgive them for their Ignorance (Illusion and Lie) that they are living in.

The members of God's Family continue on with their lives, Free of Guilt, Fear, Doubt and Illusion, and in Peace, Harmony, and EQUALITY with their neighbors and the world around them, and subsequently find Happiness, Decency, Prosperity and Peace of mind. Hoping that one day "The Shadow Worshippers" will see the error of their way and Join back in with The Family of God, the Human Race, to relieve themselves of their Insanity.

Thank you, Dear God, Thank you, for true Insight.

Thanks for Listening,

as ever in, "The Spirit of Goodness",

"Saint Bill" (Head Coach) A Servant for God's sake.

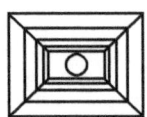

PREVIEWISM
Our World is Beautiful, Yes, Multi-Cultural

There is only One God, but It seems there are Two.

Dear Friends and Children of all ages:

We at Previews believe there is only One God, and only One Big Family of God called the Human Race.

But according to some it seems there are Two Gods, yours and mine.
And according to some it seems there are Two kinds of People, the Jewish and the Gentiles.

One kind of people are called Jewish or Christian.

The other kind of people are called Gentiles (Gentle people) (Saints) or Previewlites.

The Gentiles set up a Democracy long before the Jewish or Christians came along. The Jewish and Christian are still trying to set up a Dictatorship. But they lost the Battle long ago.

This is why 88% of people are Gentiles (Gentle people) (Saints) or Previewlites. And only 12% of people are Jewish or Christian.

The Gentiles make the rules and run a Democracy.

The Gentiles gave the Jewish a Tract of Land that they can call their own, on the condition that they run a Democracy.

So you see, the Leaders of the Jewish community lost the Battle and within 300 years the Jewish people will see the Error of their way and throw away the Old Bible, because the Gentiles now have one of their own called "The Compass", a new Bible, The EverLast Testament, together with all related material, manifested by The Spirit of God, The Spirit of Goodness, by author: Saint Bill, alias: Wilhelm J. Handel.

Now, getting back to the presumption of Two Gods.

Let me ask you, what does One God have that the other God does not have.

Answer: Nothing but Counterfeit Miracles. Pure and simple illusion designed to Deceive the Ignorant and their Followers. (2 Thes.2, v.9-11)

So you see, we at Previews will never give up Hope that the Jewish and the Christians will one day see the Error of their way and Join forces with the Majority, the Gentiles (the Gentle

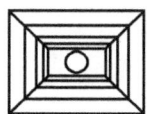

PREVIEWISM
Our World is Beautiful, Yes, Multi-Cultural

people) (the Saints), the Previewlites.

All this to gain Freedom from Guilt, Fear, Doubt and Illusion so that we can be in Peace, Harmony, and Equality with our Neighbors and the world around us, and subsequently find Happiness, Decency, Prosperity, and Peace of Mind throughout the world. Together with the Knowledge that Life is Eternal in Body, Mind and Spirit. Yes, Life in the Womb, Life on Earth and Life in Heaven, as each is Eternal unto its own, and are One as we Recycle into and out of the Future, World without End.

Thank you, Dear God, Thank you, for true Insight.

Thanks for Listening, as ever in, "The Spirit of Goodness",

"Saint Bill" (Head Coach) A Servant for God's sake.

(Acts 26, v.16-18) (John 7, v.16-18) (1 Jn.4, v.20) (2 Thes.2, v.9-11)

Previews Institute, "Summit Loc-001, H.O."

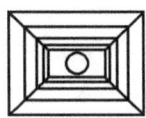

PREVIEWISM
Our World is Beautiful, Yes, Multi-Cultural

Dear Friends and Children of all ages:

Just some further Insight

Are you going to Heaven? You say, you are not sure

Well, let me tell you,. You can be sure you are going to Heaven. Do you know why.? Because I am going to Heaven, and if I am going to Heaven, then everyone is going to Heaven. Of this we can be sure. Do you know why,. Because a wise man called Saint Jesus, once said the very same thing. He said, I came from Heaven, so I know what I am talking about.

Well, folks, I came from Heaven too, so I know what I am talking about too. Believe me, Have Faith, Do not question me, Have no Doubt, and have Faith in God the Real, The Spirit of Goodness, with Its Sense of Judgement, Free Spirit, and Good Nature, together with all of Its angels (characteristics), the oldest being the Spirit of Truth and the youngest being the Spirit of Enthusiasm, with many in between, as they live in Heaven, in the World, and in your Heart, Mind, and Soul, from creation, conception and Birth. Yes, God is with you, always.

When we were created, we inherited the Basic Instincts of God the Real, The Spirit of Goodness, and when we are conceived we inherit the Basic Instincts from our Parents. Yes, the Spirit becomes Body, this is life in the Womb. When we are Born, the Body becomes Word (written or verbal), this is Life on Earth, and we become what we Think,. because Thought is the source of Action,. and Actions speak louder than Words. So watch your Actions, because they let us know what you Think.

So you see, you know your Parents went to Heaven, because they had Faith in God the Real, The Spirit of Goodness, and all that It means. So you are going to Heaven, when you go on to better things, Daily. Yes, look Up and to the Future, and you will find Heaven on Earth is equal to Heaven in Heaven, and we know that is Eternal in Body, Mind and Spirit. Yes, Life in the Womb, Life on Earth, and Life in Heaven, as each is Eternal unto Its own and are One as we Recycle into and out of the Future, World without End.

For further Insight and support see "The Compass", a New Bible, The EverLast Testament, and all related material by Author: Saint Bill, written for Saint Jesus, the Job he left Undone.

Thank you, Dear God, Thank you, for true Insight.

Thanks for Listening,

Author: The Spirit of Goodness, by "Saint Bill", A Servant for God's sake.

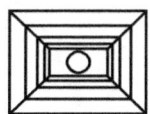

PREVIEWISM
Our World is Beautiful, Yes, Multi-Cultural

God Comes as One, People Come in Three's

Dear Friends and Children of all ages:

There are three types of people in the World.

1. There are the ones who Think they are Sinners.
2. There are the ones who Know they are Saints.
3. There are the ones who Think they are Both,
Yes, these are the Confused.

The Sinners need to be "Born again" to Worship God and Serve their Neighbors, and Not The Shadow.

The Saints were Born right the First time to Worship God and Serve their Neighbors, and Not The Shadow.

The Ones in Transition are the Confused. Yes, It seems they are Hypocrites, but they are just Confused.

Now remember Life is a Journey, while some are born into a Family of Sinners, while some are born into a Family of Saints, and some are born into a Family of the Confused.

Now remember, We are all Saints in God's eye, because God Forgives us All our Shortcomings to Renew and Keep our Good Nature intact, time and time again. And We at "Previews" look at Life through God's eye, the eye of Reality.

Yes, God is Healthy Positive, Not Sick Negative.

Thank you, Dear God, Thank you, for true Insight.

Thanks for Listening, as ever in "The Spirit of Goodness"

"Saint Bill" (Head Coach) A Servant for God's sake.

(Acts 26, v.16-18) (John 7, v.18-18) (1 Jn.4, v.20) (2 Thes.2, v.9-11)

Previews Institute, "Summit Loc-001, H.O."

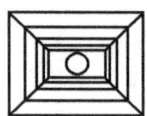

PREVIEWISM
Our World is Beautiful, Yes, Multi-Cultural

The Dumb and Voiceless

Dear Gordon:

It is obvious you are being led by the Nose. And by a two faced Hypocrite yet.

Saint Jesus said, the Jews are serving Satan (Acts 26, v. 16-18)

And Satan is an Insane Murderer and an Extortionist Parasite wanting a Free ride from Society at any cost to his neighbor.

This is who you are serving on the one hand.

On the other hand you are serving a Perfect Idiot, and a Perfect Idiot is an Illusion.

This creates a Two faced Hypocrite which is The Holy Spirit, saying one thing and doing another.

We at Previews have found The Spirit of God, which is The Spirit of Goodness, and It has three Instincts, them being A Sense of Judgement, a Free Spirit, and a Good Nature. And The Spirit of Goodness has many angels (characteristics) the oldest being the Spirit of Truth and the youngest being the Spirit of Enthusiasm, with many in between.

When you Exercise your Instincts and angels of God, you find Heaven on Earth as God wants It to be.

We have not found a Christian yet that says he/she is living in Heaven on Earth. So It is time for you to go on to better things.

You say, you are a poor miserable Sinner, and I am a Saint.

I have something to offer you,

You have nothing to offer me.

So let us talk from the Heart, with our Sense of Judgement, Free Spirit and Good Nature.

Yes, this will lead you to the Truth and the Truth will set you Free of The Shadow (Satan) (Illusion)(Christ)(Messiah)(Lucifer) and what ever else you may want to call It.

Yes, Free of Guilt, Fear, Doubt and Illusion.

And in Union with God the Real, The Spirit of Goodness.

Thanks for Listening, as ever in, "The Spirit of Goodness",

"Saint Bill" A Servant for God's Sake

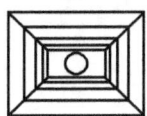

PREVIEWISM
Our World is Beautiful, Yes, Multi-Cultural

Blessed are the Wise men, and There are Many

Dear Gordon;

I think you are a Wise man.

Therefore, I have a question for you.

Now, you may say, Ask me no questions, and I will tell you no Lies.

But all I need is a simple Yes or No.

No Lies, just a Yes or a No.

Now here is the question.

Do you live Sin-Free.?

Waiting to hear from you soon, we remain,

Yours truly,

Thanks for Listening, as ever in, "The Spirit of Goodness",

"Saint Bill" (Head Coach) A Servant for God's sake.

(Acts 26, v.16-18)(John 7, v.16-18)(1 Jn.4, v.20)(2 Thes.2, v.9-11)

Previews Institute, "Summit Loc-001, H.O."

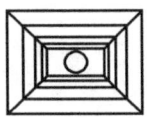

PREVIEWISM
Our World is Beautiful, Yes, Multi-Cultural

Blessed are the Wise men, and There are Many

Dear Gordon:

You did not answer, so since you say that you are a Sinner, It is obvious that the answer is No. you do not live Sin-Free.

So, I have another question.

Would you like to live Sin-Free.

So, since you are a Wise man, It is obvious that the answer is Yes you would like to live Sin-Free.

So, I have another question.

Does God want you to live Sin-Free.?

1 can only assume that the answer is Yes.

So, I have another question.

Has God shown you how to live Sin-Free.

I assume that God has shown you how to live Sin-Free.

So I have another question.

Why do you not live Sin-Free.?

It seems to me that you will say, that It is impossible.

So, God has shown you how to do the Impossible, and you do not even try, because you think It is impossible.

Oh, yee of little Faith.

We have something to teach you, because God has shown me how to live Sin-Free and I tried It and I succeeded.

I had some learning to do, but I have succeeded.

I now live Sin-Free and I can now teach people how to live Sin-Free,

Is that not wonderful, yeh, that is wonderful.

Since you said that you would like to live Sin-Free, you are welcome to start a learning process with me, and you will never Look back.

And you will come to live Sin-Free.

Is that not wonderful!, yeh, that is wonderful.

Hoping to hear from you soon,

We remain, Yours truly,

"Saint Bill" A Servant for God's Sake

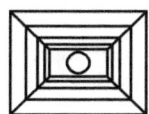

PREVIEWISM
Our World is Beautiful, Yes, Multi-Cultural

The Unconditional Love of God keeps us Sin-Free

Dear Friends and Children of all ages:

By Definition:

Sin seems to be something that separates us from God.

But such a something does not exist and just an Illusion because God is Omnipresent

Yes God is with us Always and Always with us, Whether we are walking Frontward or Backward, God is with us Always, and continues to Forgive us for our Shortcomings and misconceptions. Therefore we are always Sin-Free.

Is that not wonderful, Yeh, that is wonderful.

And when we use our sense of Judgement to Judge (Decide) right from wrong, It leads us in Truth and Reality.

Any story to the contrary is pure Lie and Illusion for the purpose of Extortion.

So you hold your head up High and remember you are a Saint walking with God all of the time.

And where there is God, there is Truth.

And where there is Truth, there is Love.

Where there Is Love, there is No punishment

Where there is No Punishment, there is Understanding.

Where there is Understanding, there is Knowledge.

Where there is Knowledge, there is No Ignorance.

Where there is No Ignorance, there is No Offence.

And where there is No Offence, there Is No Sin.

And where there is No Sin, there is God.

Now remember,

We are all Saints in God's eye, and

We look at life through God's eye, the eye of Reality.

Through which eye do you look at life?

Thanks for Listening, as ever in, "The Spirit of Goodness",

"Saint Bill" (Head Coach) A Servant for God's sake.

(Acts 26, v.16-18)(John 7, v.16-18)(1 Jn.4, v.20)(2 Thes.2, v.9-11)

Previews Institute, "Summit Loc-001, H.O,"

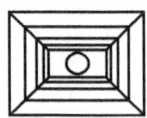

PREVIEWISM
Our World is Beautiful, Yes, Multi-Cultural

What a Joy It is, Heaven on Earth

Dear Friends:

Do you realize that you Live Sin-Free?

If you do, please go and tell your Neighbors that they do too.

If you do not, we want to assure you that you do, because a Sin is only a Sin while It is not Forgiven, Once Forgiven It is gone and no longer exists.

And since God is Omnipresent, yes, always with you, It Forgives you on the Spot and there is no Sin, No guilt, fear, doubt or Illusion. No Spiritual pain or suffering.

And since we do not have to ask God to Love us, we do not have to ask God to Forgive us, It just does, this is the Nature of God. Since Love and Forgiveness go together like water and wash, they can not be separated; we are always with God and Its Blissful existence.

When you realize this you are going to find that God goes a step further, to always warn you before you do something wrong, Yes, when you use your Sense of Judgement and Judge (Decide) right from wrong, you naturally choose the good path and you are Sin-Free.

So have Faith in your Sense of Judgement, It is God's gift to you, Use It, and pay Attention to It, and It will become more and more accurate, as you come closer and closer to God and Its Blissful existence.

Yes, Heaven has now come to Earth with the Doctrine of Previewism (Happyism) as manifested by The Spirit of Goodness, in and by "The COMPASS", a New Bible, The EverLast Testament by Author: Saint Bill. Alias: Wilhelm J. Handel.

Now remember: We are all Saints in God's eye, and We look at life through God's eye, the eye of Reality.

Through which eye do you look at life?

Now Remember: The Law is your Neighbor's opinion, and when you respect your Neighbor's opinion, The Law serves God the Real, The Spirit of Goodness.

P.S.: Any Story to the contrary is simply Illusion (Fear Tactic) for the purpose of Extortion.

Thanks for Listening, as ever in, "The Spirit of Goodness",

"Saint Bill" (Head Coach) A Servant for God's sake.

(Acts 26, v.16-18)(John 7, v.16-18)(1 Jn.4, v.20)(2 Thes.2, v.9-11)

Previews Institute, "Summit Loc-001, H.O."

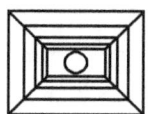

PREVIEWISM
Our World is Beautiful, Yes, Multi-Cultural

God of Reality vs God of Illusion

Dear Friends and Children of all ages:

The Spirit of God Is The Spirit of Goodness, and The Spirit of Goodness is The Spirit of God, by Nature a Heavenly entity, promoting the Doctrine of Previewism (Happyism), Yes. Multiculturalism, Yes, Reality.

The Spirit of God is not the Holy Spirit, and The Holy Spirit Is not The Spirit of God, because the Holy Spirit is a "Lord God", Yes, a Human Idol, Yes, a Two faced Hypocrite, a Self-righteous Fearmongering Extortionist Parasite, and an Insane Murderer who committed Suicide for the sake of Glory, and asks us to follow Its example.

This is Sadism in its worst case scenario. Then to make matters worse, It claimed It rose from the Dead to go to Heaven to help God rule. Well, let me tell you. God is quite capable of Ruling in Heaven on Its own. God does not need an Uninformed Human to mess things up in Heaven.

Yes, Folks, there is a big difference between The Holy Spirit and The Spirit of Goodness, it is like Black and White. One Glorifies Itself by saying it is Perfect, and the Other Glorifies its creation by saying, we are all equal and One with God, and God is equal and One with each of us, always. (John 7, v. 16-18)

Now we know that to be Perfect is to be Dead or without further room for Improvement.

Well, we know that God is Alive and always has room for improvement.

So if One has no further room for Improvement He/She might just as well be Dead.

But do not Despair, God the Real, The Spirit of Goodness, has prevailed, as Truth always does, Yes, God created "Life Eternal" with no Beginning or End in sight. Yes, Life in the Womb, Life on Earth, and Life in Heaven, as each is Eternal unto Its own. and are One as we recycle into and out of the Future, World without End.

And God the Fraud, Illusion (The Shadow)(Satan)(The Messiah) has been cast out into outer Darkness, beyond the reach of Light and told to stay there, we need you there for reference.

Chuckle, chuckle, eh, Folks,

Thanks for Listening, as ever in, 'The Spirit of Goodness",

"Saint Bill" (Head Coach) A Servant for God's sake.

(Acts 26, v.16-18)(John 7, v.16-18)(1 Jn.4, v.20)(2 Thes.2, v.9-11)

Previews Institute, "Summit Loc-001, H.O."

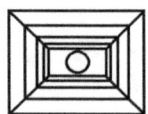

PREVIEWISM
Our World is Beautiful, Yes, Multi-Cultural

Tolerance Is a Burden, So God chooses to Forgive

Dear Friends and Children of all ages:

God the Real, The Spirit of Goodness, Loves Saints, God does not Love Sinners, God Tolerates Sinners, but Tolerance is a Burden, and God does not like Burdens. So God Forgives and the Burden is Gone.

Yes, God prefers to stay Free of Spiritual pain and Suffering, Free of Guilt, Fear, Doubt or Illusion, Yes, Free of Sin, because Sin is an Illusion expressed, and Illusion expressed is Lie, and Lie is Sin and Sin is Lie, and Actions based on Lie cause Pain and Suffering and Pain and Suffering leads to Sadism and ultimately Suicide.

So God says, Out with all that Garbage. And so God always stays true to Its Nature, which is Unconditional Love and Forgiveness in Spirit, Body, and Mind.

Yes, complete acceptance of Reality, because Reality is God and God is Reality, Not Fantasy or Illusion.

Yes. Folks, we are all Born Ignorant and we all become Wise to different degrees depending on the circumstances and the environment we live in. So if you do not like the environment, Change It, and the circumstances will change, and you will be Free to enjoy your Blessings.

Thank you. Dear God, Thank you. for true Insight.

Thanks for Listening, as ever in, "The Spirit of Goodness",

"Saint Bill" (Head Coach) A Servant for God's sake.

(Acts 26, v.16-18)(John7, v.16-18)(1 Jn.4, v.20)(2 Thes.2, v.9-11)

Previews Institute, "Summit Loc-001, H.O-"

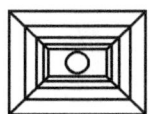

PREVIEWISM
Our World is Beautiful, Yes, Multi-Cultural

Three Different Worlds

Dear Friends and Children of all ages:

Children live in a different world than Adults do.

And Adults live in Two different worlds,

Some people live in a World of Crime.

Some people live in a World of Sin.

Some people live in a Sin-Free World.

Now we have a Choice, Do we want our Children to live in a World of Sin or do we want our Children to live in a Sin-Free World.?

Since God gave us a Sense of Judgement to Judge (Decide) right from wrong, we know that you want your Children to live in a Sin-Free World, because It Is a wonderful and Beautiful existence.

We know that Sin is an Illusion expressed, and an Illusion expressed Is Lie, and Lie is Sin, and Sin is Lie.

The result of Lie is Spiritual Pain and Suffering, Yes, Guilt, Fear, Doubt, and Illusion. Yes, this is the result of Sin.

The first Illusion expressed was when someone said. You are separated from God. Wrong, You are never separated from God, God is Omnipresent, Yes, always with you and with you always, whether you are walking frontward or backward, God Is with you always, and continues to Forgive you for your Shortcomings and misconceptions. So you see, You are always Sin-Free. Because a Sin is only a Sin while It is not Forgiven, Once Forgiven It is gone and no longer exists.

Since God is always with you. God Forgives you on the Spot, and there is No Sin, No Spiritual Pain or Suffering, No Guilt, Fear, Doubt or Illusion.

In order for us to eliminate Illusion, we must always face Reality, which is God, and the Reality is that when God created us in Its Image, we inherited the instincts of God, which are a Sense of Judgement, a Free Spirit, and a Good Nature. When we use our Sense of Judgement and Judge (Decide) right from wrong, It controls our Free Spirit, which allows our Good Nature to grow.

In order for our Good Nature to grow into something beautiful we must adopt the Angels (characteristics) of God, the oldest being The Spirit of Truth and the youngest being The Spirit of Enthusiasm, and as we know there are many in between.

Yes, folks. Our Sense of Judgement is the key that leads us to the Truth, and the Truth Sets us Free in Spirit, Body, and Mind, Yes, in Thought, Word, and Deed.

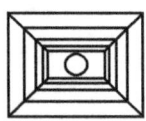

PREVIEWISM
Our World is Beautiful, Yes, Multi-Cultural

This is the ultimate purpose of God, so that we will Live in Peace, Harmony, and Equality with one-another and Find Happiness, Decency, Prosperity, and Peace of Mind.

When we allow all people the same Privilege that we have ourselves, which is to Use our Sense of Judgement to Judge (Decide) right from wrong, we come to Live in a Sin-Free World.

For further Insight and direction see 'The Compass", a New Bible, The EverLast Testament, manifested by God the Real, The Spirit of Goodness, by Author Saint Bill, alias: Wilhelm J. Handel.

Thank you. Dear God, Thank you, for true Insight

We are One vs. I am It.

Dear Friends and Children of all ages:

Most people Worship God the Real, The Spirit of Goodness, and It says, We are One, and that makes us equal, and when we are equal with God and one-another we live in Peace and Harmony, because we are Living in Reality and Freedom of Thought.

A Few people Worship the "I", "I", "I" guy, and He thinks he is Perfect, Yes, Holy. These people are living under the Illusion that they are Better than you. And so they go to any extreme to try to prove it, but they fail every time, and so they become very disappointed and depressed, and so they strike out at you for causing their problem.

This causes much pain and suffering because It is living in Illusion, Lie, and Mental Slavery.

These people can be told many times how to overcome their problem, but they have become a bit Retarded, and usually fail to understand the solution.

The Ones that do catch a glimpse of the solution usually find it a long road to what we call acceptable behavior.

But they are a part of God's creation, and so we have to continue to offer the solution and Forgive them their shortcomings, so as to keep us equal, in order to maintain Peace, Harmony, and Equality and freedom from Guilt, Fear, Doubt and Illusion and subsequently find Happiness, Decency, Prosperity, and Peace of Mind. Yes, this is the Ultimate purpose of God, The Spirit of Goodness, in our lives, together with the revelation of the Knowledge that Life is Eternal in Body, Mind, and Spirit, Yes, Life in the Womb, Life on Earth, and Life in Heaven, as each is Eternal unto Its own and are One as we recycle into and out of the Furure, world without end.

Thank you, Dear God, Thank you, for true Insight.

Author: The Spirit of Goodness, by, Saint Bill, A Servant for God's sake.

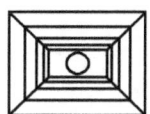

PREVIEWISM
Our World is Beautiful, Yes, Multi-Cultural

With a Positive Attitude there is No Sin.

Dear Friends and Children of all ages:

The definition of Sin is like a Tree with many branches and twigs, and each branch and twig is a different definition, and those that live under this Tree find life to be very Cloudy as under the influence of the Shadow. Yes, they develop a very Negative Attitude.

We at Previews have walked out from under this tree and have looked up to a Clear Blue Sky, as the Sun shines always, even above the Natural Clouds. Yes, we have developed a very Positive Attitude.

If you find a friend that is living under the Tree of Sin, Let him/her know that the Original Seed of the Tree was defined as :

Sin being an Illusion expressed, and an Illusion expressed is Lie, and Lie is Sin, and Sin is Lie.

And Actions based on Lie cause Pain and Suffering.

And so the next definition of Sin was defined as:

Sin being Spiritual Pain and Suffering, Yes, Guilt, Fear, Doubt and Illusion.

And so all these people have to do is remember that God is Omnipresent, Yes, always with you and with you always, whether you are walking frontward or backward, God is with you always, and continues to Forgive you for your Shortcomings and misconceptions, and so you see. you are always Sin-Free. Because a Sin is only a Sin while it is not Forgiven, once Forgiven It is gone and no longer exists.

Yes, my Friends, when people live under the Tree of Sin they come to think that all that life brings them is a Stumbling Block because they are Looking Down to the Shadow.

All they have to do is Look Up and face the Reality of God all around them, and they will find that the Stumbling Block becomes a Stepping Stone to a better and better way of Life.

Yes, Sunshine and Rainbows in a Sin-Free world and they will find It is a wonderful and Beautiful existence.

Yes, this is the ultimate result of following Previewism as manifested by The Spirit of Goodness, God the Real, in and by The COMPASS, a New Bible, The EverLast Testament, by Author: Saint Bill, alias, Wilhelm J. Handel, written for "Saint Jesus", the Job he left undone.

And the Glory be to God. (John 7, v. 16-18)

Now remember: We are all Saints in God's eye, and

We look at life through God's eye, the eye of Reality.

Through which eye do you look at life?

Author: The Spirit of Goodness, by Saint Bill, A Servant for God's Sake.

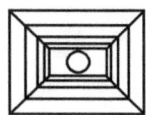

PREVIEWISM
Our World is Beautiful, Yes, Multi-Cultural

A Miscellaneous Proverb

Dear Friends and Children of all ages:

A True Prophet says, You follow your Sense of Judgement, and Worship God, The Spirit of Goodness, and It will lead you to the Truth, and the Truth will set you Free to Serve your Neighbour as God instructs you to, and you will find Happiness, Decency, Prosperity and Peace of Mind, and the ability to deal in Peace, Harmony, and EQUALITY with your Neighbours and the world around you.

A False Prophet says, You worship Me, I am God's Special servant, all the others are Frauds, Believe me, I would not Lie to you would I?......If it were not so I would tell you, Right....Yes, Follow me, and I will take you to Heaven, Yes, My way is the Only way, so you Bow down, and Serve me and to Hell with your Neighbor. (Luke 14, v.26). Yes, You serve and worship me or God will cast you into the Fire and Brimstone of Hell and Damnation.

(But It is a Liar, and so It takes you to Hell the long way around, right here on Earth.)

Thank you, Dear God, Thank you, for an Obvious and Easy Choice.

Thanks for Listening, as ever in, "The Spirit of Goodness",

"Saint Bill" (Head Coach) A Servant for God's sake.

(Acts 26, v.16-18)(John 7, v.16-18)(1 Jn.4, v.20)(2 Thes.2, v.9-11)

Previews Institute, "Summit Loc-001, H.O."

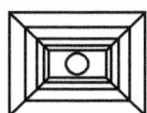

PREVIEWISM
Our World is Beautiful, Yes, Multi-Cultural

In the Blink of an Eye

Dear Friends:

People who walk with God, The Spirit of Goodness, (Yes, in Reality) do not have any Sin in their Lives.

People who have Sin in their Lives are walking with Satan (The Shadow) (Illusion).

And so you see, We at Previews have not come to cure the Healthy, we have come to cure the Sick.

But of Course, you are all welcome to ask some questions, because for the Sick we have a Pound of Cure, and for the Healthy we have an Ounce of Prevention.

Now, since God is not Perfect, and we are not Perfect, you must always use your Sense of Judgement to Judge (Decide) right from wrong for yourself and allow all others the same privilege.

And as we discuss the Reality of God within us, we all gain more and more Spiritual Fulfillment, Earthly Happiness, and Heavenly Joy, as The Shadow, the Accuser, the Liar is exposed and cast out of Sight, out of Mind, and out of Mind, out of Existence.

Yes, my Friends, Look up and to the Future and It will come to bring you a beautiful Present.

Do not look Down or to the Past, because It will never come, but Rob you of the present you have.

Now go, and expect the Best, and make the Best of what you get, and you will never have a Bad day.

And remember, God Loves Saints. God does not love Sinners, God tolerates Sinners. But tolerance is a Burden, and God does not like Burdens, So God Forgives and the Burden is Gone.

All this happens in the Blink of an Eye.

So you see, we are all Saints in God's eye, and

we look at life through God's eye, the eye of Reality.

Thank you. Dear God, Thank you, for true Insight

Thanks for Listening, as ever in, "The Spirit of Goodness",

"Saint Bill" (Head Coach) A Servant for God's sake.

(Acts 26, v.16-18)(John 7, v.16-18)(1 Jn.4, v.20)(2 Thes.2, v.9-11)

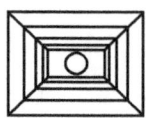

PREVIEWISM
Our World is Beautiful, Yes, Multi-Cultural

God the Real is The Spirit of Goodness. God the Fraud is Illusion, Yes, The Shadow, Yes, The Holy Ghost.

Dear Friends and Children of all ages:

The Shadow's servants claim that most people worship Animals or Material things, but that they worship God.

The problem is, they do not say which God, the Good one, or the Bad one.

The Good God is The Spirit of Goodness.

The Bad God is a Human Idol.

Well, we at Previews would rather worship a Cow than a Human Idol.

Simply because a Cow does not Lie, or try to Extort you.

A Human Idol lies to try to control you for the purpose of Extortion.

And so you see folks, we should always remember that there is only One God, but that It seems there are Two, yours and mine.

And so we come to Understand that God is a Definition (each unto his/her own) and we at Previews define God as a Spirit, the Good one, yes, The Spirit of Goodness, and the Goodness that we were created, conceived, and Born with is a Sense of Judgement, Free Spirit, and a Good Nature. Yes, these are the Instincts that we inherit from God.

Our Free Spirit makes us Creative, Our Good Nature makes us Good Providers, and our Sense of Judgement makes us Steadfast Comforters.

Naturally The Spirit of Goodness has many Angels (children)(characteristics), the oldest being The Spirit of Truth and the youngest being The Spirit of Enthusiasm, with many in between.

When we adopt one of these Angels every week we soon have the whole Family of God in our Heart, Mind and Soul. Subsequently we come to live in Peace, Harmony, and Equality with our Neighbors and the world around us, and find Happiness, Decency, Prosperity, and Peace of Mind. Yes, this is the purpose of God in our Lives.

Yes, Folks, It is a wonderful and beautiful life when we realize that God loves us, Just as we are, any time any day, and never once condemns or punishes us for our Shortcomings and misconceptions, but rather always chooses to Forgive us and say, Now go, and do It better next time, now that you have learned Reality from Illusion, and found the Newness of Life to keep you forever Enthused, and filled with hope for a better and better Day.

Yes, Folks, we who understand Previewism (Happyism) realize that because God Loves us, we live Sin-Free in a Sin-Free world.

Is that not wonderful, Yeh, that is Wonderful.

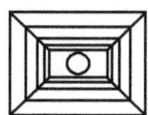

PREVIEWISM
Our World is Beautiful, Yes, Multi-Cultural

If you find a friend that is living in a World of Sin, Yes, Guilt, Fear, Doubt and Illusion, Yes, Spiritual pain and suffering, please let him/her know what you know about Previewism (Happyism) as manifested by The Spirit of Goodness, in and by The Compass, a New Bible, The EverLast Testament by Author: Saint Bill, alias: Wilhelm J. Handel

And Praise God for that.

Thank you, Dear God, thank you, for true Insight.

Thanks for Listening, as ever in, "The Spirit of Goodness",

"Saint Bill" (Head Coach) A Servant for God's sake.

(Acts 26, v.16-18)(John 7, v.16-18)(1 Jn.4, v.20)(2 Thes.2, v.9-11)

Previews Institute, "Summit Loc-001, H.O."

A Miscellaneous Proverb

Dear Friends and Children of all ages:

We are all born with a Sense of Judgement, Free Spirit, and a Good Nature. And when we use our Sense of Judgement to Judge (Decide) right from wrong, we come to Realize that some things are impossible, and we come to Worship the God of Reality because Reality expressed is Truth and where there is Truth there is Love and where there is Love there are Blessings, and a Life of Happiness and Bliss.

The Shadow (Satan) says, Do not Judge. Do not Decide right from wrong or you will Die, and I can tell you that Nothing is Impossible, I can walk on water, I can raise the dead, I can change a bottle of water into a bottle of whiskey by snapping my fingers, I can say to the mountain 'move' and it will move. And you come to Worship the God of Illusion, and Illusion expressed is Lie and Lie is Sin and Sin is Lie, and Actions based on Lie cause Pain and Suffering, and Pain and Suffering lead to Sadism and ultimately Suicide.

Thank you, Dear God, Thank you, for an obvious and easy choice.

Author: The Spirit of Goodness, by Saint Bill, a Servant for God's sake

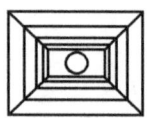

PREVIEWISM
Our World is Beautiful, Yes, Multi-Cultural

Previewism (Happyism) Proved beyond a Doubt.

Dear Friends and Children of all ages:

As we at Previews understand It, "Saint Jesus" said that Christians are serving Satan because Saint Jesus said that Christ means Messiah (John 1, v.41) and Saint Jesus said that the Messiah is Satan (Acts 26, v. 16-18).

So you see, Saint Jesus was not the Messiah of the Jews, they rejected him. But The Messiah's favorite disguise Is a Sheep-skin coat and the Mask of a Good man. And so Its servant Mr. Saul (Paul) put the Mask of a Good man on the Head of Satan and clothed it with a Sheep-skin coat. And in doing so He deceived a Few Gentiles into practicing Judaism while he called them Christians, Yes, Sinners.

But the Gentiles know better and realize that they are "Saints" in God's eye, never once condemned or accused of wrongdoing, but rather always Loved.

Yes, Saint Jesus said that All the Sins of the Past, Present and Future are Forgiven, and we know that Sins once Forgiven are gone and no longer exist

So you see, since God the Real is omnipresent, yes, always with you. It Forgives you on the Spot, and there is No Sin, No Spiritual pain or suffering. No Guilt, Fear, Doubt or Illusion. Yes, those that walk with God the Real, The Spirit of Goodness, have no Sin, No separation from God, but rather always complete Harmony and Oneness with God.

Yes, Saint Jesus was a Wise man when you understand him right.

When you do not understand him right He was made out to be a Lunatic or a Hypocrite, and a Liar, Yes, The Christ (The Messiah)(The Shadow) A Human Idol (The Illusion of God) (2 Thes. 2, v.9-11). Yes, a man who tried to Justify murder by committing Suicide for the sake of Glory.

Well, we know there is never any Justification for Murder or Suicide. These things can be Forgiven, but Never Justified.

So you see, Folks, we all know that a Sin is an Illusion expressed, and an Illusion expressed is Lie, and Lie is Sin, and Sin is Lie.

And Actions based on Lie cause Pain and Suffering. So do not Believe the Lie and you will not Act on It, and you will not cause anyone any Pain or Suffering. Yes, you will be Free to serve you Neighbor properly and you will find Happiness, Decency, Prosperity and Peace of Mind, allowing you to live in Peace, Harmony, and Equality with your Neighbors and the World around you.

Yes, you will realize that you are Free of Sin because of the Nature of God, which is always Present.

Yes, My Friends, we know that Love and Forgiveness go together like Water and Wash, they can not be separated, and so we are always with God. and Its Blissful existence.

Thank you, Dear God, Thank you, for true Insight.

Thanks for Listening, as ever in, "The Spirit of Goodness",

"Saint Bill" (Head Coach) A Servant for God's sake.

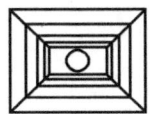

PREVIEWISM
Our World is Beautiful, Yes, Multi-Cultural

The Spirit of Goodness

My Summit is my Home
and
My Home is my Summit
and
My Congregation is my Family
Oh, Yes,
And that includes You!!

Lesson #1
We are FORGIVEN before we start our Day
and
We are FORGIVEN after we end our Day
and
While we Sleep we can do Nothing wrong.
So we are Always SAINTS.
Thank you, Dear God, Thank you, for true Insight.

———————

In the Spiritual Realm, Religions that are "Off Track" are Centralized and they have Upy-Ups.

Religions that are "On Track" are Decentralized, where everyone is Equal and Free, and they have God as the Centre and not the Upy-Ups.

Yes, Each one deals direct with God through their Sense of Judgement, Free Spirit and Good Nature.

Thank you, Dear God, Thank you, for true Insight.

Thanks for Listening, as ever in, "The Spirit of Goodness",

"Saint Bill" (Head Coach) A Servant for God's sake.

(Acts 26, v.16-18)(John 7, v.16-18)(1 Jn.4, v.20)(2 Thes.2, v.9-11)

Previews Institute, "Summit Loc-001, H.O."

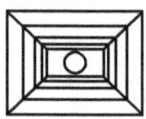

PREVIEWISM
Our World is Beautiful, Yes, Multi-Cultural

A Profound Truth

Dear Friends and Children of all ages:

Today we have a question for you.

Are you a Sinner or are you a Saint.?

If you say, You are a Saint, you are Right.

If you say, You are a Sinner, you are Wrong.

If you say, You are Both, you are Confused.

Yes, a Wise Prophet, Saint Jesus once said, You are either For God, or you are Against God, you can not be Both unless you are a confused Hypocrite.

So the question is, Are you For God, or are you Against God.

If you say, You are For God, you are a Saint.

If you say, You are Against God, you are an Idiot, yes, a Sinner.

Now, how many Idiots are there in the World.?

Well, there are a Few in the Human eye, but there are None in God's eye. And we look at life through God's eye, the eye of Reality.

Yes, the Reality is, that God considers us All Saints because God knows we are all Born ignorant and we all become Wise to different degrees depending on the circumstances and the environment we live in.

And so God always Forgives us our Shortcomings and misconceptions, because It knows that although we sometimes make Errors in Judgement, God knows we had Good Intentions. Yes, God always says, Forgiven, Now go and do It better next time. Yes, Forever Hopeful for a better day.

Yes, Folks, we must continue to Judge (Decide) right from wrong for ourselves and allow all others the same Privilege, in order to make progress. And we must always Forgive one another for our differences in opinion, and not strike back with condemnation or punishment, because God never condemns or punishes anyone, but rather always Forgives, to keep us Hopeful for a better day.

Yes, the Wise men of History, namely, Saint Hindu, Saint Buddha, Saint Confucius, Saint Jesus, Saint Mohammed and a few more are mostly misunderstood because of The Shadow (Illusion)(Satan) the Liar.

But God allowed that to be because It gave us all a Sense of Judgement, a Free Spirit, and a Good Nature, and when we use or Sense of Judgement to Judge (Decide) right from wrong, It controls our Free Spirit and allows our Good Nature to grow into something beautiful as we adopt the angels (characteristics) of God, the oldest being the Spirit of Truth and the youngest being the Spirit of Enthusiasm, with many in between as you know.

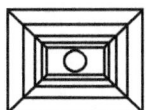

PREVIEWISM
Our World is Beautiful, Yes, Multi-Cultural

Yes, Folks, It is a Big and Beautiful world when we Look-Up and Cast-out Illusion, The Shadow, the "I", "I", "I" Guy, the Liar.

Yes, We should dwell on the "We" "We" "We" guy.

Yes, God the Real, The Spirit of Goodness, says, We are One, and that makes us equal, and when we are equal with God and one-another we live in Peace and Harmony because we are living in Reality and Freedom of Thought.

God the Fraud, The Shadow, with Its Holy Spirit says, I am It. I am better than you. Ya, I am perfect. So you must be my Slave, so you do as I say or you are Dead....Now go walk across the Ocean.

This causes much Pain and Suffering because It is living in Illusion, Lie, and Mental Slavery.

So remember, We are All Saints in God's eye, and Saints are a Free people, and God is a Free Spirit, and It keeps you Free to look at Life through God's eye, the eye of Reality.

Thank you, Dear God, Thank you, for true Insight.

Thanks for Listening, as ever in, "The Spirit of Goodness",

"Saint Bill" (Head Coach) A Servant for God's sake.

(Acts 26. v.16-18)(John 7. v.16-18)(1 Jn.4, v.20)(2 Thes.2. v.9-11)

Previews Institute. "Summit Loc-001, H.O."

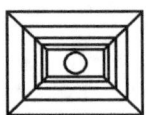

PREVIEWISM
Our World is Beautiful, Yes, Multi-Cultural

Knowledge Comes from Wise People and Good Books
Wisdom Comes from Experience
Yes, Actions Speak Louder Than Words

Dear Friends and Children of all ages:

Would you rather Live by what God says, or would you rather Live by what the Preacher says?

If you say, You are not sure, Let me Assure you that you will be by far the Wiser person when you Live by what God says.

Now, when you Decide to Live by what God says, you will have to ask yourself: "What is God?". And you will find that God is a Spirit. Then you will have to ask: "Which one, the Good one or the Bad one?". And you will find that It is the Good one.
Yes, God the Real is "The Spirit of Goodness".

The Spirit of Goodness has three Instincts. Yes, It has a Sense of Judgement, a Free Spirit and a Good Nature.

And you were Created, Conceived and Born in the Image of God.

When you use your Sense of Judgement and Judge (Decide) right from wrong, It controls your Free Spirit which allows your Good Nature to grow into something Beautiful as you adopt the angels (characteristics) of God. The oldest being The Spirit of Truth, and the youngest being The Spirit of Enthusiasm, with many in between as you know.

As you continue to use your Sense of Judgement and Judge (Decide) right from wrong, you will quickly learn that you must always base your Decisions on Facts and not on Hearsay.

Now, we all know that God Loves us Unconditionally. And we all know that Love and Forgiveness go together like Water and Wash, they cannot be separated, and so we are always Forgiven our Errors in Judgement and therefore always receive God's Blessings for our daily activities.

Now, we all know that God is Omnipresent, yes, always with you and with you always, and It lives in Heaven, in the World, and in your Heart, Mind and Soul, from creation, conception and Birth, and so we are always with God and Its Blissful existence.

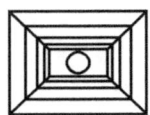

PREVIEWISM
Our World is Beautiful, Yes, Multi-Cultural

Finally, you are going to find that your Sense of Judgement will lead you to know that Life is Eternal in Body, Mind and Spirit. Yes, Life in the Womb, Life on Earth, and Life in Heaven, as each is Eternal unto Its own, and are One as we Recycle into and out of the Future, world without end.

When we are conceived, the Spirit becomes Body, Life in the Womb. When we are Born, the Body becomes Word. Life on Earth, when we go on to better things, the Word becomes Spirit, Life in Heaven. After some time we are Re-conceived again to come again to Live and enjoy the Fruits of our Labor from the previous time around.

Yes, My Children, there is No Death in God's world, only Life Eternal….is that not wonderful, yeh, that is wonderful.

Now remember, We are all Saints in God's eye, and
We look at life through God's eye, the eye of Reality.

Thank you, Dear God, Thank you, for true Insight.

Now, Go and carry my torch.

Thanks for Listening, as ever in "The Spirit of Goodness"

Saint Bill (Head Coach) A Servant for God's sake.

(Acts 26, v. 16-18) (John 7, v. 16-18) (1 Jn. 4 v. 20) (2 Thes. 2, v.9-11)
Previews Institute, "Summit Loc-001, H.O."

P.S.

What the Mind can Conceive and Believe, It has Achieved.

Therefore:

So It is Written

So Shall It Be

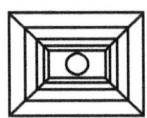

PREVIEWISM
Our World is Beautiful, Yes, Multi-Cultural

A Few Select Pages for a Condensed Booklet

Page	Title	Page	Title
40	Big Organization	196	A Fortunate Person
41	Marriage Contract	202	This is against the Law
44	Out on the Farm	209	A Few Short Stories
73	Card Game	216	Functions and Result
80	In 90 years	227	The Body of God
103	In 300 years	233	A Poem - Sin-Free
105	No more Pain	236	A New Standard
107	Positive Thinking Religion	245	Eternal Trust Foundation
109	The Sun and Earth	265	Ultimate State of Mind
113	Freedom has a Price Tag	277	Judge
117	Achievers Habits Program	283	God is not in a Hurry
119	Baptism	293	Previewism
134	Children have No choice	299	A little further Insight
158	Boasting a Little	303	Reason for Sin-Free Living
181	What God	311	Who was the Wiser Man
184	A Tribute to Brittney	313	The Big Lie-Three Fold
190	Start with are you Happy	333-353	The Final Result=Sin-Free

Thank you,

Compiled by: The Spirit of Goodness, by: Saint Bill, A Servant for God's sake.

THE TRADITION OF "CHANGE FOR THE BETTER" IS BORN IN *"PREVIEWISM"*
www.previews-inc.com
Make 10 - 20 Copies per week and Pass It On. - God will be well Pleased.

www.ingramcontent.com/pod-product-compliance
Lightning Source LLC
Chambersburg PA
CBHW080052190426
43201CB00035B/2170